THE RECOVERY REVOLUTION

CLAIRE D. CLARK

THE RECOVERY REVOLUTION

The Battle Over Addiction Treatment
in the United States

Columbia University Press / New York

Columbia University Press
Publishers Since 1893
New York   Chichester, West Sussex
cup.columbia.edu

Library of Congress Cataloging-in-Publication Data

Names: Clark, Claire D., author.
Title: The recovery revolution : the battle over addiction treatment in
  the United States / Claire D. Clark.
Description: New York : Columbia University Press, [2017] | Includes
  bibliographical references and index.
Identifiers: LCCN 2016041877 (print) | LCCN 2016043072 (ebook) |
  ISBN 9780231176385 (cloth : alk. paper) | ISBN 9780231544436 (e-book)
Subjects: | MESH: Substance-Related Disorders—therapy | Substance-Related
  Disorders—history | Substance Abuse Treatment Centers—history |
  Therapeutic Community | Self-Help Groups | Drug and Narcotic
  Control—history | History, 20th Century | History, 21st Century |
  United States
Classification: LCC HV5825 (print) | LCC HV5825 (ebook) |
  NLM WM 11 AA1 | DDC 362.290973—dc23
LC record available at https://lccn.loc.gov/2016041877

Cover design: Fifth Letter
Cover image: ©Fred Lyon/Getty Images

For Mike and Molly

CONTENTS

INTRODUCTION
The Roots of Revolution

PART I
REVOLUTION

1. SELLING SYNANON

2. SYNANON RASHOMON

CONTENTS

PART II
CO-OPTATION

PART III
INDUSTRIALIZATION

LIST OF ILLUSTRATIONS

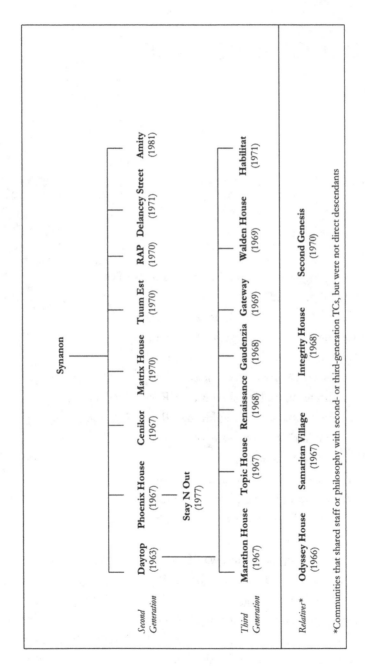

FIGURE F.1

Genealogy of Therapeutic Communities in the United States

(Not comprehensive.)

Second Generation

Synanon

Daytop (1963)   Phoenix House (1967)   Cenikor (1967)   Matrix House (1970)   Tuum Est (1970)   RAP (1970)   Delancey Street (1971)   Amity (1981)

Stay N Out (1977)

Third Generation

Marathon House (1967)   Topic House (1967)   Renaissance (1968)   Gaudenzia (1968)   Gateway (1969)   Walden House (1969)   Habilitat (1971)

Relatives*

Odyssey House (1966)   Samaritan Village (1967)   Integrity House (1968)   Second Genesis (1970)

*Communities that shared staff or philosophy with second- or third-generation TCs, but were not direct descendants

PREFACE

THE MAJORITY OF PEOPLE with substance-use problems resolve them without formal addiction treatment or twelve-step support groups. In the early 1960s, researchers observed that most individuals who were labeled addicts by medical or criminal-justice authorities had stopped taking drugs by the time they reached their midthirties—a phenomenon that became known as "maturing out" of addiction.[1] Later scholars found that people were often able to bring their use under control without treatment by replacing psychoactive substances with work or educational pursuits and reviving relationships that did not revolve around drugs.[2]

But a smaller population, for tangled biological, psychological, and social reasons, needed more systematic help with breaking self-destructive behavioral patterns. When medicine failed to provide it, they organized themselves.

And medicine failed often. Each time medical providers devised progressive treatment models for "inebriates," "addicts," or "alcoholics," their efforts were frustrated; even the most enlightened reforms eventually reincorporated punitive management strategies.[3] For more than a century, addiction treatments ranged from mildly disciplinary to downright abusive. Hospitals and asylums ran token economies and used forced restraints, such as straightjackets and shackles. The criminal-justice system has long meted out therapy as well as punishment.

Today's policy reformers and liberal critics characterize punitive and moralizing solutions to drug use as the product of conservative political agendas or a new front for racial oppression.[4] There is an element of truth in both these histories, but they are incomplete. As I searched archives, visited addiction-treatment centers, and met and interviewed treatment leaders, I discovered a story as complicated as the treatment system, one in which recovering addicts—alternately hailed as radicals, heroes, and villains—had agency and, ultimately, a hand in their own subjugation.

I also came to believe that the moral treatment model could not be simply dismissed on the basis of its recent politics. The roots of an abstinence-based, value-laden approach to addiction run deeper than the Reagan revolution and the rise of a New Right coalition of free-market boosters and social conservatives. Industrious, abstemious treatment centers first emerged in the late 1800s, not the 1980s. Victorian-era treatment providers promised to scientifically recalibrate residents' characters, which they believed could be unbalanced by bad habits such as drinking, smoking, and sexual promiscuity. For individuals and families trapped in a cycle of shameful and self-destructive behavior, the possibility of redemption could not be oversold.

As the field of psychology developed, yesterday's virtues transformed into today's personality traits: "intemperate" became "neurotic," and "dutiful" was rechristened "conscientious." But addiction was still understood as an inability to align individual behavior with ideals and long-term goals, making treatment a moral enterprise, as it remains today.

It is not, however, a monopolistic enterprise. Past and present treatment providers prescribe a variety of different approaches to addiction. Experts in the field today say that the key to recovery is finding the right match between client and clinician rather than the one true cure for addiction.[5]

As yet, there is no single cure for addiction. This claim may disappoint readers of this book, especially those invested in particular treatment models. As a historian, I do not have a professional stake in any therapeutic approach. There are few clinical recommendations in these pages.

I instead investigate the origins of our therapeutic options. How did addiction treatment become unevenly distributed across the medical and criminal-justice systems? Why have treatment-industry gains failed, so far, to translate into more humane attitudes toward people with addiction?

The answer begins in the 1960s and ends with the unfinished work of the recovery revolution.

ON SOURCES AND METHODS

Historians are preoccupied with sources; because I trained primarily as a historian of medicine, so am I. Although this book draws from an extensive collection of evidence, history is by nature a selective endeavor. When investigating our topics, we read the classics in our fields, excavate overlooked materials, talk to the living, and commune with the dead. But in the end it is impossible to incorporate every source, so we make decisions about which materials to cite and highlight. Transparency about those decisions is a disciplinary imperative. Our rationale is practical as well as ethical: historical knowledge progresses along the paper trails left behind by previous scholars.

There are at least three historiographic debates buried in the bibliography: the interpretation of multimedia materials, the use of oral histories and interviews, and the difficulty of reconstructing the histories of marginalized groups.

Photographs and films often serve a descriptive purpose in historical work by illustrating, for example, the appearance of significant individuals or important locations. Although multimedia material helped me visualize key people and places, I tried not to treat pictures as literal depictions of the past. The book instead draws attention to the way images of addiction treatment were produced, promoted, and received and to the active roles that recovering addicts played in this process. I also put representations in historical context: images that once played as progressive seem horribly retrograde because past activists were working within different political and historical constraints. Dramatic stories about "dope fiends'" hard-won redemption raised public consciousness about the viability of addiction treatment in the 1960s, but in time their radical narrative became the dominant one. As contemporary groups such as Faces and Voices of Recovery later pointed out, that narrative also became counterproductive to a progressive recovery agenda.

This book draws from oral histories of people in recovery conducted in the 1960s, 1980s, 2000s, and 2010s. Yet the book is not an oral-history project; I did not speak with every Synanon resident or therapeutic-community leader. I spoke to enough sources to learn that each has a unique perspective and story to tell, by turns hilarious, thrilling, and painful. Because memory is fallible, I privileged contemporaneous sources when they were available and turned to retrospective interviews to fill in the gaps in the historical record. This book argues that sensationalism can undermine even the best intentions of treatment advocates, so I chose not to dwell on interviewees' recollections of their darkest private moments. I instead selected statements that demonstrate how the views held by treatment leaders and people in recovery related to broader historical trends and contributed to the development of treatment policies.

Addiction treatment has gone—and can still go—badly awry. In order for the treatment field to progress, we need to find a way to reckon with past mistakes without unwittingly reinforcing prejudicial assumptions that all addiction treatment is futile or that people with addiction histories are universally untrustworthy. History has demonstrated the need for continued vigilance about the mistreatment of vulnerable populations enrolled in treatment programs, whether their treatment providers are peer counselors or more mainstream medical professionals.

In selecting treatment centers for analysis, I emphasized influential centers and common developmental themes rather than cataloging every therapeutic community's evolution. A comprehensive institutional history of therapeutic communities might feature many more organizations and trace the model's global influence as each new community opened in England, Europe, and South America. Writing a history of this sort would be challenging because no centralized archive of therapeutic-community materials currently exists and historical records tend to vanish when treatment centers merge or close.

When the treatment industry of the nineteenth century collapsed, a wealth of sources was lost to history. In the years since then, curators have struggled to preserve material about addiction treatment, a topic still on the fringes of both medicine and U.S. history. In writing *Slaying the Dragon*, a sweeping history of addiction treatment, the historian and clinician William White found no printed record of some of the recovery movement's pivotal moments; still other records vanished in the sixteen years between the publication of the first and second editions of his book. From the time I began my research until the time of my book's publication, the archives of at least one treatment center were lost and found.

The preservation of these elusive sources is essential for future scholarship—for comprehensive addiction-treatment and policy histories, for commemoration and reflection, for clinical teaching, and for alternative interpretations of the story told here. For this reason, the University of Kentucky has begun the Therapeutic Communities Collection, an archive that will be professionally preserved, digitized, and made available on the Web. If you are reading this book and have material to contribute, I invite you to contact Special Collections.

THE RECOVERY REVOLUTION

INTRODUCTION

The Roots of Revolution

T HERE'S NOTHING MUCH to say about me," Charlie Hamer told the Hollywood screenwriter Guy Endore in 1960. "I'm just an old con. Been in and out of jail most of my life for just about every crime you can think of." Hamer was born on a ranch in Oklahoma in 1903 and picked up an opium habit from Chinese railroad laborers who settled in the area. Decades later he could still describe the exotic drug paraphernalia and the rose scent he associated with the smoke. "After the Harrison Act made narcotics a federal offense, opium had to go," said Hamer. "That odor was a dead giveaway. The narcotics officers couldn't miss it. Morphine, cocaine, and then heroin took the place of opium. Quicker and safer."[1]

For Hamer, though, the unscented substances provided only temporary relief from a life of crime. He moved from the countryside to urban centers, and as state surveillance of drug-related activity escalated, his offenses kept pace with his cravings. Hamer's habit reflected a generational trend: other young, single men sought to avoid police detection by switching from opiates associated with ethnic minorities to those largely preferred by white, middle-class women, and the laws shifted around them. When heroin became a substance of recreational abuse among working-class men with a tolerance for Victorian-era vices, drug use emerged as a serious social problem.[2]

A series of laws passed in the first two decades of the twentieth century imposed increasing regulations on the prescription and possession of morphine and heroin. By 1920, the federal government made medical maintenance of opiate dependency under the supervision of a physician illegal; other forms of treatment for substance dependence also contracted. For more than forty years, the government adopted a simple, supply-side addiction policy that sought to control substance use by punishing users and dealers. During this era of strict narcotics control, clearly defined rules governed substance use and contributed to the creation of the archetypal addict who is driven by visceral craving and associated with crime.[3] Scientific research and popular culture reinforced this image of the heroin addict, and limited and ineffectual treatment methods further supported the notion that addiction was a fundamentally incurable condition. By the early 1960s, however, the weaknesses of the punitive, centralized drug-policy paradigm started to show. Pressure came from above: Harry J. Anslinger's reign as commissioner of the Federal Bureau of Narcotics and Dangerous Drugs came to an end, and bellwether states such as New York and California challenged the bureau's policies and began experimenting with new approaches to sentencing and treatment.[4] Forces also applied pressure from below: a small community of self-described "ex-addicts"[5] claimed they could succeed where bureaucrats failed. They had conceived a cure for the intractable problem of heroin addiction, one that habilitated even career addicts such as Charlie Hamer.[6]

This community, called Synanon, successfully sold the cure. Screenwriters such as Endore, magazines such as *Life*, and politicians such as Connecticut senator Thomas Dodd Sr. (D) were fascinated by the group's ability to dramatically refashion the psyches of the most incorrigible addicts. The Synanon treatment not only enabled residents to abstain from heroin but also theoretically allowed them to achieve near-total character reformation. Synanon's new peer-based treatment methods radicalized the principles of Alcoholics Anonymous (AA) and served as a protest against the medical establishment's constrained treatment options. They led to the rebirth of a national addiction-treatment industry that had largely disintegrated by the time Charlie Hamer discovered Chinese smoking opium.

* * *

In the chapters that follow, I describe how illicit drug use transformed from a fringe issue associated with supposedly incurable and immoral addicts such as Hamer to a central concern of middle-class households. Rising rates of youthful substance use in the 1960s and 1970s fueled an industry built on the timeworn image of the American junkie. In the early 1960s, Synanon's ex-addicts designed a radical new form of addiction treatment in response to the client profile of the older "hard-core" heroin user; by the following decade, hundreds of new treatment centers would apply these therapeutic methods to adolescents who used other substances. "Group pressure by ex-addicts forces, cajoles and motivates the addict first to act as an adult, then to think as an adult, and finally, to feel as an adult," explained one center's brochure. "If this process is repeated long enough, the alteration of personality becomes authentic and self-sustaining."[7]

THE END OF INEBRIETY

Before addicts, there were *inebriates*; before addiction-treatment centers, twelve-step programs, and hospital detoxification units, there were asylums. A medical explanation for the habitual and compulsive consumption of psychoactive substances gained ground in the decades following the American Civil War. The diagnosis had a name—"inebriety"—and in 1870 an association of professionals assembled to treat and study it.[8] Inebriate asylums, sanitariums, lodges, and institutes flourished in the late nineteenth and early twentieth centuries. In addition to treating opium habitués, tobacco users, and alcoholics, the new treatment centers also produced medical research about the singular condition that afflicted the groups. The field's flagship journal, the *Quarterly Journal of Inebriety*, was edited by T. D. Crothers, who served as the assistant physician at the public New York State Inebriate Asylum (the first of its kind) and later as superintendent of the private Walnut Hill Asylum in Hartford, Connecticut. Like Crothers, many of the journal's scientific authors also served as managers of treatment programs; some programs placed advertisements alongside articles in the journal.[9] Leaders of the new inebriate homes were

FIGURE 0.1

A Keeley Institute treatment center, undated. The Keeley Institute was one
of the most prominent inebriety treatment chains in the late 1800s
and early 1900s.

Source: Courtesy of the Missouri Valley Special Collections, Kansas City Public Library,
Kansas City, Missouri.

passionate and charismatic advocates for the medical treatment of chemical dependence. They could also be self-promotional ideologues, given
to squabbling about treatment philosophies and willfully ignorant of the
field's ethical lapses. By 1925, the professional association had folded, and
the network of inebriate homes collapsed.[10]

Prohibition had something to do with the collapse. A study conducted
by the Scientific Temperance Federation in 1922 examined a sample of pre-
Prohibition alcoholism-treatment providers; approximately 80 percent of
the centers had disappeared, closed, or decided to treat other conditions.

The number of inebriety treatment providers dwindled to twenty-seven.[11] Although inebriety asylums differed from the mental asylums promoted by mid-nineteenth-century reformers, they suffered the same fate.[12] Asylums operated under the premise that some combination of pastoral setting, spiritual cultivation, healthy recreation, and habitual labor could reform residents' troublesome temperaments. Although historians credit nineteenth-century asylums with promoting a "moral model" of mental-health care, in practice superintendent-researchers believed socially unacceptable behaviors and emotions had treatable biological causes. They claimed to calm the nervous system and purify the spirit at the same time.

As institutions failed to realize this utopian promise, the theory that inebriety was a curable medical condition suffered. In the early twentieth century, progressive reformers, seeking to purify wayward youths and control the growth of seedy communities, came to view substance use as a kind of moral contagion. When the Treasury Department surveyed local health officials about the nature of addiction in 1918, the majority believed the condition was a vice, not a disease.[13]

Reformers concluded that legal restriction, not personal reformation, was the best way to control chemical dependence. Public funding for treatment withered as local activists proposed bans on alcohol, tobacco, and nonmedical opiate and cocaine use.[14] The Harrison Narcotics Tax Act regulated the nonmedical use of opiates and cocaine beginning in 1914; amendments to the act increased drug restrictions. By 1924, the federal government forbade the prescription of opiates to addicts, maintenance therapy, and heroin importation. In 1920, the Eighteenth Amendment to the Constitution prohibited the production, transportation, and sale of alcohol. Offenders were sent to prisons rather than to sanitariums. If inebriety could not be treated, perhaps it could be outlawed.

So went the logic of enforcers such as Harry J. Anslinger, who began his career as an international antidrug campaigner within a few months of Crothers's death in 1918.[15] Anslinger would become, according to his critics, the nation's leading proponent of "dope fiend mythology."[16] In 1930, he took political advantage of public controversies surrounding the Federal Bureau of Prohibition and emerged as the first commissioner of the newly created Federal Bureau of Narcotics. As an employee of the Treasury Department, Anslinger promoted strict supply-side controls to curb substance use; he dismissed demand-side tactics such as education and treatment.[17] When state conventions repealed alcohol prohibition in 1933, Anslinger retained his post as the nation's leading antinarcotics officer. He would preside over an era of addiction hypocrisy: alcohol would be sold and celebrated; narcotics would be vilified.

Diagnoses aligned with policy. General terms such as *inebriety* and *intemperance* split into substance-specific classifications.[18] Alcoholics professed a weakness for liquor, beer, or wine. Addicts copped to heroin or morphine use. The two groups—pathetic drunkards and dangerous dope fiends—supposedly had little in common.

According to the historian John Burnham, the repeal of alcohol prohibition accelerated social challenges to the dominant nineteenth-century notions about character and respectability. Victorian elites, the ruling class from the mid-1800s until the early twentieth century, largely believed good character could be cultivated through self-restraint and spiritual practice.[19] They did not view bad habits—for example, excessive drinking, cigarette smoking, recreational drug use, gambling, and cursing—as harmless pastimes or isolated pursuits. Each bad habit weakened the will (and the nervous system), opening the door to others. Inebriety was a Victorian concept. The modern "atmosphere is full of psychological germs, calculated to inflict the nervous system and produce disease," concluded the American Association for the Study and Cure of Inebriety in 1893. Treatment involved countering these toxic trends through "the best conditions of forced healthy living."[20]

This moral enterprise collapsed over the course of the twentieth century as business leaders unbundled the underworld vices and sold them off one by one to a growing mass market of compromised consumers. The "vice-industrial complex," Burnham argues, liberated mainstream American mores long before the cultural battles of the permissive sixties.[21] Other scholars have since concurred: the sixties were no radical shift.[22] They were instead the climax of a Toynbeean story in which previously rebellious underclass practices infiltrate the ruling classes and lead to an age of excess.[23] Some reformed addicts of the era, who knew the dangers of hipster culture too well, made a similar assessment.

THE POLITICS OF ADDICTION TREATMENT

By the 1950s, a growing subculture of illicit-drug users took on new identities as fiends and junkies. New pharmacological and psychiatric research on heroin users affirmed the idea that addicts were devious, contagious, and difficult to cure.[24] As social norms regarding premarital sex, alcohol use, and cigarette smoking relaxed in the mid–twentieth century, the opiate user became a lonely icon of illicit vice. Enforcers and researchers explained that addicts posed a threat to the social order. The addict characterized during the strict era of narcotics control tested many tenets of modern progress. Addiction defied individual autonomy, rational consumption, and the useful application of scientific discoveries.[25]

Most importantly, addicts apparently resisted the advances of modern medicine. The treatment methods favored by inebriate homes were replaced by Freudian talk therapy, behaviorism, and hospital detoxification programs, each of which failed to emerge as a long-term cure for narcotic addiction. Inspired by science as well as by politics, addiction treatments were new technologies. Historical circumstances influenced whether the technologies took aim at patients' psyches, behavior, or biology.

From the 1930s until the mid-1960s, the federal government consolidated these varieties of addiction treatment in penitentiaries located in Lexington, Kentucky, and Fort Worth, Texas. The criminalization of opiate use and the decline in treatment options led to a surge of addicted inmates within the prison population in the 1920s. Wardens at federal prisons found the addicts troublesome. They supported a bill, introduced by the Republican congressman Stephen Porter (PA) in 1928, to quarantine and rehabilitate addicts in specially designated penitentiaries.[26] Like many long-gone inebriate asylums, the new penitentiaries would engage addicts in a regular schedule of recreation and pastoral labor. Unlike the inebriate homes—a

FIGURE 0.2

Lexington Narcotic Farm dedication, 1935. Photograph by Lafayette Studios.

Source: Courtesy of the University of Kentucky Libraries Special Collections Research Center, Lexington, Kentucky.

vulnerable village of private and locally funded enterprises—the penitentiaries were a national project. They were managed by a newly created division of the Public Health Service and designed as a showcase for the nation's best psychiatric research.[27] When the Lexington "Narcotic Farm" finally opened in 1935, officials presented the hospital as a "New Deal for the drug addict."[28]

The deal provided addicts with voluntary and court-ordered treatment; the penitentiaries eventually incorporated a range of therapies, including talk therapy, twelve-step support groups, and vocational labor. In return, addicts provided researchers with data. Would sorting addicts into classes (such as iatrogenic or psychopathic addicts)[29] help explain treatment outcomes? Could researchers separate biological and psychological drug dependence? Some patients volunteered to serve as subjects in basic biological research studies; beginning in the 1940s, a separate wing of the Lexington facility housed the Addiction Research Center, a National

Institute of Mental Health (NIMH) laboratory that conducted drug experiments. [30] The federal narcotics hospitals were cathedrals to the era's faith in experts. After World War II, that faith foundered as addiction rates rose and the patients' high relapse rates gained notoriety.[31] Nevertheless, the hospitals' experts continued to cultivate the belief that centralized, scientific government programs could solve social problems.[32]

This philosophy had a name, "technocracy," which became an epithet in the 1960s.[33] According to Theodore Roszack, a leading cultural critic at the time, the U.S. government increasingly relied on scientific experts to justify domestic and internal policies; officials often chose to ignore the unintended consequences of technological advancement. As a technocratic project, the narcotics farms' failed treatment experiments reaped distressing results. Officials labeled drug users "addicts" and corralled them into two central locations; once in those locations, the addicts internalized the label. Rather than permanently breaking addicts of their drug-seeking habits, the farms functioned as a temporary escape from the addicts' everyday environments and from tougher correctional settings. Residents described Lexington as a fraternal "fantastic lodge" where they swapped instructive stories about hustling and scoring.[34] Meanwhile, their repeated stints in prisons and hospitals fostered their skepticism about therapeutic technocrats.

The few midcentury treatment institutions unwittingly primed addicts for an alternative cure. They cited bad experiences with private psychiatrists, shock treatments, and short-term hospital detoxification.[35] "It isn't true that Riverside Hospital didn't cure dope addicts," one ex-addict said sarcastically in the mid-1960s. "In fact Riverside cured me twice. I was also cured at Bellevue and again at Manhattan. The reason I've been cured so often is because [sic] none of these cures lasted any longer than it took me to reach my connection once I was discharged as cured."[36]

THE TREATMENT REVOLUTION

Synanon's promoters claimed that the commune's methods marked a radical departure from the ineffective addiction cures available at other institutions.

FIGURE 0.3

Theodore Roszack, "Synanon: The Therapeutic Community," *Los Angeles Free Press*, August 27, 1964.

Source: Author's personal collection. Courtesy of the *LA Free Press*. See LAFreePress.com for further information about the *LA Free Press* archive.

Its treatment radicalism railed against experts' medical-criminal therapies by reviving an older concept of addiction. Scholars and former residents called Synanon's treatment philosophy positively Victorian.[37] In 1959, one reporter claimed that Synanon stood for "Sinners Anonymous"—an allusion to the nineteenth-century notion that the opiate habit is likely linked to other moral misdemeanors.[38]

The name also evoked Alcoholics Anonymous (AA). In 1958, a recovering alcoholic named Charles "Chuck" Dederich spun Synanon off from an AA group in the Los Angeles area. Dederich was inspired by AA's peer-led therapy, but he claimed its nonjudgmental process of "sharing" was too gentle to affect heroin addicts hardened by their criminal careers, underworld associations, and socially unacceptable substance choice.[39] Dederich instead developed a group process that used confrontation and ridicule to force participants to confront their moral defects. The confrontations took place in an intense, rule-governed familial environment that supported addicts' efforts to replace old, maladaptive defenses with new habits and coping patterns. Whereas AA was a nonresidential mutual-aid society that ran on a gift economy, Synanon's founder was a former oil salesman who hoped his innovative treatment model would turn a profit. Dederich said he chose the name "Synanon" because it "looked good on the side of a truck."[40]

Synanon members protested technocratic midcentury addiction treatment and planned to disrupt it with a market-based solution. The organization's early members included longtime survivors such as Charlie Hamer and younger urban men who encountered heroin along with jazz in the late 1940s and 1950s. The hipsters could have been members of J. Milton Yinger's "contraculture"; in 1960, the sociologist applied the term to groups—such as adolescent delinquents—who live by values in direct opposition to the dominant culture.[41] By the end of the decade, the hipster and beatnik subcultures blossomed into "hippies." Theodore Roszack repackaged the term *contraculture* as *counterculture*, which he described as a vital international movement poised to upend the mechanistic and supposedly dehumanizing value structure of modern society.[42]

Believers in Synanon's treatment model argued that psychoactive chemicals had thoroughly corrupted mainstream culture; they claimed resisting, not ingesting, drugs was countercultural. By the late 1960s, alcohol and prescription-drug abuse appeared problematic. Illicit-drug use was on the rise.[43] The institutions created to deal with addicts' dire problem had seemingly worsened it. In 1969, an ex-addict advocate explained the political significance of the new Synanon-inspired treatment centers to Congress. The nation's misguided drug treatments represented "a failure of America's democracy. A failure of our wasting all this time sending people to the moon and not concentrating on things around here."[44]

From this perspective, the establishment's ineffective drug treatments symbolized the limitations of the consensus politics that had emerged from the New Deal and World War II.

The mutual-aid model pioneered by Synanon would appeal to groups on both sides of the growing cultural and political divide. With its rock soundtrack and conspicuous hair, the counterculture seemed like an apolitical response to the confines of consensus-driven liberalism. But countercultural pastimes encouraged adherents to imagine what sort of society might replace the ruling technocracy.[45]

Two competing visions stood out. Libertarians sought to regain control of their choices from the federal government's supposedly coercive policies; communitarians wanted to foster authentic relationships that defied societal expectations. Both impulses are reflected in unflattering historical interpretations of the counterculture as either market oriented or navel gazing. They reappear in the derisive definition of Synanon: a cult with Coca-Cola ambitions.[46]

Taken together or separately, the libertarianism and communitarianism of the 1960s had utopian implications: for the sake of humanity's future, both the market and the psyche needed to be freed from society's dysfunctional regulations. Despite their futuristic claims, the Synanon-inspired therapeutic communities (TCs) of the 1960s had ancestors. Their founders were motivated by the Episcopalian Oxford Group and its spin-off AA, both of which combined group confession with a can-do attitude toward business.[47] In addition to the reformatory ideals of the asylum movement, leaders found inspiration in nineteenth-century communes such as Oneida, which ran its own industries and used mutual criticism in an attempt to attain Christian perfection.[48] And they were well aware that America was often imagined as a shining city on a hill, a Puritanical utopian experiment first begun in the 1600s.[49]

In the 1960s, treatment pioneers were finally able to turn mutual aid into a saleable product. At federal conferences and congressional hearings, ex-addicts agitated experts and sensationalized reporters. They voiced a strong preference for long-term residential treatments that relied on their personal expertise—a hard-knocks education that some professionals today might call "recovery." The movement toward ex-addict-led treatment models gained traction as graduates of early TCs exported the model to other states and countries.[50]

The movement's accomplishments twist the typical stories about the thwarted radical movements of the 1960s. Unlike thousands of other communes that folded by the late 1970s, TCs gained legitimacy and grew.[51] Most leftist activists helped liberalize cultural attitudes but failed to incite radical economic changes.[52] In contrast, ex-addicts' campaigns revolutionized the treatment marketplace—but they did so by reinforcing stereotypes about drug users and nurturing the idealistic dream of a drug-free America.

Their revolution fills in the details that have mostly dropped out of our drug-policy origin stories. Rather than focusing on treatment activists' efforts, some scholars have traced the source of our troubles to President Richard M. Nixon, who expanded drug-related policing along with treatment.[53] Others view the treatment expansion of the 1970s as a response to public panic about addicted Vietnam veterans, and still others see the drug-policy debates of the late twentieth century as just one battlefield in the larger culture wars between social conservatives and permissive liberals.[54] The most widespread account reduces drug policies to racial politics: historically, we have cracked down on minority populations and found a way to treat affluent white ones.[55]

Race, wars, presidents, partisan politics: all played roles in shaping our current treatment system. But they interacted with the TC activists who, by inventing and advocating for a particular treatment model at an opportune time, were equally influential.

This is their story in three parts: "Revolution," "Co-optation," and "Industrialization."

Synanon led the revolt by capitalizing on the liberal optimism and progressive mental-health policies that accompanied John F. Kennedy's presidency. In the mid-1960s, Synanon began advertising its therapeutic lifestyle to nonaddicted spiritual seekers. Meanwhile, Synanon graduates and affiliates professionalized its model in new TC treatment centers. The TCs attracted national attention, and new stakeholders co-opted their therapeutic approach. TCs received a sizeable federal investment when the Nixon administration expanded treatment to control the heroin epidemics and related crime surges of the late 1960s and early 1970s. Although Synanon and some other centers roiled with violent internal crises in the 1970s, a private treatment industry emerged from their ashes in the 1980s. As the treatment industry grew more profitable in the 1980s, 1990s, and early 2000s, early treatment leaders continued to fight: this time, they faced new competition from other providers, the necessity of developing new revenue streams, and pressure to capitalize on legislative trends. Yet the revolutionary model's continued appeal to establishment liberals and conservatives allowed the rhetoric of treatment radicalism to outlive the upheaval of the 1960s and shape the drug policies of the decades to come.

PART I

REVOLUTION

1

SELLING SYNANON

S YNANON PIONEERED THE hippie business," said its founder, Charles
Dederich. The group modeled communal living before it became
fashionable. Yet Dederich viewed latter-day hippies as hypocrites
who "took what they liked from the established world and then tuned in,
turned on, and dropped out." Their communes were not self-sufficient; their
righteous spirituality disguised immaturity. "What's holy about getting
loaded to your eyelashes and leaving your garbage to pile up and breed flies
while your plumbing goes out of whack and your girls get babies and the
clap at the same time?"[1]

That was the sort of no-nonsense language residents could expect at
Synanon. Like a stern father, Dederich promised to create an orderly residential environment that would teach drug users to behave responsibly.
Run entirely by reformed addicts, the Synanon group soon billed itself as a
"tunnel back to the human race" for heroin addicts trapped in a degenerate
subculture. Synanon's recovering addicts opposed AA's gentle method of
group "sharing"; they preferred to use "attack" therapy to force each other
to confront their sins and defects. The confrontations took place in an intense, rule-governed familial environment that apparently altered the habits of the most hardened addicts. For the early residents who recovered
there, the experience was revolutionary. "What I want to point out you,"
said one ex-addict advocate in the 1960s, "is that what *happened* [to me] at

Synanon did not happen at the Menninger Clinic in Topeka; the Institute of Living in Hartford; three times in Lexington, Kentucky; New York; Metropolitan Hospital; Manhattan General; the Holbrook Sanitarium; or the Westport Sanitarium."[2]

This ex-addict's litany of institutional failures was comprehensive; drug addicts in the late 1950s and early 1960s had few treatment options. The Victorian-era sanitariums that emerged to treat the disease of "inebriety" collapsed by the early twentieth century. A few hollowed state asylums, hospital detoxification centers, and therapeutic federal penitentiaries remained, but by the 1960s patients and the public had come to view these facilities' treatment offerings as futile. Dederich saw the crumbling treatment system as ripe for disruption. Struggling addicts, desperate for a treatment alternative, helped Dederich create one at Synanon. Together, they successfully marketed the organization as a radical and glamorous new form of addiction treatment.

Dederich described his therapeutic experiment as "a new form of communication, a new trade, a new kind of people, a new branch of knowledge, that would possibly have as great an impact on the world as Freud's discoveries in psychoanalysis at the end of the nineteenth century."[3] In Dederich's lifetime, the influence of psychoanalytic ideas expanded beyond the realm of mental-health services to the business world. Marketers appealed to Eros in advertising campaigns; executives applied Carl Jung's Myers-Briggs Typology Index to workplace management. Although Dederich would gain notoriety as a cult leader by the end of the 1970s, his decisions were usually the result of managerial, rather than divine, inspiration.

After helping journalists uncover Synanon's most problematic practices, the sociologist Richard Ofshe concluded that Dederich's management choices drove the organization's development.[4] Synanon first began as an AA-influenced fellowship of recovering alcoholics and addicts (January–September 1958), quickly established a residential TC (September 1958–1968), expanded into a self-declared social movement (1969–1975), and, finally, devolved into a controversial, corporatist new religion (1976–1992). In the last phase, Synanon also came to symbolize the excesses of experiments with spiritual exploration and alternative living in the 1960s and 1970s. "A once-respected drug program turned into a kooky cult," reported *Time* in late 1977.[5] Synanon leaders ordered residents to enter into open marriages, undergo vasectomies, and prepare for battle against the organization's enemies. Professionals warned that Synanon's fate should serve as a "signal for caution" to addiction-treatment centers based on its model.[6]

While scholars and critics fixated on Synanon's connection to cults or communitarian religious movements, generations of treatment centers that followed Synanon sorted out the mixed blessings of their therapeutic inheritance. Early critics argued that the hierarchical treatment model prevalent in TCs, "while freer than many custodial facilities," still presented ample opportunity for the coercion of residents through "ridicule, abrasive encounters, social ostracism, stripping of defenses," and so on.[7] Yet TC proponents ultimately provided evidence that an intense social environment, if managed appropriately, improved clients' outcomes.[8]

Synanon's new therapeutic model directly challenged the drug-treatment status quo. The few recognized drug-treatment facilities—however dubious their cure rates—were authorized by a bureaucracy of medical professionals, criminal-justice referrals, and government funders. In contrast, Synanon's quest for legitimacy initially relied on charismatic leadership. The organization's growing membership of drug-free former addicts congregated around Dederich and gave his treatment methods credibility. Had Dederich's community been unable to attract the interest of establishment figures such as government officials, researchers, reporters, and business leaders, Synanon's early members might have lost interest in the movement. Had he been quick to offer the treatment model to the authorities who wished to modify it, the recovery revolution may have been moderated—or, as sociologist Max Weber put it, "routinized."[9] It instead took more than a decade for TC treatment to become routine.

Until then, treatment radicals' integrity correlated with their leader's charisma. Dederich's business plan shaped Synanon's treatment structure. His personality inspired a provocative new way to think about addiction and its treatment.

Charles E. Dederich was born in Toledo, Ohio, in 1913 and was fatherless less than ten years later. Dederich's mother married a well-off engineer soon after her husband's death, altering the family's financial circumstances and Dederich's status in the household. They moved into a large Victorian house, and Dederich was sent to private Catholic schools and briefly to college at Notre Dame. He had difficulty adjusting to Notre Dame, and his grades were poor. He returned to his hometown, found work at Gulf Oil's office, married, and had a son he named Charles Jr. As a traveling salesman for Gulf, Dederich became a heavy social drinker, and for a time cocktails capped off his business deals. In 1944, he contracted meningitis and fell into a coma that lasted two weeks. He survived after doctors performed a mastoidectomy that left him with facial deformities and tics. A droopy eye, partly paralyzed mouth, and brush with death sent Dederich into a deep depression; his habitual alcohol abuse progressed to alcoholism.[10] Seeking renewal, he moved his wife and son to Los Angeles, California, where he divorced, remarried, and had a daughter, Jady, by his second wife. His increasingly problematic drinking made it difficult for him to maintain employment.[11] In 1956, Dederich's second wife left him, and—taking her parting suggestion to heart—he attended his first AA meeting. "Once she was sure that I had a fighting chance of taking care of myself, we divided everything up," said Dederich. "She took the inside of the house, and I took the outside."[12]

Dederich's wit made him a sought-after AA speaker. He maintained his abstinence from alcohol by attending an AA meeting each day. He landed an office job at an aircraft-manufacturing company in Santa Barbara but quickly grew restless. Citing a new revelation from a tattered copy of his favorite essay, "Self-Reliance" by Ralph Waldo Emerson, Dederich quit his job, returned to Los Angeles, and dedicated himself to creating a new enterprise that would cure other alcoholics. Emerson was a leader of the mid-nineteenth-century transcendentalist movement, which advanced the idea that the cultivation of the individual mind and spirit was the best route to the divine. Emerson's essay urged readers to be skeptical about living according to traditional belief structures and societal constraints.[13]

Dederich offered an alternative to square, Salvation Army–style evangelism. He tried to convince a local AA clubhouse to transform the meeting space into a kind of "way-out hep jazz AA club" that would cater to a younger demographic and welcome addicts as well as alcoholics.[14] The AA stalwarts rejected Dederich's proposal. By 1957, however, he had nevertheless gathered a small fellowship of recovering alcoholics and addicts in a dilapidated storefront in Venice Beach. They paid the rent with one member's disability pension. Although Dederich's group continued to attend local AA meetings, privately their rollicking, confrontational arguments evolved into a distinct form of therapy. In 1958, Dederich pushed the members of his group to formalize their association. The alcoholic members, in keeping with AA tradition, wanted to maintain an informal, nonproprietary, voluntary association and resisted Dederich's plan to incorporate.[15] The AA traditionalists, said Dederich, were "gumming up my deal" with their emphasis on God and gift economy. "They still thought it was an AA club and they would come in and put a dime on the counter and drink 30 cups of coffee and use our shower."[16] The addicts followed Dederich, and, together with four other members, he drafted an organizational charter and filed the necessary paperwork. In 1958, the Venice Beach flophouse became a nonprofit corporation. Dederich originally called the organization the "Tender Loving Care Club" but soon changed the name to "Synanon"— a brand that brought to mind the old-fashioned concept of "sin," the twelve-step precedent of "anonymous," and the group's therapeutic "symposiums"—because he had a vision of the group's logo "in print, on letterheads, and on our literature."[17]

At first, members subsisted on donuts and stale sandwiches donated by local vendors.[18] Gradually, the organization attracted new members, positive press coverage, and bigger donors. After Dederich's split with alcoholic members, Synanon became focused on courting heroin users. According to Synanon's press coverage and internal bookkeeping, residents in the early 1960s were prototypical hipster heroin addicts: they were mostly working-class white men from traditional immigrant communities in urban centers. Enamored of jazz and cynical about their futures, they had started using drugs in adolescence and entered Synanon in their late twenties.[19] Synanon also admitted a smaller number of women and African Americans, and Dederich believed that "hustling" for funds and attention taught all the organization's addicts—regardless of race, gender, age, or addiction history—to channel their survival skills into a responsible enterprise. By 1968, Synanon had more than one thousand residents and locations in San Francisco, Santa Monica, New York, and Detroit.[20]

Dederich initially claimed his entrepreneurial vision was equal parts Emerson and lysergic acid diethylamide (LSD). In the 1950s, several human experiments demonstrated that LSD, a derivative of a grain fungus with hallucinogenic properties, was an effective treatment for alcoholics. Researchers hypothesized that the hallucinogenic experience facilitated by LSD mimicked the experience of delirium tremens, a condition caused by withdrawal from alcohol and often accompanied by visual hallucinations. For some alcoholics, the nightmarish delirium functioned as a shock that influenced a subsequent commitment to recovery. AA cofounder Bill Wilson endorsed and participated in LSD experiments.

One of the researchers who administered LSD to Bill Wilson was Keith Ditman of the University of California at Los Angeles (UCLA). Together with Sidney Cohen, the psychiatrist who would later become a leading official at the NIMH, Ditman conducted experiments to test whether LSD aids alcoholism treatment. Charles Dederich, then in early recovery from alcoholism and eager for novel therapeutic experiences, enrolled in Ditman and Cohen's LSD study.[21] In Dederich's account, a transcendent experience on LSD led to a series of "calmer breakthroughs" in the months following the experiment.[22] In the mid-1960s, Dederich emphasized LSD's ability to help him see beyond the prescribed limits of traditional institutions.[23] But in a friendly retrospective conversation with Cohen, he concentrated on the drug's therapeutic utility. Dederich said that the clarity he gained in Cohen's medical experiment helped him transform from an unfocused "fanatic" to a clean-shirted, "dedicated man."[24]

A month before his conversation with Dederich in 1966, Cohen warned a U.S. Senate subcommittee about the dangers of recreational LSD use.[25] By then the drug had migrated from psychiatrists' "clinics to [college] campus[es]."[26] As LSD morphed from a promising psychiatric treatment to a street substance of abuse, Synanon began to recruit polydrug-using youth who had taken multiple doses of LSD.[27] For these new residents, Dederich decided, LSD couldn't be considered an appropriate therapeutic tool. Instead, Synanon used variations of the confrontational therapy tactics that had worked well on the original group of hardened heroin addicts in the early 1960s. Leaders expanded Synanon's confrontational therapy groups into days-long "marathons" or "dissipation" sessions that broke down the ego without the aid of drugs. The famous humanistic psychologist Abraham Maslow agreed with Synanon's leaders: group therapy was a good alternative to hallucinogens.[28] The short-term dissipation of the self helped individuals gain new perspectives on their problems and stifling preconceptions. Participants supposedly emerged more self-reliant or—to use Maslow's term—"self-actualized."[29]

Synanon's shorter sessions also helped residents of all ages "grow up." Several times a week residents gathered for group confrontations. They originally called the sessions "synanons"—supposedly inspired by a tongue-tied resident's riff on "seminar" or "symposium"—but later decided to call the meetings "games."[30] The hard-fought confrontations provided an outlet for residents to express their daily frustrations. The sessions also used humor, ridicule, and rage to force participants to confront their personal failings. In one of the first sessions, several founding Synanon members admitted they were using drugs on the sly. In an environment such as the federal Lexington Narcotic Hospital, they might have hidden their habits from the therapist. But the encounter's ego-crushing peer pressure made it difficult to evade detection. In a Synanon session, Dederich explained, "There is no escape through chemicals, techniques of avoidance come to nothing, the con-wise criminal finds himself thwarted at every turn, and the high verbal professional can't find enough words to talk his way around things."[31] Synanon's members confessed and committed themselves to clean living.

Most of these members kept their promise.[32] Their ability to do so bolstered Dederich's claim that compulsive drug seeking was a maladaptive response to social pressures. The treatment was simple: Synanon "points out [addicts'] stupidity in the hope that they will learn how to grow up and function like adults," said Dederich.[33] The technique worked for other supposed symptoms of immaturity, avoidance, and indulgence, including countercultural hedonism. One Synanon member had been arrested seven times for public protesting; she said she was "addicted to peace demonstrating and marches." She was immersed in hippie culture and "did everything they did but grow a beard" until Synanon helped change her self-presentation, worldview, and behavior.[34] It did so without any drugs, within a surrogate-family setting, and with considerable style and drama. In the 1960s, these strategies became excellent selling points.

* * *

Synanon opened its doors to tours by elected officials and addiction researchers. Some were sold on the therapeutic model; others were less certain. In 1963, officials in the New York City Department of Corrections were considering investing in a Synanon-style program.

Richard McGee, a leader in midcentury prison reform and an administrator in California's Youth and Adolescent Corrections Agency, wrote a confidential letter to New York corrections commissioner Anna Kross in May 1963. McGee warned Kross to be suspicious of Synanon's positive press. "When Senator Dodd of Connecticut was in California holding hearings on this matter a year ago, he was completely taken in by the press-agentry of Mr. Dederich and wrote a laudatory speech into the *Congressional Record*," wrote McGee. "Unofficial information is that he is now very embarrassed by having gone out on a limb without careful investigation."[35]

Nearly a century earlier, the establishment of the *Congressional Record* had turned congressional proceedings into "a sort of variety performance, where nothing is supposed to be real except the pay," complained one public servant at the time.[36] When the complaint reappeared as evidence in historian Daniel Boorstin's book *The Image* in 1962, political culture had grown more dramatic. Full-fledged professions of advertising and public relations arose from the local variety shows used to sell medicine and home goods in the nineteenth century. Although the new industries brought advertisements to a mass audience, their twentieth-century campaigns often reproduced the contradictory Victorian strategy of celebrating self-discipline while simultaneously reveling in the primitive or profane. This evangelical script for personal transformation persisted even after advertising consolidated in professional firms that presented self-improvement in more scientific terms.[37]

Twentieth-century advertisers attempted to use the new science of psychology to rationalize their manipulation of market audiences, but they could never completely manage their trade's carnival qualities. In advertising, even straightforward language and statistics took on a degree of artifice.[38] Whether confronted with the nineteenth-century nostrums of the medicine show or the products highlighted by the World War I newsreel, audiences could never be entirely sure that salesmen's claims were true—in fact, ambiguity had always been part of advertising's appeal.[39] The adoption of photography and cinema, which aimed to document reality more accurately, only heightened audience incredulity.

Boorstin and others argue that by the 1960s new media professionals were not only documenting history but also manufacturing it. Public-relations firms regularly staged "pseudoevents," marketing or entertainment gambits that audiences perceived as authentic and significant.[40] Successful pseudoevents were self-fulfilling prophecies; if a hotel wanted to increase its prestige, it simply needed to present itself as prestigious. Much as AA entreated its members to "act as if" they possessed psychological health in order to achieve it, public-relations pioneer Edward Bernays advised an aspirational hotelier to persuade a committee of high-profile community members to host an anniversary celebration big enough to attract media attention. The event, wrote Boorstin, "gave the hotel the prestige to which it was pretending."[41]

The media impact of pseudoevents depended on audience curiosity rather than on gullibility. Is the news story real or fake? Ambiguity generates ongoing public interest. Much as hoteliers produced prestige, Synanon House's staged tours implied that the organization was a significant new form of drug treatment; news coverage of the tours reinforced that idea. But from the moment Synanon appeared in the press in the late 1950s, readers puzzled about whether to believe media accounts of its cure.

In the late 1950s, the recovered heroin addict was a curiosity. Early Synanon members played into the sensationalism that often accompanied depictions of the social problem of addiction; one reporter described Dederich as a "cross between P. T. Barnum and Florence Nightingale," a neo-Victorian hybrid of grand self-presentation and altruistic intention.[42] Without the aid of public-relations professionals, Synanon members instigated local news coverage of a Santa Monica zoning controversy. They rallied celebrities, politicians, and academics to help Synanon resist wealthy opponents' attempts to prevent the organization from occupying a new property on Santa Monica Beach. The conflict was initially a local issue that interested beachfront homeowners, but Synanon used it as a platform for promoting the promise of its therapeutic method. Images first described in the *Santa Monica Evening Outlook* were later repeated in articles, photo essays, and films by national media outlets such as *Time*, *The Nation*, and *Life*.[43] Following the paper trail, academics arrived to investigate the organization's novel treatment strategy. As scholars continued to study Synanon, their findings also circled through a series of popular media outlets. The tension between Synanon as a verifiable, therapeutic breakthrough and stagey revival of a nineteenth-century confessional lengthened the pseudo-event into an era. From 1958 to 1968, Synanon members sold the organization's addiction cure as the solution to the nation's drug-abuse problem.

SYNANON'S ICONS

"Unique Club Seeks to Whip Narcotics," declared one of the first articles published about Synanon, which appeared in the *Evening Outlook* in January 1959, just months after the organization was founded. Reporter R. D. Fox described the Venice Beach club's unconventional atmosphere and followed the description with a twist: the club's residents "are not 'beatniks.' They are not 'Bohemians.' They are narcotics addicts trying to cure themselves." The only requirement for membership, noted Fox, is the experience of "hitting bottom" and the desire to "start climbing the ladder back to normal society—back to the world of the 'squares.'" Although members of AA began their "steps" to sobriety from a similarly low point, Fox reported, Synanon stood for "Sin, Anonymous."[44] In contrast to AA, Synanon claimed to offer a more comprehensive characterological makeover, one that combined public humiliation for wrongdoing with growth-motivated educational sessions that drew lessons from Bible passages, popular psychology and sociology texts, and nineteenth-century transcendentalists such as Emerson.[45] These sessions took place in intimate living quarters, which Fox described as an efficient "ship-board type" atmosphere. Fox observed that a life preserver hanging on the clubhouse had the words "'S.S. Hang Tough' painted in neat letters in place of a ship's name. It means keep trying, don't give up."[46] The "Hang Tough" life preserver became an enduring symbol of Synanon's novel therapeutic philosophy; two years later, the preserver still hung on the wall, and a *Time* reporter used the image to introduce a portrait of Dederich.[47]

The "hang tough" directive worked for scholars as well as for supposedly "hardened" addicts. Shortly after the first *Evening Outlook* articles appeared, a graduate student in sociology at UCLA joined Synanon. Rita "Ricky" Volkman was the first nonaddict to participate in Synanon games and the first scholar to study the organization in depth. Volkman initially found the games "tremendously exciting" but resisted the idea that they were relevant to her life as an accomplished, middle-class young woman. Participation in the games gradually began to break down her self-image of a "lovely and highly educated young girl, just stuffed with sweetness and light." Volkman's confrontations with the ex-addicts caused an identity crisis as she came to view her polished self-image as an illusion, "another kind of dope I had been taking all my life." Stripped of her previous source of self-confidence, Volkman considered abandoning her research project. She sat in her car and prepared to drive away when she "remembered that 'Hang Tough' motto that one of the addicts has painted on a ship's life preserver. I would swing the wheel of my car hard and drive right back, determined to see it through."[48]

Synanon permitted other writers to take part in early encounter groups. Less than two years after the first *Outlook* article appeared, Walker Winslow, a prominent journalist and recovering alcoholic who had chronicled the Menninger family and their influence on psychotherapy, moved into Synanon with plans to complete a book on the organization's therapeutic method. Although Winslow anticipated that outsiders might consider living with ex-addicts "an adventure" or a "novel way of gathering morbid material," he experienced Synanon as a "a new dynamic of family life that each day brings some fresh reward." The uncompromising honesty evident in Synanon's therapy sessions could also be found on its house tours. Synanon guides, wrote Winslow, "followed the injunction 'display before you are investigated,' and let officials and professional people stroll where they will and talk to whomever they wish."[49] Synanon leaders incorporated positive press coverage into their tours for journalists and officials. The media attention attracted newsmakers along with new residents.

Winslow covered the *Evening Outlook* reports. The paper reversed its positive assessment of Synanon when the ex-addicts relocated from a seedy Venice storefront to an armory building on Santa Monica Beach. Winslow posited that the *Evening Outlook*'s editors catered to wealthy Santa Monica residents that made up the paper's primary readership.[50] The city condemned the Venice beach facility in 1959—Dederich later conceded that the small storefront wasn't designed to house twenty-five people—and members of a local theatrical club volunteered to fund Synanon's rent if it found a suitable new building. The planned move to beachfront property met with fierce opposition from Synanon's new neighbors, who attended Santa Monica City Council meetings and urged the city attorney to file investigations for health and zoning violations. In August 1959, Synanon was charged with a misdemeanor zoning violation for operating a hospital without a license, and the theatrical club withdrew its support. The local dispute spurred a national public-relations campaign.

Synanon residents drafted letters to Governor Edmund Brown and President John F. Kennedy. The Synanon file maintained by the NIMH included more than fifty letters from Synanon residents and supporters as well as Synanon's own offprints of positive news coverage from *The Nation*, *Manas*, *Sepia*, *Downbeat*, and *Time*.[51] Synanon members perfected testimonials that emphasized the longevity of their abstinence from drugs. In a letter to President Kennedy, ex-addict Charlie Hamer offered his two drug-free years in Synanon as evidence that the organization was "the first workable approach to this terrible problem that has yet been discovered." Rather than asking for federal funds, Hamer and others urged Kennedy to "help us preserve the right to help ourselves."[52] At a Santa Monica City Council meeting, reported Winslow, "member after member of Synanon got up, after the manner of Salvation Army 'testifiers,' and told his or her story. Tears began to flow on both sides. Even the *Outlook* editorial writer was softened."[53]

Whereas Salvation Army testimonials were aimed at pious observers, Synanon members sought to convince the editors. As Synanon expanded, the extensive media coverage of its therapeutic lifestyle became difficult to distinguish from the actual inner workings of its media-rich environment. In 1964, the tour offered to a *San Francisco Chronicle* reporter followed an established script. By then, Synanon's display of positive news clippings blanketed a large corkboard near Synanon's office, where an ex-addict, serving as a guide, greeted the reporter with a firm handshake. Before offering his own recovery testimonial, the guide screened a short *Steve Allen Show* television clip about Synanon, which described members' domestic duties, intense group interactions, artistic pursuits, and therapeutic philosophy ("An addict is a child that has a need for a firm loving hand," said Dederich's screen image).[54] When the guide finally offered his own testimonial, he punctuated his recovery story with a few rough statistics about Synanon's cure rate, pausing occasionally to point at the first academic book about Synanon to reprint Dederich's figures, *So Fair a House* by Daniel Casriel.[55] The *Chronicle* article did not dwell on the data. It instead included a familiar observation—the S.S. "Hang Tough" life preserver hanging over Synanon's mantle—and a title pasted from the pages of a *Life* magazine photo essay, "A Tunnel Back to the Human Race."[56]

The *Life* article had brought Synanon's addiction treatment to a national audience. The weekly picture magazine had debuted to a wide readership in 1936 and doubled its circulation to two million by the following year.[57] The *Santa Monica Independent* reported that the Synanon essay was the "largest black and white documentary that *Life* has ever done"; the photographer took more than seven thousand photos.[58] Critics anticipated that the story would have considerable reach. One Santa Monica doctor wrote to Bureau of Narcotics commissioner Harry J. Anslinger, complaining that the *Life* article would bring the organization's problematic pitch to a national audience. Synanon "conducts a constant appeal to the youth community," he wrote, through its "beatnik atmosphere" and constant invitations to "fraternize with the addicts and thereby show what wonderful people they were."[59] The criticism had some merit; after seeing the *Life* essay, one young woman fantasized about using an eyebrow pencil to imitate track marks so she could gain admission to Synanon.[60] Even residents in the federal government's rehabilitation facility at Lexington, Kentucky, received *Life*. The unforgettable Synanon issue circulated in group therapy sessions. After a post-Lexington relapse, one addict asked his brother to help him get to Synanon: "in the back of my mind I remembered the article from Lexington," he said.[61]

FIGURE 1.1

Grey Villet, "A Tunnel Back Into the Human Race," *Life*, March 9, 1962.

Source: Reprinted courtesy of Getty Images.

The attention generated by the article began to alter Synanon's management structure. In the early 1960s, Synanon had three stages; residents moved up to greater degrees of responsibility and independence, concluding with a graduation. By 1965, Synanon phased out the final graduation stage. Synanon promoter Zev Putterman argued that the *Life* article forced Synanon to innovate. It had to launch new industries to support an influx of residents attracted by the photo essay.[62] It developed new business projects—such as gas stations as well as new treatment facilities in San Francisco and Connecticut—that required leadership and staff. Synanon had an incentive to retain its most experienced ex-addicts as leaders.

"*PEYTON PLACE* FOR DOPE FIENDS"

The earliest ex-addicts in Synanon achieved celebrity. Other media outlets repeated the images presented in *Life*. *Life*'s photos were recycled as décor in Synanon House's foyer; they appeared as part of the set when the Synanon band played on the television show *Jazz Scene USA*; and they hovered in the background of director Richard Quine's motion picture about the group. The movie *Synanon*, released by Columbia Pictures in 1965, dramatized *Life*'s journalistic photo essay and illustrated the therapeutic rationale that Synanon members promoted.[63] In his review of the film, *Saturday Review* reporter Hollis Alpert echoed local Santa Monica critics when he argued that the movie's attempt to make addicts sympathetic glamorized them. "Be *proud* to be an addict," he wrote sarcastically. "Hollywood is on your side. Why, that whole fan magazine crowd is doing it, and if your own family can't or won't help you, if society at large turns its collective head, don't worry[,] man. There's always Synanon."[64]

Columbia's publicity campaign further muddled the studio's artistic intention. At times, the movie was promoted as a serious film about rehabilitation but at others as an exploitation of teen fascination with hard-drug use.[65] The advertisements catered to audiences' desire to see "real" stories of suffering and redemption. Promotional material for the film featured two pages of biographies. The first page, titled "Cast Histories," featured headshots and résumés of the actors featured in the film; the second, "Case Histories," displayed headshots and rap sheets of the recovering addicts from Synanon who were awarded supporting roles.[66] As a promotional tie-in, the Columbia press book urged theater owners to ask former addicts to tell their stories on local radio or television spots.[67]

One aspect of the film struck *Life* author Richard Stolley as "unsettling": watching "actors play real people." Director Richard Quine enlisted Synanon residents as extras and supporting actors, and he styled the lead actors after real Synanon residents featured in the article. Nevertheless, Stolley gave the film an enthusiastic endorsement, asserting that its faithful adaptation of his text grounded it in truth. "Too melodramatic? Not in my experience," wrote Stolley. "Although there is ample drama, it is not the showbiz kind; it is the drama of a superb documentary, which it essentially is."[68] Although the actors' performances might verge on the extreme, Stolley defended the film's authenticity on the basis of the plotlines, which were based on true events.

In fact, *Synanon* is a docudrama. *Life* magazine and Time-Life film depicted the real-life dramas of Synanon's residents; the Columbia movie fictionalized them.[69] By definition, docudramas deploy melodrama—a narrative form that relies on stock characters and tightly written, pathos-filled plots—to deliver social critique. Docudramas place an intimate, familiar domestic setting within the context of corrupt and powerful social systems. Cinema scholar Steven Lipkin argues that the docudrama's ability to resolve its fictionalized, domestic plotline suggests that the "lost moral structure" that characterizes the film's social setting "can be recovered and restored."[70]

Synanon's plotlines were driven by the residents' real stories of redemption, which took place within a ship-shape domestic setting. Ex-addicts described Synanon as an exit from lives of prostitution, theft, drug dealing, and alienation, and their stories helped Dederich sell the organization as a "tunnel back to the human race." This line became the title for the *Life* feature, the subtitle of an academic book about Synanon, and the tagline for the Columbia film.[71]

The metaphorical tunnel went through Synanon's living room. *Life*'s photo essay, like earlier journalistic tours of Synanon, took the viewer through the domestic spaces of Synanon House. Photographer Grey Villet captured meals, chores, and conversations. These images established the normalcy of the ex-addicts' communal life. The mundane aspects of Synanon's private life made the contrasting images of sensational "game" therapy sessions more credible. Addicts were a curiosity. A radical new therapy with the potential to reform them? That was newsworthy. "We snatch all the covers off our dirty little secrets," read one subhead in an ex-addict's voice. The *Life* article explained how the seemingly over-the-top, tough-love interactions created an environment that fostered domestic tranquility.[72]

Author Richard Stolley viewed *Life*'s close-ups of ex-addicts' confrontations through a therapeutic lens: "Out of his own agonizing honesty, the addict reaches a more realistic and, surprisingly, a more comfortable feeling about himself and his shortcomings."[73] As a studio film, *Synanon* dramatized the residents' confrontations for entertainment purposes. Syn-

FIGURE 1.2

Grey Villet, "A Tunnel Back Into the Human Race," *Life*, March 9, 1962.
"We snatch all the covers off our dirty little secrets."

Source: Reprinted courtesy of Getty Images.

anon's own public-relations campaign nevertheless benefited from the docu-drama approach. The film suggested that by redeeming a small cohort of addicted residents in a private therapeutic setting, Synanon's treatment methods could counteract the prevailing drug culture. The repetition of Synanon's theories also helped sustain public interest about the veracity of its cure.

Some aspects of the film were strategic distortions, designed to bring Synanon's therapy to a wider audience. Dederich and his supporters sought movie deals from the time Synanon started; at one point, they pitched a script about the Santa Monica zoning dispute. When Columbia finally acquired the rights to the Synanon story, the production company promoted the adaptation as a bold move. "Synanon sold the motion picture rights to three different companies," the film's program explained. "In each case, options were dropped when controversy raged around the brave efforts of this institution." Instead of avoiding controversy, Columbia planned to capitalize on it.[74] Edmund O'Brien lobbied for the role of Chuck Dederich, whom he described as "the most total personality I've ever met." But the Dederich character did not make an ideal leading man. "Columbia was interested in making money," said O'Brien. Producers inserted a doomed love story into the Synanon narrative in order to make the picture commercially viable. "Chuck [Dederich] wanted the [therapeutic] methodology truly represented. Then if a boy–girl story was necessary for the box office, he agreed to that," said O'Brien.[75]

Although the movie wasn't a box-office success, Synanon managed to benefit from it.[76] Dederich negotiated compensation for Synanon's role in the film's production. ("I have no way of putting a price on the peculiar 'gut level' technical advice that is available here," he wrote to Richard Quine, the film's director before the film was released. "So what do I do? What is the matter with a lump sum in the neighborhood of $100,000 or $125,000 to cover all these things, help in rewriting, working with actors, etc.[?]")[77] Columbia hosted a benefit premiere at Santa Monica's Aero Theatre and donated the proceeds to Synanon.[78] Synanon's own San Francisco premiere featured Synanon members, actor Chuck Connors, the Synanon band, and a display featuring a scholarly book about Synanon, *Synanon: The Tunnel Back* by Lewis Yablonsky.[79] Synanon members took advantage of the Hollywood publicity machine and blamed the cinematic excesses on the entertainment industry. "We know more about living than Hollywood does," said one ex-addict in a panel discussion following a San Francisco screening. "All they know is how to make one kind of movie, *Peyton Place* for dope fiends."[80]

A "JUNKET WITH THE NATIONAL INSTITUTE OF MENTAL HEALTH"

Incredible depictions of Synanon's therapeutic method also attracted scholars. Ricky Volkman's adviser, criminologist Donald Cressey, described her work on the group to criminologist Lewis Yablonsky. Cressey convinced Yablonsky that a "radical set of circumstances" might be required to solve an intractable problem such as drug addiction.[81]

Yablonsky observed Synanon in 1961. In 1962, Yablonsky and psychiatrist Daniel Casriel joined Dederich at a Senate subcommittee meeting on juvenile delinquency. Casriel had visited Synanon while undertaking a nationwide survey of innovative addiction-treatment methods. Dederich described Casriel's tour in salesman's terms: Casriel discovered Synanon as part of his "junket with the National Institute of Mental Health," said Dederich. "This 'junket,'" agreed Casriel, "has been one of the most worthwhile and rewarding experiences of my life. I think [Synanon] is the greatest breakthrough psychiatry has seen since Freud."[82]

Former psychiatric patients agreed. Seven Synanon members submitted their case histories to Congress, summarizing the years of drug use, criminal history, and therapeutic failures they accrued before achieving months or years "clean" in Synanon. Like the ex-addicts who emphasized the failures of previous treatments, Yablonsky and Casriel described their disappointing experiences researching and treating addicts in institutions such as Riverside and Metropolitan Hospitals. Thomas Dodd Sr., chair of the Senate subcommittee, had invited the men to testify before it. Dodd was a conservative Democratic senator from Connecticut who, along with Estes Kefauver (D–TN), convened a series of hearings about the influence of media on adolescent violence. His subcommittee on juvenile delinquency would go on to explore the effects of drugs on youth. In 1962, he concluded the subcommittee's examination of Synanon with a rousing endorsement that was later reprinted in the *Congressional Record*.

"The central ingredient of Synanon" is not present "in any treatment methods attempted in correctional institutions, psychiatric clinics or even the two Federal hospitals for drug addicts," declared Dodd. That ingredient, he concluded, is the "family type social climate where hardened drug addicts help each other get a grip on life." Synanon's ability to function as a "substitute for the right kind of family most addicts never had" served as Dodd's central selling point to his fellow politicians. Dodd claimed he was not highlighting the seven Synanon members as "horrible examples, or to exploit their difficulties"; his stated goal was to "draw inspiration" from the ex-addicts' experiences and urge federal agencies such as the NIMH to "experiment with the Synanon idea."[83]

Controlled experiments proved difficult. Synanon members resisted efforts to quantify or replicate the organization's processes. Dederich said he "didn't believe in statistics"; he favored participant observation instead.[84] In 1961, Synanon leaders refused to furnish California's Narcotics Commission with client records.[85] But Synanon's opposition to statistical analysis did not prevent the organization from developing what Boorstin at the time called a "corporate image," a brand identity built on "over-simplified, sociological concepts such as 'status,' 'other–direction,' etc."[86]

FIGURE 1.3

The Columbia Pictures press book for the motion picture *Synanon* (Columbia Pictures, 1965).

Source: Courtesy of Columbia Pictures/Sony. Copyright © 1965, renewed 1993, Columbia Pictures Industries. All rights reserved.

Yablonsky's research argued that "status," not pseudofamilial relations, was at the center of the Synanon model. Former addicts could earn
recognition for achievements that ran contrary to the reinforcement they
previously received for abiding by the code of the "street." These ex-addicts
served as achievable role models for new Synanon recruits, who could move
up to positions of leadership and authority in the organization as they ma-
tured. In Synanon, developing a new, drug-free identity became a way to gain
status. Although early critics of the organization observed that residents'
adoption of a strict behavioral code resembled the brainwashing tactics of an
army boot camp, Zen monastery, or Maoist re-education camp, Synanon
members argued that their growth in the program was not simply a response
to external stimuli.[87] "Outer-directed" individuals, explained sociologist
David Riesman in his popular book *The Lonely Crowd* (1950), reacted to
their circumstances, allowing the social expectations placed on them to
shape their desires and identity. Riesman argued that the bureaucracies
of the 1950s tended to favor the outer-directed personality type because these
individuals could be easily convinced to adopt the goals and values of large
organizations. In contrast, "inner-directed" individuals had a strong, autonomous sense of their own identity, values, and unique human potential.[88] After
Synanon residents rejected their former identities as addicts, they theoretically went through a process of discovery and emerged with a more authentic sense of self. "In the space of just a few short months," wrote one
reporter, "former addicts have passed through two stages of transformation corresponding approximately to Riesman's change from 'outer-direc-
tion' to 'inner direction.'"[89]

Synanon members spoke social science lingo but largely rejected the
scientific method. This tactic was in keeping with the marketing trends of
the time, as dry, data-driven advertisements gave way to a style of self-
expression and nonconformity.[90] Yablonsky, who later became Synanon's
director of research, intuited the trend when he argued that there was a "possible danger in using standard methods of research on Synanon." The danger
was part placebo effect, part public-relations problem. Systematic attempts to
study the residents could "conceivably impair the aura of positive expectation
and success that surrounds Synanon," wrote Yablonsky. Part of the reason
Synanon was able to attract and reform new residents, Yablonsky argued,

was that addicts believed the cure would work.[91] "Attitudes are more important than facts," declared one prominent sign in Synanon House.[92]

Addicts who did not believe Synanon's method would work quickly departed, and the organization did not follow up with residents who gave up on the therapy after a few short days or weeks. The records that the organization provided to the New Jersey Study Commission in 1964 indicate that around 50 percent of Synanon residents left within the first six months—not enough time to reform an addictive personality by Synanon's standards.[93] Although Synanon guarded its rosters, an internal population history conducted in November of that year anticipated later studies of TC efficacy. The longer residents stayed in Synanon, the less likely they were to drop out: the dropout rate fell to 40 percent for those who stayed three months, 32 percent for those who stayed six months, and less than 25 percent for those who stayed a year or longer. As of 1964, of the 1,180 members who had joined Synanon since 1958, 463 (39.3 percent) were in residence or had graduated in good standing.[94] By the standards of Synanon's contemporaries, that cure rate was more than respectable.[95]

But good data paled in comparison to compelling visual evidence—such as a beachside class picture of Synanon's reformed addicts, the opening shot in a Time-Life documentary film. The photo reinforced Synanon's preferred numerical argument: that the organization had "the largest number of clean addicts in one place as anyplace else in the world."[96] The talking point came with an important caveat: "outside an institution." Because Synanon residency was voluntary, the members argued that it differed from coercive total institutions such as prisons and hospitals. Synanon's promoters claimed that its successful but unconventional therapeutic methods made it difficult for the organization to obtain federal government support.

Not that Synanon didn't try. Synanon followed Dodd's suggestion to his fellow senators and, with Yablonsky's help, applied for NIMH funding. When the reviewers rejected Synanon's application in favor of other TCs based on its model, its leaders turned to industry. According to supporter Guy Endore, the organization "was forced to depend on the charity of thousands of modest donors, plus some few—some very few—larger donors such as the Mellon Family."[97]

SPONSORS OF SYNANON

The Sponsors of Synanon (known by the acronym SOS) list in 1964 included entertainers such as Steve Allen, Ruth and Milton Berle, and Jack Lemmon; media professionals such as *Life* reporter Richard Stolley and *Manas* magazine publisher Henry Geiger; as well as criminology and mental health researchers such as Karl Menninger, Donald Cressey, and Lewis Yablonsky.[98] By the mid-1960s, Synanon cited several large companies as major investors, including Burlington Industries, Singer, Haggar, and Maidenform.[99] Synanon's so-called hustling program began when the first residents begged for modest donations of food and clothing. Within a few years, the hustling program had grown into an efficient operation. Synanon members advised companies to dispose of unsold food and merchandise by donating them to Synanon. Salespeople emphasized that because Synanon was charitable enterprise, the donations were eligible for tax write-offs.

Synanon supporters often made an economic argument for their treatment method. A pamphlet soliciting monetary donations described the "billions of dollars wasted" on ineffective educational programs that failed to prevent or cure drug addiction. "This is because of our neglect in teaching adulthood and fundamental morality, [which form] Synanon's basic curriculum," wrote fund-raisers. A detachable return card provided blank spaces where potential donors could contribute to Synanon by indicating how long they would "like to keep one drug addict off the streets." According to the card, Synanon rehabilitated a single addict for the cost of approximately $3 a day, $20 a week, $80 a month, and $1,000 a year.[100]

By 1963, Synanon had an impressive fund-raising record. That year the organization received approximately $800,000 in donations of goods and services and $200,000 in cash.[101] In Synanon, fund-raising was part of the treatment. Synanon's ex-addicts gained the confidence to seek out powerful, moneyed individuals. "I could go to the president of most banks and get an appointment, or crash a senator's office because he's never sure how many votes I represent," remembered John Maher, a former Synanon member who later founded his own TC. At Synanon, Maher learned to transition smoothly from corporate meetings to countercultural

FIGURE 1.4

"Attitudes are more important than facts." In Gene Dauber and Jim Hoffman, "New Hope for the Addict: Synanon," *Pageant*, January 1964 (offprint).

Source: Author's personal collection.

Without pain, without histrionics, an organization of addicts destroys one of the myths of our times and brings new life to men at the edge of death. Here, in story and pictures, is proof that the 'impossible' is true.............

NEW HOPE FOR THE ADDICT: SYNANON

PHOTOGRAPHED FOR PAGEANT BY GENE DAUBER
TEXT BY JIM HOFFMAN

■ "His EYES WATER as though he had hay fever; he yawns and mucus runs from his nose. Still later his muscles begin to twitch violently. He has violent pains in his stomach, has diarrhea, his legs and arms jerk.

"He curls up in bed or on the floor and puts on as many blankets as he can find even in the hottest weather. Because he cannot retain food or liquid in his stomach, he loses weight rapidly —as much as ten pounds within twenty-four hours. About the third day without the drug, he is in the very depths of torment.

"He is unkempt, disheveled, dirty, neglecting all thought of personal hygiene. Even after he begins to recover from these violent reactions to the drug, he still is unable to sleep and suffers from weakness and nervousness and has muscle pains for weeks."

This lurid description of a heroin addict, or "hype," in the throes of withdrawal from the use of drugs comes directly from experts most fa-

Below seminar theme, Sandy P. kicks habit "cold turkey"—no help from drugs

miliar with the process—the members of the Federal Narcotics bureau. With slight variations, it also constitutes a typical picture of an addict in a hallway, jail, or hospital withdrawing from the use of morphine or opium, or of a "pill-head" in a sanitarium who has been deprived of "goof balls" (the barbiturate depressants) or of pep pills (the amphetamine stimulants).

It describes what happens to the habit-kicking addict everywhere—except at one place: Synanon.

Sandy P., not old enough to vote, was a junkie and pill-head, who'd been hooked for nine months. He came to Synanon Westport in Connecticut—the overcrowded East Coast outpost and way station for the main Synanon houses at Santa Monica and San Diego, California, and Reno, Nevada—shortly after undergoing "detoxification" at a hospital, a cure that didn't take. Three days after his discharge he'd taken another fix. (Ninety to 95 per cent of addicts who kick the habit in jails, hospitals, and sanitariums get hooked again in short order.)

At Synanon, Sandy suffered none of

123

gatherings, "addressing huge college rallies while the mob cheers, 'Right on!'"[102]

In addition to soliciting donations and drumming up popular support, Synanon started its own industries in the early 1960s, beginning with a series of gas stations in the Los Angeles area. In 1964, Synanon leaders asked Walker Winslow to compose several advertisements for trade journals.[103] Even the organization's gas station ads relied on Synanon's characteristic tension between reality and self-promotion. With cheeky self-referentiality, the ad for Synanon's Texaco station declared, "Synanon service doesn't come naturally! Obviously this photograph didn't just happen. We planned it, posed it, pressed the uniforms, even brought along a birdie for our guys to look at."[104] The ad concluded that Synanon members were equally conscientious about achieving good results with the cars they serviced, citing the stations' sales records and customer satisfaction as evidence.

Synanon was led, managed, and supported by the work of its ex-addict residents, whose earnings pored back into the nonprofit endeavor. Labor was central to Synanon's mode of rehabilitation, and its rehabilitative mission justified Synanon's nonprofit status. Ideally, working at gas stations or soliciting donations helped train residents for the adult responsibilities they had evaded while in the grip of addiction. Other plans for Synanon's expansion were more overtly therapeutic enterprises. In 1961, Synanon piloted the Terminal Island Project off the coast of Los Angeles. At the island's penitentiary, Synanon members led confrontational game sessions for prisoners and established a small, Synanon-type community inside the prison.[105] Inmates were initially doubtful about the program until "some of the Synanons began to kick off and do something with the guys who got with it," said Candy Latson, a Synanon member who led the effort.[106] A few Synanon members had once been Terminal Island inmates; they returned to the prison to make the case for the Synanon program as a viable prison reform. Ex-addict James Middleton argued that former inmates were uniquely qualified to bridge the communication gap that invariably separated prisoners from the correctional employees who attempted to coercively reform them. "It is conceivable to me that someday Synanon could become an established part of the prison system throughout the United States," predicted Middleton.[107]

The program ran for two years before encountering resistance from administrators who did not want Synanon inmates living together on a single cellblock.[108] Although prison leadership removed Synanon from the program, the model Synanon initiated continued when Terminal Island became a federal drug-treatment site under the Narcotic Addict Rehabilitation Act of 1966. According to a report later published by the National Institute on Drug Abuse, the Terminal Island program was the earliest precursor to the implementation of TCs in prisons.[109] In the meantime, Synanon members moved on to Nevada. After seeing Yablonsky give a presentation on Synanon's program at a regional psychology conference, a Nevada State Prison psychologist visited Synanon in California. He reported back to his superiors, who were sold on the program. Within weeks, Synanon members opened a house in Reno and introduced Synanon sessions into the state prison setting.[110]

The program generated more positive publicity. In Reno, Synanon's "tunnel to the human race" led to underground caves where the confrontational therapy sessions were held. Walter Cronkite's documentary series *Twentieth Century* followed Latson into the prison's cellar. On March 13, 1966, the show broadcast the remarkable transformation that occurred upstairs in the Synanon prison halls. On Synanon's row above ground, the cells were wide open; inside, inmates played chess, hung art on their walls, and listened to classical music. The confrontational sessions apparently civilized the Synanon cellblock. Latson, a seasoned Synanon leader, argued that the therapy groups he led could address sins other than addiction. The program's narrator asserted that Latson brought a revolutionary idea into the prison: "the idea that crime, like dope, is an addiction to stupidity."[111] By using the game sessions to break down the prisoners' defenses—the same defenses Latson had unlearned in Synanon—Latson reportedly helped the inmates evolve beyond the impulsive and immature behavior that characterized their pasts.

At the same time, Synanon established new locations for its voluntary therapeutic program. Several Synanon members moved north to San Francisco, where they recruited addicts into the program, forged bonds with sympathetic audiences, and solicited donors. In 1964, the San Francisco chapter of SOS invited Dederich to establish a Synanon residence in the area. With help from sponsors, Synanon acquired an old warehouse near the water, and Synanon's ex-addicts carried out a full-scale renovation. Synanon soon expanded its Bay Area operation by purchasing an estate in Marin County. The organization predictably faced opposition from local residents, but this time it had experience in making its case. Synanon affiliate and attorney Dan Garrett argued that Synanon's rapid expansion from "a raggedy bunch of Beatniks occupying a storefront to a multimillion dollar enterprise spanning the entire United States" was possible "precisely because it has never permitted the slightest compromise with morality."[112] Garrett successfully argued that the familial qualities of Synanon's rehabilitative enterprise justified the use of properties zoned as residential, such as the estate in Marin.

By the mid-1960s, the Synanon family had homes on both coasts. Synanon's public-relations campaigns contrasted the healing environs of the California beachfront with the hardscrabble streets of New York City. In a press release announcing the new San Francisco location in November 1964, Dederich claimed that he could "have 3,000 addicts off the New York streets in 18 months."[113] Synanon also established a small residence in Westport, Connecticut, as an intake center for the California locations. In 1964, Dederich estimated that about half of Synanon's population came from New York, "the junk capital of the world." He said that more than 50 percent of the East Coast addicts who had arrived at Synanon since 1959 were "living drug-free lives."[114]

Synanon's public-relations agents shaped the organization's pitch for niche media outlets in New York City. The vice president of the San Francisco SOS chapter sent "exclusive" press releases about Synanon's planned expansion in 1964 to editors at the *New York Post*, the Spanish publication *La Prensa*, *Businessweek*, and *Jet*. For *La Prensa* and *Jet*, Synanon emphasized the inspiring recovery stories of Puerto Rican and African American residents; for *Businessweek*, the organization noted that Synanon began with "the total capital of $32 and a dozen addicts" and "doubled its size each year." The letter to the *New York Post* highlighted Dederich's "colorful, positive, and important personality" and promoted his planned confrontations with city officials as the "New York invasion."[115]

According to the letter to the *New York Post*, Dederich traveled to New York at the invitation of a New York Supreme Court judge; he brought along "several ex-addicts taken off the streets of New York" to "act as an indication of the effective work of Synanon."[116] Within a year, local officials would support several new drug-treatment centers based on the Synanon model, but Dederich's media assault failed to generate direct support for a large Synanon-run center in New York.

A REHABILITATION DESTINATION

Synanon's intake centers relied on persuading individual addicts rather than invading competing institutions where addicts were admitted. The treatment failures that colored many Synanon members' biographies were based in real social circumstances: in the early 1960s, effective addiction treatment was practically nonexistent. By 1965, thirty-four states still had *no* special facilities for addicts.[117] Although Synanon House was hardly luxurious—residents were expected to work, bunk together, and subsist on donated food and clothing—the beachfront locations were a draw for addicts accustomed to the hustle of the city or the boredom of pastoral cures in the federal penitentiary hospitals in Lexington and Fort Worth. Local Santa Monica papers reported that Synanon quickly established a reputation through underground networks of drug users.[118] After being discharged from Lexington, one addict learned about the Synanon cure from a drug-using friend who "made their set-up sound like Utopia."[119]

By the mid-1960s, Synanon had gained enough acclaim to begin charging some addicts for admission. Rates varied but were rumored to run between $500 and $1,000 (equivalent to about $3,500 and $7,000 in today's dollars).[120] One addict who was unable to raise the funds to enter Synanon griped, "I don't give a damn whether it calls itself a social movement or the French Revolution. It's just the country club of junkie places."[121]

In the years before Synanon became a social movement, its leaders marketed the country-club lifestyle to nonaddicts. Synanon ran confrontational therapy groups for nonaddicts as early as 1961, when members helped a Santa Monica minister use Synanon's confrontational techniques as a form of couples' therapy.[122] In 1966, Synanon opened its first "game club"; for the price of a monetary donation to Synanon, nonaddicts could gain admission to Synanon's confrontational therapy groups—and enjoy Synanon's facilities near the beach.[123] The game-club campaign signaled a shift away from the organization's original mission. Synanon's decision to start charging for services—first for drug treatment and then for general admission to its confrontational therapy sessions—was an early sign that the organization would no longer be marketed as the last-minute salvation of working-class drug addicts.

"You may be able to buy a private beach club membership, or a sauna, or entertainment, or whatever, elsewhere," read a letter to new Santa Monica Synanon club members. "You cannot, however, buy the Synanon game elsewhere at any price!"[124] An ex-addict who managed the Santa Monica game club sold the confrontational groups as a form of recreation: "a social function, a setting for relaxation," and a "way of managing apathy."[125] Synanon expanded its message to focus on reeducation for the disenchanted masses rather than on drug rehabilitation for an underworld minority. One Synanon public-service announcement proposal directed members to "play down drugs, etc. Emphasize group interaction." Synanon would be sold to nonaddicted members as a new form of education: the "communiversity." "The Synanon Foundation has developed a re-education process which supplies the individual with moral and intellectual tools, enabling him to cope with a changing world," stated the radio spot.[126]

The sales approach worked. In 1967, approximately one thousand nonaddicts engaged in confrontational therapy groups at clubs in Santa Monica, San Diego, San Francisco, Reno, Detroit, and New York; seven hundred people were on waiting lists to join.[127] A San Francisco news station produced a two-part documentary on the clubs, advertising the utility of confrontational group sessions for managing interpersonal relationships in schools, businesses, and marriages.[128] After the documentary aired, the San Francisco club received eighty-five new applications.[129] One San Francisco area director promoted the Synanon game as a promising method for "unearthing possible approaches to such gigantic social questions as racial conflict and the generation gap." Synanon "still counters addiction as a side effect of its full time educational process," said the director. But in the late 1960s its "scope expanded considerably."[130] Synanon became part of what one critic called "America's one growth industry": the human-potential movement. Synanon game sessions, such as "T-groups, encounters, marathons, and sensitivity training workshops, spread across the landscape like real estate developments in Southern California."[131] By 1968, the year Synanon became a social movement, the organization had 3,400 nonresident members.[132]

SYNANON AND SOCIAL MOVEMENTS

In 1968, Synanon celebrated its tenth anniversary as a rehabilitation mecca. At the party, Synanon's leaders announced its new mission. Hundreds of Synanon members met near Synanon's former location at the rear of the Pacific Coast Highway and formed a human chain for a walk back to the newer palatial residence on Santa Monica beach. Whereas Synanon's brand had once relied on its association with supposedly irredeemable addicts such as Charlie Hamer, Synanon newsletters now presented the beachfront formation as the new "Synanon personified: old and young, black and white, ex–dope fiend and businessman." The media event highlighted a decade of positive news and documentary footage of Synanon. Later that evening, celebrants were "treated to a display of old Synanon films, newsreel clippings, and some film strips which would not have been seen since Synanon's early days."[133]

The screenings played on the prestige of past media attention. Synanon's big reveal to contemporary media outlets, however, was the debut of the organization's new statistical tool. In a press release for the event, Synanon announced its own metric for the success of its rehabilitative enterprise. Rather than concentrating on the number of cured addicts, Synanon introduced the "clean man day," which members defined as the cumulative number of days that Synanon's ex-addicts remained drug free, crime free, and outside of hospitals and jails.[134] Later critics noted that Synanon's "clean man" calculation depended on ex-addicts' continued residence inside Synanon: After all, hadn't many addicts accumulated a number of crime- and drug-free days in jails or hospitals, only to relapse following their release?[135] Synanon contended in an anniversary press release that its program's central virtue, in comparison to established institutions, was its cost. Synanon rehabilitated addicts at no expense to taxpayers and at a much lower daily rate than other institutions.[136] Synanon's earlier resistance to data could have created dramatic anticipation for its quantitative debut, but the press release quickly changed the topic. Although Synanon's directors now had the numbers to defend their claims of efficacy, they also "had the unpleasant and unproductive experience of being treated as statistics in the various arms of the bureaucracy." As a result, they "felt that Synanon's growth in human terms over the past ten years was of greater consequence."[137]

The declaration was no contradiction; by tying economic arguments to personal growth, this Synanon press release was in keeping with new management trends. The technocratic, bureaucratic management style that had dominated corporate culture at midcentury was shifting in favor of new approaches that valued creativity, individual expression, and work fulfillment. Dederich and other Synanon members embraced the work of psychologist Abraham Maslow in the early and mid-1960s. According to historian Jessica Grogan, Maslow, the founder of humanistic psychology, was inspired by the New Left movements of the 1960s, in particular the civil rights and antiwar movements. The individuals who participated in these movements challenged and surpassed the limitations that society placed on them. Grogan argues that Maslow's optimistic theory about the universal human capacity for spiritual connection, fulfillment, and joy was "reinforced almost daily by the parade of individuals who pronounced, in what sounded to Maslow like a distinctly Maslowian style, a new era of the self."[138] Maslow must have heard stylish declarations when he visited and lectured at Synanon in 1966; he later classified Synanon and one of its spin-offs as examples of "Eupsychia"—utopian societies that fostered rather than stifled spiritual and psychological growth.[139] Although his humanistic theory had roots in the New Left, Maslow quickly shifted his attention from utopian societies to the corporate world, publishing his book *Eupsychian*

Management in 1965. According to Grogan, his "warmest reception came from executives" who believed humanistic psychology could improve employee productivity[140]

Maslow was more than welcome at Synanon; according to Dederich, "Maslow" became a household name among the ex-addicts in the early 1960s—on par with "Sinatra."[141] Synanon members often discussed Maslow's work on self-actualization, and Maslow agreed with Synanon's method of stripping away the particular social and cultural influences that impeded addicts' self-realization. Self-actualizing people in every culture, Maslow told his Synanon audience, have discovered that the "ultimate verities are in our guts."[142] The confrontational therapy practiced by Synanon and similar groups, Maslow wrote elsewhere, "ripped aside the veil of the half-blind world" by "cleaning out the defenses, the rationalizations, the evasions and politenesses of the world."[143] Significantly, rather than concentrate on Synanon as an idyllic, separatist society that cultivated the discovery of universal truth, Maslow focused on the organization's potential to transform the business of mental-health care. In an uncharacteristically positive war metaphor, Maslow declared that Synanon was "in the process of torpedoing the entire world of psychiatry, and within ten years will completely replace psychiatry."[144]

Synanon presented confrontational therapy games as a boon to human relations; according to Synanon's promoters, the games offered a way to increase personal satisfaction and organizational productivity. The documentary produced for a San Francisco television station pitched Synanon's games as a great "tool for business managers" and explained that the tool had already been tested in Synanon's many enterprises. At the time of the documentary's release, Maslow's well-received Quality of Work Life programs made the factory into a site of self-fulfillment, not labor alienation;[145] Synanon representatives echoed this insight. Workplace game sessions allowed business leaders to learn the details about floor-level plant operations while providing workers with an opportunity to blow off steam. As a result, one representative concluded, the encounters could help corporations realize their "human potential *as organizations*."[146]

Synanon members also promoted Maslow's suggestion that the ex-addicts' influence on the psychiatric establishment might have larger social and political implications. At a lecture for a Synanon-inspired TC in New York, Maslow argued that the organization's graduates were uniquely qualified for a "new kind of job opening up," "an activists' job that demands experience rather than book training." The lay professionals who excelled in this new profession were not "the people with PhDs"; they were "the people who have been on the streets and know what it is all about themselves."[147] The prediction reflected Synanon's critique of technocratic responses to social problems such as addiction. Maslow championed the ex-addicts' ability to see beyond the establishment's limited vision for drug treatment and urged Dederich to "groom some young people for politics."[148]

Synanon members later framed their group confrontations as a way to overcome the divisive cultural conflicts of the late 1960s. One poem, printed over an image of empty directors' chairs arranged in a circle, mused that Synanon's encounters offered a potential solution for rebellious youthful drug use, prison riots, college protests, and inner-city racial confrontations. Synanon could fill the chairs with the warring parties and get "all the people talking to each other."[149]

Synanon's new identity as a social movement was fraught with tension between the stated desire to transform society and the motivation to recruit residents. Even as Synanon used its purported success with heroin addicts to sell its therapeutic model to new audiences, Dederich ousted old-timer addicts. Although Synanon would continue to attract new drug-treatment clients, the organization focused on polydrug-using youth and middle-class professionals trying to kick a variety of bad habits. Quitting drugs was a prerequisite for radical personal and social transformation; it was no longer the organization's main purpose. Dederich saw old-school ex-addicts as a reminder of Synanon's low-class past. He claimed they interfered with the organization's productivity and undermined its updated image.[150]

Synanon leaders believed that their therapeutic model had the potential to revolutionize sectors of society such as business and education, but they fiercely resented the emergence of other addiction-treatment centers based on Synanon's philosophy. Because Synanon maintained the mystery about the details of its operating procedures, Dederich argued that his model was impossible to replicate. "How do you imitate something that you don't fully understand?" he asked rhetorically.[151]

Later TCs inspired by the Synanon model would use many of the same promotional strategies pioneered by the commune: practiced tours of tidy domestic settings, personal stories of redemption, and imagery depicting addiction treatment as a process of rebirth and maturation. They would also face challenges from proponents of other treatment models such as methadone, who argued that the labor- and time-intensive residential TC cure did not place enough emphasis on integrating addicts into society. Whereas later TCs aimed to return addicts to society after they had been sufficiently reeducated, Synanon members increasingly argued that society itself was sick. In so doing, Synanon tapped into nonaddicted spiritual seekers' seemingly conflicting desire: to transform society by dropping out of it. The press release announcing Synanon's new incarnation as a social movement declared that the organization was "absorbing people into the *responsible community*."[152] Synanon's seemingly retrograde moral philosophy—with its focus on self-reliance, rules, rigorous self-examination, and family values— had a novelty quality that nevertheless appealed to influential supporters in politics, academia, corrections, and media. In 1962, the countercultural magazine *Manas* disseminated Synanon's self-fulfilling prophecy: "The Synanon method seems destined for large-scale application—in prisons, in public hospitals, and independently, in a growing number of communities."[153] As Dederich also predicted, each of these stakeholders would have different interpretations of his controversial cure for drug addiction.

2

SYNANON RASHOMON

P OSSIBLY, A PART of our society is so sick that it can't stand seeing people organize to *get well*," wrote reporter Walker Winslow in 1961.[1]
But if a social group were united in its opposition to mutual aid,
by the 1960s that sector was shrinking. Unlike radical separatist groups
who believed American society needed to be bulldozed and built anew,
Synanon's ex-addict advocates made inroads into the criminal-justice
system, academia, and government.[2] According to Winslow, establishment
skeptics shared a single sickness: a complacency with technocratic bloat. In
contrast, the authorities that embraced Synanon's cure did so for an assort-
ment of reasons.[3]

Although Synanon's promoters emphasized aspects of their therapeutic
lifestyle to suit different audiences, they could not completely control what
observers saw in the waterfront residences, uninhibited group-therapy
sessions, regimented daily routines, and testimonials of character reformation. Like the characters in *Rashomon* (1950), the relativistic film by
Japanese director Akira Kurosawa, Synanon's supporters viewed the therapeutic events through the lens of their own preconceptions. When they
explained what they witnessed, the stories reflected their agendas. They
agreed on only one point: "A visitor to Synanon," wrote Winslow, "might
have thought it to be anything but a hospital."[4] Synanon's anti-institutional
attitude galvanized establishment reforms. "I like to think of Synanon as a

convict program rather than an institution program," said one prison-program participant.[5]

THE CRIMINAL-JUSTICE ESTABLISHMENT

Synanon started its first prison program at a transitional moment in the history of corrections. Along with asylums and almshouses, the United States began erecting penitentiaries in the 1800s. The penitentiary's original goal was personal reformation through enforced solitude or manual labor or some combination of the two.

By the end of the Civil War, reformers argued that U.S. prisons had already been corrupted, transformed from spaces of spiritual reformation into brutish sites for slave labor. These reformers promoted the philosophy that warehousing socially disenfranchised members of society fostered criminality. By the early twentieth century, progressive prison reformers had introduced value-laden classification systems for prisoners based on their social risks of recidivism. They also launched the reformatory initiatives that would serve as models for post–World War II prisoner-education programs. [6] They believed in continuously measuring prisoners' characterological improvement, emphasized the importance of education in nurturing personal reformation, and believed prisoners' wills could be reshaped through psychological persuasion rather than through older behavioral techniques such as lashing, restraints, and simulated drowning.

Many Synanon members had participated in progressive educational and therapeutic experiments during their previous periods of incarceration. When they led prison-based Synanon groups in the early 1960s, they capitalized on the growing perception that the present liberal prison-based social programs were permissive and ineffectual. Criminologists such as Synanon supporter Lewis Yablonsky confirmed Synanon members' claims that most prison-based group-therapy programs unintentionally indoctrinated inmates into a deviant subculture.

Prisons in California, where Synanon began its programming efforts, embodied the "rehabilitative ideal" of midcentury U.S. corrections.[7] That ideal began to crumble with Ronald Reagan's landslide gubernatorial election in 1966. Reagan's media-savvy campaign packaged a punitive turn as a common-sense response to student and racial protests. Almost a decade later, the California Department of Corrections (CDC) adopted mandatory sentencing and officially abandoned the rehabilitative mission.[8] The sociologist Kerwin Kaye (writing as Kerwin Kaye Brook) argues that the correctional establishment's receptivity to Synanon's hierarchical structure and tougher therapeutic encounters anticipated the backlash against supposedly permissive correctional environments. The first TCs in U.S. prisons were not modeled on Synanon; they resembled the "democratic" TC model pioneered by psychiatrist Maxwell Jones in the United Kingdom.[9] Richard McGee, the director of the CDC and champion of the "rehabilitative ideal," hired Jones as a consultant, and California initially implemented democratic TC prison programs based on Jones's approach.[10] These programs supposedly improved upon intermittent group-therapy sessions by transforming the entire prison environment into a "therapeutic milieu." In this rehabilitative setting, prison workers and prisoners shared equal responsibility for creating a total environment that encouraged personal growth. In contrast to later Synanon-style TCs, democratic TCs' professionals tactfully moderated the confrontational therapy sessions and played supportive roles in both individual and group therapies. Synanon's hierarchical "level system," in which prisoners gained liberties and luxuries through good behavior, was also noticeably absent in democratic TCs. According to Kaye, the comparatively liberated environment of democratic TCs ultimately "fostered Black radicalism" and "created 'problems' for McGee and other prison officials."[11] The few vocal officials who embraced Synanon's hierarchical, authoritarian spin on the TC concept viewed its adjustments as a possible solution to the political problems arising from the more democratic model of prison reform.

"People ask why I don't go to Birmingham and help the sit-iners," said Candy Latson, an African American leader of Synanon prison programs in California and Nevada. "I'm doing my job here."[12] The Birmingham civil rights campaign, led by Martin Luther King Jr. and the Southern Christian Leadership Conference, brought national attention to the ways in which business and criminal-justice authorities used intimidation and violence to protect racial segregation. Latson's suggestion that he was "doing his job" had a double meaning: it implied that Synanon's prison-reform program was a form of social justice work while distancing Latson from the fraught civil rights conflicts of the day.

In the 1960s, prisoners' access to radical texts and like-minded inmates would transform cellblocks into incubators of revolutionary leftist dissent, giving birth to best-selling leaders such as Malcolm X, Eldridge Cleaver, and George Jackson.[13] Yet few of the authorities who supported Synanon's program in the early 1960s viewed Latson's job as a political or institutional threat. As *Time* reported in March 1963, Synanon's open cells were decorated with "reproductions of Van Gogh and work done by inmates instead of calendar nudes."[14] Progressive wardens, notes the historian Lee Bernstein, still tended to view prison cultural programs as a way to distract inmates, prevent protest, and temper dissent—in other words, as a disciplinary tool.[15]

Jack Fogliani, the warden who brought Synanon to Nevada's state prison in Carson City, attributed the reduction in inmate "fights, disturbances, and complaints" to Synanon's prison program, which he believed helped inmates develop the maturity to work through their conflicts independently and without resorting to violence.[16] "[Synanon] makes meaningful changes for us" that "effect the whole prison," said one inmate.[17] "We're 100 percent behind this program," said Nevada governor Grant Sawyer, "and want to do everything we can to help it along."[18]

But the hierarchical system employed by Synanon and similar programs developed inmates' "maturity" by reserving the right to grant or revoke privileges—such as open cells and recreational activities—based on program participation and behavior. While these incentives for joining Synanon remained in place in the Nevada prison, program participation was high. But when the correctional paradigm shifted from rehabilitation to custody in the mid-1960s, the state prison outlawed programs that conferred "special treatment" on any group of prisoners. Prison officials hypothesized that the discontinuation of "earned privileges" caused Synanon membership to "dwindle to the point that the program was discontinued."[19]

Synanon's relationship with the criminal-justice system carried on, however. Although Synanon's ex-addicts frequently emphasized how other treatment programs had failed them, addicts were far more likely to be sent to standard prisons than they were to receive specialized addiction rehabilitation in detoxification units, psychiatric hospitals, or federal centers like those in Lexington and Fort Worth.[20] For that reason, members of Synanon's initial target population—"hard-core" addicts or "dope fiends"— usually had histories with law enforcement. Synanon sought the support of parole officers who had the power to supply Synanon with a steady client base of released addicts who remained under state supervision.

The Southern California Parole Officers Association was among Dederich's first audiences, and the paper he read to them in October 1958 later became Synanon gospel. In his speech, Dederich described Synanon's "autocratic structure," designed with the "19th century family setup" in mind. He argued that the verbally "brutal" therapeutic encounters effectively reformed addicts' behavior and helped them "realize that a loving father must be a firm father." Four years later Dederich noted that his paper was no manifesto—it was simply a "framework for discussion" with the officers in attendance. Nevertheless, scholars and critics continued to cite the document as the primary source of Synanon's therapeutic philosophy.[21]

Although the paper presents an early version of Synanon's concept of addiction and recovery, it was probably intended to convince corrections officers that Synanon was a suitable placement site for new parolees. Early press coverage of Synanon implicates corrections officers in the organization's controversies. The Santa Monica police chief seriously worried that the organization was "attracting felons and narcos,"[22] but one probation officer expressed ambivalence about Synanon's place as a treatment alternative: "About all I'd say is that it's highly unorthodox," he said. "But you can't quarrel that these addicts are off the stuff and seem to be staying off."[23] Less than a year after Dederich delivered his paper, he received an endorsement from a state parole officer, who praised Synanon's work with three parolees from state prisons and favorably compared its rehabilitative program to the available treatments in the California State prisons and the federal programs in Lexington and Fort Worth.[24]

Probation and parole officers in New York and California began to refer clients with drug problems to Synanon. The officers had pragmatic reasons for supporting Synanon: when their cases stayed under Synanon's fatherly supervision, they tended to keep out of trouble. [25] Despite the support from individual officers, Synanon had difficulty garnering bureaucratic support. CDC officials viewed Synanon's antiprofessional stance as a threat. When California assemblyman John O'Connell steered a favorable subcommittee investigation of Synanon, a medical official from the CDC fiercely criticized the notion that the government might support a therapeutic enterprise managed by nonprofessionals. [26] The CDC ultimately removed seven parolees from residence in Synanon.

Synanon leaders used the removal to rally supporters to their cause. [27] A group of Berkeley students disrupted a CDC presentation by passing out Synanon's informational flyers. While CDC officials described plans to launch their own "Synanon-type program," the protesters effectively championed Synanon's peer-led privatization of addiction treatment. Their protest turned out to be an accurate prediction: "Any individual, even a public ward, should be able to seek rehabilitation by any legitimate means. That private organization may assume the responsibility of any person who chooses to seek its assistance," declared the protesters' handout. [28]

At the time, however, legitimacy was precisely what Synanon lacked. California required probationers in its treatment programs to undergo random drug tests (first with a drug called Naline and later with urine chromatography). Synanon vehemently resisted any form of drug testing and argued that its total institutional environment, which was predicated on a drug-free philosophy, guaranteed that no members were using psychoactive substances. Dederich and his fellow Synanon members argued that their therapeutic lifestyle required members to commit themselves to the practice of searching, brutal honesty and conformity to the community's fixed moral norms. In this setting, the rationale went, any lapse in sobriety could not be disguised for long. For Dederich, the condition of random drug screening probably also represented a loss of control. Drug-testing programs would grant external authorities the right to determine the status and progress of Synanon members on the basis of their tests.

CDC officials believed Synanon's unscientific approach to probationer rehabilitation engendered "morbid dependency" rather than a gradual transition to independent living. [29] To circumvent perceived CDC bias, Dederich knew he would need to appeal to other authorities. Synanon directors selected a parolee, Gil Faucette, as a legal challenge to the CDC's policy. In 1966, county probation officials waived Naline tests for Synanon parolees, but Faucette knew that staying in Synanon was still a violation of the requirements for his state parole. If the judge looked unfavorably on Synanon's antitesting argument, Faucette faced a return to prison.[30] Luckily for Faucette and Synanon, the judge upheld the organization's claim that irregular drug tests destroyed the "sense of trust" that Synanon's model of rehabilitation required.[31] Although the case further alienated Synanon from CDC officials, the American Civil Liberties Union defended Synanon's claim that its rigorous treatment required little government oversight.[32]

The parole debate highlighted a central Synanon paradox. The organization's rhetoric led supporters to believe that Synanon was a reaction against the failed carceral solutions to drug addiction, especially supposedly enlightened rehabilitation programs like those attempted in Lexington and the CDC's new center in Corona, founded in 1961. But supporters in corrections recognized that Synanon never questioned the value of the larger social project of reforming hardened addicts; what Synanon offered was a different way to discipline them. In contrast to programs that exemplified a "*re*habilitative ideal," Synanon and similar programs aimed for *habilitation*.[33] The structured environment and cathartic attack-therapy sessions did not simply correct a few minor neuroses; they broke down the addict's personality and remade it, this time in the context of a neo-Victorian moral habitus. The technique fascinated midcentury social scientists because it implied what they already suspected: the cure for addiction is social and cultural.

THE SCHOLARS

The notion that psychiatric diagnoses may be social constructions was not a product of "the counterculture's loopy excesses," writes the historian Michael Staub. "Antipsychiatrists" of the 1960s—writers such as R. D.

Laing, Erving Goffman, Thomas Szasz, and Michel Foucault—posited new theories about the societal roots of mental disorders. [34] But mainstream psychiatry had embraced "social diagnoses" even earlier: after World War II, the rise of Nazism and communism motivated government-funded research on the interplay between social and psychological disorders.[35] The premise that civic problems such as drug use and crime had social causes underwrote entire disciplines, such as sociology, criminology, and the fashionable new postwar field "social psychology." Synanon's contention that the right combination of social forces could reshape behavior and personality would have come as no surprise to prominent social psychologists of the time, such as Stanley Milgram and Philip Zimbardo, whose infamous experiments were based on the same assumption.[36]

Nor did Synanon's social cure come as a shock to criminologist Donald Cressey, who viewed the organization's early success with a small group of heroin addicts as validation for his own theories. Cressey was a renowned criminologist who had earned his doctorate under the supervision of Indiana University criminologist Edwin Sutherland in the 1940s. Sutherland had developed an influential theory that criminal behavior is learned, not innate. In his paradigm, a criminal education is achieved through a process called "differential association," in which law-breaking techniques, motivations, and justifications are reinforced by close-knit social groups. In an influential essay published in 1955,[37] Cressey employed Sutherland's principle of differential association. He critiqued correctional programs that focused on altering individual criminals' psychology; correctional treatment programs should instead target the social codes of groups, Cressey argued. He hypothesized that "the most effective mechanism for exerting group pressure on members will be found in groups so organized that criminals are induced to join with non-criminals for the purposes of changing other criminals."[38] Press coverage of Synanon often paraphrased one of Cressey's central arguments: "the way to change Criminal A is to get him to change Criminal B."[39]

When Rita Volkman introduced Cressey to the Synanon commune, he saw his theory at work in Synanon's confrontational "games." Volkman and Cressey combined the data for her master's thesis, which she collected in 1959 and 1960, with Cressey's observations from his own weekly visits, which began in July 1960 and lasted for a year. Their article, published in the influential *American Journal of Sociology* in 1963, presented the Synanon case study as evidence that supported each of Cressey's earlier guidelines for group corrections. Synanon's reform processes, it claimed, "unwittingly" attempted to implement the features mentioned in the ideal correctional program described by Cressey in 1955. Volkman and Cressey argued that Synanon alienated members from deviant group norms, indoctrinated them into a new anticrime subculture, fostered group cohesion around the new subculture, socially rewarded obedience to anticriminal norms, and even used former criminals as change agents in group therapy sessions. Rather than depicting Synanon as the most promising cure for drug addiction (which was how Synanon members interpreted Volkman and Cressey's results), the article presented the problem of drug addiction itself as a "crude test" of Sutherland's theory of differential association and Cressey's sociological principles.[40] It wouldn't be the last time that research on the therapy model would reinforce the concept that drug users were deviant. Synanon's subcultural cure for drug addicts with criminal pasts suggested that the scholars' abstract social theories of deviance had a practical application.

For Lewis Yablonsky, criminology research was personal. Like many of the ex-addict Synanon members recruited from the East Coast, Yablonsky grew up in a rough neighborhood near New York City. A brief stint as a hobbyist gambler sparked his interest in social deviance, and after discovering a sociology textbook at the public library, he decided to make sociology his profession. He abandoned his undergraduate training in business and engineering and began graduate school at New York University, where he studied youth gangs while working in a juvenile jail and managing a city-wide violence-prevention program.[41]

Yablonsky was working as an assistant professor at the University of Massachusetts in Amherst when he met Cressey at a conference in the summer of 1960. Over drinks at a local bar, Cressey "sketched a vivid picture of the [Synanon] group, loudly arguing philosophical concepts and amateur psychology into all hours of the night," Yablonsky wrote later.[42] A few months after their conversation, the phone rang with what Yablonsky described as a "Hollywood phone call."[43] It was an invitation to take

Cressey's place at UCLA for the year and pick up the Synanon research project.

On Yablonsky's first visit to Synanon, Charlie Hamer's gripping story and Synanon House's spotless atmosphere convinced him the group was worth studying. Unlike Rita Volkman, who was shaken by the group encounters, Yablonsky relished Synanon's confrontational therapy sessions. "I related easily to other Synanon residents because of my early socialization with my Newark buddies," Yablonsky wrote. He viewed deviance as largely situational. One man—whom Yablonsky had found incorrigible in his previous studies of New York gangs—had been utterly transformed by Synanon. "My friends in Synanon were not my criminal cohorts. They were individuals attempting to quit their past lives as junkies and criminals," he wrote.[44]

In 1961, Yablonsky fell in love with a Synanon resident. His personal and professional lives became part of Synanon's story. "If Synanon worked—we worked," he reflected. "If it was like all the other failed [drug-treatment] methodologies I knew—marrying Donna was a major mistake in my life."[45] Yablonsky became an enthusiastic expert on Synanon's methods.

At one lecture given a few years later, Yablonsky joked that conventional social scientists perceived his book on Synanon as "deviant research" rather than "research on deviance." But Yablonsky defended his personal investment in his research subject, claiming that his scholarship was enriched by his decision to relate to Synanon "first as a human being, not in the phony way in which anthropologists do field studies."[46] In fact, Synanon did not welcome detached academic observers; beginning with Volkman's original study, Synanon expected scholars to actively participate in therapeutic confrontations. Although Synanon was not fond of statistics, the organization's policies were not hostile to research; in fact, Synanon's guidelines suited subsets of research trends in the 1960s—such as anthropological participant observation and humanistic psychology—that challenged the conventional divisions between researcher and subject.[47] Whereas traditional psychiatry taught practitioners to guard against countertransference, the social scientists who studied group interactions in Synanon would have to embrace the premise of the new humanistic psychology: that they, too, should be changed by their participation in therapeutic encounters.

Whether psychiatry was capable of transformation was still an open question. "You can't come here for a few weeks like [psychiatrist] Dr. Casriel, dash off a little book, and then establish a Synanon," complained Dederich.[48] In 1962, Daniel Casriel was surveying the available addiction-treatment models for a planned halfway house in New York. He arrived at Synanon along with an illustrious research team.[49] By then, Yablonsky was well entrenched as Synanon's director of research. After hearing a short presentation from Yablonsky, Casriel came to believe Synanon was a "major breakthrough in the treatment of addiction." Casriel moved into Synanon and became, he boasted, "the first psychiatrist to live at Synanon and study the movement in detail and depth as a participant-observer."[50] Casriel's account, *So Fair a House: The Story of Synanon*, was published barely a year later, when his plans to open a Synanon-style center in New York were well under way.

Before his Synanon visit, Casriel had spent more than a decade working as a community psychiatrist with drug addicts and drug-dependent juvenile delinquents in the best facilities in New York. [51] He concluded that addicts were incurable and proposed two possible solutions to the problem of addiction: "Put [the addict] away either in hospitals or jails for the rest of his life, or give him all the heroin he wants." The Synanon model convinced Casriel that there was a way out of that vicious circle: the "radical difference" he saw in Synanon members persuaded him that "Synanon holds the solution to the enigma of drug addiction."[52] But where Cressey had seen social theory at work in Synanon, the psychoanalytically trained Casriel found Freud.

Casriel believed that the Synanon "movement," "unknowingly using the psychodynamics and basic teachings of Sigmund Freud, has developed a system of therapy that may revolutionize our present method of treatment of certain types of personality disorders." For Casriel, Synanon's success was derived from the "paternalistic family structure" led by Dederich. This organizational model enabled addicts to experience a "rebirth" and then guided them through the Freudian stages of development (oral, anal, phallic, and latency periods).[53] In this way, Casriel's conversion story remained faithful to the common psychiatric view that addiction is the expression of an underlying, individual psychological disturbance caused by insufficient psychosexual development.

If faulty personality development could be traced back to childhood and the family, then Dederich's claim that Synanon's subculture treated addicts as children who need firm, loving guidance followed a Freudian logic. Although Casriel admired the ex-addicts' ability to create a familial milieu, he also thought the Synanon model ought to be integrated with traditional psychiatry. "The psychiatrist's aid to Synanon should start at the top," wrote Casriel, who believed psychiatric professionals should be responsible for assessing and supervising treatment centers' peer leaders.[54] In New York, Casriel cofounded a Synanon-style TC, where he was able to advance his own psychodynamic theory of addiction.[55]

At another Synanon location in northern California, Mitchell "Mitch" Rosenthal became the second psychiatrist to adopt Synanon's structure following an intense period of observation. Rosenthal was managing a British-style psychiatric TC in a naval hospital when two Synanon members visited the unit to make the pitch for their treatment model.[56] Rosenthal was receptive. In addition to joining Synanon's groups as a participant, Rosenthal counseled individual Synanon members alongside Dederich.[57] Rosenthal tried and failed to restructure the naval TC in the Synanon style before moving to New York, where, like Casriel, he helped establish a Synanon-modeled treatment center. "I had become impressed, as a psychoanalytically oriented psychiatrist, with the tremendous power of this new form of social psychiatry," recalled Rosenthal, who focused more on the "power" of the "group encounter" than on the authoritarian father figure's influence. "I thought that kind of approach could be [useful] to many different populations that we might describe in general as being socially disordered."[58]

Rosenthal's receptivity to group therapies befitted his military background; in the United States, group-therapy pioneers such as Karl Menninger and Carl Rogers developed their techniques in military settings.[59] Unlike Synanon's communal confrontations, however, these previous professional approaches to group therapy were technocratic; they were designed to address the trauma experienced by servicemen and were implemented in a bureaucratic context that favored rationalization, planning, and large-scale social engineering. In contrast, Synanon's groups seemed to scholars like a spontaneous, revolutionary method for addressing loftier social problems.

For psychologist Abraham Maslow, mental health meant more than taming neuroses and restoring an individual's ability to function socially. Psychological well-being was entwined with feelings of spiritual fulfillment, social belonging, and acceptance; these states could be achieved only once an individual's basic physical and psychological needs had been fulfilled. From Maslow's point of view, Synanon's residential environment met residents' fundamental requirements. The organization's encounter groups then provided a venue in which residents could experience a radical shift in perspective—a sense of harmony, oneness, and understanding that Maslow called a "peak experience." The Synanon encounter was a transformative spiritual event that enabled participants to transcend the societal expectations that impeded personal growth.

Although Maslow died in 1970, the humanistic social scientists he inspired continued to promote Synanon's methods. Steven Simon, a doctoral student in Harvard's Department of Social Relations, followed Maslow's advice to a group of undergraduates: "Go West to Synanon!"[60] In an article published in the *Journal of Humanistic Psychology* in 1978, Simon argued that the Synanon lifestyle, as adapted to include nonaddict residents, had "implications for building humanistic organizations." For Simon, the dichotomy of the social rules that applied inside and outside of the confrontational therapy sessions helped foster holistic psychological growth by forcing residents to "integrate new personality and behavioral elements." In short, "for dope fiends, a Synanon gaming organization offers obedience training," and "for squares it offers assertion training."[61] A social work student at UCLA who studied Synanon's appeal to nonaddicts similarly viewed the lifestyle as a corrective to the technocratic excesses of postwar culture—such as materialism and conformity—that Yablonsky called "robopathology."[62] For middle-class youth who were becoming attuned to the racism and sexism that characterized their ordinary upbringing, Synanon offered an attractive form of deprogramming.

THE COUNTERCULTURE

In the late 1960s, therapeutic encounter groups spread far beyond Synanon. Group confrontations had become a daily habit at psychedelic, counter-cultural communes and the politicized, New Left variety.[63] Like later historians who questioned the distinction between politically engaged New Left radicals and the hedonistic idealists of the counterculture, journalist Tom Wolfe viewed the two groups as part of the same religious movement—a "holy roll" driven by the unprecedented expansion of the middle class following World War II.[64]

College students also fueled the youth revolutions. The attack therapy that communes practiced, Wolfe noticed, resembled the traditional high-brow hazing in the Ivy League's secret societies. During the 1960s, federal investment in public universities and the expansion of college to women and minority groups meant that the college experience was no longer limited to elites. By the end of the decade, college enrollment had increased 120 percent.[65] In one New Left origin story, newly empowered college students at the University of California at Berkeley and the University of Michigan linked calls for university reforms—such as free speech and campus governance—to broader issues such as civil rights and peace activism.[66] Even Timothy Leary's countercultural directive to "drop out" implied access to the institutions of higher learning that he urged his acolytes to reject.[67] But for Synanon in the early 1960s, any association with institutions of higher learning helped confer respectability.

The most influential Synanon observers favorably likened Synanon to college. "It looked like a campus co-ed situation," thought Lewis Yablonsky during his first trip to Synanon, "except it was integrated."[68] At Synanon, Daniel Casriel similarly recalled, house members "acted as if they were preparing for an open-house party on an average college campus." They looked nothing like the "guarded, sullen, lost souls" confined in other psychiatric or criminal treatment facilities.[69] For addicts whose opportunities for higher education had been limited by their drug habits, Synanon's seminars and encounters offered an avenue for growth. "I call them my college days," remembered one recovered resident who arrived at Synanon for drug treatment sometime around his eighteenth birthday. He described twenty-four-hour "marathon" sessions followed by philosophical discussions called "reaches."[70] Dederich similarly described the secret of his therapeutic breakthrough: "we're nothing but a college bull session blown up into an institution."[71]

For students mildly disillusioned with traditional education, Synanon offered a way to explore a new lifestyle—to "drop out"—while still maintaining enrollment in established institutions. For some middle-class students accustomed to summer camps or dormitories, the communal living arrangement came naturally. One undergraduate who studied for a semester at Synanon remembered adjusting quickly to the mess-hall meals and dormlike sleeping quarters. She returned to Synanon the following year, after considering her postgraduate options: "Europe, grad school, or Synanon."[72]

The economic security of the postwar years made communes and graduate school equivalent choices for an expanding class of college graduates.[73] The historian Timothy Miller roughly estimates that in the 1960s communes numbered in the "tens of thousands," but most had disbanded by 1975.[74] Although most communes did not evolve into institutions, the brief trend in experimental living had lasting cultural influence. Communal life piled up stereotypes: in addition to the encounter sessions Synanon helped popularize, the communal lifestyle supposedly supported a freewheeling attitude toward sex, drugs, and rock and roll. Public expressions of these countercultural values played out in media depictions of hippie gatherings such as the music festivals at Woodstock and Altamont.[75]

Synanon predated the countercultural communes, and the organization's antidrug stance, structured lifestyle, and comfortable relationship with capitalism challenged popular preconceptions about what communal life looked like. As the "dysfunctional" behaviors that previously defined the drug-using underworld seeped into mainstream society in the 1960s, Dederich's claim that Synanon's values-driven lifestyle was the true counterculture gained credibility. Just as the hip posturing of heroin-using subcultures supposedly impeded the psychological growth of some original Synanon residents, hippie performativity stood in the way of the authenticity and connection that youthful seekers chased. "[I] came straight from

Greenwich Village and my hair was down to here," said one Synanon member. "They cut my hair and took away my sunglasses and told me to talk to people. Well, I couldn't do it."[76] This testimonial implied that some social revolutionaries were also conformists: the hippie counterculture was equally capable, in its own way, of stifling genuine self-expression.

With that argument, Synanon conjured up the sixties zeitgeist: the "romance of the outsider." According to historian Grace Elizabeth Hale, this new romanticism was "politically promiscuous"—equally attractive to right- and left-wing activists who positioned themselves in opposition to conventional society. During the 1960s and 1970s, Hale argues, Elvis, William F. Buckley, Tom Hayden, Bob Dylan, Stokely Carmichael, Lonnie Frisbee, and Jerry Falwell claimed rebel status.[77] We could add Charles Dederich and his followers to the list. Who could be more excluded from mainstream society than drug addicts—the *archetypal* outsider group?[78]

Perhaps the only group more deviant than heroin users was black heroin users. In 1962, Dederich proclaimed Synanon "the most successful experiment in integrated living in a segregated area in the world."[79] The claim had credence. Dederich's loving, interracial marriage with Betty Coleman was formalized in 1963 and served as a powerful symbol of the community's commitment to racial equality.[80] By 1964, more than 10 percent of Synanon's residents were black. Long before Tom Wolfe lampooned the "radical chic" of black militancy in 1970,[81] Synanon emphasized the racially integrated environment it provided for recovering drug addicts.

Integration also worked as a selling point. In addition to fascinating the Hollywood elite, Synanon received favorable attention from the black press. By all reports, Synanon "games" not only cured drug addicts of their character deficiencies but also helped members get over the racial hang-ups that stifled their psychological growth. "A young Negro girl with an inferiority complex" was "lashed" by fellow game players, reported *Ebony* magazine in 1963: " 'You just can't admit to yourself that you might have been chosen to do the job because you were qualified!' A southern white man received similar treatment: 'How can you be from Texas and not be prejudiced?' "[82]

Although Synanon generally viewed racial issues as secondary to psychological ones, when civil rights trends changed, Synanon changed with them. In the early 1960s, journalists depicted Synanon as a model of integrated living and an ideal setting for Sidney Poitier's next film project.[83] By the late 1960s, Synanon opened an Oakland branch and forged relationships with Black Panthers by moderating their confrontational therapy sessions, supplying donated food for breakfast programs, and hosting afterschool activities for neighborhood youth.[84]

At this point, California was a hotbed of community activism. In 1965, the newly inaugurated U.S. Office of Economic Opportunity established a jobs-training program largely geared toward inner-city youth. Rather than impose programming on disadvantaged communities, the Kennedy–Johnson administration sought to involve indigenous inner-city leaders as community organizers. In 1967, there were forty-four Community Action Agencies in California, including ten in the Bay Area that were staffed primarily by members from underrepresented minority groups.[85]

Lewis Yablonsky helped shape the Office of Economic Opportunity's logic of community-based leadership. He served as a consultant for Sargent Shriver's Job Corps program and in 1965 recommended that the program adopt Synanon's tactics for antidelinquency jobs-training and education programs. Yablonsky rejected the program's initial plan to locate the training programs in rural locations and to employ government officials to conduct them; he argued instead that leaders from urban communities should manage training and discipline.[86] Synanon's ex-addict leaders, who had little luck with applications for direct government grants, secured local funding for youth programs from the Office of Economic Opportunity jobs-training program. In 1967, Synanon members were enlisted to provide drug education for two schools in East Los Angeles. In Las Vegas, officials hired Synanon members to moderate racial confrontations among high school students.[87]

Nevertheless, some members who left Synanon to found their own TCs thought Synanon was not sufficiently attuned to the needs of ethnic communities beset by drug addiction.[88] John Maher, the founder of the Delancey Street TC in San Francisco, believed that Synanon members capitalized on confrontation but lacked genuine community engagement. "The three organizations that have cured more drug addicts are, in order, Red China, the Black Muslims, and Synanon," said Maher. "But they have done so only at the tremendous cost of imposing total conformity" and embracing separatism.[89]

Some female Synanon members interpreted Synanon's emerging separatism, new boot-camp training regimen, and heady therapy confrontations as a form of feminist consciousness raising. "Think Synanon: we are the true revolution!" the women chanted as they marched in step. "This is the first time I've had to confront the Feminine Mystique and knock it off," declared one participant.[90] Other aspects of Synanon's social movement lifestyle also promoted women's liberation from traditional gender roles. Betty Dederich invented the "hatchery," a communal form of child rearing that supposedly freed women from the responsibilities associated with being an infant's sole caretaker. Women-only "games" featured frank discussions about bodies and sex. In her tour of various encounter groups, journalist Jane Howard noted that the consciousness-raising sessions held by women's liberation groups—with their stated intention to speak bitterness about their suffering and circumstances, just as social outcasts were taught to do in Maoist reeducation centers—were the most politically radical faction of the human-potential movement.[91] But as early as 1970, critics questioned the paranoid conservative notion that the human-potential movement was a dangerous "blend of brainwash and sex orgy." "Here as elsewhere," concluded critic Robert Claiborne in *The Nation*, "the Right credits the Left with far more enterprise than it actually possesses."[92]

Later critics largely concurred. In the early 1970s, Wolfe hypothesized that "in the long run, historians will regard the entire New Left experience as not so much a political as a religious episode wrapped in semi military gear and guerrilla talk."[93] In the short run, scholars such as Christopher Lasch argue that America's cultural revolution ushered in an era of narcissism: consciousness-raising groups and encounters were ultimately about personal improvement, not social change.[94] Although Synanon's outsider status may have been attractive to putative misfits, some members simply saw the organization's activities as a self-help tool. "To be married and be able to communicate with each other is definitely a peak experience," reflected one woman in a written assignment following a Synanon workshop in 1974.[95] To others, Synanon offered a completely transformative therapy, a subculture so radical that it could refashion personality and negate prejudicial social conditioning. And as Synanon's counterculture romanced seekers and outsiders, the organization's oppositional style half-convinced the political establishment that Dederich had discovered the solution to drug addiction. Over the coming decades, aspects of Synanon's new moral model of addiction would influence officials' interpretations of the nation's drug problems.

GOVERNMENT AUTHORITIES

Dederich's providential political timing overwhelmed officials' doubts about his treatment methods. The optimism of the Kennedy era extended even to drug addicts. The president fulfilled his campaign promise to convene a White House Conference on Drug Abuse in September 1962.[96] The gathering brought together elected officials, public-health experts, and criminal-justice leaders in the hopes of reforming the nation's punitive approach to drug use.

Rising rates of heroin use in the 1950s had inspired a federal crackdown on drug users and dealers: both the Boggs Act of 1951 and the Narcotic Control Act of 1956 imposed mandatory-minimum prison sentences for some drug offenses. Meanwhile, enlightened postwar rehabilitation programs in New York and California had offered alternative methods for addressing the addiction problem. In 1952, New York City opened Riverside Hospital, a 141-bed facility for juvenile narcotic addicts. Smaller units for adult addicts were also designated at Metropolitan Hospital and Manhattan State Hospital. Beginning in 1961, the California Civil Commitment program provided funding for the massive California Rehabilitation Center in Corona. Civil commitment, a legal proceeding in which addicts can be diverted out of the criminal-justice system and into state psychiatric facilities, emerged in the early twentieth century but had practically disappeared until California officials revived the practice. Following California's lead, New York enacted the Metcalf–Volker Narcotic Commitment Act in 1962.

These institutional experiments, like the Lexington and Fort Worth Narcotic Farms before them, had high relapse rates and were widely publicized as failures. [97] Synanon officials contrasted their innovative program with other institutions' bad press. Buoyed by advocacy from the New York and California leaders who argued that their states suffered from heavy drug traffic and concentrated areas of narcotics addicts, the conference floated the message that federal officials were ready to reexamine the criminal-justice approach to addiction.[98] Yet the first steps toward reform—such as the national civil-commitment legislation that U.S. senator Kenneth Keating (R–NY) introduced in 1961—still favored the kinds of designated public facilities that had repeatedly reported poor outcomes. Synanon's vocal presence at the moment of initial reform meant that the organization was later able to present a lively, viable rehabilitative alternative for politicians and professionals who were prepared to reject Bureau of Narcotics commissioner Harry Anslinger's supply-side approach to narcotics control and were embarrassed by the failures of the limited liberal institutional experiments.

"There is no divergence of opinion on the need for vastly improved techniques and programs aimed at rehabilitating addicts," pronounced John F. Kennedy in his opening remarks at the White House Conference on Drug Abuse. "The discouragingly high rate of relapse among addicts who leave our medical institutions free of physical dependence is clear evidence that more must be done."[99] The professionals' panel discussion on innovative approaches to rehabilitation featured leaders from Lexington, the California Rehabilitation Center, and major New York hospitals.

Meanwhile, Synanon members screened promotional films in a nearby room. These ex-addicts, not the experts, earned a full-page feature in the *Washington Post*. "Why has Synanon been able to succeed in some cases where hospitals, prisons, and jails have failed?" asked the reporter. "An addict never believes he can get well," responded Dederich, reinforcing the dominant political message of hope. "I tell him he can get well."[100]

The press scarcely acknowledged that even "failed" treatment programs were few in number. In 1965, the NIMH compiled a list of community services and facilities for addiction treatment. Designated addiction treatment outside state psychiatric facilities and prisons consisted of Synanon, the California Rehabilitation Center, and a small group of hospital programs in New York. Beginning in the early 1960s, officials in the U.S. Public Health Service and the NIMH began to consider restructuring the Lexington Narcotic Farm.[101] In 1966, the Narcotic Addict Rehabilitation Act (NARA) brought about institutional reforms; Lexington transitioned from its role as the nation's centralized addiction-treatment facility to a supportive entry point that would connect convicted addicts with appropriate "aftercare" in their communities. To accomplish this transition, the NIMH established state-matched grants to fund local aftercare and treatment centers necessitated by the new law.

The NIMH consulted Synanon leaders during the planning stages. In a report prepared to inform the enactment of NARA, researchers interviewed Dederich alongside research and treatment luminaries such as Lexington's research director Harris Isbell and Ray Trussel, the commissioner of hospitals for New York City; Synanon members were the only addicts whom the researchers consulted.[102] But officials remained standoffish when Synanon asked for direct support. Dederich, aware that the NIMH was dispensing grant funds to other treatment centers, wrote directly to his friend Sidney Cohen after Cohen's appointment as director of the NIMH's Division of Narcotic Addiction and Drug Abuse in 1968. "It would certainly seem that sometime during the next decade NIMH would decide to give Synanon a hand and maybe you are the guy who could get something started in that direction," wrote Dederich. "I need one helluva lot of money. Do you have any? Keep in touch whether you have or not— perhaps in your new position a real good site visit to our Santa Monica and Oakland places winding up here at Tomales Bay to boil up a shirt is indicated. Best of everything for the New Year and in your new job. Betty [Dederich's wife] still speaks of you as one of the kindest men around."[103]

Cohen responded that Synanon could get money "by becoming an aftercare agency for NARA," but "we ask for record-keeping and I suppose you don't like reports." Cohen was willing to work with Dederich if he agreed to the government's terms: "You won't get a 'helluva lot of money,' but maybe we could make a start." He concluded: "Tell Betty I'm no longer kind. This job has turned me into a guy like you."[104]

Cohen was more like Dederich than he knew. As a central administrator of NARA programs, Cohen effectively oversaw the funding for Synanon-inspired TCs across the United States. He supported Lexington's transformation into a large-scale TC in the early 1970s.[105] But Cohen, like earlier NIMH grant reviewers, was not willing to write Synanon a blank check. Synanon's ex-addicts sold the concept of effective rehabilitation and described a drug-free treatment model that resonated with timely social science research. NARA realigned the federal approach to addiction treatment and supported Synanon-style treatment centers on a national scale. Once the TC was cut from its communal roots, officials could comfortably support the model by emphasizing the aspects that suited their political agendas. And they wouldn't have to deal with Dederich, who had a habit of using polite praise from high-profile figures—such as Connecticut senator Thomas Dodd, Nevada governor Grant Sawyer, and even California gubernatorial hopeful Richard Nixon in 1962—for his own promotional purposes. (Synanon's public-relations team argued that a letter from Nixon praising Synanon for "evident effectiveness in a very worthwhile cause" counted as an endorsement, despite the candidate's protestations.)[106]

Synanon's ex-addicts made the reverse complaint: their revolutionary approach to addiction treatment had been co-opted by the establishment. Dederich, Yablonsky, and Synanon members repeated a historical analogy that Walker Winslow penned in the early 1960s: Dederich was Dorthea Dix.[107] Dix was an antebellum crusader who advocated for the rights of individuals with mental illnesses and helped establish a system of state mental hospitals. Prior to Dix's reform effort, mentally ill individuals were often placed in private homes or prisons, where they were starved, stripped, chained, and beaten. A close associate of Ralph Waldo Emerson and a proponent of the moral-treatment model developed by French psychiatrist Philippe Pinel, Dix's approach to treating mental illnesses dovetailed with Dederich's philosophies about addiction. Dix and Pinel wanted to replace physical restraints with educational techniques that could reshape the psyche, such as talk therapy, prayer in solitary confinement, and pastoral labor.[108] Synanon supporters argued that just as Dix's efforts were later co-opted by her supposed allies, the "administrators, doctors, and politicians that climbed on [Dederich's] bandwagon" would warp his good intentions. After Dix's reforms, Winslow argued, wardens continued their abusive physical practices alongside new psychological ones, this time under the pretext of curative "hospital" treatment that "gave the tormenters a protection they had never had before."[109] Dederich said he "feared" that Synanon's spin-offs would "hide behind the magic aura" of the organization's "good name." They abandoned the Synanon brand and adopted the therapies instead.[110]

PART II
CO-OPTATION

3

SELLING THE SECOND GENERATION

T HE INITIAL DISTINCTION between Synanon and its TC competitors was largely a matter of branding. Dederich set out to make Synanon "as well-known as Coca-Cola," and by the mid-1960s he succeeded. Synanon was listed in Random House's dictionary.[1] The organization's tag lines reached ordinary households via magazines and television. Conservative critic William Safire's political dictionary, first published in 1968, credited Synanon with popularizing the phrase *hang tough*; by the early 1970s, the term had crossed over from rehabilitation subcultures to the political lexicon. President Richard Nixon told his wife, Pat, to hang tough during the Watergate crisis.[2]

From another point of view, however, the 1960s were not the best time to seek Coca-Cola status; the soft-drink company faced increased competition from Pepsi's new advertising campaign. Coke and Pepsi had similar origins, and they basically peddled the same product. Coke dominated the marketplace until Pepsi's advertising firm came up with a youthful new promotional strategy in 1961. The campaign framed Coke as old, conformist, and establishment. Pepsi was the opposite: hip, rebellious, and forward looking.[3] Synanon's leadership, like Coca-Cola's, viewed the new TCs that emerged in the mid-1960s as inauthentic, Pepsi-like imitations. New TCs differentiated their treatment products from Synanon while co-opting many of Synanon's early sales techniques. ("Hang tough," read the sign above the door to a TC started by New York City's Addiction Services Agency.)[4]

The new centers inspired by Synanon dulled the organization's influence on the addiction-treatment field. By 1970, Synanon promoters could no longer claim that their branches housed the largest number of cured addicts anywhere in the world. The city of New York claimed thousands of recovery-success stories—and credited many of those successes to methadone maintenance, a biomedical addiction-treatment model. In the mid-1960s, Synanon had been a must-see stop for addiction researchers and treatment professionals.[5] But when President Richard Nixon's advisers made their rounds, they bypassed Synanon in favor of methadone clinics and spin-off TCs that former members helped establish in New York and Chicago.[6] Nixon's presidential election in 1968 marked the end of the liberal optimism that had sparked curiosity in the Synanon cure and inspired ambitious, experimental drug-treatment reforms. Historians and observers characterized the late 1960s as a crescendo of violent leftist extremism and reactionary right-wing politics.[7]

In this cultural climate, TCs became self-conscious about being perceived as cultish, leftist, or overtly like Synanon, which had revised its rehabilitative mission in 1968. Once researchers articulated the defining characteristics of the TC treatment model, they decided that Synanon had been the starting point for a new line of organizational development.[8] The New York TCs that followed called themselves the "second generation." The first group of this generation was conceived at Synanon during Daniel Casriel's visit in 1962. Despite Casriel's laudatory congressional testimonial about Synanon's treatment model, the psychiatrist and his fellow researchers did not deviate from their original plan: to apply their findings to a new experimental residential program for men with felony drug offenses. The program was managed by the Probation Department of the New York Supreme Court for the Second Judicial District; Chief Probation Officer Joseph Shelly lobbied for the lodge. These founders conferred an uncomplicated (and unhip) name upon the center: Drug Addicts Treated on Probation (DATOP).[9]

DAYTOP VILLAGE

Replicating Synanon's treatment proved more difficult than the professionals anticipated. DATOP's administrators originally attempted to hire a Synanon graduate to manage the residence, but he grew frustrated with the slow hiring process and accepted another job.[10] When that hire failed, they employed a recovering alcoholic and AA member that Synanon's allies called an "Ersatz-Dederich."[11] Despite his charismatic pretensions, the AA manager did not have Dederich's gift for discipline. Residents regularly left for work and brought drugs back to the lodge, where they lounged, glaze-eyed, in full view of the management.[12] At least four different directors tried to bring order to DATOP during its first year, without much success.[13]

Fortunately for DATOP's leaders, David Deitch—an intense, intellectual, and romantic ex-addict—left Synanon's new San Francisco location with a woman who was living in the Santa Monica house. They married and planned a move to Synanon's intake center in Westport, Connecticut, where Deitch would continue to run group sessions and promote Synanon's cure. Dederich disapproved, so Deitch left the Westport house. His departure marked the beginning of a reformation for DATOP.[14] Casriel hired Deitch first to run groups for his private practice and then as director of the reconstructed center.

Although DATOP floundered in its first year, Casriel remained convinced that the Synanon model could be duplicated under the right conditions. Synanon's members had accomplished the feat with new branches in San Francisco and Connecticut. After returning to the East Coast, Casriel continued to visit the Synanon house in Westport, where Deitch led groups. Casriel also met William O'Brien, a Catholic priest, on the steps of the Westport Synanon. O'Brien, like Lewis Yablonsky, had become interested in the problem of drug addiction after working with youthful gang members in the 1950s. He stumbled on Synanon's Connecticut location soon after it was established; he planned for a half-hour visit and ended up staying all night.[15]

Leaders were less convivial when O'Brien and Casriel attempted to broker a partnership between Synanon and the struggling DATOP. O'Brien and Casriel made a modest proposal. Synanon could assume management of the center if its leadership agreed to a few bureaucratic conditions: permit systematic research, accept collaborative relationships with credentialed health-service professionals, and temper harsh disciplinary practices. "We felt Synanon had found the formula for the recovery of life," said O'Brien, who nevertheless wanted to standardize the formula's production.[16] Dederich, however, was unwilling to reveal Synanon's recipe for success. "There is ample room for any number of imitation Synanons," explained Synanon supporter Guy Endore. But to be effective the imitators would need "the key. The savvy. The precious something."[17] Dederich's representatives rejected Casriel's requests.

Casriel and O'Brien reformulated their treatment program without the Synanon brand. The two men met with New York City mayor Robert F. Wagner, a Catholic Democrat who quickly approved their new plan for the halfway house.[18] They incorporated "DATOP Lodge" as "Daytop Village," an independent not-for-profit overseen by a board of directors—which O'Brien would later lead—not by the Probation Department. The residence would no longer serve as a "lodge" for passersby on probation; the expanded "village" would instead welcome female clients and voluntary patients without criminal records. Along with the autonomous new organizational structure and the Synanon-trained Deitch as director, the "Daytop" acronym took on a new meaning: "*D*rug *A*ddicts *Y*ield *to* *P*ersuasion." At that moment, O'Brien argued, Daytop was christened the "first of a second generation of therapeutic communities."[19]

Deitch initially used Synanon-style persuasion to transform Daytop into a TC based on principles of total honesty and chemical abstinence. He swept the house, rooted out contraband drugs and alcohol, and engaged the residents in a mass confession. That "cop-out" technique, as Deitch remembered it, carried powerful "symbolic meaning," though it was not therapeutically "artful." Deitch explained his logic at the time: "Everyone's gonna get your head shaved. Whether you like it or not, you're a part of this corrupt community, look at what we discovered, drug paraphernalia, lots of booze, and all over the facility."[20] The discovery also carried repercussions: some men still faced prison terms if they left. After the ritual, Daytop and its members "started anew" under Deitch's leadership.[21]

While Daytop's inhabitants awoke to a fresh start, the organization's early years repeated Synanon's history. With Deitch as the director, Daytop expanded rapidly. According to Casriel, Daytop was greeted with "the same welcome that Synanon [received] in its first days out in Santa Monica": picketers and protest signs reading "Junkies Go Home."[22] Undeterred, the organization moved from its original building to a spacious property overlooking Prince's Bay in Staten Island in 1965. The Swan Lake house in upstate New York opened in 1966, followed by a larger facility on Fourteenth Street in New York City in 1968. Daytop's incorporation allowed the organization to receive local and state grant funds while freeing leaders from direct control by the Probation Department.[23] The not-for-profit status also allowed Daytop to raise funds from other sources, such as private donors and concerned parents.[24] The organization quickly rose to prominence, thanks in part to Synanon-style promotions; Daytop members allowed documentarians to record their therapy sessions and dramatized their avant-garde confrontations on the off-Broadway stage.

There was one crucial difference between Daytop and Synanon: Synanon was an original, self-proclaimed revolution in addiction treatment, whereas Daytop had to contend with the precedent Synanon set. In contrast to Synanon, Daytop residents agreed to submit to drug tests and file grant reports, and its leaders took a less-hostile stance toward psychiatric theories about the nature of drug abuse. Righteous Synanon members considered such concessions an affront to a therapeutic endeavor based on rigorous honesty. Daytop members thought differently: "What's humiliating about a urinalysis? I myself would find peddling pencils [the way Synanon members do to raise money] humiliating. It's all in the way you see things."[25]

Whether Daytop members chose to "peddle pencils" or—as Synanon members charged—"piss," their method of promoting the new therapy relied on proven strategies of testimonials and therapeutic dramatization. A one-hour documentary depicting a "marathon" encounter session led by Deitch aired on ABC in 1967. "Only the possibility that insight would lead

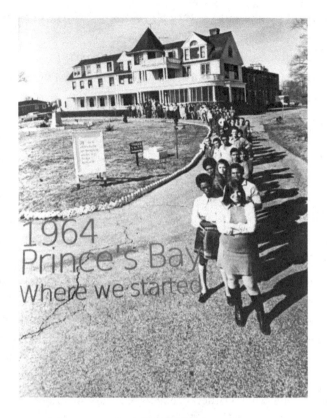

FIGURE 3.1

Daytop promotional photo, late 1960s. Reprinted in the *Daytop Quarterly*, Winter 2011.

Source: Author's personal collection.

to freedom from addiction—and that other addicts might be stimulated to seek help—justifies such an invasion of privacy," wrote one complimentary television critic.[26]

The documentary condensed more than thirty hours of footage into a prime-time feature that highlighted dramatic and deeply repressed psychological revelations. "I don't like the person inside me, whoever that is, that needs my father's love," admitted Julie, a pretty young woman who survived an intentional drug overdose, to the group. "You don't like the person inside you that needs *anybody's* love," responded Deitch. In the last therapy scene, the group offered Julie the opportunity to "grow up" by reckoning with her need to be loved and risking the rejection she long feared. Deitch directed Julie to ask the presiding psychiatrist to love her: "Will you love me, doctor?" They hugged.[27]

Julie's embrace didn't come from her father but from Efren Ramirez, a psychiatrist from Puerto Rico who would become New York City's first director of the new Addiction Services Agency (ASA). The historian Samuel Roberts has argued that John Lindsay, the Republican mayor who instituted the ASA, won the election in 1965 by challenging the treatment policies established by his Democrat predecessor, Robert F. Wagner. Wagner had turned too late from criminal to medical addiction policies, moving toward medicalization in order to weaken critiques regarding his administration's treatment of imperiled ethnic communities. In contrast, Lindsay's mayoral campaign championed pluralism and neighborhood treatment efforts. Whereas Wagner's Health Research Council excluded Puerto Rican representatives, Lindsay appointed Ramirez to a top administrative post.[28]

Daytop bridged the two administrations: the probationary halfway house established during Wagner's term quickly evolved into one of Lindsay's leading community-based treatment providers. Lindsay appointed Ramirez and an ex-addict special assistant to lead a $5.5 million treatment program in mid-1966.[29] Before joining the Lindsay administration, Ramirez had pioneered a Synanon-inspired TC program in Puerto Rico.[30] When Ramirez later appeared in New York, he seemed sold on Casriel's theory about the nature of addiction. "Drugs to the addict serve as a cushion, a protective layer," he explained in Daytop's marathon documentary. Lengthy confrontational sessions begin to heal participants by altering addicts' tendency to retreat from intimacy: "No day, no night, no sleep. Fatigue will have won over many defensive barriers."[31]

Casriel posited a theory that addicts do not react to stress according to commonly understood response mechanisms such as "fight or flight" and "fear or anger." They instead adopt a coping strategy that he called "withdrawal" or "encapsulation."[32] Effective addiction treatment begins with shedding the "encapsulating shell." Ex-addicts got behind the theory. "Be aware," Daytop residents reminded each other. "Don't be encapsulated."[33] Deitch and Casriel coauthored promotional pamphlets that described the strategy. Daytop sent pamphlets to Lindsay. Casriel submitted promotional material with another round of congressional testimony in 1969.[34]

According to a prime spot in a National Institutes of Health drug-abuse campaign film, Daytop also "took the message right to the center of the action: the ghettos, where drug use is rampant."[35] Daytop's Special Action Project Against Narcotics (SPAN) led outreach efforts in urban neighborhoods. The SPAN office in the Lower East Side of Manhattan conducted intake interviews for potential clients, confronted active drug users, and held group sessions for members who did not require residential treatment.[36] SPAN services reached ethnic enclaves and drug-culture youth. By the middle of 1968, Daytop's outreach bordered on New Left activism. "Our real job ain't got nothing to do with overcoming drugs," Deitch told a Daytop audience. "Our real job is confronting a racist community and challenging them to live the life we show by example. Daytop works because it is *not* concerned with 'overcoming drug addiction.' It's concerned with social change."[37] As Deitch made his declaration, Daytop's members had already altered the establishment's approach to addiction; its graduates were entrenched in a new, city-run system of treatment providers that would only grow larger.

PHOENIX HOUSE

In 1967, Mayor Lindsay moved Efren Ramirez's multi-million-dollar treatment effort out of the Health Services Administration. He named the psychiatrist the first commissioner of the ASA in New York City's Human Resources Administration. Lindsay's move aligned addiction treatment with other social problems such as poverty rather than with the medical establishment. Lindsay announced that the newly created agency would support Ramirez's treatment philosophy, which emphasized "the close relationship of narcotics to other social problems in neighborhoods." Ramirez explained that he intended to increase the budget for the city's programs by more than $90 million to meet his treatment goals.[38] Ramirez might have been content to continue investing in existing, independent treatment providers such as Daytop; instead, he used his mandate to found and expand a massive, city-run TC project. Phoenix House became one of the largest residential treatment programs in the country between 1967 and 1970. With 918 residents in fifteen locations, Phoenix soon rivaled Synanon and the narcotics farms.[39] (In 1970, Synanon had 1,365 residents, though not all of them were addicts; Lexington and Fort Worth had a combined patient load of 618.)[40] "Phoenix House is the largest project of its kind in the world," touted its brochure, and its history is a grassroots story like Synanon's.[41]

TCs relied on the uncommon expertise of ex-addicts who understood the essential components of the therapeutic philosophy. Synanon was still the best place to find employees who met this qualification. Ramirez asked the psychiatrist Mitchell Rosenthal to serve as his deputy, and in the spring of 1967 Rosenthal moved from California to New York. Once the framework for a new program had been established, the ASA extended generous offers of employment to Synanon graduates (one couple was reportedly offered an annual salary of $19,000 a year—the equivalent of more than $130,000 in today's dollars).[42] Daytop graduates also found work at Phoenix House and similar treatment programs; an evaluation study conducted in mid-1969 found that 75 percent of graduates were employed in the addiction-treatment field.[43] Daytop helped establish this pattern of TC employment. It held its first official graduation ceremony in 1967, and many graduates chose to remain employed at the organization.[44] Only three graduates listed on a roster of Daytop graduates in 1968 found work outside the growing treatment industry. Those employed in the treatment field outside Daytop worked with new city-run treatment programs or in Marathon House, a TC founded by Daytop graduates in Rhode Island.[45]

Another way to acquire ex-addict talent was to develop it. Phoenix House's expansion in the late 1960s was made possible by recovering addicts and supporters with roots in Synanon. A few years before Phoenix House's population boomed, Ramirez started a pilot program at the Morris Bernstein Institute. The institute was housed in a wing of the well-respected Beth Israel Medical Center, which had acquired Manhattan General

Hospital in 1964. The venerable center held addicts who displayed an underwhelming faith in addiction treatment's curative powers. When Ron Williams checked in for a month-long detoxification stint, he had no plans to break his long-term heroin habit. Then Ramirez launched his new program. "I'm going to come back tomorrow," Ramirez promised the skeptical patients. "I have a surprise for you."[46]

The surprise was a cured addict. Williams and his fellow patients had never heard of Synanon. They knew about Lexington—and, Williams remembered, thought its treatment would not work. Ramirez's clean-cut colleague testified about his drug use, prison stints, and the difficulty he had reentering society afterward. The patients were skeptical but hopeful; even if Ramirez's friend was not entirely cured, they thought, he was clearly a functional addict. He returned on several occasions and brought along other ex-addicts. They made staying clean seem possible.[47]

Williams had twenty days left in his twenty-eight-day stay when Manhattan General Hospital announced it was starting a TC. He joined the ex-addicts on a designated floor. The leaders "were gifted. You wanted them to like you. And you would do things in order to be liked," said Williams. Gradually, "your standards changed a little." Williams' twenty days became forty. Forty became sixty. Williams bonded with the other Bernstein TC residents. When the program directors announced their plan to renovate a prison on nearby Hart Island and transform it into a large-scale TC with the help of the Bernstein residents, a few ex-addicts, including Williams, refused to work in a prison. One member of the group, Julio Martinez, convinced a developer to rent them a floor of his building on Eighty-Fifth Street. If they pooled their welfare money together, they could just afford the rent. Rather than following Ramirez's men to Hart Island, these Bernstein TC graduates moved into the apartment building with plans to establish their own halfway house.[48]

The building was a wreck inhabited by "winos and addicts—and they had drugs," said Williams. The floor was crawling with roaches and rats. One of the six residents was a former Synanon member who had relapsed after leaving the organization. He intuited how to repeat Synanon's early success in Venice Beach. The roommates scrubbed the floor clean, combined their resources, and started hustling. They soon had furniture and regular food donors; they began attracting new residents. They named the house after the patient newspaper they had started together at the Bernstein Institute: Phoenix House.[49]

When Mitchell Rosenthal visited the house, the recovering residents had expanded their venture to other floors of the building, but their ambitions were still small in scope. "If you could have one thing," Rosenthal asked the Phoenix leaders, "what would it be?" Williams asked for a telephone; at the time, twenty men shared a single line. "Phones. Two or three phones," Rosenthal repeated, incredulous. "One of these days you're going to have so many phones, you won't know what to do with them."[50]

Rosenthal brought phones, funding, powerful connections, and professional experience. As he promised, Phoenix grew rapidly; it quickly "took on qualities of industry," said Williams.[51] Phoenix leaders became "professional dope fiends," complained one former Phoenix resident who later joined Synanon. "They would guru for eight hours a day, they would tell all the dope fiends how to be responsible, how to develop some kind of character and then they would leave and do whatever they did."[52] A few Synanon members criticized Phoenix House treatment as a "watered-down" version of the cure Synanon had promoted in the early 1960s. They argued that the Phoenix version had been hopelessly corrupted by its total dependence on establishment support.[53]

Rosenthal hired several of Synanon's ex-addict luminaries to establish the facility on Hart Island's prison site. Former Synanon members such as Candy Latson brought extensive Synanon prison experience to the Hart Island project, and within seven months the program had grown from fifty people to more than two hundred. The intake department was processing forty to fifty new arrivals each week. At that point, Rosenthal asked the Hart residents to train nonaddicted ASA officers in TC methods.[54] Vinny Marino lived in Synanon and Daytop before entering Phoenix House after another relapse. He went to work as an unpaid senior coordinator for the island. He led groups and renovated the facilities as part of his treatment; with the increasing patient population, he expected an eventual promotion to a paying position. Instead, Marino complained, he was "asked to show

FIGURE 3.2

Actor Hal Linden with two Phoenix House staff members in front of the
organization's Upper West Side location. Photograph by William Shrier
for *Look* magazine, May 8, 1969.

Source: Courtesy of the *Look* magazine photo collection, Library of Congress,
Washington, DC.

these squares from ASA how everything worked so they could go out and
get fatter salaries from the city."[55]

The ASA's hefty operating budget also drew scrutiny from outside the
prison; in addition to employing a handful of influential ex-addict leaders,
the ASA created an entirely new bureaucracy. A large portion of the ASA's
investment in treatment went into Phoenix House. When city leaders decided to turn Phoenix's management over to the Foundation Board in
1970, Phoenix's combined city and state funds ($4.3 million) rivaled the

ASA's entire first-year operating budget ($5.5 million).[56] But taxpayers would have to wait to see their return on investment in Phoenix and similar programs; cure in TCs was a lengthy and labor-intensive process that was often expected to take years.[57] Rosenthal knew that Phoenix would need data from rigorous evaluation studies to retain its legitimacy. He hired George De Leon, a recent PhD in psychology from Columbia, as Phoenix's in-house researcher.[58]

Like the Synanon scholars before him, De Leon was familiar with drug-using subcultures; he was a jazz musician and had seen several friends develop heroin habits. He later observed the results of his friends' encounters with Synanon and Daytop: they seemed completely reformed. As a psychologist, De Leon was keenly interested in the curative mechanisms of the TC model. His patients with everyday neuroses made only modest, incremental changes while in private psychotherapy; in contrast, the TC method apparently resulted in dramatic character transformation. The TC practice seemed like a much more rewarding pursuit.[59]

De Leon also noticed that TC proponents had made little effort to quantify their success. Using Phoenix House as his laboratory, he carried out extensive studies on the impact that the organization had on long-term emotional changes, criminal activity, and psychopathology. He later showed a relationship between the length of time that clients stayed in the TC and the degree to which they achieved a variety of therapeutic goals.[60] For example, staying in the TC for one year or more reduced residents' anticipated postprogram arrests by 70 percent. Slightly shorter stays of between three and eleven months still reduced arrests by more than 40 percent. Leaving the TC within the first three months, however, reduced arrests to merely 6.7 percent of the preprogram level.[61]

TCs needed the data. They soon faced opposition from a rigorous, biomedical, and monied new treatment method: methadone maintenance. The early New York TCs initially competed for talent, clients, and official support. By the late 1960s, however, a growing recognition that the drug methadone might solve the heroin epidemic inspired TC providers to present a unified message: "Methadone is a lie," said Judianne Densen-Gerber, the conservative director of Odyssey House.[62]

ODYSSEY HOUSE

On the surface, Judianne Densen-Gerber had little in common with the addicts she would eventually treat. In 1965, she described herself as the perfectionist daughter of intellectual professionals, the wife of the director of New York's hospital system, a pregnant mother of two, and a graduate in law and medicine. Her vita lacked the experiential learning that ex-addicts substituted for doctoral training. But when Densen-Gerber began treating an addict in the first year of her psychiatry residency at Metropolitan Hospital, she related to the feelings of alienation and distress described by her client, Tony Enriquez. Densen-Gerber did not use drugs, but she privately agonized over whether she would be capable of sustaining the competing demands of motherhood and medicine.[63]

Because everyone knew addicts couldn't be cured, leaders at Metropolitan didn't consider caring for them to be particularly demanding, and the chairman of the Psychiatry Department assigned Densen-Gerber to the drug-addict ward in lieu of maternity leave. But Densen-Gerber was inspired by her work with Enriquez and decided to take a more active role. She tried all the standard psychiatric practices—token economies, aversion and shock therapies, and drug maintenance—but met with "failure after failure."[64]

She persisted. Efren Ramirez, whom Densen-Gerber remembered meeting on a "post-partum rest visit" to Puerto Rico, assured her that it was possible to "redirect" addicts' manipulative skills to therapeutic ends. Densen-Gerber had not found the right method of redirection (the patients found ways to use drugs on her ward), but she did become convinced that the hospital's standard experimental methods were unethical. Authorities asked Densen-Gerber to persuade her patients to consent to liver biopsies for an unrelated research study. Researchers also supposedly enrolled patients, against their will, in another study that tested their neurological response following heroin administration. As a result of the study, a few became readdicted. Densen-Gerber grew increasingly disenchanted with the establishment response to addiction treatment.[65]

But her solitary efforts to inspire change still proved insufficient. She discovered that Enriquez had relapsed. In 1966, she brought him onto the ward at Metropolitan. She devised a new treatment plan. Enriquez would first receive care as an individual patient. Once he was stabilized, she wrote, she would count on him to "police the ward from within." Several weeks of turmoil eventually led to a cop-out session: fourteen residents recommitted to therapy and elected Enriquez as their president.[66] The residents decided to discontinue use of the maintenance drug cyclazocine and—contrary to the hospital's wishes and funding mandate—to begin a drug-free treatment program. This, Densen-Gerber remembered, was the beginning of Odyssey House.

"We used group-therapy techniques borrowed from everywhere, from Synanon, from Daytop, from Maxwell Jones, from whatever we could find on the subject," wrote Densen-Gerber. The patients' decision to terminate maintenance therapy caused controversy, and Metropolitan discharged them. Daytop housed the former patients while Ramirez searched for a more permanent location. When he gave up—citing bureaucratic opposition to the plan—Densen-Gerber allowed several patients to camp in her Upper East Side penthouse while they searched for an affordable group home. Over lunch, a wealthy friend of Densen-Gerber's reflected that the group "appeared to be on an odyssey." Before the TC found a building, it had its brand.[67]

The ex-addicts located a dilapidated building in East Harlem that rented for $17 a month. Odyssey House's residents fixed the broken windows, cleaned the rooms, and hustled donations of food and funds. They visited the nearby police precinct and befriended the officers. The sergeant told the *Today* show that the order Odyssey established was "an oasis in the desert."[68]

Reporters were intrigued by Odyssey House. The *Village Voice* justified the cramped, makeshift quarters: the lack of privacy "[is] intentional. No secrets are tolerated. Nothing is too personal to be discussed."[69] Authorities were less ready to recognize regimented communal living as a form medical treatment; Densen-Gerber, like Dederich before her, challenged building-code regulations as ill suited for classifying such unconventional therapeutic operations.[70]

Odyssey billed itself as a "therapeutic community," but it deviated in several ways from the Synanon model. Densen-Gerber actively participated in the confrontational group sessions, but she did not—to use Casriel's terms—shed her psychiatrist "shell." Ex-addicts could advance to roles of authority in Odyssey, but Densen-Gerber patrolled the paraprofessional divide. In 1967, under Enriquez's leadership, Odyssey residents revolted. Enriquez had graduated, received a promotion to executive director, and shortly afterward demanded that Densen-Gerber grant him total control over clinical care. As an ex-addict, he argued, he had insight that Densen-Gerber lacked. Mitchell Rosenthal, recently arrived from California, agreed. Rosenthal joined a local group of addiction-treatment providers; once there, he reportedly urged the other members to turn their agencies over to ex-addict leaders.[71] Densen-Gerber believed Rosenthal intended to use Odyssey's split as an opportunity to take control of the organization. Although the board of directors ultimately supported Densen-Gerber over Enriquez, Enriquez's walk-out called Densen-Gerber's leadership into question. Ramirez threatened to cut off Odyssey's local funds and place the organization under new leadership: Rosenthal and his group of ex-addict advisers. "Efren, she's full of this psychiatric shit," Rosenthal reportedly argued. "She's not capable of running an agency. She doesn't understand what it's all about."[72]

Densen-Gerber and Odyssey's board successfully resisted the city's attempt to restructure the program. Densen-Gerber later argued that Ramirez's Phoenix House program was an "encapsulated addict world" that was out of touch with reality. "Our residents go out into the communities, talk to drug addicts, purchase supplies, go to the movies," countered Rosenthal. "How can you call them isolated?"[73] The shape of outreach and activism reflected the leadership of different TCs. Despite Odyssey's intention to "treat the streets,"[74] the organization, unlike Synanon or Daytop, never catered to the counterculture. Densen-Gerber was unabashedly conservative—more conservative than most others in the field, she said—and she charmed powerful Republican supporters such as Governor Nelson Rockefeller.[75] When funds were not forthcoming, she also shamed politicians with public-relations campaigns. In 1968, Odyssey parents paraded a coffin in front of Mayor Lindsay's Gracie Mansion, symbolizing the imminent death of Odyssey House, which was awaiting the ASA's overdue response to a budget request.[76]

Synanon and Daytop supporters had argued that their treatment organizations served as effective substitutes for dysfunctional families. Densen-Gerber created a new niche market by promoting TC treatment designed for women and children. Densen-Gerber's arguments drew on her personal experiences as a woman, a mother, and a trained mental-health professional. In her campaigns for treatment funding, she emphasized the innocence and immaturity of the addicts under her care. "I have no problem as a mother looking at these children [who use drugs] and considering that if these were my children, I would consider [addiction] an illness, not a crime," said Densen-Gerber, who went on to argue that successful parenting was the disease's cure. She believed that poor adult models and insufficient moral supervision lead children to abuse drugs.[77] Odyssey's emphasis on instilling traditional values in parents and children could complement conservative political platforms, and Densen-Gerber challenged politicians to invest in the addition-treatment models that best reflected their values.

In 1969, Densen-Gerber claimed that Odyssey's Bronx building was overcrowded with teenage addicts seeking treatment. Because government officials refused to allocate additional funds for youth-specific treatment, she opened a private adolescent unit. "This was technically illegal," she conceded, but justified by government officials' immoral reluctance to address the problem of drug abuse among youth. Mayor Lindsay's administration took Densen-Gerber to court but reversed its opposition almost immediately. The city and state allocated funds for Odyssey's adolescent program, which maintained its growth through a combination of private and government funds.[78]

Densen-Gerber "led the crusade" for youthful addicts, reported the *New York Times*. Her campaign had an impact, anticipating the arguments of the Reagan era and inspiring her organization's rapid expansion. Scarcely a year after Odyssey established its adolescent unit in New York, the organization fielded requests to establish Odyssey Houses in New Hampshire, Massachusetts, Arizona, Utah, Virginia, and Michigan.[79] In New York City, Densen-Gerber brought "Ralphie" deJesus, a frail twelve-year-old boy, to a committee hearing in early 1970 to testify about the reality of his drug addiction. Sitting on Densen-Gerber's lap, deJesus told the city's Joint Legislative Committee on the Protection of Children and

Youth Drug Abuse that he began mainlining heroin after "learning how to do it in the street."[80] The committee was skeptical about the likely efficacy of Governor Nelson Rockefeller's new campaign to address drug abuse among youth, which did not appear to come with increased funding or new proposals for treatment. Densen-Gerber similarly criticized the decision to allocate state funds to new buildings rather than to treatment services. She made a motherly declaration: "We don't need buildings, we need bedtime stories."[81]

"Officials ought to stop sniping at the voluntary, private agencies [like Odyssey] trying to meet a need that the city, the state, and the federal government are clearly not beginning to meet," concurred the New York Times editorial board.[82] Densen-Gerber argued that federal revisions to NARA should "more fully utilize" private-sector innovations such as Odyssey's adolescent program.[83]

Odyssey's promotions turned Daytop and Synanon-style docudrama into soap-opera material. In 1970, the daytime drama One Life to Live filmed a summer series of sixteen episodes at Odyssey House, where One Life's fictional character Cathy Craig took part in confrontational therapy sessions with real teen drug users. The series followed the "troubled teenager's" arc through her journey of drug experimentation and dramatic recovery. Unlike preachy documentaries or somber news stories, One Life's summer storyline had the potential to reach bored, at-risk teenagers—or their mothers.[84]

In 1971, Odyssey added a new facility with treatment programs tailored to young girls and pregnant women.[85] Densen-Gerber was first convinced that maintenance medication was the enemy of authentic addiction recovery in Metropolitan Hospital. Youth and pregnant women were even clearer illustrations of the dangers of drug-based addiction treatment: giving a heroin substitute to innocents amounted to government-sanctioned "genocide," Densen-Gerber later argued. In 1971, she warned a tour of federal officials that the maintenance drug methadone was being diverted for illicit use and that methadone-related deaths were increasing. Densen-Gerber believed the Nixon administration supported prescribing narcotic agonists such as methadone to child addicts. She offered an alternative: "children should be inoculated with values."[86]

METHADONE'S TREATMENT-MARKET TAKEOVER

In 1965, as the newly incorporated Daytop faced the objections of Prince's Bay protesters and Densen-Gerber began her psychiatric residency at Metropolitan Hospital, two researchers published a groundbreaking study on a promising new treatment for narcotic addiction. The technical title of the article published in the *Journal of the American Medical Association*—"A Medical Treatment for Diacetylmorphine (Heroin) Addiction"—belies the extraordinary impact it had on addiction medicine and politics.[87] The study's authors, Vincent Dole and Marie Nyswander, began their work when Dole was asked to lead the New York City Research Council's Committee on Narcotics during the chair's sabbatical in 1962. At the time, Dole researched obesity and metabolism; he knew little about the field of addiction. He contacted Marie Nyswander, a psychiatrist who had worked at the Lexington Narcotic Farm and authored a sympathetic book about clinical work with addicts, *The Drug Addict as Patient*.[88] Dole secured a staff position for Nyswander at his home institution, the Rockefeller Institute. They developed an unorthodox hypothesis: narcotic addiction was not caused by a sociopathic personality that led addicts to chase craving without regard for consequences. Instead, they viewed craving as a fundamentally biological condition that could be treated with pharmaceuticals. Their research led to a reversal of the nation's ban on maintenance treatment for opiate addiction.[89]

Dole and Nyswander began with an observational study that used an approach that incensed Densen-Gerber during her residency at Metropolitan: maintaining addicts on different narcotic drugs. Dole and Nyswander soon saw that short-acting narcotics such as heroin and morphine made maintenance arduous for patients. Patients' growing dependence on the drugs varied wildly, and Nyswander found it difficult to standardize the dosage. As a result, patients often suffered through daily withdrawal as they awaited their next dose. The craving overwhelmed patients' plans to complete any other daily task—even dressing seemed like an insurmountable goal, remembered Nyswander.[90] But when Dole and Nyswander switched the patients to a longer-acting, synthetic opiate called methadone, the patients' cravings subsided. They enrolled in school and looked for work. And their criminal behavior—the most politically significant sign of sociopathy—ceased.

Based on the results from the first twenty-two methadone patients, Dole and Nyswander argued that addicts stabilized on 80–120 mg of methadone could be "blockaded" from the euphoric experience associated with heroin injection. Once exposed to narcotics, individuals theoretically underwent a permanent metabolic change and became addicts. After, they needed the drugs in a visceral way, just as "a diabetic needs insulin."[91]

But drug-free TC advocates saw methadone treatment as substituting one drug for another: they argued that addicts needed methadone like a bourbon-drinking alcoholic needs scotch.[92] TC leaders believed it took time, effort, and even some degree of discomfort to achieve maturity— yet Dole and Nyswander's patients were functioning in jobs and school in a few short months. The methadone cure ran contrary to the early TCs' philosophy.

While TC leaders were just beginning their work with small groups of initiates, the preliminary methadone study quickly generated political and scholarly attention. New York City Hospital commissioner Ray Trussel gave Dole and Nyswander an entire floor at the Bernstein Institute, which also piloted Phoenix House.[93] Dole and Nyswander's participant pool grew into the hundreds, and the positive results scaled up to higher sample sizes. The expanded studies tracked arrest records of heroin users maintained on methadone. In 1968, after measuring the employment and crime status of 750 methadone patients over a four-year period, Dole reported "unequivocally" positive results: "criminal addicts can be rehabilitated by a well-supervised maintenance program." Eighty-eight percent of the patients were "socially acceptable, maintaining arrest-free records since admission," and a subset of 59 percent had become "productive members of society" by gaining and maintaining employment.[94] This evidence suggested that methadone was a solution for crime and a workable treatment for a chronic disease. Journalists and politicians picked up the message.

Some members of the medical establishment, such as Commissioner Trussel, viewed Efren Ramirez's ASA as a challenge to the biomedical status quo. Ramirez endorsed ex-addict professionals, and his agency siphoned public funds away from hospital providers. Even worse, the ASA seemingly operated with enviable autonomy.[95] TCs' comparatively small number of reformed addicts countered the drug culture one user at a time; meanwhile, Dole and Nyswander's methadone program produced relatively rapid, widespread results. In 1968, Julius Moskowitz, a Democratic city councilman from Brooklyn, denounced Ramirez's agency as a "fraud." Moskowitz claimed Phoenix House had "not cured a single addict in the city."[96] According to likeminded critics, Ramirez's TCs were an obstacle to methadone, the only proven treatment method. The Lindsay administration tried to balance support for both treatment modalities, but they proved incompatible.[97] Ramirez resigned in 1968 and was succeeded by his protégé, Larry Allen Baer, who left the following year. In 1970, Lindsay, once among TCs' most powerful proponents, tipped the scales toward methadone. The *New York Times* reported that Phoenix House had reached its peak enrollment, but because Phoenix had supposedly produced only 140 successful graduates since its inauguration in 1966, [98] Lindsay refused to invest in increasing the TC's capacity. In contrast, methadone programs could serve far more patients and could be administered for a fraction of the cost of residential treatment. Lindsay planned to expand the number of addicts in methadone programs from around 2,500 to at least 7,500 in less than a year.[99]

Methadone's expansion outlasted Lindsay's mayoralty.[100] Under the direction of Robert Newman, New York City's methadone program grew from several thousand patients to approximately eighteen thousand by 1973.[101] In the late 1960s and early 1970s, other cities and states attempted to replicate New York's success; large-scale methadone programs in Illinois, Washington, DC, and Georgia became the training ground for the nation's first three "drug czars" (Jerome Jaffe, Robert Dupont, and Peter Bourne).[102] While TC leaders bickered, the managers of large-scale methadone programs formed an intimate club and met regularly to share their experiences with treatment expansion.

Methadone appealed to politicians and health professionals. Dole and Nyswander's studies made the controversial notion of outpatient opiate maintenance medically (and thus politically) respectable. Methadone programs used the existing medical infrastructure to deliver treatment, which meant that they could be scaled up relatively rapidly. Many of the methadone pioneers understood the programs as a public-health response: methadone was a population-based intervention that could be swiftly implemented in areas that experienced surging rates of heroin use. It even tested well in double-blind studies.[103]

Therapeutic communities, in contrast, were a labor- and time-intensive form of treatment oriented primarily toward individual and familial transformation. They were expensive, and their reliance on residential treatment and a trained workforce of peer counselors limited their ability to expand quickly enough to meet rising demand. While TCs promoted gripping stories of personal transformation, methadone programs gathered crime data. Dole and Nyswander showed that methadone treatment reduced recidivism in their patient population. The psychiatrist Robert Dupont's new methadone program in Washington, DC, brought down crime rates throughout the district.[104]

What good were TCs' "anticriminal" subcultures if they did not reliably reduce neighborhood crime rates? Confronted with such questions, TC leaders who opposed methadone on moral grounds adopted three central counterarguments in response to methadone supporters. First, they contended that the TC model's emphasis on maturation and psychological development made it a more appropriate treatment option for youth and families. Second, they noted that methadone was a limited treatment model; the drug worked only on opiate addicts and could not be used to reduce the habitual cravings associated with other illicit substances. Third, they argued that TCs could meaningfully treat the symptoms of social dysfunction (such as drug use and crime) by countering the decadent culture that produced them. This last point caused conflict among second-generation TCs such as Daytop; in the late 1960s, treatment promoters became increasingly concerned with the era's cultural politics.

DAYTOP DIVIDED

Daytop came perilously close to becoming a Synanon-like cult in 1968—or so Monsignor William O'Brien argued. As Synanon leaders made the self-conscious decision to recruit countercultural seekers, O'Brien believed Deitch was confusing Daytop's rehabilitative mission with spectacular social activism.[105] Deitch began to preach that curing the individual addict was secondary to a larger mission: transforming the inequitable and dysfunctional conditions that produced addiction. For him, the dramatic transformation of individuals within TCs—from apathetic, deluded drug users to aware, engaged adults—served as a metaphor for the sort of radical transformation needed to create a more just world. Deitch had working relationships with the Black Panthers and, like some Panthers, began to frame addiction as a tool of oppression.[106] O'Brien learned about Deitch's philosophy from an NBC documentary producer, who called with concern after several disappointing days of filming at Daytop. "We've burned the flag, we've heard all about the life of Che Guevara," the producer reportedly told O'Brien. "We haven't seen a thing about Daytop."[107]

O'Brien felt he had made a critical mistake. Years earlier he had refused to partner with Synanon when its directors rejected oversight. But Deitch had been such a competent leader at the time that Daytop board members had felt confident in giving him free reign over the organization's operations. Daytop's grantors would not be pleased if they discovered that funds meant to address the drug problem were going to political radicals.[108]

They found out soon enough. On November 17, 1968, the *New York Times* published an article with the headline "Narcotics Complex Split by Charges of Cultist Activity."[109] A few days later, the next issue of the *Village Voice* also called Daytop a cult: "Drug treatment in the Vietnam era gets politicized, cultish."[110] O'Brien denounced Deitch's therapeutic program as a "new left commune" and urged government agencies to withhold funding until Deitch had been removed and order restored.[111] O'Brien, Casriel, and some Daytop staff protested Deitch's increasingly politicized therapeutic philosophy—especially the artistic decision to make costumes out of the American flag for Daytop's anniversary celebration in late October. Casriel threatened to resign unless the board took action against Deitch. In response, Deitch fired seven staff members who opposed his leadership. The board refused Casriel's resignation and prepared to fire Deitch and his political followers. Before he could be fired, however, Deitch resigned along with sixty-one staff members. They staged a "live-in" at Daytop's property on West Fourteenth Street.[112] Signs reading "We're a Family, Not a Factory" and "Integrity, Not Compromise" decorated the windows of the former convent building where the staffers were housed.[113] While O'Brien took legal action to have the occupants removed, Deitch met with his own supporters, including the deputy commissioner of the ASA and a defeated Democratic candidate for the U.S. Senate.[114] "We are operating the same way we have for years," argued Deitch. "Now, suddenly, they call this a commune."[115] The communal kitchen and dormitory rooms that the *Times* called cultish were architectural remnants from the building's previous use as a nunnery. The Catholic O'Brien and activist Deitch clashed over the community's purpose but not its therapeutic process. "They disagree only on the crucial question of which side is obsessed with manipulation, in contrast to the side of the selfless therapeutic angels," noted the *Village Voice* reporter.[116]

Were Daytop's therapeutic confrontations in service of middle-class (and technocratic) maturation or liberatory (and dangerous) consciousness raising? O'Brien's recollection of the Daytop revolt echoes later historical interpretations of 1968: the year when the "good sixties" turned bad and enlightened liberal reforms gave way to campouts and cults. Daytop, perhaps more than any other TC at the time, was engaged with the cultural and political events of the day. More than a year before Woodstock, Daytop hosted a music festival featuring the Grateful Dead, Pete Seeger, and Janis Ian, among others; thirteen hundred people attended.[117] When protesters rocked the Democratic Convention in August 1968, Daytop members were there.[118] Six months after antiwar student protesters occupied Columbia University's campus administration buildings, Daytop members occupied the convent property and made statements in favor of peaceable resistance. While the rock opera *Hair*'s cast bestowed posies on a Broadway audience, real Daytop members walked through the aisles of their own play's off-Broadway venue and asked each audience member directly: "Will *you* love me?"[119]

Daytop's play *The Concept* opened off-Broadway on May 6, 1968, after being piloted in Atlantic City, Philadelphia, Providence, Trenton, Stanford, and Los Angeles.[120] Director Lawrence Sacharow worked with Daytop members to organize their life stories and therapeutic experiences into a full-length play. The play follows a young addict from jail to Daytop, where he undergoes the challenging process of rehabilitation. Daytop members played themselves onstage, and critics argued that their tight bond, wry humor, and rhythmic profanity kept *The Concept* from veering into soap-opera sentimentality.[121] In addition to staging the TC's dramatic group encounters, the play adopted the expressionist tactics of the avant-garde stage. Although many critics were moved by the audacious intimacy created between *Concept* actors and their audiences, one skeptic argued that the togetherness fostered by the interactive off-Broadway theater too closely resembled "T-groups, communes, and encounter sessions. In this type of atmosphere, the opportunities for charlatanism are simply enormous."[122] (When a *Village Voice* critic saw the Daytop members moving into the aisles at the play's climax, their arms extended for hugs and affirmation, she was thankful to have a balcony ticket.)[123] But most audiences were less skeptical about edgy theater's capitalist impulses. "*The Concept* is a wonderful commercial for Daytop," concluded one opening-night review, "and"—echoing *Life's* Synanon coverage—"an even better one for the human race."[124]

When Deitch left Daytop, director Lawrence Sacharow argued, *The Concept* died. The play ceased production in December 1968 after Deitch's ouster but was revived the following fall. Sacharow called the new *Concept* a "fading carbon copy"; it could never recapture the "honesty and love" that animated Deitch's Daytop and the nightly dramatic portrayal of it.[125] The authentic Daytop spirit was as lifeless as "the Hippie," the countercultural icon that the Diggers, a radical San Francisco community group, declared dead in October 1967. Just as the Diggers proclaimed the Hippie a media invention, Sacharow argued that although audiences could still see the co-opted performance of Daytop's therapy sessions, it would be a fraud.[126] But the tension between therapeutic realism and fiction only continued to drive sales. Daytop's new leadership wrote that the play remained a faithful depiction of the Daytop philosophy; *The Concept*, they argued, was still "playing to standing room only" and inspiring standing ovations.[127]

FIGURE 3.3

Daytop group photo at Swan Lake. Residents and staff from Swan Lake and Staten Island. Photograph by Charles Devlin, October 1967.

Source: Courtesy of Charles Devlin.

The treatment facilities took longer to fill. On December 3, 1968, Daytop's board regained control of the facilities using a court order; when the former staff left, they took approximately fifty residents with them.[128] Charles Devlin, Daytop's first patient, and Samuel Anglin, another ex-addict employee, had opposed Deitch's increasingly politicized leadership agenda; when he was gone, they returned to Daytop in leadership roles and worked to rebuild the organizations' legitimacy. The buildings were not operating at capacity, and important records had mysteriously disappeared during the shake-up. (A team of evaluators, surveying the available drug-treatment programs between October 1970 and February 1971, issued a scathing review of Daytop's spotty data.)[129] Yet by 1970 the organization had reassembled a handsome portfolio of grants; the State Narcotics Commission presented Daytop with a $1.5 million award, bringing Daytop's total state funds since the fallout in 1968 to almost $4 million—a generous sum touted by Governor Nelson Rockefeller at a press conference.[130] Despite TC leaders' worries about methadone, treatment funding in the early 1970s did not become a zero-sum game. After Daytop's reorganization, Casriel opened a private center where he treated wealthy, troubled, polydrug-using youths with encounter groups and primal-scream therapy.[131] In the late 1960s, other former Daytop employees also founded new treatment centers such as Marathon House, Gaudenzia House, Walden House, and Gateway House.[132]

GATEWAY TO THE WHITE HOUSE: THE ILLINOIS DRUG ABUSE PROGRAM

In 1966, Illinois still lacked adequate treatment facilities for addicts. New York, in contrast, had adopted a California-style statewide program for civil commitment several years earlier. And newer therapies were also well under way: the methadone experiment was expanding, and Daytop's roster of residents continued to grow.[133] When NARA was enacted in November 1966, Illinois, like many other states, needed to put alternatives to incarceration in place. When addiction researcher Jerome Jaffe moved from

New York to the University of Chicago a few months later, the only place an addict could detoxify was the infirmary of the county jail.[134]

Jaffe, who had trained as a psychiatrist and pharmacologist, arrived at Chicago following appointments at Lexington and Vincent Dole's laboratory at Rockefeller University. As Jaffe began to establish his Chicago research lab in early 1967, he also served as a consultant to the Illinois Narcotics Advisory Council.[135] Jaffe was a dynamic, inventive young researcher (then only in his thirties) who had already observed Lexington, Synanon, Daytop, and methadone treatments firsthand.[136] The council heeded his advice.

Jaffe proposed a research program that would have been unthinkable in New York. Although the state and city had adopted comparatively progressive drug-treatment policies, New York's treatment landscape was littered with conflicting philosophies, large personalities, and well-entrenched medical and criminal-justice interest groups. Jaffe asked: Why not pilot the treatment programs that had demonstrated promising preliminary results—methadone, TCs, detoxification, and after-care programs—and then expand the ones that hold up to rigorous evaluation? The council agreed with one condition: Jaffe had to head the program. Instead of devoting the next phase of his career to the basic and clinical studies of alpha-acetyl methadol (a methadone-like drug known as LAAM), he made Chicago the testing ground for multimodal addiction treatment.[137]

Jaffe's idea for the Illinois Drug Abuse Program (IDAP) earned Governor Richard Ogilvie's approval and the full support of Harold Vigotsky, who directed the State Department of Mental Health. With the political and financial backing of local authorities and the research resources of the University of Chicago, Jaffe recruited talented researchers such as Bob Schuster and Patrick Hughes.[138] In just a year and a half, IDAP established a detoxification ward with associated residential and day treatment facilities, more than one methadone program, and a new TC called Gateway House.[139]

Jaffe initially planned to test the modalities' efficacy by randomly assigning patients to one of the three treatment options: maintenance, detoxification, or TC care. But clients had strong opinions about which treatment model suited them and little interest in Jaffe's clinical trial. The attrition for clients assigned to undesirable treatments was "horrendous," remembered Jaffe. The plan to randomize addiction treatment was "naive."[140] Clients were more likely to be successful if they were initially motivated to comply with their treatment program.

Casriel disagreed. "We assume when [clients] come in they truly have no real motivation. One of the things we do very early is to motivate them so that they stay over several weeks," he said in a filmed debate with Jaffe, citing Daytop's impressive 90 percent retention rate. "This is of course the great paradox," replied Jaffe, "that although you have to push them into treatment that we designate as being curative, we have a waiting list of several hundred people who want to participate in a methadone treatment program."[141]

While Jaffe made TC programs available for those who demanded them, he argued that methadone was a more viable public-health solution. Methadone programs served more people, and the clients they treated returned more quickly to their communities, where they could serve as worthy examples for active addicts. Daytop's ex-addicts also addressed urban issues, countered Casriel: they "vacuumed the streets of addicts through confrontation." Daytop's SPAN workers returned to their old friends to say, "Look, Johnny, you don't have to do it anymore. You know, you don't have to be a dope fiend. You're not some peculiar enzymatic defunct human being. You just had a problem that you've never been able to face." According to Casriel, that problem was "emotional, cultural, social, and vocational." It was not metabolic.[142]

Jaffe was not opposed to assertive approaches to community outreach or to social and vocational enrichment programs; he hired David Deitch to help manage education and outreach for IDAP in 1969. But he demanded that staff in the TCs and methadone programs collaborate; they attended meetings together and shared discussions about clinical care. If the staff brought any philosophical hang-ups to IDAP, Jaffe later said, "they were smart enough to hide it from me."[143] IDAP became famous for reconciling the two opposing treatment strategies. The program allowed clients to transition from one modality to another and used some TC techniques in groups designed for methadone patients. Clients who wanted to stop taking methadone could have their dose gradually reduced in supervised TC settings.[144]

Gateway was the first TC associated with IDAP. Jaffe drew from his knowledge of the drug-treatment field and earlier observations of TCs such as Synanon and Daytop. He revisited Synanon and asked if the organization would be interested in establishing a new TC in Chicago. Dederich was not interested—not if Jaffe planned to manage the external evaluation of the center. Synanon's stance had not budged since the conversation with Casriel and O'Brien almost five years earlier. "Basically Chuck Dederich just said, 'Give us money and don't bother us,'" remembered Jaffe.[145] So Jaffe located several ex-addicts in another treatment program and sent them east to be trained at Daytop. He hired a former Synanon member to run the new organization.

Jaffe organized Gateway as a nonprofit governed by a board of directors rather than as a state-run facility. He believed that an organization with the freedom to pursue private and public funds would ultimately be more sustainable. He also thought that the ex-addict leadership needed to feel a sense of ownership for the organization to work.[146] But ownership had hazards that were not immediately obvious. Although Jaffe took a rigorous approach to treatment evaluation, IDAP also established a friendly therapeutic environment; staff, management, and patients from the programs mingled at picnics.[147] Jaffe even referred one of his own relatives to Gateway for treatment. All was well—that is, until several residents told Jaffe that Gateway's director had moved his brother into the community as an "enforcer." Gateway, like other traditional TCs, was certainly "authoritarian," said Jaffe. "That didn't bother me." Then Jaffe discovered that the director attempted to use intimidation and threats to coerce women in the community to perform sex acts.[148]

Jaffe called several meetings with Gateway's board of directors. "They were completely taken in by their so-called director of the house," said Jaffe.[149] He explained that he would withdraw the public support of IDAP funds unless the board looked for new leadership, but this threat was empty because Gateway was an independent entity, and the board could continue to raise revenue from other sources.[150] The board initially voted to retain the director and forgo state funds, a decision that left Jaffe without a traditional TC for his multimodal program. Just as Jaffe established a new TC and hired Daytop defectors Carl Charnett and Michael Darcy to run it, Gateway's board reversed course and fired the errant director. Jaffe permitted a "quiet merger" of the two organizations.[151] Charnett and Darcy reversed Gateway's chaotic course.[152]

In addition to Gateway, IDAP pioneered other treatment centers with TC elements. Tinley Park accommodated about one hundred people in a former mental-health center. Tinley offered an array of services, including detoxification, TC treatment, methadone, and transitional supportive housing for patients who needed further counseling and job training before returning to independent living.[153] Safari House also provided both outpatient methadone and residential treatment and was managed by TC graduates and former addicts who were not initially trained in the TC model.[154] The IDAP approach proved to be a highly creative endeavor that encouraged the combination of different treatment approaches and a wide variety of options for addicts who sought treatment. But it was also bureaucratic and designed with the ultimate goal of collecting evidence.

Jaffe later argued that the bureaucracy and not the intimacy between patients and staff kept the abuses inherent in the hierarchical treatment structures from escalating in IDAP TCs.[155] IDAP's close association with the University of Chicago and with the state funders meant that evaluators and medical residents regularly visited Gateway and other program sites. The multimodal approach also meant that the professionals involved with particular communities often had professional allegiances outside the TC orders.

Bureaucracy appealed to politicians who had a stake in effective solutions to the addiction problem. By the early 1970s, hard-drug use and addiction had expanded beyond the trafficking centers in New York and California and become an issue of national concern. The heroin epidemic of the late 1960s was inspired by demography as much as by geography; it was a baby-boom phenomenon.[156] The first wave of heroin users in the late 1960s had consisted mostly of black and Hispanic young men. Substance use soon began to spread among other groups—soldiers, women, middle-class youth—so Jaffe rapidly expanded IDAP, and presidential candidate Richard Nixon pledged to restore law and order.[157]

NIXON'S NEW CRISIS

Richard Nixon won the presidential election in 1968. In early June 1970, his adviser Jeffrey Donfeld took a tour of the nation's most prominent drug-treatment programs: Daytop Village, Phoenix House, a New York City methadone clinic, and IDAP in Chicago.[158] Donfeld had weathered the 1960s as a California conservative; he had opposed the free-speech movement as a law student at Berkeley and had spent the Summer of Love as an intern at Nixon's law firm.[159] Although Nixon had largely avoided discussing drug-policy specifics during the campaign in 1968, Donfeld made the drug issue his cause as a member of Nixon's domestic-policy staff. Donfeld read Dole and Nyswander's pioneering methadone results and decided that new treatment innovations could bring down crime rates. When Nixon's trusted adviser Egil "Bud" Krogh Jr. wanted to address crime in the District of Columbia, he turned to Donfeld for advice.[160] Either Donfeld's or Dole's research or both sold Krogh on methadone's ability to function as a crime intervention. Krogh gave Robert Dupont, then head of a small pilot methadone program, the authority to replicate New York's large-scale success rate with methadone. The Narcotics Treatment Administration, a multimodal program with a heavy emphasis on methadone, opened in Washington, DC, in February 1970.[161] Krogh viewed DC as a "laboratory," a natural experiment to test whether funding community-based treatment would have a positive effect on social disorder.[162] Both Donfeld and Krogh had the inkling that methadone, not TCs, would best serve Nixon's crime-fighting agenda. Nevertheless, Krogh asked Donfeld to survey several of the nation's prominent programs.

Donfeld reported that the New York program leaders were universally disparaging about competing treatment approaches: "each is a very parochial zealot believing that his program is the true panacea," he wrote.[163] IDAP's TCs were different. Tinley Park exhibited none of the "intense, moralistic, rigid approach of Daytop," observed Donfeld, who attributed the change in tone to Jaffe's cerebral management style.[164] He asked Jaffe to head a new study commission that would investigate the feasibility of establishing a national treatment program. Jaffe accepted. His commission's advice convinced Nixon adviser John Erlichman to take a proposal for national methadone expansion to the president.[165]

Nixon created a new office to tackle the drug problem—the Special Action Office for Drug Abuse Prevention (SAODAP)—and appointed Jaffe to lead it. A variety of factors in the months of 1971 paved the way for this bold new bureaucratic solution: stonewalling from the Bertram Brown's psychoanalytically inclined NIMH, which still viewed pharmaceutical methadone treatment as a fringe threat to the profession; a moral panic about drug use in Vietnam and among veterans, who obviously deserved compassion rather than criminalization; and the astonishing success of Dupont's DC methadone program, which began to bring crime down in 1970 after a frightening three-year increase that tracked a heroin epidemic from 1966 to 1969.[166]

In June, Nixon's advisers called Jaffe to the White House for a second meeting, ostensibly to further discuss his proposed plan for detoxifying troops before their return from Vietnam. Krogh and Donfeld instead brought Jaffe to a meeting with President Nixon and John Erlichman, who asked him to explain the details of the IDAP approach and questioned the relative merits of methadone and TC treatment. When Jaffe mentioned that his program included TCs "like Synanon and Daytop," Nixon vaguely remembered Synanon. Jaffe dismissed the group's relevance to drug treatment: "It's a very controversial group that's effective for a very select group. But they have most of their time available to go around writing speeches about how they've been converted. There's a certain evangelical quality to it—which is not bad, but the difficulty is that they are not very critical about themselves and they are all too willing to denigrate other approaches."[167]

But Jaffe also conceded that TCs had a place in a national treatment plan. He repeated two arguments in TCs' favor. First, methadone programs could serve heroin addicts, yet many youthful drug abusers used a variety of substances. Most who used heroin had only recently developed the habit. Second, giving methadone to young heroin users was politically unpalatable, and Jaffe had psychiatric misgivings about it as well. He described the ideal federal plan put forth in his commission's report: scale up methadone treatment into a nationwide program and fund multimodal, IDAP-style systems in cities with documented drug abuse problems and

FIGURE 3.4

Richard Nixon (*second from left*) and Jerome Jaffe (*third from left*), "Report on Drug Briefing." Photograph by White House press photographer Oliver Atkins, June 17, 1971.

Source: Courtesy of the Nixon Presidential Library and Museum, Yorba Linda, California.

few treatment programs.[168] On June 17, 1971, Nixon announced the creation of the new office, Jaffe's appointment, and a new federal budget of $105 million designated for addiction treatment. Nixon's cabinet may have underwritten this budget with methadone in mind, but TC advocates would also be eligible for the unprecedented influx of funding.

Treatment advocates predicted the further federalization of community treatment, a process that arguably had begun with the matching grants associated with NARA during the Johnson administration. Congressional subcommittee hearings in 1969 and 1971 debated the merits of each treatment model.[169] TC and methadone advocates presented results from their local programs, argued for funding each model on a national scale, and positioned themselves for new funding opportunities. New Yorkers repeated their arguments for a national audience.

Daniel Casriel told Congress, "Methadone will prevent stealing, but it doesn't cure [the addict's] personality. No chemical does. The thing that drove them to search out heroin is still driving them. Long before they took heroin they were not functioning effectively, either vocationally or socially."[170] TC advocates called methadone a crutch, a Band-Aid, a handkerchief, and an alcohol rub.[171] It looked like medicine but failed to address the underlying causes of addiction, which TC advocates believed were spiritual and characterological. Critics told horror stories about children getting into methadone-laced orange juice[172] and expressed concern for the well-being of fetuses exposed to the drug in utero—statements made long before fetal alcohol syndrome was a widely recognized condition.[173] Born into a chemically saturated culture, innocents with the propensity for chemical addiction would need a therapeutic retreat to get out of it.

Vincent Dole challenged this theory at a congressional subcommittee hearing in 1971. His pilot-study data failed to convince his conservative audience, so Dole used an anecdote to argue that addicts could be referred to methadone maintenance as a form of civil commitment. Dole told the story of a "tough Irish kid," a high-school dropout and heroin addict, who had been jailed twice for stealing and who had failed at previous attempts at detoxification. Seven years into methadone treatment, the "kid" had a wife, a family, and a college degree in aeronautical engineering. "Now," Dole asked Representative Robert McClory (R–IL), "is he rehabilitated?"[174]

"My answer to that," replied McClory, "would be that from the standpoint of rehabilitation from narcotics, no, he isn't." The boy's continued reliance on the drug—perceived as an "easy way out" of addiction—undermined Dole's uplifting story. McClory continued, "Sure, we can rehabilitate persons by putting them on another form of drugs or, I suppose, through the British system of letting heroin be received free of charge and thereby rehabilitate a criminal. He won't be out stealing in order to support his addiction. But that isn't the kind of rehabilitation we had in mind: no."[175]

Some conservatives had in mind McClory's preferred "slow gradual [program] which required a lot of spiritual and mental rehabilitation, a change in attitude and thinking, an aftercare program." Dole's data failed to move McClory, who admitted that he would sooner send his son to a TC-style, NARA-designated research center than to Dole's methadone program.[176]

Ex-addicts (some of them former Synanon members) employed by TCs in the late 1960s critiqued the depravity of a drug-saturated mainstream culture. They crafted these critiques of mainstream culture even as they promoted the TC model's efficacy in helping ex-addicts conform to it. In 1969, ex-addict and former Daytop resident Samuel Anglin minimized the importance of chemical effects and emphasized the influence of a dysfunctional culture: "We have to find out what it is in our culture and the attitudes of our culture that encourages drug abuse. And you see it on television and everything else: you take the little blue pill if you get up tight. You see it about Compoz: it doesn't bother him, the war and everything, because he takes Compoz. If we keep dealing with this problem chemically, we will in 20 years have a bunch of people sitting around tranquilized not caring about anything."[177]

Conservative and liberal drug-free ideologues disagreed on which issues were worth examining, but both sets of arguments considered the physical properties of the chemicals less important than their symbolic function as a form of false consciousness. Monsignor William O'Brien, like Anglin, viewed the TC as a response to the "loneliness and alienation" of modern life. "The elimination of the symptom," he proclaimed, "be it substance abuse or other disorders, is only part of the treatment."[178] TC advocates framed the "truth" at the center of addiction recovery as the total alignment of personal behavior with the community's particular moral philosophy. TCs could be perceived as a promising treatment model as long as their philosophies were uncontroversial and the methods used to achieve behavior change seemed reasonable.

"Uncontroversial" suddenly meant "conservative"—institutionally and politically. TCs, which Synanon graduates envisioned as a reaction against the traditional psychiatric treatments embodied by the Lexington Narcotic Farm and hospital wards, briefly allied with the establishment in the fight against methadone. Psychiatrists such as Casriel, Ramirez, Densen-Gerber, and even Sidney Cohen—who would attempt to revitalize Lexington using the TC model—helped legitimize many of the therapeutic methods that Synanon developed. To politicians, the TC approach for treating addiction proved most acceptable when residents were socialized into appropriate religious and gender roles along with their new abstemious behaviors. For better or worse, the most radical aspects of Synanon's model of social experimentation—which involved alternative family, labor, and educational structures—were not replicated using federal funds. In addition, the "community" itself became a bounded entity, delineated by funding structures as well as by walls. Deitch's model of the TC resident as a "change agent" who challenged mainstream culture and affected local neighborhoods was short-lived; as TCs became established as legitimate agencies, "community" was largely reduced to an efficacious method of delivering addiction treatment for the individuals who entered it.[179] This efficacy was defined in terms of individual recidivism, not social or cultural changes. Though TC advocates raised awareness about a drug-saturated society, for the most part politicians turned their attention back to incorrigible individuals. In a discussion of the expansion of civil commitment for addiction treatment in 1971, one Republican congressman concluded that addiction is an epidemic. Forced treatment was a justifiable "quarantine of people who are sick and infect others with this sickness wherever they go."[180] Addiction was framed as a problem of contagious agents rather than social environments. Rhetorically, transformative countercultures became quarantine wards.

With addiction rates still rising, especially among youth, more wards were needed. The differences between the patient populations of methadone and TC programs became evident: methadone providers tended to treat older, nonwhite patients with lengthier drug-use histories; Synanon's therapeutic model was designed to remake the "hard-core" career opiate addict, but second-generation TCs began shifting their focus to young polydrug users by the late 1960s. The first nationwide efficacy studies confirmed Jaffe's discovery in Chicago: it was difficult to compare outcomes in TCs and methadone programs because clients selected treatments based on their personal taste and motivation—two factors that were shaped by the treatment providers' increasingly savvy public relations.[181]

Providers' treatment philosophies would continue to drive policy even after rigorous evaluation data became widely available. This was true despite favorable outcomes worthy of front-page news: in the Drug Abuse Reporting Program's multifaceted analysis of the positive effects of drug treatment, the "standard," Synanon-style TC treatment outranked eleven other treatment models.[182] The treatment model was more than a symbolic improvement on past attempts: it held up scientifically in comparison with its contemporaries. At the same time, methadone treatments achieved impressive during-treatment results with special populations, such as older heroin addicts.[183] Narcotic addiction treatments were evaluated on a holistic range of variables, including their ability to influence alcohol and nonopiate drug use, to lead to employment, or to reduce arrests.

The early Drug Abuse Reporting Program studies suggested that drug treatment in the aggregate had negligible effects on arrests and jail time.[184] Although medical authorities such as Dole and Nyswander measured crime outcomes, they also hoped that methadone could be used to attract and maintain street addicts in rehabilitation programs. Methadone might link street addicts to other social services; metabolic stability could become the basis for social uplift. Unfortunately, the Nixon administration hoped to emphasize lower crime rates, not drug users' moral or even socioeconomic progress. Methadone advocates accordingly pitched the clinics as part of an "anticrime" initiative rather than as a "rehabilitation" program. Critic Edward Jay Epstein wrote, "The net result was that those with the technical competence to see the limits of methadone treatment chose not to deflate the unrealistic claim that methadone would substantially reduce crime."[185]

Ex-addict TC advocates who lacked "technical competence" had nevertheless pointed out that methadone, as a single-drug solution to heroin dependence, was useless in treating the supposed personality defects that might also lead to psychedelic or stimulant addiction. By the early 1970s, however, the public—even the liberal community that initially promoted methadone treatment—was becoming less worried about alleviating the condition of addiction than in addressing its consequences. Popular-media coverage of addiction treatment was no longer so hopeful.[186] The *New York Times* featured a Lower East Side resident with little interest in the basic causes of addiction or in the humane treatment of addicts. "I wouldn't care if someone came along with a machine gun and killed all of them," he said in 1971. "I've been robbed, my wife has been robbed—I'm sorry, I just don't care anymore."[187] Unfortunately—as methadone-maintenance advocates well knew—a simple chemical solution was an inadequate response to the era's trends in drug use and crime. Some historians argue that when New

York's Rockefeller Drugs Laws ushered in mandatory prison sentences for minor drug offenses in 1973, the treatment revolution was over before it started.[188] Conservatives such as California governor Ronald Reagan attempted to defund local methadone clinics and favored other measures for controlling drug-related crime.[189] As Nixon and other political leaders in the 1970s soon learned, no medicine could arrest the bedlam of the bad sixties.

4

LEFT, RIGHT, AND CHAOS

F OR DRUG CZAR Robert Dupont, Nixon's election in 1968 coincided
with the beginning of the "Drug Abuse Decade." In Dupont's internal history of the drug-abuse field, addiction research and treatment
progressed over the next ten years; Dupont broke the progress into periods.
During the "Incubation Period" from 1968 until 1971, drug use emerged as
a social problem due largely to concerns about addicted servicemen, rising
rates of drug abuse among youth, and an association with rising crime
rates. Local experiments with methadone maintenance and TC treatments
attracted federal attention. The Controlled Substances Act, a sweeping
drug-policy reform with increased funding for both treatment and policing, sailed through Congress in 1970. In 1971, the creation of the SAODAP
and its rapid expansion of drug treatment ushered in the "Chaotic Growth"
period. According to Dupont, the chaos lasted until 1974, when the new
National Institute on Drug Abuse (NIDA) affirmed federal experts' authority and consolidated addiction-treatment efforts. The end of the upheaval
of the sixties inaugurated the "Progressive Maturity" period (1973–1978)
for drug-abuse professionals. Federal funding stabilized; "public concern
remained high but was much less hysterical," wrote Dupont at the end of
the decade.[1]

Hysterical, paranoid, estranged: the public mood had a profound impact on the development of addiction research and treatment during

Nixon's presidency. Nixon was an effective, if reluctant, chaperone of progressive drug policies. [2] But his surveillance tactics inspired liberals' suspicions. Controversial therapies tainted drug-treatment efforts. Revelations and hypotheses about government projects involving behavior modification and brainwashing coincided with Nixon's downfall.

The image of Nixon as a dark conspirator circulated in the radical Left's underground press long before *Washington Post* reporters linked the White House to the break-in of the Democratic Campaign Headquarters in the Watergate Hotel on June 17, 1972.[3] The ex-addict employees in a government-run treatment center were not permitted to the read the papers' depictions of government conspiracy. But they secretly subscribed to the theories.

REVOLUTION IN LEXINGTON

The federal Public Health Service hospital known as the Lexington Narcotic Farm had just undertaken a massive reorganization project when a small group of addicts claimed an unused room in the hospital and began to run their own confrontational therapy sessions. The passage of NARA in 1966 and the expansion of community-based treatment that followed rendered Lexington's treatment model obsolete. Charles Dederich's friend Sidney Cohen, then the acting director of the NIMH Division of Narcotic Addiction and Drug Abuse, assembled a committee to investigate whether Lexington could be transformed into an institution-wide TC. Cohen named his colleague Harold T. Conrad to the committee. In 1968, Lexington's treatment wings became the Clinical Research Center (CRC); Conrad became the hospital chief and associate director of the NIMH Division of Narcotic Addiction and Drug Abuse.[4] In 1969, the prison bars came down, and each hospital wing prepared to operate according to the open TC concept. "We've gone from maximum security to maximum freedom," proclaimed Conrad to the press.[5] When Lexington's leadership discovered a faction of ex-addicts from the Numen House wing holding confrontational therapy groups in November 1969, they encouraged the residents and made space for their group. The group members decorated their designated room by painting the walls with graphic psychedelic images of drug-use depravity. Five months later they moved into a one-hundred-bed building on the Lexington grounds. They called it Matrix House.[6]

The leaders found the word *matrix* in the dictionary: "something within which something else originates or develops."[7] Matrix grew out of the group sessions led by Numen House members under the informal name "the Lighthouse." The liberated new therapeutic environment made it easier than ever to smuggle in contraband substances, and some participants in the Lighthouse group continued to use them. A few residents decided to replace heroin or meth habits with marijuana or acid, swapping their "dirty dope fiend" identities for "groovy dope fiend" postures, said Terry, a Lighthouse founder and former Synanon member. "We just decided we don't use dope, period. Not smack, not speed, not acid, not pot."[8] Along with Jon Wildes, another ex-addict leader who had been in Synanon, Terry pressured the other members to "cop out" and take a drug-free pledge.[9] They formed a new group, Lighthouse II, from the pledging members. Lexington administrators formally recognized the new group, which grew from a small band of four to almost twenty members.[10]

The Matrix founders "were rock stars," remembered former resident Dick Shea. Jon Wildes claimed his band had opened for Iron Butterfly,[11] and Matrix's style evolved accordingly. Members replaced the feces, dirty straightjackets, and filth of a former asylum building with tie-dyed bedspreads, bell-bottoms, and patchouli. They buffered the floors to a shine until they looked like glass reflecting the walls' bright paint colors.[12] "Matrix House was like walking into somebody's rather large San Francisco apartment," remembered one medical officer.[13]

Or a college dormitory. Residents decorated individual rooms with colorful curtains, bedspreads, and music posters. Officials praised the campus atmosphere, tie-dye and all, in internal quarterly reports.[14] Images of Matrix members lounging on the grass in discussion circles appeared in government publications and news articles. Matrix, read one newspaper caption, is "just like a college campus except that the curriculum is an 18 month course in survival."[15] Matrix's demographics in 1970 were more collegiate, too—compared to residents in the professionally run communities in the CRC, Matrix residents were younger and had more education, fewer arrests, and shorter drug histories.[16]

Matrix's mode of reeducation differed from "Kentucky College," the nickname former Lexington residents had long ago assigned to the institution's apparently ineffectual treatment; "K-Y" inadvertently schooled naive addicts in street skills such as hustling, smuggling, and stealing.[17] Rather than reinforcing addicts' old skills, Matrix House members prohibited "street talk" and promised to follow the Synanon pattern to reconstruct residents' psyches in a more wholesome fashion.[18] Matrix promoters emphasized the new community's similarity to Synanon. "At Lexington, we've adopted many of the Synanon methods," Conrad told the press.[19] He used the same pitch for a congressional appropriations committee: the "emergence of the addict as an active participant in his treatment is one of the most encouraging developments on the treatment scene in the last 5 years."[20] Matrix House's informal first director, Terry, departed, and Conrad hired four ex-addicts—Jon Wildes, Jay Therrien, Vernon Farrington, and Carl Salley—as federal employees to manage the house.[21] "We are becoming valuable, and probably within the next year Matrix will have as big a national reputation as Synanon if things keep going the way they have gone," cofounder Wildes told anthropologist Robert S. Weppner.[22]

Weppner served as Matrix's in-house anthropologist. He closely observed the community's development from July through October 1970; at the end of October, he moved into the house for a week and experienced the initiation process firsthand. As part of Lexington's restructuring, the CRC had revived its mission to engage in innovative treatment research. From 1969 until the CRC's closure in 1974, three staff anthropologists studied Lexington's organizational culture. Conrad touted the planned Matrix House research as a unique opportunity to study the ex-addict-led TC in a controlled institutional setting.[23] Although Synanon had abandoned its strictly therapeutic enterprise for a more sweeping social movement— and second-generation communities had begun downplaying Synanon similarities—the Matrix residents' plan to re-create Synanon suited the CRC's search for a new research agenda.

The Matrix founders' enthusiasm initially won over Weppner. He published a flattering report of the organization's first year of development,

Lexington

The National Institute of Mental Health

FIGURE 4.1

Lexington Narcotic Hospital brochure, 1970.

Source: Courtesy of National Archives and Records Administration–Southeast, Morrow, Georgia.

concluding that it had "grown beyond the experimental stage" and served as a model for "other treatment units at Lexington" and beyond.[24] But if Matrix served as a model, it was not always an attractive one. Although Matrix generated curiosity following its move to a freestanding building in April 1970, it had a more difficult time attracting residents; it was never able to fill more than half the slots in its one-hundred-resident building.

The rate at which residents "split" from Matrix climbed from around 40 percent at the end of the organization's first year to more than 50 percent by March 1971; at that point, two codirectors, Therrien and Salley, attempted to oust Wildes from the house leadership. When Conrad backed Wildes in the dispute, Therrien and Salley left with several other residents, thus increasing the "split rate," and Wildes assumed total authority over the dwindling community. Weppner grew critical of Wildes's increasingly dictatorial rule, and in May Wildes terminated the researcher's association with Matrix.[25]

Although Wildes recruited a few nonaddict residents from visits to community sites and local colleges, most "squares," including Weppner and his wife, were not interested in living the Matrix lifestyle full-time. With Weppner's departure, Matrix residents became insulated from external scrutiny. Wildes's philosophy became politicized, and the dramatic therapeutic tactics he used to remake the psyches of Matrix residents escalated. Most of the developments exaggerated Matrix's initial concepts. In an early publicity packet for Matrix House, Wildes had confessed that his drug use resulted from a displaced revolutionary fervor; this impulse, now channeled into realizing the Matrix philosophy, would remake society.[26] As Wildes developed political causes, he monitored residents' reading material—the preferred Synanon library of "Emerson, Thoreau, and Yablonsky" expanded to include work by Abbie Hoffman and Chairman Mao.[27] Matrix House began making small contributions—possibly from the leaders' government paychecks or small donations from public-speaking engagements—to organizations such as the Black Panthers and the American Indian Movement.[28] Margie Smith, a resident who moved into Matrix shortly after Wildes assumed the role of sole director, watched the community radicalize. Matrix developed a new "esprit de corps," and an "almost militaristic faction within Matrix" donned berets, said Smith.[29] Wildes took up arms.

Wildes did not have permission to possess a gun, but he told Matrix members that the house was under threat.[30] In December 1971, a Lexington staff physician reported that Wildes had threatened him with a gun. A second report followed a few days later. Conrad gave Wildes and the rest of the Matrix House residents six months to close their operation at

Lexington.[31] "We are encouraging [Matrix House] to seek independence and eventually to plan on separation from the federal government with the development of self-sustaining Matrix programs in communities where interest and support are available," wrote Conrad in his annual report for 1971. "Until this is accomplished, we shall continue to do in-house research and study the entire self-help movement and lifestyle."[32]

According to former Matrix residents, Conrad was aware that Wildes had added compulsory nudity to the TC's typical structure of confrontational therapy, intentional humiliation, and hierarchical system of household duties.[33] Wildes ostensibly forbade sexual relations among the residents; the nudity that Conrad observed supposedly symbolized the residents' psychological liberation, not their sexual freedom. In March 1972, Wildes ordered residents to cross-dress and then to remove their clothes. Resident Dick Shea remembered the ritual as an "innocent" event; the "'Anti-American' spirit" of the role playing had a "therapeutic value," he later argued.[34] Other observers saw something more sinister. One evening Wildes decided to punish resident Marshall Green—observers differ regarding his justification—and reportedly ordered the naked man to hold up a large wooden cross. Green was subsequently admitted to Lexington's health clinic, his flesh singed with burns from Wildes's cigarette.[35]

A few days later an officer from the Federal Bureau of Investigation (FBI) told the hospital director that Matrix House members were secretly supporting other revolutionary groups. On March 16, 1972, Lexington's guards raided Matrix House and discovered the community had a collection of radical literature and material for incendiary bombs. Marty Panone, a nonaddicted resident who escaped before the raid, remembered the rationale for making the bombs: "The society is gonna come at us and we had to learn to protect ourselves."[36] It was a self-fulfilling prophecy.

Wildes's paranoia was reciprocal. Matrix revelations emerged just in time for locals to reimagine Wildes as Kentucky's Charles Manson.[37] Weppner later hypothesized that FBI surveillance of black radical groups had led agents to the groups' supporters in Matrix.[38] Some Matrix House members, like other radical factions, suspected the government was spying on them. But leftist groups such as Students for a Democratic Society, once cast as "paranoid," later came to find out "that they indeed were bugged; not only were they bugged, but they were set up," remembered vindicated Matrix resident Margie Smith. "Keep in mind this is the same administration that had [the muckraking reporter] Jack Anderson on a hit list and [carried out] Watergate."[39]

Several Matrix leaders were federal employees, so they might have anticipated some government oversight. Four months after the raid, a federal grand jury finally began an investigation of Matrix. It culminated in a trial the following April: "Former Drug Patients Relate Sex, Violence," read the headline of an Associated Press story in a local Kentucky paper, overshadowing a smaller column to its right titled "Watergate Unsettled."[40] U.S. District Court judge H. David Hermansdorfer settled the case in less than two weeks. Wildes was convicted of violating the Federal Firearms Act, assaulting a patient, and enacting lewdness on a government reservation. He was initially sentenced to thirty-six and a half years in prison.[41] Hermansdorfer ordered a more extensive investigation into the inner workings of the CRC. In 1975, that jury concluded that Conrad had been "derelict in his duties" by failing to provide adequate supervision of Matrix House's operations—"notwithstanding what may have been the accepted practice in similar institutions throughout the United States."[42]

INTERNAL POLITICS

The practices at other TCs had motivated Conrad to hire Wildes and his colleagues. In a Labor–Management Committee meeting in 1970, Conrad outlined the proposal to employ ex-addicts. No ex-addict residents would agree to manage a TC with only room and board as compensation, he explained—not as long as leadership by ex-addicts remained a "hot commodity" among state and municipal government and private treatment providers. TCs outside Lexington were prepared to pay handsome salaries to luminary ex-addict leaders, explained Conrad.[43] Hiring a few experienced ex-addicts in permanent staff positions would also provide the organizational consistency necessary for establishing a new TC. If the community proved successful, Conrad hoped the entrepreneurial ex-addicts would expand their ranks and establish new TCs.[44] After the passage of NARA, Lexington operated at half capacity.[45]

Federal officials promoted the decision to hire former addicts as progress. A press release from the U.S. Department of Health, Education, and Welfare (HEW) championed the new hires: HEW secretary Elliot Richardson reportedly argued, "It would be folly to ignore the valuable resources many ex-addicts bring to rehabilitation programs." The NIMH had urged the Civil Service Commission to revise the regulations prohibiting the employment of ex-addicts; the CRC became the first agency to act on the new regulations by hiring Wildes, Therrien, Farrington, and Salley to manage a "Synanon program." NIMH director Bertram Brown framed the move as an improvement in the areas of "equal employment and consumer participation."[46]

Matrix employees set up a public-relations office that ran on the Synanon model.[47] They recorded confrontational therapy sessions and supplied communities across the country with tapes. They ran training programs at other ex-addict-led centers and made appearances on local television stations. They hosted reporters and representatives from other government branches.[48] One reporter wrote to Conrad with fond reflections of her "absorbing experience" at Matrix; Conrad forwarded clippings from her series of published reports to the director of the NIMH. "Although the stories were generated by a 'failure' who ran away from Matrix House, on the whole I think the Matrix people 'turned on' the reporter sufficiently to get good press even out of that," he wrote.[49] Matrix members joined Synanon representatives for an educational event hosted by the Mayo Clinic in Rochester, Minnesota. Conrad could "personally testify" to NIMH leadership in May 1970: the residents "are doing a tremendous job."[50]

Other Lexington workers had their doubts. Sidney Louis, an air force veteran and nurse with a graduate degree in psychiatric hospital supervision, led the CRC's Education Department. He critiqued the hospital for enlisting unvetted ex-addict speakers as participants in community and school-based educational events; attractive and charismatic ex-addicts could undermine professionals' efforts to convey the harms of drug use. Louis began compiling criteria for speakers after "having been burned a number of times by having a patient I didn't know accompany me to a program."[51]

Conrad, in contrast, happily invited Matrix members to join him on public-speaking events that garnered press attention. Along with Matrix House's public-relations team, Conrad worked to channel the energy associated with a growing movement of community-based, ex-addict-led treatment centers; Matrix's brochures emphasized the new organization's adoption of the Synanon and Daytop model of drug treatment.[52] But in 1970 Matrix's campaign lagged behind other second-generation TCs. Weppner later viewed Matrix as an unoriginal "vintage model of Synanon, perhaps a 1965 version."[53] Conrad "urged" resistant Lexington employees to attend Matrix's Synanon-style open houses;[54] meanwhile, Synanon, now a social movement, had discontinued facilities tours. "Guided tours during the work day create an 'institutional' situation for both residents and visitors," concluded the Synanon Speakers' Bureau.[55]

A few longtime Lexington workers resented any attempts to remake the institutional environment. Even before the establishment of Synanon-style, ex-addict-led Matrix House, Lexington employees reportedly resented the planned transformation of NARA wings into more democratic TCs inspired by the British psychiatrist Maxwell Jones. The workers had been trained as jailers and supervisors, not as coparticipants in a total therapeutic environment. "The staff has not jelled to the program and many of them are looking forward to their termination date in June," wrote the chief of one NARA wing in early 1970.[56]

Lexington's reorganization brought an influx of new young physicians. Veteran nurse Sidney Louis believed many of the young doctors volunteered to serve as commissioned officers in the Public Health Service at Lexington in order to avoid deployment to Vietnam. Lexington's therapeutic programs, therefore, were too idealistic and "poorly conceived by young doctors with no background in administration," wrote Louis.[57] Lexington's guards, who were mostly conservative and southern, disapproved of Matrix members' long hair and psychedelic style. Older guards reportedly considered Matrix House "communistic."[58]

According to Louis, Conrad paid little attention to internal politics. He preferred to work from his office and rarely conversed with the staff. He restructured the organizational chart and placed the new ex-addict hires on the second tier; they ran an autonomous unit and reported only to

Conrad's office.[59] "There was no illusion of supervision," said Matrix House physician Jack Croughan. "They were given the mission to establish a truly self-help unit, and I think the project was designed to see if it could be done in a very good fashion without a lot of administrative intrusion."[60] For Louis, this managerial approach created "a near perfect culture medium for the disaster which was growing at Matrix House"—an assessment shared by Weppner and the grand jury that investigated Matrix.[61]

In a letter to the grand-jury investigators, NIMH chief Bertram Brown defended Conrad's leadership but revised his earlier opinion regarding the value of ex-addict employees: "it should be pointed out that the indictments involve only addict patients or former ex-addict patients rather than regular staff members." Brown noted that Robert Dupont's new agency[62] had since conducted overview of the CRC's treatment programs and made recommendations. "It was learned from the Matrix House experience that when patients are allowed to conduct their own affairs, special difficulties arise because of Federal responsibilities for close monitoring and supervision of its treatment and research programs," wrote Brown.[63] Brown's statement suggested that decentralized or privatized ex-addict-led programs might involve fewer "difficulties." The government closed the federally managed CRC treatment program in 1974.

Lexington's other research arm, the Addiction Research Center (ARC), continued to operate following the CRC's closure. According to historian Nancy Campbell, the biomedical researchers who staffed the ARC resented Lexington's transition into a TC. Just as Lexington's guards did not want be therapists, basic scientists such as Peter Mansky became equally perturbed about the prospect of becoming jailers. Before NARA, ARC researchers conducted medical experiments on addicted prisoners recruited from Lexington's general population. But under NARA's new civil-commitment program, Lexington patients' sentences were too short to permit experimentation (Lexington scientists would not treat patients with experimental drugs within six months of their release date). The scientists had to recruit research subjects who were serving longer sentences from other federal prisons.[64] By 1970, the ARC's human subjects were the only federal prisoners remaining at Lexington. The scientists placed research subjects under lockdown behind heavy bars and gates, whereas TC residents freely roamed the grounds. The ARC's pioneering research had produced discoveries regarding the abuse potential of various pharmaceuticals and the mechanisms involved in relapse,[65] yet the government had inexplicably chosen to reinvest in clinical research. ARC researchers, along with other basic scientists in the early 1970s, perceived treatment evaluation as scientifically weak. The decision to reorient Lexington around treatment research led to conflict between the ARC and the larger institution.[66] The ARC experiments, like the Matrix House treatment, generated ethical controversy. But experts respected the ARC's scientific reputation, and they ultimately decided to rehabilitate it; in 1979, the ARC moved from Lexington to Baltimore and was restructured as the intramural research enterprise at NIDA.[67]

In 1973, Robert Dupont supervised NIDA's formation. NIDA merged the ARC, the cabinet-level SAODAP, and the NIMH Division of Narcotic Addiction and Drug Abuse. Dupont wrote later that in addition to the ARC's basic science researchers, the new organization brought together two disparate new traditions of treatment research: SAODAP's "young anti-bureaucrat devotees to quick decisive action" and the NIMH's "professional[s] who had mastered the arcane intricacies of the bureaucracy of HEW."[68] The arranged marriage made both groups beholden to the same political pressures. NIDA largely maintained the SAODAP tradition of funding extramural treatment research—a rational enterprise that nevertheless developed its own ethical challenges when critics questioned NIDA's political motivation for privileging particular grant applications.[69]

Lexington's intramural therapeutic and scientific experiments coincided with a crisis of legitimacy in the U.S. prison system.[70] The conflict between old guards and young doctors reflected the renewed debate between proponents of retributive and rehabilitative corrections. Lexington's TC proponents did not predict the resurgence of mandatory-minimum drug sentences or the widespread appeal of a carceral model of social control. "We stress the mature use of increased freedom, and conversely, to imply the need for a return to a prison system is pandering to impulsive kids, a 'cop-out' on manhood," wrote the chief overseeing a new Lexington TC in 1970.[71] The Lexington chief, like proponents of Synanon's early prison TCs, emphasized the shortcomings of simplistic criminal-justice approaches that unintentionally bred further criminality. But by 1974 the verdict was in: the government transferred Lexington to the Federal Bureau of Prisons. Bureau officials reinstalled the prison bars that had been stashed away on Lexington's grounds.

EXTERNAL POLITICS

The raid at Matrix House in 1972 took place six months after New York governor Nelson Rockefeller quashed an uprising in the Attica State Prison. The televised brutality of the Attica uprising brought long-standing academic debates about the fairness and efficacy of the correctional system into public view. For a polarized viewership, the event proved the prison was either a retrograde, racist relic that should be abolished or a necessary warehouse for irredeemable criminals that clearly posed a serious threat to civilized society.[72]

Liberal academics and activists who took the first view hoped a deinstitutionalization movement for prisons would follow the transition to community-based care in the mental-health system. To their later regret, they levied a fierce critique against the indeterminate sentence, which granted parole boards the ability to end a prison term based on their assessment of whether a prisoner had been adequately "rehabilitated." The subjective nature of this form of sentencing was vulnerable to conscious and unconscious biases and abuse.[73] As early Synanon members and supporters once charged, much prison rehabilitation was playacting: those who pretended to go along with the system earned release, whereas those who protested against it could be held in prison indefinitely. If individuals had committed only nonviolent crimes to feed their addictions, the TC and methadone-treatment pioneers argued, it made more sense to address criminality by diverting addicts to community-based therapy. Lexington's TC proponents argued that ex-addict peers trained in the Synanon model had special insight into the veracity of addicts' character transformation. If the prison could be made to look like a TC, the distinction between the two would eventually evaporate. The addict prison, like the mental asylum, would be rendered obsolete.[74]

At the same time, other critics of rehabilitative corrections took aim at indeterminate sentencing for entirely different reasons. Hard-line proponents of retributive justice emphasized punishment for its own sake.[75] Like the liberals and radicals, hard-line critics rejected the notion that the correctional-justice system should be used for rehabilitation; they also rejected a more moderate and utilitarian view that prison sentences should help deter future crime. Hard-liners instead advocated for fixed sentences that communicated the nonnegotiable consequences of individual moral violations. In 1973, Governor Nelson Rockefeller championed mandatory-minimum sentences for drug charges; possessing four ounces of heroin, morphine, cocaine, or cannabis earned offenders at least fifteen years in prison. The former champion of rehabilitation became responsible for the resurrection of the carceral solution for drug abuse. Other conservative governors followed Rockefeller's example. By the end of the decade, straightforward punishment and incapacitation, not rehabilitation, had become the primary purpose of prison work.[76]

Other uses for prisons came under scrutiny in the early 1970s when left-wing journalist Jessica Mitford exposed the horrific biomedical experiments conducted on prisoners. Mitford's book *Kind and Usual Punishment*, published in 1973, also delivered a trenchant critique of coercive psychotherapies.[77] As home to both Matrix House—a reeducation effort run amok—and the ARC, which administered drugs to confirmed addicts for decades, Lexington exemplified the ethical violations that beset the nation's prisons. Matrix House caught the attention of the Associated Press. The ARC's experiments entered public consciousness following controversial revelations about government-funded experiments on African American men afflicted with syphilis in Tuskegee, Alabama.

U.S. Senate subcommittee hearings on human experimentation called these decades-old research studies into question. The civil rights movement and the antiwar Left had raised public awareness about racial disparities and the moral shortcomings of Cold War military logic.[78] The Senate investigation of government research efforts also coincided with the Watergate crisis. FBI associate director Mark Felt ("Deep Throat") broke the latter story. Felt was no friend to left-wing groups; he unapologetically led illegal surveillance of left-wing groups such as the Weather Underground and Black Panthers. But when Nixon passed Felt over for an expected promotion—twice—Felt, in turn, passed along the details of the FBI's Watergate investigation to Bob Woodward and Carl Bernstein at the *Washington Post*.[79] The revelations that followed tapped into a bipartisan backlash against the unchecked power of the federal government.

Nixon's critics had questioned his misuse of federal power well before Watergate. His drug-control strategies, for example, verged on militancy. Nixon expanded law enforcement along with treatment. The number of federal agents in the Federal Bureau of Narcotics and Dangerous Drugs grew from four hundred to two thousand between 1969 and 1971.[80] When bureau director John Ingersoll resisted the pressure to devote these new resources to low-level drug arrests rather than to international traffickers, Nixon created a new cabinet-level office, just as he had done with SAODAP. The Office of Drug Abuse Law Enforcement was inaugurated in 1971 with just four hundred officers and an eighteen-month sunset provision. The office was a showpiece, not a permanent drug-control solution, but it capably displayed the administration's aggressive new crime-fighting weapons: no-knock raids, preventive detention, the power to jail witnesses who refused to testify in grand-jury drug cases, and wiretaps.[81]

Historians such as Kathleen Frydl argue that many of Nixon's dramatic drug-related encroachments on civil liberties entered a stage that had already been set by President Lyndon Johnson and his predecessors. In 1968, the regulation of narcotics moved from the Department of the Treasury, which treated drug distribution as a trade problem, to the new Bureau of Narcotics and Dangerous Drugs, housed in the Department of Justice.[82] Johnson also expanded the Office of Law Enforcement Assistance. The expanded Law Enforcement Assistance Administration (LEAA) supported liberal social efforts such as community policing, educational programs, and even a few TCs; it also helped outfit state and local law enforcement agencies with the tools for quasi-military policing.

Under Nixon, the LEAA's federal funding mechanism provided incentives for tougher street policing. The brand of aggressive street-level enforcement later promoted by the Office of Drug Abuse Law Enforcement became the province of local police departments, now emboldened with new weaponry and federal support. The Los Angeles Police Department requested a submarine; Birmingham, Alabama, wanted an armored personnel carrier.[83] Massachusetts drug-treatment commissioner Matthew Dumont ominously argued that Nixon's extraordinary policing and surveillance efforts quickly subsumed treatment: "All of the equipment, technology, and bureaucracy designed to predict, identify, isolate, monitor, and control the drug addict will be found to have other utility."[84]

The most searching critique of federal drug-control efforts, behavioral research and treatment, and Watergate came from Sam Ervin, a Democratic senator from North Carolina. Ervin, a watchdog for civil liberties violations with a blind spot regarding desegregation, was a vociferous opponent of the no-knock raids pioneered by Rockefeller in the mid-1960s. Ervin chaired the Senate Watergate Committee and played a pivotal role in gathering evidence that led to Nixon's resignation. In 1973, he also released the results of a government investigation into coercive behavioral research.

TREATMENT ETHICS AT THE END OF THE 1960S

The Senate Subcommittee on Constitutional Rights, chaired by Sam Ervin, held a series of hearings on the constitutional rights of the mentally ill in the early 1960s. By the 1970s, the committee had also begun questioning whether current carceral conditions violated prisoners' constitutional rights. Beginning in 1971, Ervin and other committee members grew concerned about the use of new behavioral technologies on "captive" populations of mental patients and prisoners. They launched an investigation into the wide variety of government-funded approaches to behavior modification. Ervin discovered that HEW, the Federal Bureau of Prisons, LEAA, the Veterans Administration, the Department of Defense, the Department of Labor, and the National Science Foundation supported a wide range of behavior-modification programs—such as psychosurgery, chemical castration, and attack therapy. Ervin asked leaders in each agency to describe how the funded programs were ethically evaluated and monitored. HEW was the only agency with an ethical review process in place.

Three months after Nixon's resignation, the subcommittee published the results of its investigation. *Individual Rights and the Federal Role in Behavior Modification* collected the letters and articles from the critics of federal behavior-modification programs alongside agency officials' overwhelmingly ineffectual replies to Ervin's inquiries regarding ethical oversight.[85] The report described several frightening programs: a behaviorist prison project in which misbehaving inmates were stripped naked and shackled to their beds; planned LEAA research into radio receivers that could "determine the location, activities, and even the thoughts" of possible offenders;[86] and the Veterans' Administration's ongoing practice of performing "therapeutic" lobotomies. Ervin framed the report's results as a reproach to reactionary politics: "The widespread civil disobedience of the nineteen sixties caused many to despair of more indirect methods of 'behavior modification' such as rehabilitation and understanding." A new emphasis on violence prevention spawned new agencies, such as the LEAA, which privileged "immediate and efficient means" to correct antisocial behavior above "more time-consuming attempts to understand its sources."[87] The boom in federal funds for methadone and TC programs in the early Nixon years was due in large part to their explicit links to criminological results: methadone served as a crime-fighting tool, and TCs seemed to inspire permanent personality change.

In an article published in the *Hastings Center Report* in 1975, the ethicist Gerald Klerman affirmed the TC's function as a tough but progressive form of behavior modification. The reeducation TCs offered supported the lofty goals of deinstitutionalization and decarceration. Yet the use of TC treatment to achieve these ideals raised dystopian questions. The outcry against the new tools of behavior control stemmed from the fear that they "will restrict the individuality and political freedom not only of the inmates in publicly created institutions, but also of the citizens outside who had helped create them."[88] According to this frightful logic, restrictive institutions would be rendered irrelevant by new behavioral technologies that could "convert the community into the ultimate institution, a totalitarian society," à la *1984* or *A Clockwork Orange.*[89] Some TC leaders' stated intention to transform society stoked the fear.[90] The students at an HEW-funded TC featured in Ervin's report "have an informing system similar to that in Nazi Germany," complained one guidance counselor.[91] "Please let me not say that the Communist party is in control [of the organization]," wrote one concerned citizen. "But us not be [*sic*] so ignorant as to believe that they are not."[92]

The TC named "the Seed" was not a Nazi or Communist enterprise, but the ethical problems with its treatment approaches could not simply be dismissed as a conspiracist fantasy. Ervin explained that he had timed the release of *Individual Rights* to coincide with the formation of Senator Edward "Ted" Kennedy's (D–MA) National Commission for the Protection of Human Subjects of Biomedical and Behavioral Research; the report's findings would inform further investigation of government-funded research. Kennedy's committee hearings surpassed Ervin's in shock value and impact and eventually led to national principles for medical research ethics (outlined in *Belmont Report: Ethical Principles and Guidelines for the Protection of Human Subjects of Research*)[93] and a decentralized bureaucracy to enforce them (Institutional Review Boards). The new regulations streamlined the review process already in place at HEW and placed similar guidelines on other forms of government-funded research.

A series of hearings exposed troubling details of coercive and covert government research. In 1975 and 1977, Senator Frank Church (D–ID) held hearings investigating the secret Central Intelligence Agency program MK-ULTRA, which administered LSD and other "chemical weapons" to both knowledgeable and naive test subjects. Some MK-ULTRA funds supported the ARC's experiments in Lexington. Ex-addict patients Eddie Flowers and James Henderson Childs testified that researchers had coerced their participation: As addicts, how could they have been expected to turn down the opportunity to take drugs? Flowers and Childs claimed that their ability to consent to research was compromised by their visceral craving for drugs. Although Lexington researchers argued that they followed a scrupulous consent procedure, the research subjects' testimony grouped Lexington with the most notorious cases in the history of bioethics.[94]

Complaints about the NIDA-funded Seed program emerged during the Matrix House crisis and threatened to taint the entire TC concept. Anthropologist Robert Weppner left Lexington, disgusted, and relocated to South Florida to work as a researcher in the Dade County drug program. The Seed had already sprung up by the time Weppner arrived there—first in Broward County (Fort Lauderdale and the surrounding area) in 1970 and then in Dade County (Miami) in 1972. The rapid growth of TCs appeared to fulfill proponents' early goals. A decade earlier, psychiatrist Daniel Casriel had emphasized the importance of developing peer-counselor talent. "We are in need of people to 'seed' new Synanons throughout the country," wrote Casriel.[95]

The Seed's founder, Art Barker, was a former stand-up comedian, not a Synanon graduate. Like Charles Dederich, Barker was a recovering alcoholic. He worked briefly in an alcoholism program in the New York area before winding his way to South Florida, where he founded the Seed, a "daycare" program designed to reform adolescent drug abusers.[96] Other TCs such as Odyssey House and Daytop offered programs for adolescent or young-adult drug users, but these residential programs simply tailored the TC concept to a younger population. In contrast, the Seed placed young clients into foster homes led by parents who had enrolled their own children in the program, which allowed the organization to operate as a "nonresidential" treatment provider even though clients were under full-time supervision by foster families. The informal Seed foster system operated separately from the state foster system; parents signed paperwork that voluntarily turned their children over to the care of the nonprofit corporation, which then placed them in "Seed families." After the clients underwent a minimum of two weeks of nonstop intensive attack therapy, or "rap sessions," the Seed staff evaluated whether they could return home. Clients who returned home entered a three-month aftercare phase that included mandatory attendance at rap sessions three evenings a week and one full day on the weekend.[97]

Although some concerned parents sought out the Seed's treatment for their children (one article estimated that about two-thirds of the Seed's clients were brought in by parents),[98] in Dade County an overwhelming number of referrals came from judges. According to the Seed's own statistics, more than three-quarters of clients were "users" or "abusers" rather than "addicts." Pot, barbiturates, psychedelics, and amphetamines were the drugs that clients most commonly used and abused.[99] Heroin and opiates were at the bottom of the list. Weppner and James Inciardi later used the Dade County case study in an argument for marijuana decriminalization. In the 1970s, nonresidential TCs in Dade thrived on the courts' diversion of young, male, occasional marijuana users into treatment. From 1971 to 1975, marijuana arrests (mostly possession charges) accounted for more than 60 percent of all drug arrests, with the rate rising each year.[100] Weppner and Inciardi estimated that Dade County spent $10.5 million annually in combined state, county, and federal funds on drug treatment and control.[101] The decriminalization of marijuana would strike a blow to the treatment–criminal justice–industrial complex; treatment centers could expect to lose millions of dollars along with their marijuana-using clientele. But Weppner and Inciardi argued that those funds would be better spent on programs that had a greater public-health impact. The Dade County medical examiner had not recorded a single death from marijuana.[102]

As long as Dade County officials remained intent on eradicating all illicit drug use, the community would continue to invest in TCs.[103] Both Dade and Broward were traditionally conservative counties, and the Christian Right's political influence grew in South Florida in the 1970s.[104] The Seed promised to transform long-haired, pot-smoking, wayward youth into clean-cut, God-fearing citizens. It delivered its message with considerable showmanship. While the Dade County Health Council deliberated about whether to grant the Seed a license for a new Miami branch, five hundred Seed youth sat outside the building singing a Seed anthem to the tune of "Greensleeves": "The Seed, the Seed, is all we need to stay off the junk and the pills and weed."[105]

Yet, according to a state survey, 17 percent of Seed clients had never used drugs of any sort.[106] Ben Shepphard, a physician and drug-rehabilitation professional, served as a consulting doctor for the Seed before concluding that the treatment program amounted to "brainwashing" children who posed minor disciplinary problems to their parents.[107] Although the Seed attracted considerable support from powerful parents pleased with the program's results, drug-abuse professionals in South Florida did not consider the Seed a model TC.[108] The organization took an oppositional attitude toward fellow drug-treatment providers. More than one evaluator recommended that the Seed adopt a more collegial and collaborative relationship with other organizations.[109] In a letter to the Dade County Health Planning Council, a concerned couple drew a distinction between the treatment their son received at the Seed—which culminated in his suicide attempt—and the more professional and supportive program offered by another provider, which also employed ex-addicts. "To describe the differences between The Seed program and Here's Help is like describing the difference between black and white or day and night," wrote the parents.[110]

From a federal standpoint, the Seed's distinctiveness made it worthy of funding. The Seed launched in Fort Lauderdale with an annual NIMH grant of $230,000 and an additional $35,000 from the LEAA; two additional LEAA grants supported the Seed's expansion into Dade and Pinellas Counties.[111] The NIMH had difficulty monitoring the Seed from the time it first approved the grant. A clinical-treatment specialist who managed the grant monies explained that the NIMH supported the project in order to learn more about "non-traditional treatment modalities" and to remain responsive to new trends in the field.[112] NIMH grant reviewers originally pointed out substantial problems with the Seed's program structure: the program was "built around one man"; the grantee's understanding of heroin and barbiturate withdrawal was medically "erroneous"; an appropriate system for medical referrals was lacking; the program had not supplied evidence of its effectiveness; and the administrative and fiscal structure was ill defined. But the grantors unanimously approved NIMH funding under the condition that Barker address these issues.[113]

During the first year of the grant, the NIMH directed the Seed to meet the conditions of the original grant by establishing a referral system, hiring a full-time drug-abuse professional and an evaluator, and developing an organization chart and fiscal plan. Barker took small steps toward meeting these goals, and the NIMH, following deliberation with both SAODAP and Florida's drug-abuse office, decided to renew the grant for a second year.[114]

Then the NIMH received a letter from Sam Ervin. As officials compiled material to comply with Ervin's request for materials regarding the

Seed, they discovered that Seed officials had checked "yes" to the question about whether the organization placed human subjects at risk. This checkmark on the second-year grant-renewal form transformed the program from a nontraditional "demonstration project" to an experiment. This new designation subjected the Seed to another round of review, and the third-year continuation of the grant became conditional upon the National Institutes of Health assessment of the risk posed to Seed research subjects.[115] Rather than await the results of the review, Barker rejected the federal funds—from the LEAA as well as the NIMH. By divesting the Seed of federal funds, Barker wrote, he would eliminate the "excessive demands, harassment, and bureaucracy created by these numerous agencies" and gain "the necessary autonomy for The Seed to continue its innovative and dynamic leadership in fulfilling its only purpose—saving kids!!!" Ervin republished Barker's fervent rejection in the *Individual Rights* report.[116]

The report also included two opposing accounts of the Seed's treatment program published by the *St. Petersburg Times* in 1973. A former runaway explained that the Seed's program of total honesty reversed her life trajectory, which had included "living in Haight Ashbury for a while, capturing an ROTC building at the University of Kentucky, being in a psychiatric hospital, selling about $1,000 a week of cocaine and being 'strung out' on a racetrack job in Florida where she heard about the Seed."[117] But Seed leaders encouraged clients with less-sensational histories to simply make up more-sensational ones. Former clients recounted how they were coerced into making explicit sexual confessions designed to humiliate them. One client escaped from the program after being locked in a room by his "foster" family. He called his real parents, who took him back to the Seed, where leaders ordered his father to beat him. Convinced that the boy was on drugs and the beating a matter of life and death, the father punched his son repeatedly while Seed staffers looked on.[118]

* * *

In May 1972, Lois Chatham, chief of the Narcotic Addict Rehabilitation Branch, warned NIMH director Bertram Brown about possible controversy arising from the Seed. Chatham had learned that Seed director Art

Barker had crowed that he had total control over the NIMH funds and "the political clout to go with it." In response, Chatham wrote, the local community had begun questioning Barker's competence and asking whether his grant "was approved as a political gesture." The statements seemed to support the theory that Barker's patriotic drug-prevention program was a form of secret government programming. "If this situation persists, I am confident the Broward County Narcotic Council, local professionals, and health care agencies will begin to formulate a plan of action that will ultimately involve this Institute," wrote Chatham.[119]

Ervin's investigation predictably led to the end of the Seed. Before the publication of *Individual Rights* in November 1974, the Seed met with local and state resistance. The Dade County Health Planning Council advised against licensing the Seed, and Barker closed the Dade branches and relocated clients to the licensed branches in nearby Fort Lauderdale (Broward County) in 1973. That summer, Florida governor Reuben Askew, a "New South" Democrat, asked Tampa judge Herboth S. Ryder, chair of a special subcommittee of the Florida State Drug Abuse Advisory Council, to conduct a review of the state's licensing procedures along with a special study of the Seed. Before the review was requested, the committee recommended licensing the Seed despite concerns about the safety of the foster homes and the professionalism of the Seed staff.[120] The publication of *Individual Rights* affirmed the Seed's local critics and embarrassed prominent supporters.[121] The Seed's nontraditional treatment model had garnered endorsements from high-profile figures; state legislators, judges, doctors, the chairman of the Broward County School Board, and the lieutenant governor had served on the Seed's board of directors.[122] Believers in the treatment model blamed the controversies on Barker's eccentricities. Seed boosters and graduates ousted Barker and planned to restructure the program under a new name.[123] The "Chaotic Period" of drug-treatment expansion thus came to a close.

The mid-1970s were a period of contraction. Second-generation TCs were not only concerned about their possible association with the controversies in Kentucky and Florida but also suddenly faced devastating reductions in public funds. By the end of 1974, drug-free residential TCs across the country enrolled fifteen thousand clients. Having reaped the benefits of treatment expansion in the early 1970s, TC leaders were unprepared for the economic recession, inflation, and funding cutbacks that befell the field from 1974 to 1976.[124] The high cost of long-term residential treatment (about $5,000 a slot, in contrast to $1,500 in a typical methadone program) made TCs especially vulnerable to local, state, and federal cutbacks.[125] The consolidation of federal drug-treatment efforts probably also contributed to the contraction in federal funds. In 1973, NIMH grant reviewers unanimously awarded Odyssey House a $65,000 grant for a research proposal that did not state the hypotheses, methods, sampling procedure, underlying theory, or timetable.[126] Future reviewers would be less generous.

In 1973, the ASA in New York became a high-profile case study in mismanagement when Democratic comptroller Abraham Beame published a report that detailed waste and corruption in the city-funded treatment programs.[127] Beame's allegations bolstered his successful mayoral campaign in 1974, which emphasized his shrewd approach to city finance. Ironically, Beame oversaw New York's massive financial crisis, inheriting a $1.5 million deficit and narrowly avoiding a devastating default on the city's debts. Beame's staff cuts to the ASA in 1974 foreshadowed the massive contraction of government support as former mayor John Lindsay's unfunded programs buckled under the weight of fiscal realities. A NIDA review of the ASA's federal treatment grant in 1974 revealed that New York programs cost more per treatment slot than programs in any other metropolitan area, and the ASA program's cost per treatment slot was more than double the city average.[128]

As the in-house researcher at the ASA's flagship treatment program Phoenix House, George De Leon had a stake in the TC model's survival. In 1975, a variety of prominent TCs such as Phoenix, Daytop, Odyssey, and Gateway formed a nonprofit professional association called the Therapeutic Communities of America. In January 1976, De Leon and NIDA official George Beschner held a planning conference. NIDA and Therapeutic Communities of America cosponsored the conference, which presented the TC as a unified and professional treatment approach. Conference participants discussed the ethics of TC treatment, the need for rigorous evaluation, and possible responses to the addiction-treatment industry's changing economic climate. The conference report concluded that the TC was "at a crossroads." One path followed the Synanon approach: TCs could maintain purity and autonomy by rejecting federal funds and maintaining "an existence of modest self-reliance."[129] By 1976, Synanon had begun its transformation from rehabilitation enterprise to new religion; the erratic behavior of Synanon's leaders and their increasingly militant control over residents began to drive away less-dedicated members in droves. "We're not going to mess with the old-time, turn-the-other-cheek religious postures," Dederich told residents. "Our religious posture is: Don't mess with us."[130] TC leaders believed an insular strategy would almost certainly lead to the contraction of the TC modality and limit its impact on society at large. It would be a dead end.

The other road merged with the health-care establishment. The newly professionalized TC could claim space as a "significant (albeit unique) health care institution" and "assume a more visible place in the health care arena."[131] Charismatic leaders such as Synanon's Charles Dederich, Daytop's David Deitch, Odyssey House's Judianne Densen-Gerber, Matrix's Jon Wildes, and the Seed's Art Barker had been savvy promoters of their individual treatment enterprises. Institutions appeared in their "lengthened shadows."[132] These charismatic personalities had inspired and imperiled the first TCs. Now the hierarchical, drug-free, long-term, peer-based treatment structure needed bureaucratic legitimacy. By the end of Dupont's "Drug Abuse Decade," the drug-free TC philosophy would—with a few important modifications—mature into national policy.

PART III

INDUSTRIALIZATION

5

SELLING A DRUG-FREE AMERICA

A T A DINNER party in 1972, William Fine, son of a Hollywood scion, fashion magazine publisher, and antiminiskirt entrepreneur, struck up a conversation with New York governor Nelson Rockefeller. Fine was invested in the growing drug problem at the time: he was chairman of Phoenix House, and his son had struggled with drug addiction. Rockefeller suggested Fine visit Japan to see how that country had managed to bring down addiction rates. Fine reported back to Rockefeller. Although Japan had successfully orchestrated one of the first multifaceted drug-control strategies in response to a post–World War II amphetamine crisis, Rockefeller, who was by then a beleaguered champion of addiction treatment, focused on the punitive part of Fine's report: Japan had mandatory life sentences for drug dealers. That policy matched the calls for action that filled Rockefeller's mailbox. The New York electorate had grown angry about expensive programs that focused on rehabilitating users rather than stopping drug traffic into cities and suburbs. Rockefeller was contemplating a fourth presidential run in 1976 and thought toughening his drug policy would be a good political strategy.[1]

California governor Ronald Reagan, who also had his sights on the Republican nomination in 1976, was equally intrigued by Fine's ideas. At another party, Fine mentioned his report to Reagan, who asked to review a copy. But Rockefeller refused to share the centerpiece of his new campaign strategy. He planned to present his harsh new drug laws as evidence of his transformation from a genteel political moderate to a law-and-order Republican.[2]

That evidence failed to convince Republicans that Rockefeller was electable. He served as Gerald Ford's vice president after Richard Nixon's resignation, but Ford ousted him from the ticket for the election in 1976. (That year Ford narrowly won the Republican nomination in a close race with Reagan before losing the general election to Georgia governor Jimmy Carter.) Rockefeller died in 1979, but his drug-control tactics lived on: the Fine-inspired national drug strategy thrived during Reagan's presidency. And the Reagans would have many more dinners with Phoenix House supporters.

Although Nancy Reagan visited the TC Daytop during the presidential campaign in 1980, drug treatment then was a chancy cause for a conservative First Lady and an aggressively cheerful Reagan administration.[3] Treatment was a gloomy topic, and it was strongly associated with the chaos of the Nixon era and Gerald Ford's politically troublesome wife, Betty, who had entered treatment for alcoholism and prescription drug addiction in 1978.

By 1979, even President Jimmy Carter's administration recognized that the political momentum was behind prevention of drug abuse among teens, not treatment for adults. One of Carter's leading drug advisers, Lee Dogoloff, made his career in the emerging treatment field of the 1960s and 1970s. He helped write the Ford administration's White Paper on Drug Abuse in 1975, which proposed that the government's primary drug-policy responsibility was rehabilitating hard-drug users, not preventing marijuana use. But in less than five years, Dogoloff had reversed his opinion, arguing that a firmer stance on prevention among youth and marijuana criminalization would give the chagrined Carter presidency "a sense of competence again."[4] It might also win Carter the support of a grassroots movement of parent activists who were distressed by rising rates of marijuana use among teenagers in the 1970s. Highly educated, suburban parents such as Thomas "Buddy" Gleaton, Sue Rusche, and Marsha Keith Schuchard associated the drug use among adolescents in their communities with the permissive society that emerged from the upheaval of the

1960s. They believed the best way to prevent drug use was to turn back the cultural tide, and so they formed activist associations such as Families in Action and Parents' Resource Institute on Drug Education. "We were the real counterculture," said Schuchard, who was originally a strong Carter supporter.[5]

But such confrontational talking points ultimately suited the Reagans better than the Carters, whose moral vision was less muscular. "Our revolution," proclaimed President Reagan after beating Carter in the election in 1980, "is the first to say the people are the masters and the government is their servant."[6] To Reagan revolutionaries, mastering government meant tightening support for social programs and freeing the private sector from high taxes and regulation. Reagan's first budget, the Omnibus Budget Reconciliation Act of 1981, made the rhetoric a reality. A billion dollars in grants to assist states with Medicaid coverage disappeared; a million citizens were no longer eligible for food stamps; hundreds of thousands lost welfare benefits. In August 1981 at his majestic California ranch, Reagan held a signing ceremony for both his budget act and the Economic Recovery and Tax Act, which cut taxes on capital gains, slashed the effective corporate tax rate, and significantly reduced the marginal income tax rate for the highest earners.[7]

Although the cuts to social programs were poised to take effect that fall, the First Lady appeared busy redecorating the White House, ordering expensive china and clothes, and socializing with British royalty. To critics who thought Ronald Reagan's ideal America looked more Dickensian than utopian, his wife became a useful symbol. Print and television news outlets placed her apparent excesses in stark contrast to American families struggling in the midst of an economic recession. Nancy Reagan's advisers needed a way to rehabilitate her image as icy, spendthrift, and out of touch.[8]

They settled on the drug problem. Mickey Ziffren, a board member at Phoenix House and an acquaintance of Nancy Reagan, first suggested the idea in 1981.[9] Mrs. Reagan's adviser Ann Wrobleski attended a conference held by Schuchard and Gleaton's group Parents' Resource Institute on Drug Education and got behind their prevention agenda.[10] Once Mrs. Reagan had been thoroughly briefed on drug prevention and treatment,

Wrobleski scheduled her public appearances with parents' groups and at TCs.[11] The First Lady praised TC residents for their self-determination and the treatment centers for their resourcefulness.

"Mrs. Reagan, during the last few months, has agreed to lend her name to fundraising facilities she has visited," wrote Wrobleski to fellow staff. "The fundraising is especially important in light of the federal funding cuts for treatment centers." In 1982, Nancy Reagan attended private fundraisers at Phoenix House in April, Gateway in May, and Second Genesis in June. [12] By February of that year, the First Lady's advisers had settled on the right public-relations strategy for her: "we really perfected the Nancy Reagan drug trip," remembered Wrobleski.[13]

THE NANCY REAGAN DRUG TOUR

On her first official trip, Mrs. Reagan visited Second Genesis, a TC in a Maryland suburb. The TC was established in 1970, named by its ex-addict residents, and, according to its promotional material in the 1980s, inspired by Synanon and Phoenix House.[14] At a prearranged "rap session" with residents, Mrs. Reagan asked several questions that she would repeat at each treatment center she visited. Had the residents begun using marijuana before progressing to harder drugs? Did they think marijuana should be legalized? The answers were almost always unanimous: yes and no. The First Lady was initially uneasy about courting the press, but Carlton Turner, her husband's drug-policy director, encouraged her to stick with the plan. The *Washington Post*'s recap of Mrs. Reagan's visit hit all three points Turner wanted to promote: marijuana is a gateway to harder drugs; the liberal media has socially sanctioned "soft" drug use; and decriminalization is a dangerous trend.[15]

In May 1982, residents at Gateway agreed with these positions, but it was becoming evident that Mrs. Reagan's visits to second-generation TCs came with historical baggage. "The program Mrs. Reagan chose to visit got a lot of attention at the end of the sixties," said one local newscaster covering the visit. "Today, it's almost an institution, one that's had its share of success."[16] In the recessionary environment of the early 1980s, the program noted, that success was in jeopardy. In an interview, Gateway's president criticized President Reagan for his budget cuts. The news story ended with the hope that Mrs. Reagan's visit meant more federal support would be forthcoming.

Other coverage was less optimistic. "Drug abuse has had its day in the sun," Gateway founder and former drug czar Jerome Jaffe told the *Los Angeles Times*. "The programs had their bite of the apple. Now it is going to defense and other areas the people who elected Reagan wanted it for."[17] The Reagan administration cut 26.3 percent of all the federal funds dispersed by NIDA, a crushing blow for the community-based treatment centers run on tight budgets. In this context, the reaction of TC leaders to the First Lady's antidrug campaign ranged from outraged to enthusiastic. "We ought to get Mrs. Reagan and Dear Abby and two of the food writers from the *New York Times* together to solve the drug problem once and for all," said Delancey Street's John Maher sarcastically. "For the moment, I'd have to say Mrs. Reagan's impact in the world of drugs hasn't really been felt. Her husband's impact has been felt. It's going to be terrible for all the good little programs that need federal money to stay in business."[18]

Daytop's president William O'Brien later described the First Lady as a diplomat to the drug-treatment world—a "diplomat without portfolio."[19] The centers that benefited from Reagan's early campaigning figured out how to use her public-relations efforts to generate other sources of revenue. "I didn't expect money to come with her," remembered Phoenix House founder Mitchell Rosenthal. "But I know how to raise it; if she was in the parade, I knew how to get people to march."[20] In the 1984–1985 fiscal year, a $50,000 donation from the First Lady at a charity tennis tournament helped Phoenix House establish the Nancy Reagan Drug Abuse Fund. The treatment center's fund-raising goals reached record levels, with the Development Fund reporting revenues of $1.67 million dollars.[21]

The First Lady's attendance at fund-raising dinners was a "big plus," said one Second Genesis board member. But "the graduates are really their own best salesmen."[22] President Reagan's advisers were not certain that adult ex-addicts were the best spokespeople for the administration's drug policy, however.

Carlton Turner, the parent-movement advocate appointed as Reagan's senior adviser for drug policy in July 1981, expressed doubts about associating Mrs. Reagan too closely with reformed adult heroin addicts. Turner was a marijuana researcher, and his bailiwick was preventing teenagers' drug use. Former drug czar and NIDA chief Robert Dupont praised Turner's appointment, noting that he was "the first head of the White House Drug Office whose experience is in marijuana rather than heroin. He would also be the first presidential drug advisor who finds his political support among the worried middle-class parents of teenagers, rather than the drug abuse treatment fraternity."[23]

"The Federal priority has been on heroin treatment and control with little emphasis on prevention before the young person graduates to heroin," Turner wrote to Wrobleski in August 1981. "We need to concentrate on the two main starter drugs, alcohol and marijuana." He discouraged Wrobleski from enlisting reformed adult addicts in Mrs. Reagan's campaign. "You cannot be certain they, especially reformed heroin users, will not go back to drugs. From a gut view, a 'reformed user' is the best person in the world to deal with drugs because of the clean image. How about using young reformed users that are not celebrities to convince the kids not to use drugs and use a 'clean' positive hero figure for media appeal?"[24]

One of the best places to find young reformed drug users was a treatment organization in Florida named "Straight, Incorporated," where, according to Wrobleski, Mrs. Reagan's approach to drug-treatment tour was perfected in February 1982. Straight was cofounded by shopping-mall tycoon and prominent Republican donor Mel Sembler, whose marijuana-using son received counseling at the Seed before that center stopped treating teenagers in 1976.[25] Straight's treatment sites were ready made for Reagan-era photo opportunities. "It's very name is emblematic of the drug war's goal," journalist Maia Szalavitz later observed, "whereas the Seed sounds like it could be a hippie commune."[26]

Straight had even earlier precursors than the Seed of the 1970s; its philosophical lineage extended to the Victorian era. In the mid–nineteenth century, philanthropists and correctional leaders who had grown disenchanted with the large juvenile reformatories built at the turn of the century borrowed a new treatment model from Europe.[27] In the "cottage" reforma-

FIGURE 5.1

Nancy Reagan speaking before schoolchildren at a rally and "rap session"
at Bentley College in Waltham, Massachusetts. Photograph by White House
press photographer Mary Ann Fackelman, August 8, 1985.

Source: Courtesy of the Ronald Reagan Presidential Library and Museum,
Simi Valley, California.

tory model, troubled youths were placed in model homes, where surrogate
parents would align their emotional responses and habits with the morals
of middle- and upper-class Protestant culture. "Each house is to be a *family*,"
declared the trustees of one institution. "The government and discipline
are strictly parental," with the goal of teaching the young residents "industry, self-reliance, morality and religion, and preparing them to go forth
qualified to become useful and respectful members of society." This education would be achieved without physical restraints, "bars or bolts," but "by
the more sure and effective restraining power—*the cords of love*."[28]

Specialized juvenile courts, another alternative model of youth reformation, attracted new supporters by the turn of the twentieth century. Like
cottage reformatories, juvenile courts emphasized delivering rehabilitation
in domestic rather than institutional settings; probation officers monitored

the households of wayward youths and attempted to use state surveillance to reshape family dynamics. Keeping youth out of prisons was a goal of both treatment models.[29]

The Seed and Straight shared similarities with these nineteenth-century innovations. In addition to housing teens at group facilities, the treatment centers placed them in cottage-style "foster" families who would help cultivate a tough-love parenting philosophy. The private centers attracted concerned parents who voluntarily enrolled their children in treatment, but they also received referrals from the school counselors and courts that sought a domestic alternative to reform schools and juvenile detention centers.

Treatment for middle-class youth expanded in response to the antidrug panic of the 1980s, but the scope of the problems with the private adolescent-treatment industry did not become clear until investigations by government officials and journalists such as Szalavitz in the 2000s. According to a report published by the U.S. Government Accountability Office in 2007, program abuses were not isolated instances or limited to a few treatment centers; rather, investigators found thousands of reports of abuse from centers across the country. In 2005 alone, more than 1,600 staff members in thirty-three states were charged with allegations of abuse.[30] The community-based therapy that had been revived to treat the "hardest"-drug users in the 1960s somehow became harder, not softer, when applied to at-risk teens.

* * *

Straight's medical director, Miller Newton, worked in alcoholism treatment in the 1960s and 1970s. So did his wife. In 1979, they discovered their youngest son had a drug problem and enrolled him in Straight. This personal experience with drug abuse challenged everything Newton thought he knew about treatment and drug use, which he had previously associated with "slum heroin addicts from the 50s and hippies from the 60s." "Teenage drug use today is distinct and different phenomenon from either the 50s or 60s," he wrote in 1981.[31] It would require a new approach.

Straight's emphasis on rehabilitating young drug users was more militant than Nixon-era TCs that had also treated adolescents, such as Phoenix House and Odyssey House. While the Reagan administration sought to distance the First Lady from former hard-drug users and the treatment centers that served them, Therapeutic Communities of America, the professional organization formed partly in response to treatment abuses in the mid-1970s, denied Straight's application for membership.[32] From the beginning, Straight was beset by allegations that it practiced inhumane treatment methods such as forced imprisonment (which leaders acknowledged) and physical, sexual, and psychological abuses (which they denied). As if to assure critics that Straight would not become another Synanon, an external evaluator determined that the organization was not "guided by a charismatic guru" whose thinking is "wooly, utopian, and magical, and his programs potentially dangerous." Straight is not a cult, the report concluded, because it is "relentlessly normative. The goal is the re-establishment of the family unit."[33]

While Straight's evaluator decided the organization was anti-utopian, its promoters advanced a clear vision of what Straight could do for families. Its pamphlets promised to fulfill the "dream for every parent": a drug-free household and the resolution of familial dysfunction.[34] It made the promise without regard for clinical criteria, failing to distinguish between teens who used alcohol or marijuana occasionally and those whose substance use had led to more serious problems. According to Straight's promotional material, "the best form of prevention is intervention."[35] All teens required the same rigorous treatment program.

Like other TCs that had involved parents in family counseling since the early 1970s, Straight depended on the cooperation of parents to function. Just as some second-generation TCs were placing increasing emphasis on credentialing staff and improving bureaucracy, Straight opened its doors, staffed by former Seed members and their parents.[36] Panicked parents signed their children into Straight and allowed the organization to hold them there. Critics argued that the parents should need a court order to have children committed to a treatment center, but supporters viewed middle-class families' desire for mandated treatment as a private matter. "If an agency or an organization is applying 'coercion' to the drug user, then by all means legal rights must be respected," wrote Straight supporter and former NIDA chief Robert Dupont. "If a family or a friend is applying the 'coercion' (I would call it 'persuasion'), different standards must be invoked: nonviolent standards of love and caring. Tough love is the term used. It is an accurate term."[37]

The accuracy of this vocabulary would be challenged repeatedly beginning in 1978, when several former Straight employees expressed misgivings about the treatment center's methods. Miller Newton, who was promoted from involved parent to Straight's national clinical director in 1982, helped oversee Straight's expansion to Atlanta, Cincinnati, Sarasota, Florida, and Springfield, Virginia, bringing a group of parents to help seed each new location. He was trailed by allegations of abuse. The allegations became lawsuits, and in 1983 a jury awarded college student Fred Collins $40,000 for being confined against his will and $180,000 in punitive damages for the painful effects of Straight's treatment, which had left Collins anxious, depressed, estranged from his family, and suffering from traumatic nightmares.

At the trial, Collins's fellow resident Leigh Blight testified that in response to a minor infraction Newton had cursed at her, thrown her to the floor, and made her the center of a three-day marathon therapy session, during which time she was repeatedly humiliated—by, for example, being forced to clean her feces from the toilet bowl with her bare hands—and began to hallucinate from sleep deprivation.[38]

The organization responded by encouraging Newton's resignation. The Reagan administration responded by downplaying the allegations. After the Collins verdict, a Straight adviser wrote to Carlton Turner, summarizing the recommendations he made to William Oliver, Straight's executive director. The first piece of advice was to minimize Newton's visibility to the press: "The program needs to be perceived as a parents program, not a Miller Newton program." But for the decade following Newton's departure, former Straight residents filed similar lawsuits until the organization finally collapsed, due in part to the financial burden of settling so many civil claims.[39]

Nancy Reagan's visits helped Straight centers fend off critics while making her wildly popular with the public. In 1984, the Reagan–Bush reelection committee paid for a visit to Cincinnati's Straight location, where residents sang "Straight Is It" to the tune of "Coke Is It," while Mrs. Reagan and the parents filed into the meeting room.[40] At each Straight visit, Mrs. Reagan would watch the group meeting as teens testified about the ravages of drug use and their hard-won reformation before reconciling with their parents. She would cry along with the parents in attendance and offer a few encouraging words. She repeated the script again in Springfield, Virginia, in 1985, this time accompanied by Princess Diana.[41] The public no longer seemed bothered by Mrs. Reagan's associations with royalty; by then, her poll numbers had surpassed the president's, topping 70 percent in the months before this particular visit.[42]

Although Straight had powerful supporters, its controversial treatment methods were no government conspiracy; controversy initially helped rally the organization's base. "Every positive worthwhile effort in the history of man that has confronted an amoral society has drawn criticism," wrote one Straight parent and supporter in an advertisement published after Collins's suit.[43] "Straight has admitted to violating some administrative regulations," wrote two parents in response to a network television exposé; "however the thousands they have saved far outweigh the minor violations they have been accused of."[44]

Others disagreed. Policy scholar Arnold Trebach published his book *Why We Are Losing the Great Drug War* in 1987; it depicted Straight's privatized, loosely regulated, and donor-backed centers as an example of all that was wrong with treatment in Reagan's America. But Reagan had given conservatives a convincing new credo: anything liberals thought was wrong must be right.

Mrs. Reagan's antidrug pageantry gave Reagan a platform for more serious policy reform. At the signing ceremony for the Anti–Drug Abuse Act of 1986, the president saluted his wife, "a special person who has turned the fight against drugs into a national crusade" whose goal is "nothing less than a drug-free America."[45]

And so the personal became political, and treatment rhetoric once again took on a utopian tinge. "We must move from the denial of 'not my kid' to the commitment of 'not my country,'" wrote Straight's executive director William Oliver. "We recognize fully that if the tide of the drug epidemic is not turned within this generation of children, the American dream will become the American nightmare."[46]

RONALD REAGAN'S DRUG WAR

President Reagan credited his wife with "mobilizing the American people" in the fight against drugs "long before the polls began to register our citizens' concern."[47] Over the course of Reagan's presidency, it became clear to Republican leaders that the drug issue placated social conservatives as well as driving the polls. "Politically drugs is the only issue strong enough to occupy the attention of the nation and overwhelm the difficulties inherent in the abortion issue," wrote James Burke, the former CEO of Johnson & Johnson and president of the Partnership for a Drug-Free America (PDFA) in a private memo to George H. W. Bush.[48] Republican operative Lee Atwater, chair of the Republican National Committee, admitted as much in a letter to party leaders in September 1989. "In 50 years of polling, it is virtually unprecedented for Americans to rank a social issue as the most important problem facing the nation," he wrote. By the end of the 1980s, however, concern about illegal drugs trumped "fears about trade deficits, inflation, unemployment, abortion, and fear of war."[49]

Atwater's emphasis on fear evoked the drug war's strategic shift. In the late 1980s, drug policy took a punitive turn, and political rhetoric crossed the line from the melodramatic to the macabre. The talking points during Reagan's first term were mostly optimistic—a word Reagan himself used in his initial declaration of a "war on drugs" in 1982. On the same radio address, the First Lady celebrated parent-movement prevention efforts and spotlighted innocent teens who had been saved from becoming "shells of their former selves."[50] The language in the early days of the drug war was almost religious. "We brought in a walking chemical," said one Straight parent not long after Nancy Reagan's first visit. "Now we have a walking miracle."[51]

Linking drug policy to the restoration of the ideal nuclear family may have made up for some of Reagan's shortcomings in the eyes of evangelicals (for all the president's platitudes, he was divorced, an erratic church-goer, an estranged parent, and an idle anti-abortion crusader).[52] Drugs became a family issue around which the president and First Lady presented a unified front. By the election season in 1984, Nancy Reagan had traveled fifty-five thousand miles to forty-three cities in twenty-six states to spread the drug-free gospel. She had received eleven awards and given twenty-eight speeches and ninety-one media interviews.[53] In 1983, the president made his own trip to Cenikor, a privately funded second-generation TC in Texas.[54]

Cenikor was founded in a Colorado State penitentiary by James "Luke" Austin (whose real name was James Sanborn Thompson) in 1967. Austin said he got the idea for Cenikor from Synanon, where he briefly worked in California before splitting and, having failed to internalize the community's lessons, being convicted for assault with a deadly weapon in Colorado.[55] He initially called his self-help group of Colorado inmates a Synanon spin-off. But, according to one internal history of Cenikor, "Synanon was not thought of highly in the Colorado Penal System," and prison leaders denied Austin's request to start a group with the Synanon name. Austin responded by renaming the group the Center of the Core of the Individual, shortened to "Cenikor," and reframing the confrontational sessions as "re-ality therapy," a modality developed by psychiatrist Milton Glaser in the 1960s.[56] The penitentiary approved the Cenikor program.

After two years of incarceration and about one year leading the in-prison Cenikor program, Austin was released. He married, and he and his wife, Doris (Dottie), incorporated Cenikor on May 27, 1968. A generous donation from the businessman Charles Kettering III financed the first major Cenikor facility, which had previously housed a Denver bakery. In 1972, the Austins moved the business to Houston, where private philan-thropy drove the organization's rapid expansion (the center did not receive government funds and was fully supported through donations and its own service-industry ventures).[57]

As had happened with other TCs, the business's expansion caused complications. Austin, his wife, and a third board member were responsi-ble for Cenikor's finances. Investigations by the Houston district attorney, a state senator, and the Internal Revenue Service found the Austins had been misappropriating funds. Their lavish expenditures seriously threatened the organization's tax-exempt status. After the Austins were reprimanded, in 1977 several newly appointed board members discovered that the couple had made unauthorized credit card charges. Both of the Austins were fired, and board members Ken Barun, Doug Sadbury, and Edward Fresquez took control of the organization. Cenikor withstood the financial challenges left in the wake of the Austins' departure. It also withstood an actual assault: in July 1978, Luke Austin was arrested for attempting to take over the Houston and Denver facilities with tear gas, weapons, and a group of paid followers.[58]

By 1983, Cenikor had regained stability. The organization's operating budget increased from $600,000 in 1977 to $4.4 million, and its liabilities decreased from $2.5 million to $500,000. The Reagans' visits that year completed Cenikor's "re-birthing process," concluded one annual report. In April, the president came to Houston; the First Lady later made separate visits to Colorado and a new intake facility in Fort Worth.[59] Despite its earlier growing pains, the center was now "self-sufficient," concluded Cenikor's report of the president's visit. "It is this strong sense of independence and self-sufficiency that reinforces one of President Reagan's most deeply held beliefs: the belief in the viability of private sector initiative."[60]

"I believe in the philosophy that Cenikor symbolizes," the president told the residents. "This center is self-sufficient, just like all of you will be. Cenikor receives no Federal money and so no Federal strings come attached. And, maybe you're not aware of how much of an advantage that can be. Even though I'm part of the Federal establishment, sometimes there are two ways of doing things—the right way and the way they do it in Washington."[61]

Reagan framed recovery as self-reliance, and, blending old-fashioned moralizing with human-potential movement optimism, he told Cenikor's recovering residents that "the only limits to your achievement are self-imposed." While residents completed the hard work of rehabilitation, society would be "eagerly awaiting your return."[62]

What would treatment residents do once reintegrated? Demand-side drug policies such as treatment were the home front of the drug war, and Reagan preferred to spend federal dollars on the battlefield: interdiction

FIGURE 5.2

Ronald Reagan visits Cenikor, April 29, 1983.

Source: Reprinted with the permission of the Cenikor Foundation.

and prosecution. Nevertheless, recovered addicts had rhetorical value. In a speech explaining why most of the emergency funds provided by the Anti–Drug Abuse Act were allocated to supply-side drug-control strategies, Reagan likened cured addicts to returning combat veterans and called on them to share their war stories. Those who had been "cured through treatment and self-help" had a "critical role to play" in the drug war, said Reagan. "You can help others by telling your story and providing a willing hand to those in need."[63]

But in the months leading up to the passage of the Anti–Drug Abuse Act of 1986, some public treatment programs desperately needed a hand from the government. In New York, more than 1,000 people were on waiting lists for the city's twenty-five publicly funded residential treatment centers. Between May and August, Daytop's wait list quadrupled, from 125 to 500 people, due largely to rapidly rising rates of powder and crack cocaine use.[64]

When crack, a potent, smokeable form of cocaine, first appeared in New York City in December 1983, most of the consumers in the area were white urban professionals and middle-class suburban youth. But because crack was cheaper than powder cocaine, it spread to lower-class neighborhoods and quickly addicted residents. By the end of 1986, the drug had taken root in distressed New York neighborhoods. It had spread from its Caribbean origins to Atlanta, Boston, Detroit, Houston, Los Angeles, Kansas City, Miami, New York City, Newark, San Francisco, Seattle, St. Louis, Dallas, Denver, Minneapolis, and Phoenix.[65] The news coverage was terrifying. According to one *Newsweek* report, Forty-Second Street in New York City was "like staring into the inferno," "a nonstop choreography of craving, dealing and despair," orchestrated by, among others, "a big-shouldered Trinidadian wearing gold chains and a diamond-studded bracelet with his name engraved on it." His clients were "scavengers, the losers from turf wars in the outlying neighborhoods" whose habits had forced them "into the most dangerous and wide-open drug hustle of them all."[66]

For those with means, powder cocaine was even more readily available, thanks to an explosion of South American production in the 1970s and traffickers' abilities to rapidly adapt to U.S. interdiction efforts. It was on hand in June 1986 at a party near the University of Maryland, where college basketball star and first-round NBA draft pick Len Bias was celebrating the day after his signing ceremony with the Boston Celtics. It was in the possession of Don Rogers, a former All-American college football player and safety for the NFL's Cleveland Browns, the day before his wedding that same month. Both Bias and Rogers overdosed, little more than a week apart, disabusing the nation of the notion that powder cocaine had few negative health effects.[67]

The media frenzy surrounding a sudden urban epidemic of crack traffic and the dramatic cocaine-related deaths of two promising young sports stars "changed the mood of the country," said drug adviser Carlton Turner.[68] The public was ready to retaliate against the perceived scourge of stimulants. In the months before the midterm elections, congressional Democrats and Republicans jockeyed over which party would take the lead in introducing new legislation to address the cocaine crisis. The Anti–Drug Abuse Act of 1986, signed by President Reagan in October, was an emergency bipartisan measure that allocated an additional $1.7 billion dollars in federal funds to the $2.2 billion already annually committed to combating drug traffic and abuse. Among other measures, the act also imposed mandatory-minimum prison sentences for illicit drug trafficking and intentional sentencing disparities for powder and crack cocaine (which congressional leaders viewed as the driving force in a new drug epidemic). Under the new legislation, first-time drug dealers would automatically receive five- or ten-year sentences, depending on the classification and amount of the drug they were convicted of trafficking.

"This legislation is not intended as a means of filling our jails with drug users," said President Reagan in his remarks on signing the act, which promised a one-time increase in federal block grants to the states for publicly supported treatment. "What we must do as a society is identify those who use drugs, reach out to them, help them quit, and give them the support they need."[69]

* * *

Intentional or not, the legislation passed during Reagan's presidency had a profound impact on the U.S. prison population. In 1983, researchers at the Department of Justice warned that "prison populations would increase dramatically" if the nation systematically embraced determinate sentencing. The report asserted, moreover, that fixed federal sentencing guidelines for specific criminal offenses, like those that soon emerged from the Sentencing Reform Act of 1984, would have a limited impact on crime reduction.[70]

Tougher sentences and a prison-building boom did affect public perception. Journalists noted that the national investment in drug education and treatment could take years to produce results; in contrast, retributive justice was swift. Even the campaign for public opinion took a more assertive turn. The PDFA was launched in 1986 by a group of successful advertising executives who intended to use cutting-edge marketing strategies to "unsell" illicit drugs. PDFA raised funds from corporate contributions and enlisted the pro bono assistance of Madison Avenue advertising agencies such as Ogilvy and Mather; J. Walter Thompson; and Batten, Barton,

Durstine, and Osbourne. Within five years, PDFA had become the second-largest advertiser in the country, second only to McDonald's.[71] Deglamorizing illicit drugs could not be accomplished by an ordinary advertising campaign, said the chairman of the organization's creative review board. It required "an incessant bombardment" of images. "The advertising we produce must generate a negative attitude—a social revulsion—to what is now a smile and a wink at the higher end of the socioeconomic spectrum and a fatalistic shrug at the lower levels of social or economic deprivation."[72]

Both the perceived risk of drug use and the rates of abstention went up throughout the 1980s. If the shift in opinion was due in part to the PDFA's efforts, some researchers argued it came with a cost: prevention was purchased at the expense of treatment. In the effort to unsell drugs, the PDFA measured its campaign's success by the degree to which survey respondents considered drug users to be "aggressive, depressed losers." Some researchers argued that the stigmatization of drug users helped legitimate a criminal-justice response to addiction and discouraged the expansion of community-based treatment centers, whose residents would appear even more undesirable in light of the ads.[73] The focus on discouraging middle-class recreational drug use also neglected disadvantaged populations and seriously addicted youth, argued Daytop cofounder William O'Brien in 1993.[74]

Even so, drug-free treatment-center representatives were part of the coalition of Reagan drug-policy supporters convened at the Conference for a Drug Free America in 1987. The conference, another mandate of the Anti–Drug Abuse Act, brought together parent advocates, researchers, treatment leaders, and representatives from corrections to prepare a report and recommendations for the president. The top treatment programs and resources recommended in the final report included Narcotics Anonymous and the second-generation TCs Second Genesis, Amity, Cenikor, Phoenix House, and the coalition Therapeutic Communities of America.[75]

Although treatment providers appeared in the report's appendix, people in recovery from serious addictions were off-stage during the conference's publicized opening events. In her opening words, Nancy Reagan asserted that even casual drug users were undeserving of sympathy. Redemption was out; retribution was in. The First Lady told several violent stories of drug-related deaths, including a vivid retelling of the slaying of Stephanie

Roper, a college senior from suburban Maryland who was raped, shot, and set on fire by two men under the influence of alcohol, marijuana, and phencyclidine hydrochloride (better known as PCP) in 1982. The leniency of the murderers' sentence had galvanized the movement for determinate sentencing, and the Ropers were celebrated at the conference's opening session. By Mrs. Reagan's logic, drug users' complicity with a brutal, illicit trade made even those who had not personally committed violent acts culpable. "I'm saying if you're a casual user, you're an accomplice to murder," Nancy Reagan told the conference audience in her opening address.[76]

Conference leaders presented the new emphasis on "user responsibility" as a corrective to the policy strategies of the 1960s and 1970s. "The mental health community took over the [drug] problem in the 1960s and 1970s[,] labeling users as sick and basically not responsible for their use," the introduction to the conference's final report asserted. "Americans relied on treatment as the answer to the drug problem and deluded themselves that treatment was working well."[77]

Any "threats to the recent gains" in decreased tolerance for illicit drug use that occurred during Reagan's presidency—trends such as drug-related crime, overdose deaths, addicted infants, and even Acquired Immunodeficiency Syndrome (AIDS)—also reflected "the long-term consequences of the permissive attitudes of the 1960s and 1970s," according to the administration's official assessment of its drug-policy legacy in 1988.[78] To address these public health indicators, Reagan's successor, George H. W. Bush, appointed the first presidential drug adviser with no experience in medical practice or research—an adviser eminently qualified to address drug use as a cultural rather than clinical problem.

GEORGE BUSH'S DRUG CZAR

Ten days after Vice President George Herbert Walker Bush defeated Massachusetts Democrat Michael Dukakis in the presidential election in 1988, Ronald Reagan signed another round of antidrug legislation. The Anti–Drug Abuse Act of 1988 was dedicated to Nancy, whom Reagan described as his "co-captain" in the drug war.[79] It made drug-related murders a capital offense punishable by death. The act also included a provision for the next president: it created the Office of National Drug Control Policy.[80] The new office would showcase the Bush administration's commitment to building on the drug policies of the Reagan years. Internal leadership on drug issues had begun to falter after Carlton Turner left the Reagan administration at the end of 1986, so the new office's directorship was a high-profile, cabinet-level position. The press speculated about whom Bush would choose for the post.[81]

Donald Macdonald hoped he would be selected for the job. Macdonald was a pediatrician from Clearwater, Florida, who became involved in anti-drug activism after his son completed the Straight program. Macdonald's promotional work for Straight captured Nancy Reagan's attention and led him to Washington. In 1984, he was appointed director of the Alcohol, Drug Abuse, and Mental Health Administration. After Turner's departure, Macdonald became Reagan's central drug adviser.[82]

But Bush needed to design his own drug strategy, one that was firm but not overly indebted to his predecessor. The month after the inauguration, Robert Dupont sent Bush a list of suggestions for crafting his own "personal approach to drug abuse." Among them: "Do not make a handful of well-publicized visits to treatment centers." "Do not use the phrase 'Say "No" to Drugs.' It is superficial and cute." Dupont argued that it was possible to "reject drug use" without "rejecting (or hating) drug users, as people. They need love and support." He urged Bush to form relationships with people in recovery—out of the public eye—and to hire a young person in recovery for his personal staff, someone who could help him relate to people and organizations dedicated to treatment and prevention.[83]

For his director of drug policy, Bush hired William "Bill" Bennett, Reagan's heavy-smoking former secretary of education. Bennett was well known nationally for his bombastic oratorical style and social conservatism. (He once bragged that leftist, Ivy League audiences considered him "sexist, elitist, imperialist, bourgeois, ethnocentric, racist, selfish and solipsistic.")[84] Although Bush had won the election in 1988 in part by painting his Democratic opponent Dukakis as a soft-on-crime liberal, his patrician delivery of the Right's more extreme talking points was occasionally awkward. Bush's drug-war platform has "struck terror in the hearts of drug kingpins," syndicated columnist Mike Royko wrote sarcastically several months before the election. "They know it's a terrible thing to be flogged to death with a tennis racket."[85]

Bennett's vitriol, in contrast, was believable—so believable that Bush's advisers worried the new czar was staging a coup and using his post as preparation for a presidential run. In a memo comparing Bennett's national drug-control strategy to Bush's campaign statements, White House counsel C. Boyden Gray concluded in August 1989, "Recent press reports have focused on *Director Bennett's* potentially controversial 'tough cop' approach. Everyone, especially the press, needs to be forcefully reminded that this is the platform on which the President of the United States was *elected*."[86]

Both Bennett's supporters and critics described his job as a "rhetorical post," and the new director stated that his primary objective was raising public awareness about the dangers of drug use. His strategy for educating the electorate looked like consciousness raising in reverse, reported one journalist. Whereas the "consciousness-raising" tactics of the 1960s and 1970s came from disempowered outsiders who were pushing for policy change, Bennett was "on the inside of the policymaking establishment trying to raise the consciousness of those on the outside."[87] By the late 1980s, the once-radical claims of TC advocates were springing from Bennett's bully pulpit.

In a speech written for religious leaders, Bennett said he believed the drug crisis was fundamentally a "crisis of authority" brought about by a decline in traditional values. He summed up his solution in two words: "*consequences* and *confrontation*." The legal consequences for drug use should be swift and decisive. The best form of prevention, Bennett argued, "is through intervention, not government." Intervention, he explained, is also an essential component of drug treatment: "Successful programs almost always force the addict to confront and internalize the fact of his addiction." Only then can an addict be "habilitated" (not rehabilitated) by "demolishing bad habits and implanting good ones in their stead."[88]

Bennett, who was still doing battle with the sixties, sounded like a TC pamphlet printed twenty years earlier. One editorial writer argued that Bennett's retrograde perspective meant he was bound to overlook the drug issues that deserved serious consideration in the 1990s, such as the relation-ship between AIDS and drug use or the feasibility of supporting clean-needle exchanges for drug users. For his drug adviser, Bush had "picked someone whose expertise has been regurgitating the past to misapply it to the present," the editorial concluded.[89]

Although Bennett sometimes sounded like a TC leader of the early 1960s, he was much less enthusiastic about supporting addiction treat-ment. When the first wave of ex-addict leaders put the value of habilitation in economic terms, they contrasted their treatment model with the cost to society in petty crime (for a person in active addiction) and institutional-ization or incarceration (if incapacitated by the state). In a press conference discussing his drug-control priorities, Bennett argued for the importance of funding new prisons to house the one to two million addicts deemed untreatable. "It's clear you can't save everybody," he said. "Let me make a point about cost benefit because, no doubt, someone is going to come along and say that $20,000 for a prison cell could be used to send that person to Brown. I don't know how Brown feels about that, but, that aside, there's another argument here that's very important. The Bureau of Justice has estimated that the cost of not putting a drug felon in prison is $200,000 to $220,000 a year to society."[90]

* * *

While Bennett denied the need to expand government-funded treatment capacity, TCs survived. In 1987, TCs were the most popular treatment type, enrolling more clients than detoxification, maintenance, or multiple-modality treatment centers. The Drug Control Strategy released by Bennett's office in 1989 praised Phoenix House and Daytop Village for their ability to treat cocaine addicts in the absence of pharmacological interventions.[91] (In an assertion that belied a subtle antimaintenance orientation, the doc-ument also described patients who required long-term methadone-main-tenance therapy as "only partially" victorious over their addiction.)[92] But Reagan's presidency had made it apparent to treatment leaders that oratori-cal support was one thing; economic support was another. By 1987, almost half (44 percent) of the nation's drug-treatment expenditures were borne by the private sector; the other 23 and 33 percent came from federal and state governments, respectively.[93]

As treatment centers privatized in the late 1980s and early 1990s, the domestic economy began to falter. Along with the Office of National Drug Control Policy, Bush also inherited Reagan's $155.1 billion budget deficit.[94] Bush decided to curb deficit spending and in early 1991 struck a deal with Democrats to phase out some exemptions for high-income tax earners and increase the marginal tax rate in return for budget cuts. The compromise cost him popularity with Republicans just as the economy entered a mild recession. In the late 1980s and early 1990s, the pains of deindustrialization and globalization began to be felt by white-collar workers. Between 1990 and 1992, white-collar layoffs exceeded blue-collar layoffs for the first time; more than a million middle-class corporate employees lost their jobs.[95] While crack cocaine still blighted the inner city, middle-class Americans turned their attention to corporate restructuring in office parks. Middle-class voters were becoming more worried about the bottom line of their bank accounts than about rates of marijuana use; besides, by the early 1990s marijuana use was steadily declining among high school youth.[96]

With his mission ostensibly accomplished, Bennett decamped for the speakers' circuit.[97] He left office in November 1990, a few months after Bush launched a military intervention in the Persian Gulf in response to the Iraqi army's occupation of Kuwait. The Gulf War concluded on February 28, 1991, shortly after Bush reached the budget compromise. Although economic and foreign-policy pressures had begun to take precedence over drug-control efforts, Bush named Bennett's replacement in late 1990. He chose former Florida governor Bob Martinez, who had just lost his re-election campaign to Democrat Lawton Chiles.

Bush called Martinez's appointment a "battlefield promotion for a leader who has earned his stripes on the front lines of the drug war."[98] Martinez was born in Tampa, Florida. He became the city's mayor in 1980 and left office to make a successful run for state governor in 1986. Florida was a drug-policy flashpoint in the 1980s, home to demand-side campaign stops such as the first Straight treatment center and to supply-side initiatives such as Vice President George H. W. Bush's South Florida Task Force, a federal–state law enforcement partnership designed to target kingpins trafficking cocaine and marijuana through Miami.[99] As governor, Martinez advocated for stronger domestic drug penalties and for the use of military forces to combat drug traffickers abroad. He developed a working relationship with Bush, whose son Jeb served as his secretary of commerce and chairman for his reelection campaign. Robyn E. Blumer, a Martinez supporter and director of Florida's branch of the American Civil Liberties Union, justified Bush's appointment to the *New York Times*: "We have a loyal Republican who is suddenly out of a job, a former governor where the drug war was fought. He's qualified to the same degree that Bennett, a former Secretary of Education, was qualified."[100]

Martinez may have lacked Bennett's bluster, but he could point to his four years of experience enacting tough-on-drugs policies. "As a governor who signed more than 130 death warrants, he understands tough choices and the need for penalties as tough as the criminals that we face," said Bush at the press conference following Martinez's appointment. While Bush likened Florida to a fatal "battlefield," both Martinez and the commission that reported to him on the drug issue called the state a drug-policy "laboratory."[101] Like other bellwether Sun Belt states such as Arizona and California, Florida adopted harsh experimental methods to address drug control in the 1980s.[102]

According to a talking-point memo outlining Martinez's demand-side bona fides, his accomplishments included "doubling Florida's prison capacity, constructing more beds than in the previous 20 years, and increasing the prison budget from $417 million to $1 billion." As an alternative to incarceration, Martinez developed a boot-camp program for nonviolent offenders and a second, TC-style, three-phase treatment program that included residential treatment, employment experience, and probationary supervision.[103]

Martinez's critics noted that signing death warrants and raising the number of drug-related incarcerations from less than three thousand to more than sixteen thousand didn't prevent the state from having the highest crime rate in the nation. At the last count before Martinez took his national post, Florida was spending 16 percent less than the national average on treatment.[104]

As Martinez entered the last years of his governorship, a new partner-ship between law enforcement and drug treatment was forming in Miami. A group of Miami-Dade County legal professionals, led by coordinator Tim Murray and judges such as Herbert Klein and Stanley Goldstein, proposed a program that would divert first-time, nonviolent offenders who commit drug-related crimes from prison to a strict program of treatment; they called it a "drug court." Miami-Dade County supplied funding to test the program by raising traffic fines and parking fees, but in the absence of a long-term, reliable revenue stream the established treatment centers in the area weren't initially interested in participating. Early clients of Miami-Dade's drug-court program received treatment in a double-wide trailer. Positive national press soon caught the attention of Florida's state attorney general, Janet Reno. Funding followed. Treatment providers began to seek out partnerships with drug-court programs; the model spread to other Florida counties and was replicated in other states. By 1993, the drug-court movement had moved out of the double-wide and into the White House.[105]

6

COURTS AND MARKETS

WELCOME TO HUMANITY, and you look great," a Dade County drug-court judge told a neatly dressed woman defendant who had made her initial court appearance just a month earlier, bruised, unwashed, and under the influence of crack. The prosecutor, pleased with the defendant's transformation, agreed: "In this court all of us are public defenders, really."[1]

Dade County attorney Hugh Rodham actually held the title. In 1991, he arranged for his brother-in-law to tour the court with Tim Murray, then the director of Dade County's Office of Substance Abuse Control. "He [the brother-in-law] was very curious and asked a lot of questions," Murray later told a reporter. "I thought he was just Hugh's brother-in-law. I said, 'So what do you do for a living, Bill?'" "I'm the governor of Arkansas," Bill Clinton replied.[2]

Clinton, who had spent nearly a decade as the governor of one of the nation's poorest and least-populous southern states, was planning a presidential run. "All my life, I have been an agent of change," Clinton would claim on the campaign trail, citing his progressive beliefs in racial equality and publicly funded health care and education.[3] But Clinton's gubernatorial record was more conciliatory than his rhetoric. During his first term as governor from 1979 to 1981, Clinton pushed for several new progressive initiatives, including the expansion of rural health clinics, environmental regulations, and new taxes and fees to pay for infrastructure improvements. The overly ambitious agenda helped Clinton's Republican opponent defeat him in the election in 1980. When Clinton returned to the governor's seat in 1983, he chose to focus on less-divisive issues, such as fostering private economic development and improving public education.[4] He adopted some conservative positions on welfare and criminal justice. In the late 1980s, he worked with President Ronald Reagan and leading governors to help broker federal welfare-reform legislation.[5] After making the disastrous decision to commute the death sentence of a convicted murder who had killed again following his release from prison, Clinton pledged to be tough on crime.

As a presidential candidate, Clinton made a point of returning from the campaign trail to oversee the execution of Ricky Ray Rector, an African American man so mentally impaired that he famously asked his executors to save a portion of his last meal for the following day.[6] Once elected, Clinton endorsed a federal "three strikes" law that mandated prison terms for multiple offenses. He supported new penalties for drug convictions, such as denying federal financial aid for college and access to public housing. He failed to offer a strong critique of the growing national prison population, which increased from 329,821 to 823,414 between 1980 and 1991.[7] Liberal critics faulted Clinton for embracing an anticrime strategy that disproportionately affected low-income and minority communities. But in the early and mid-1990s, opponents of mass incarceration were outnumbered.[8]

Reflecting on his administration almost two decades later, as criticism of the carceral state mounted and his wife, Hillary, made a presidential campaign promise to pursue criminal-justice-system reforms, Clinton explained his previous policies. He implied that he had not completely embraced the retributive idea of justice; he had instead viewed prisons as a vehicle for psychological treatment and individual reformation. The problem was the funding. "[We put] so many people in prison that there wasn't enough money left to educate them, train them for new jobs and increase the chances when they came out that they could live productive lives," said Clinton.[9] In a foreword to a collection of essays on criminal-justice-system reform published in 2015, Clinton called for shortening prison terms and reinvesting funds in "prison education programs that practically eliminate recidivism."[10] The argument wasn't a radical reversal of Clinton's initial judgment.

In 1994, while campaigning for treatment and prevention components of the drug-control funds in the Violent Crime Control and Law Enforcement Act, Clinton made a speech before the inmates in a ninety-day drug-treatment program at Prince George's County Correctional Center. He told the crowd he intimately understood the dual problems of addiction and incarceration: he had grown up with an alcoholic stepfather, and his half-brother's cocaine problems resulted in prison time. He explained that his drug strategy would be directed at "the most tenacious and damaging aspect of America's drug use problem: chronic, hard-core drug use and the violence it spawns."[11] The county's director of corrections told reporters that Clinton was the first president to hold a drug-policy press conference at a confinement facility.[12]

Like the advocates of the prison-based treatment Clinton championed, drug-court supporters hailed their criminal-justice intervention as an innovative breakthrough. Drug courts were a policy compromise that satisfied both liberal advocates of treatment and fiscal conservatives unhappy with the expense of incarceration. Janet Reno, who was confirmed as Clinton's attorney general in 1993, advanced the drug-court cause on a national scale.[13]

But some conservatives who had sold constituents on the concept of zero tolerance called Reno out of touch. "She has this utopian belief in the perfectibility of mankind," said Bruce Fein, a former Justice Department official under President Reagan. "We simply do not know enough about human nature and the motivation of people who commit violent crime."[14] Those who shared Fein's philosophy questioned the court system's ability to determine which offenders could be "welcomed to humanity."

Dade County's first drug-court program was designed for first-time, nonviolent offenders; the county's Office of Substance Control director Tim Murray called them "virgins and Boy Scouts."[15] Once the program showed successful outcomes with the lower-risk groups, it could be expanded to more serious cases. The Clinton administration's investment in delivering rehabilitation through the criminal-justice system was a recommitment to addressing the root causes of hard-drug users that, officials argued, the Reagan and Bush administrations had abandoned.[16]

But Clinton's policies were not a clean "break with the past," as some drug-court champions contended.[17] In many ways, they revived the moral philosophy of rehabilitative (or habilitative) corrections advanced by TC advocates in the 1960s, 1970s, and 1980s. Although some scholars credit the drug-court movement of the 1990s for renewing corrections-based addiction treatment, the comeback of therapeutic correction had actually occurred several years earlier. The Anti–Drug Abuse Act of 1986—which enacted federal mandatory minimum sentences for the possession of small amounts of illicit drugs, imposed harsh new standards for parole, and allocated $97 million to build new prisons—is usually viewed as the crowning piece of drug-war legislation. But the act also allocated $241 million for addiction treatment. The allocation helped fund Project Reform, an influential multisite study on the efficacy of prison-based TCs for drug offenders.[18]

The expansion of rehabilitative corrections in the 1980s and 1990s, first through prison programs and then through drug courts, took place as the private treatment industry continued to grow. "I hate to see treatment get associated solely with the criminal justice system," said Linda Wolf Jones, the executive director of Therapeutic Communities of America in 1998. "We don't want people to feel they have to commit a crime to get treatment."[19] But for many drug users, especially racial minorities and people without economic means, Wolf Jones's worries became a reality. An arrest was the clearest entry to rehabilitation. The simplest way to access long-term treatment was through the prison system.

REFORM AND RECOVERY IN THE U.S. PRISON SYSTEM

A year before the crack scare and the passage of the Anti–Drug Abuse Act of 1986, Ronald Reagan blessed the ninth World Conference of Therapeutic Communities in San Francisco, California. Conference presentations by TC leaders considered how the TC should evolve to meet the needs of more affluent clients who might be able to pay for treatment services. Presenters also discussed how to meet their traditional client base of severely addicted, long-term drug users where they were: prisons. Researchers gave talks with titles such as "The TCs' Role in the Privatization of Corrections" and "Therapeutics and Incarceration: They Said It Couldn't Be Done."[20]

Those who doubted therapeutic incarceration formed an unlikely coalition of activists, elected representatives from both political parties, and criminologists. In the mid-1970s, investigations by journalists such as Jessica Mitford and by elected officials such as Congressman Sam Ervin challenged the ethics of prison-based behavioral research, which critics argued was often coercive and inhumane. At the same time, mounting public skepticism about the correctional system's ability to rehabilitate prisoners caused both liberals and conservatives to abandon psychotherapeutic prison projects.[21] In 1975, researchers Douglas Lipton, Robert Martinson, and Judith Wilks published an influential study on the effectiveness of treatment in prison. The study, along with a related essay published by Martinson in *Public Interest* the previous year, affirmed the growing public suspicion that "nothing works" in offender rehabilitation. By the end of the decade, the nation had shifted from a treatment model to a justice, or "just deserts," model of incarceration.[22] The prevailing attitude in corrections was that effective treatment "couldn't be done."

TC advocates challenged that view, and their prison-based treatment model endured throughout the just-deserts era; in 1979, a NIDA study found that TCs were the most prominent therapy model in prisons, serving 42 percent of all inmates enrolled in drug treatment.[23] Despite the ethical concerns about prison research that emerged in the 1970s, TC studies continued apace. In 1977, Phoenix House graduate Ron Williams helped found Stay N Out, a grant-funded, nine- to twelve-month TC for inmates at the Arthur Kill Correctional Facility on Staten Island and the Bayview Correctional Facility in Manhattan.[24] Harry Wexler, a psychologist and researcher mentored by Phoenix House researcher George De Leon, produced outcome evaluations with promising findings. Like the community-based TC research conducted by De Leon and others in the late 1960s and early 1970s, the prison-based TC research focused on variables such as abstinence from drugs, psychopathology, and recidivism. These traditional moral qualities had been the focus of research for decades, but, unlike past generations of criminologists, drug-treatment researchers in the 1970s and

1980s were able to show that treatment could significantly alter these variables over a long period of time. In 1979, Wexler found that participants in two prison-based TCs outperformed those in a comparison group on measures of drug use and criminality following their release.[25]

The study was the foundation for Project Reform and its successor, Project Recovery. These two prison-treatment and evaluation projects spanned presidential administrations from Ronald Reagan to Bill Clinton. With funds allocated by the Anti–Drug Abuse Act, the Federal Bureau of Justice Administration funded Reform (also called the Comprehensive State Department of Corrections Treatment Strategy for Drug Abuse) from 1987 until 1991. During that time, eleven state departments of corrections developed and implemented state plans for treatment. In 1991, the federal Center for Substance Abuse Treatment continued the technical assistance projects for an additional eighteen months and expanded participation to fourteen states. The continuation grant was named Project Recovery.[26]

By 1993, the effectiveness of in-prison TCs was well demonstrated, and the Center for Substance Abuse Treatment funded the expansion of the TC intervention developed in the two projects. Clinton's Violent Crime Control Act of 1994 provided further funds for in-prison drug treatment.[27] The Clinton administration's drug-strategy talking points leading up to the election in 1996 singled out studies of successful prison-based TC programs—Stay N Out in New York, Amity in California, and Continuum in Delaware—as evidence of the president's subtly Nixonian commitment to "breaking the cycle of crime and drugs."[28]

The coauthor of the influential Stay N Out studies was Douglas Lipton. Disturbed by the punitive fallout from his previous research, Lipton partnered with Wexler to counter the retributive trend in corrections.[29] Assessing the success of prison-based TCs a little more one year after the passage of the Violent Crime Control Act, Lipton wrote that the "most important aspect of Project Reform" was the "catalytic effect" the research had on the correctional community. The project collaborators enlightened wardens, judges, and even some elected officials about the possible benefits of prison-based treatment.[30] By the mid-1990s, studies showed that almost 80 percent of Stay N Out program participants were employed, drug free, and arrest free five years after their release; this rate was significantly higher than the rates for inmates who received milieu therapy, counseling, or no treatment.[31] Lipton concluded that the mounting evidence in favor of prison-based TCs led to the "inescapable conclusion that treatment lowers crime and health costs as well as related social and criminal justice costs."[32]

But that conclusion escaped some critics; one congressional Republican representative opposed the Violent Crime Control Act's expansion of prison-based treatment, arguing that the programs amounted to nothing more than "hug a thug."[33] On the political left, both academics and drug-policy reformers remained skeptical about whether the hopeful therapeutic rhetoric about correctional system TCs matched the lived reality of participating in them.[34]

In the 1990s, veteran TC leaders remembered the risks that came with rapid expansion. Linda Wolf Jones, president of Therapeutic Communities of America, cautioned that an influx of federal funding for treatment might attract opportunists and lead to "scandals, farces, and failures" that would tarnish the TC model.[35] Concerns about a repeat of the scandals that took place in the 1970s inspired treatment leaders to develop ethics guidelines for the next generation of prison programs. Rather than diluting or amending the traditional TC model, TC leaders set standards for implementing it faithfully. "It is essential," the federal guidance report began, "that programs operating as TCs have a solid grounding" in TC history and theory. According to the new prison program standards, the TC philosophy should be put into practice through, for example, TC orientation material given to each resident upon entry; "the display of TC slogans and teachings" that "promote prosocial values of 'right living'"; and a "prevailing attitude in the community that the participant needs to make major, serious life changes, rather than [that] the person is 'sick' and in need of care."[36]

That traditional attitude may have once sounded tough, but by the 1990s TCs were no longer the most demanding prison programs around. Some politicians embraced prison-based "boot camps" and a treatment model called "shock incarceration" as the solution to prison overcrowding. Boot camps, modeled on military indoctrination and reformatory school discipline, emphasized physically challenging exercises and drills over group-therapy sessions or counseling. Shock incarceration aimed to reduce the prison population by trading sentence length for more punishing conditions. In theory, intense physical exertion and sensory deprivation would scare offenders straight. In actuality, the evidence in favor of more brutal carceral methods was bleak. According to a National Institute of Justice report, by late 1988 shock-incarceration programs were operating in nine states; none had been evaluated. The lack of evaluation mattered little to these programs' supporters, however. "Shock incarceration's appeal is broad and easily generated," the report opened. "Media coverage invariably conveys visual images that are consistent with the public's desire to punish criminals—e.g. staff shouting in an inmate's face, or inmates performing hard labor or grueling exercises."[37]

Some TC leaders chafed at the sudden popular support for prison camps. In a letter to the *New York Times*, TC leader and Samaritan Village president Richard Pruss questioned the paper's endorsement of work camps, arguing that there was no evidence that "hastily erected" camps in upper New York State prisons "would yield results in reform and rehabilitation comparable to . . . the well-established and expertly staffed network of therapeutic communities."[38]

Even amid the boot-camp craze, however, the traditional TC model caught the media's attention. Press coverage of Stay N Out appeared in outlets such as *Businessweek* and the *Wall Street Journal*. The articles often focused on Lipton's economic case for treatment in prison. Lipton repeatedly argued that Stay N Out's recidivism prevention paid for the additional cost of administration within two to three years of an inmate's release.[39]

Advocates of prison-based TCs also appealed to the heart. Skeptical correctional officers at Arthur Kill Prison were initially swayed by the Stay N Out program after a former inmate and early graduate of Stay N Out and Phoenix House became a counselor in the prison program. Prison workers rarely see success stories; the reformed-convict counselors became a reminder that recovery was possible.[40]

Supportive politicians blended emotional and economic arguments. In 1990, Charles Schumer, a Brooklyn Democrat and chairman of the U.S. House Subcommittee on Criminal Justice, was confident that if his constituents and congressional colleagues met Stay N Out's recovering leaders such as Ron Williams, they could be convinced to replicate the program.[41] A few years later Texas governor Ann Richards, impressed by her conversations with Stay N Out inmates, returned home and began planning to add eighteen thousand treatment beds throughout the state, some of them managed by New York Therapeutic Communities.[42] Richards, a recovering alcoholic, said her commitment to treatment grew out of "what I feel in my heart and what I have experienced in my own life." But "the selling point we used was, we have got to keep these people from coming back, committing more crime, and unless we do something this is going to cost more and more."[43]

With time, Sun Belt states such as Texas grew surprisingly receptive to prison-based treatment. In Arizona and California, the two states that hosted Synanon's prison programs in the 1960s, the prison population soared in the 1980s and 1990s. Between 1980 and 1994, Arizona's incarceration rate more than doubled from 161 to 459 per 100,000 residents.[44] The number of prisoners in California grew almost sixfold, from 24,500 to 124,800.[45] But therapy was not officials' first response to this trend.

Some officials instead touted the harsh conditions that awaited new inmates. Governor Fife Symington III of Arizona fulfilled a campaign promise to reinstitute chain gangs in 1995; the following year he adamantly opposed a successful ballot initiative that mandated treatment rather than incarceration for first- and second-time drug offenders. While liberal leaders such as hedge-fund manager George Soros and medical marijuana activist Peter Lewis campaigned for the ballot initiative, advocates of an explicitly "tough and cheap" approach to corrections staged alternatives to treatment. The sheriff of Maricopa County (Phoenix) publicized the poor conditions of his "Tent City"—a fenced temporary prison compound of crammed-together Korean army tents, baking under the Arizona sun—as an "innovation." He bragged about purchasing green bologna and other expired food to serve the prisoners.[46] The conditions were not new to the Arizona prison system; the public pride in them was.

Across the nation, as incarceration rates soared and prison conditions deteriorated, prisoners in California, the former cradle of the rehabilitative ideal, fell silent. Historians of corrections have argued that "treatment eras" are characterized by a concern with both internal prison conditions and the larger social circumstances that produce crime. Eric Cummins explains that convicts' stories—literature detailing criminals' childhood deprivation, misdeeds, capture, and reform through imprisonment—serve several purposes. The tales raise general awareness about social problems such as poverty, broken families, and lack of opportunity. They also serve as cautionary tales for listeners and as a form of penitence for tellers. When the stories cease to function in this way, writes Cummins, "it is a sign that something has gone seriously wrong in the functioning of the rehabilitative prison."[47] When the stories stop altogether, it is a sign the treatment era is over.

Cummins presents Black Panther and Synanon supporter Eldridge Cleaver as a counterintuitive model for the activist revival of therapeutic corrections. Cleaver's memoir *Soul on Ice*, published in 1968, had galvanized a radical prison-reform movement that questioned the racial injustice of not only the correctional system but also the entire U.S. government. The prison movement's association with the Panthers and more radical domestic terrorist groups such as the Black and Symbionese Liberation Armies helped inspire the backlash against prisoner education and therapy. When Cleaver returned to the United States in 1975 after several years of self-imposed exile following an armed assault on Oakland police officers, he disavowed his past radicalism, took on the retrograde role of Penitent Thief, "and became a modern treatment-era regenerated convict," writes Cummins.[48] For Cummins, the sincerity of Cleaver's neo-Victorian testimonial was less important than its success (he was sentenced to probation).

Resurrecting the redemptive message nationally was no easy feat. Yet in 1997 the *Los Angeles Times* ran a lengthy feature article that concluded "even skeptics" were "impressed with treatment that uses brutally honest encounter groups and ex-offenders as counselors." One successful prison TC graduate, who previously dealt drugs in South Central Los Angeles, described his identity transformation: "Volron [my street name] was a bad person. He died in prison."[49]

Volron went through a two-year recovery process in a TC in California's Richard J. Donovan State Prison run by the Amity treatment center. The Amity program was led by two former Synanon members: Rod Mullen, a nonaddict and former student activist at the University of California at

Berkeley, and Naya Arbiter, who had sought treatment at Synanon while in her teens. Both went on to work in the TC treatment field. By the late 1980s, the Arizona-based Amity Foundation was managing a demonstration project in the Pima County Jail funded by the Bureau of Justice Administration.[50]

The director of the California Department of Corrections, James Rowland, had previously collaborated with Mullen on treatment programs for juvenile offenders. He asked Mullen to tour several CDC sites and make a presentation about the feasibility of implementing in-prison substance-abuse treatment. Mullen's Amity report convinced CDC leaders to participate in Project Recovery and to enlist Amity to implement treatment. Like Stay N Out's founder Ron Williams, Mullen revised the views of correctional establishment nonbelievers. John Ratelle, the doubting warden at the Donovan Prison near San Diego where the Amity program was to be housed, listened to former CDC inmates explain why the Pima County program worked. According to one report, the California program would ultimately be shaped by Ratelle's "hard-nosed attitude and unstinting support."[51]

Not every skeptic in the justice establishment was convinced. In 1989, just as Amity began preparing to implement its California program, officials at the Bureau of Justice Administration called for funding cuts to prison-based treatment programs. *The Nation* reported that George H. W. Bush's attorney general Dick Thornburgh and his assistants Richard Abell and Clifford White were wedded to the "nothing works" ideology. To reduce prison overcrowding, these federal officials reportedly preferred inexpensive innovations such as boot camps and cheap modular prisons to TCs.[52] Compared to correctional leaders who wanted punishment to come harsh and cheap, Clinton's commitment to the reform project seemed progressive.

But progressives, including Clinton, were ultimately disappointed with the scope of the results. Although prison-based treatment expanded in the 1990s, it never scaled up to meet the needs of the incarcerated population with substance-use disorders. From 1990 until 1996, the number of state and federal inmates in need of treatment grew, but the proportion of inmates in treatment continued to hover around 20 percent.[53] When an independent

California commission investigated methods to reduce prison overcrowding in 1998, it returned with a favorable report on the Amity program. The legislature committed to expanding the program to nearly ten thousand beds by the end of 1999.[54] Unlike Synanon's past prison projects in California and Arizona, which had trouble recruiting residents, Amity struggled to keep pace with demand. In 1996, it received hundreds of monthly applications for a few open slots.[55]

While inmates with substance-use disorders clamored for treatment, drug-court advocates argued that other offenders could be coerced into recovery. For addiction professionals, the political decision to link treatment to the court system would come at a cost.

THE BUSINESS OF DRUG COURTS

The new programs that used the courts to divert substance-using offenders from prison to treatment had precedents. One effort, Treatment Alternatives to Street Crime, had been created by SAODAP under Jerome Jaffe's direction in the 1970s and managed by Robert Dupont. "I never felt that the prison sentence was the enemy of the addicted person," said Dupont in a later interview. "I wanted to use the leverage of that prison sentence for pro-social purposes."[56] Dupont argued that real consequences taught responsibility and encouraged a serious commitment to a treatment program.

Some judges had long held the same belief. Individual judges had often used court-mandated treatment to divert low-risk defendants away from prison or made treatment compliance a condition of probation for people found guilty of offenses. Second-generation centers benefited from developing relationships with treatment-friendly judges.

But the trend toward mandatory minimum sentencing in the late 1970s and 1980s curtailed judges' authority to assign treatment rather than punishment. At the same time, the rising drug-related caseload in high-trafficking areas such as Miami made traditional case processing nearly impossible. At the first national drug-court conference, proponents argued that efficiency was the court's premier innovation. Streamlining the treatment-referral process through a designated drug court would alleviate the burden on a legal system strained by a surge of drug charges.[57]

Creating new formal courts for processing drug-related charges changed the relationship between the treatment and judicial systems. Judges, who might once have simply assigned treatment as a condition of parole, began to take more active roles in the treatment process. "Rather than referring certain offenders 'out' to treatment, the drug court brings treatment to center stage in the criminal process and, in fact, into the criminal courtroom," wrote criminal-justice scholar John S. Goldkamp in a federally commissioned working paper in 1993.[58]

The press credited courts, not counselors, with offering an alternative to jail by "mixing 'tough love' with treatment."[59] Early coverage of Miami-Dade's drug court focused on founding judge Stanley Goldstein, a Brooklyn native and former police officer whose bench style was described by *USA Today* as a "hybrid of Kojak and Father Knows Best."[60] "I scare the hell out of people," Goldstein told the *Saint Petersburg Times*. "I can't help it, but I do. If I don't give them individual attention, it won't work."[61]

Drug-court leaders counseled their fellow judges to cultivate a "tough" but "concerned" persona and to view the relationship between the judge and client as a form of "parenting."[62] Sociologist James L. Nolan argues that drug-court judges were activists in both attitude and action. The "assertive and compassionate" drug-court judge stood in stark contrast to an older ideal of adjudication in which the judge adopts a "restrained and impartial" demeanor.[63]

The tough-love performance was also a reclamation of judicial authority. "Drug courts mark a turning back of the judicial clock to a time when judges ran their own calendars and were responsible for their court's operations and the defendant had to answer directly and immediately to the judge for their [sic] conduct," wrote drug-court leader Judge Jeffrey Tauber.[64] Judges rather than treatment providers would determine the length and type of treatment. They would make the final call about whether a relapse should trigger a mild sanction or a prison term. In some areas, treatment providers who partnered with drug courts would be required to open patients' private medical records to judicial and public scrutiny.[65]

Placing treatment under the purview of the judicial system improved the court's ability to quickly process cases, but the relationships between court programs and treatment providers were not always smooth.

Because drug courts began as a local affair, there was no single way to set one up. By the early 2000s, two dominant models of service delivery had emerged: brokerage and in house.[66] Under the brokerage model, clients are referred to community-based treatment providers; the court serves a supervisory role by, for example, monitoring program progress and drug testing. In contrast, under the in-house model the court pays for and directly manages treatment services. Both brokerage and in-house drug-treatment providers struggled to find ways to integrate their funding, organizational decision making, and treatment philosophies with the court system.

Some types of treatment were more philosophically compatible with drug courts than others. In a survey of both internal and external drug-court treatment programs in 1999, 90 percent or more reported offering detoxification, self-help, residential, intensive outpatient, or community- or jail-based TC programs. Only 39 percent offered methadone maintenance; just 25 percent offered other pharmacological interventions.[67]

The underrepresentation of pharmacological approaches to addiction treatment led critics to question the moral basis of the drug-court movement.[68] One reporter concluded that in contrast to tested voluntary community-based treatment programs such as methadone maintenance and TCs, the drug-court delivery method was an "act of faith"; graduates of a District of Columbia drug court were in fact given an *Acts of Faith* meditation book along with their diplomas.[69]

Drug-court advocates promoted treatment with general platitudes about its capacity for redemption and glossed over the technical aspects of various treatment models. The desired outcome of drug courts—namely, lower rates of recidivism—was evaluated starting in the model's early days. But according to a survey of studies on drug-court programs in the 1990s and early 2000s, researchers tended to focus on court procedures and processes rather than on the comparative effectiveness of the different treatment models the courts employed.[70] Aside from some early controversy about leading judges' preference for acupuncture-based addiction treatment,[71] the relationship between a drug court's success and its preferred treatment model was rarely explicitly debated. Experiments and advocates focused on a different dichotomy: treatment or no treatment.

As Clinton's second presidential term came to a close, leaders questioned whether federal support for drug-court programs would continue.[72] Nearly a decade after the first contemporary drug court was founded in Miami, such courts were operating in forty-eight states; in 1997–1998, the number of courts in the planning or operational stages more than tripled to 430.[73] Many relied on a combination of funding sources and could not survive with local support alone.

In April 2000, Stephen Belenko, a Columbia University–affiliated criminologist who authored an influential survey of research on the effectiveness of drug-court treatment, submitted testimony in favor of the model at a congressional hearing on drug-treatment options in the justice system. Belenko and a range of other drug-court advocates, including drug-court judge Jeffrey Tauber and psychiatrist and former DC drug-court clinician Sally Satel, focused their attention on the need for continued funding and on philosophical and economic justifications for court-coerced treatment.[74]

Unlike the fraught hearings about treatment funding in the early 1970s, these treatment advocates' testimonials did not directly address the differences between various treatment models. No former addicts or treatment-center directors were present. Yet as the testimonials proceeded, TC logic appeared in drug-court advocates' general endorsements of both treatment and coercion.

Belenko cited an impact study of a Daytop-affiliated Kings County drug court in New York. The study's design was modeled on TC research; the results showed that 37 percent of drug-court participants were rearrested during the eighteen-month follow-up period in contrast to 54 percent of the comparison group sample.[75] Tauber noted that drug courts are designed on "reality-based" principles, including the importance of "immediate and upfront intervention," comprehensive supervision, and long-term treatment lasting a year or more.[76] "To illustrate the clinical realities of treatment, consider the therapeutic community," Satel stated. She argued that Phoenix House's researcher George De Leon had showed that time in treatment was the best predictor of long-term recovery and that using the threat of sanctions or punishment to enroll and maintain a user in treatment during an initial period of resistance only improved the likelihood of success. "Drug courts effect a marriage of the so-called medical (voluntary treatment) and moral (sanction-oriented) approaches to addiction—a combination that works better for hard-core addicts than either alone," concluded Satel.[77]

Other analysts with libertarian leanings drew different conclusions from the drug-treatment research. Groups who were politically opposed to government programs found all the treatment research unconvincing. In 1991, an assessment issued by the fiscally conservative Heritage Foundation took issue with any federal investment in drug treatment, whether voluntary or court mandated. The study argued that the "explosive" growth in federal spending on treatment under the Reagan and Bush administrations was unwarranted. The authors asserted that publicly funded drug-treatment facilities "are poorly run, fail to follow standard treatment practices, and function as 'revolving doors' for addicts seeking respite from the criminal justice system." They presented the private treatment industry and voluntary associations such as AA—or, even better, AA-inspired treatment centers—as an alternative. "Drug treatment should be privatized, and private-sector providers should be encouraged to seek drug abusers in need of treatment," read the report's list of recommendations. "Twelve step should be recognized."[78]

THE RISE OF TWELVE-STEP TREATMENT

Skeptics of twelve-step treatment believed the model had gained far more credibility than it deserved. Detractors of AA voiced concerns almost as soon as the first groups were established. Reporter Jack Alexander, who published a *Saturday Evening Post* article in 1941, confessed that he was initially doubtful about the organization and "convinced AA's [*sic*] were pulling his leg." Four years later, defending his influential report on the "drunkard's best friend," Alexander conceded that public skepticism about the group remained strong: "a lot of people are annoyed by [the group's] sometimes ludicrous strivings and its dead-pan thumping of the sobriety tub."[79]

But by 1950 AA had achieved popular success. The humble fellowship was founded in private parlors and church basements, but within a few years it also had a home in Hollywood (the first group there was founded on the Warner Bros. lot in the early 1940s) and in the hospital system (co-founder Dr. Bob Smith began working in St. Thomas's Hospital in 1939).[80] The grassroots organization influenced education and advocacy groups such as the National Council on Alcoholism (founded in 1944), which launched successful public-relations campaigns, and institutes such as Yale's Center of Alcohol Studies (founded in 1935), which produced new scientific research on the disease. AA inspired people afflicted with related addictions to adjust the steps to fit their problems. Fifty years after AA's formation in 1935, sufferers could find fellowships devoted to overcoming narcotics, cocaine, overeating, gambling, codependency, and sex. The tendency to turn bad habits into diagnoses amounted to nothing less than the "diseasing of America," proclaimed twelve-step critic and psychologist Stanton Peele in 1989. Peele, along with other critics such as Charles Bufe and Herbert Fingarette, called alcoholism a cultural construction and AA a cult.[81] Critics argued that the disease model for addiction disempowered the diagnosed and encouraged a defeatist attitude about the social causes of substance use. They also noted that the twelve-step disease model dominated a treatment industry that sought to profit from the growing range of addictive disorders. By the 1990s and early 2000s, more than 90 percent of rehabilitation centers in the United States were based on the twelve steps.[82]

Twelve-step treatment centers succeeded the TCs that had consciously distinguished themselves from anonymous groups in the 1960s and 1970s. Unlike the voluntary associations of anonymous members, TCs originally billed themselves as treatment centers. They had patient rosters, paid staff, government grants, and evaluation data. AA supporters began medicalizing mutual aid in the 1940s and 1950s, but compared to the TCs that soon followed, their early efforts were modest.

Twelve-step treatment grew from the AA groups housed in Minnesota's Wilmar State Psychiatric Hospital, the influence of an AA-based treatment center in Minneapolis called Pioneer House, and the efforts of the private treatment center Hazelden, which was founded in 1949 as a "sanitorium for the curable alcoholics of the professional class."[83] The "Minnesota Model" of treatment emerged from the three centers. The model was characterized as a "multidisciplinary" treatment that combined a three- to four-week residential program of AA rituals and literature with medical supervision and counseling by nonalcoholic mental-health professionals. The Minnesota-based programs embraced recovering counselors and encouraged them to share their personal experiences with the twelve-step program. Word of AA-based treatment gradually spread through networks of program devotees and researchers in the 1950s and early 1960s. Minnesota became a capital for alcoholism-treatment professionals and a center of activity for halfway-house founders.[84]

But when the federal government restructured support for mental-health and addictions treatment in the late 1960s and early 1970s, the investment in alcoholism-treatment centers lagged behind the support for programs that specialized in drug addiction. Since the repeal of Prohibition and the development of the federal narcotics hospitals in the late 1930s, government investment in addiction programs had outpaced spending on alcoholism programs. The disparity between drug and alcohol funding was only exacerbated by the creation of SAODAP, NIDA, and the National Institute on Alcohol and Alcoholism in the early 1970s. In 1972, the federal government spent twice as much on drug addiction (nearly $1,200 million in 2010 dollars) as on alcoholism ($600 million); in 2008, it spent nearly the same ratio, $800 million on drug programs versus $400 on alcoholism programs.[85]

The historian Grischa Metlay argues that politics accounted for the support gap. Illicit drug use had ties to criminal activity and overdose deaths; the chronic-disease burden associated with alcohol use appeared less dramatic. Nixon used his executive position to endow SAODAP with both funding and freedom from legislative bickering. The funding continued to flow to NIDA after SAODAP was restructured.[86]

In contrast, the campaign for an alcoholism institute came from the legislative branch of government, with Senator Harold Hughes (D–ID), a recovering alcoholic and AA supporter, as its loudest champion. Nixon fought the creation of the institute and periodically attempted to slash its funding. Even after its creation in 1970, the National Institute on Alcohol and Alcoholism faced internal opposition and steep competition for resources within the NIMH bureaucracy. AA-influenced organizations such as the National Council on Alcoholism and the Center of Alcohol Studies sought to change public opinion by promoting a disease concept of alcoholism, evoking empathy for alcoholics, and bringing attention to the disease burden of chronic drinking. The sober public-health message was no match for the political arguments and personalities that were mobilized in favor of drug-treatment programs.[87]

In public testimony before a House subcommittee in 1991, former First Lady Betty Ford criticized the George H. W. Bush administration for neglecting the scope of the alcohol problem. "The focus has shifted to cocaine and crack to the extent of ignoring alcohol, the No. 1 drug of addiction in this country," she protested.[88] Ford was a prominent advocate who in 1978 had sought treatment for alcoholism and prescription drug use. She included her recovery story in a memoir published later that year and cofounded in 1982 the treatment center that bore her name. The Betty Ford Center in California followed the Minnesota Model by treating patients with alcohol and drug problems together under the catch-all diagnosis of "chemical dependency." Like other Minnesota-inspired programs, the Ford Center emphasized the twelve steps and the twenty-eight-day stay, shunned maintenance drugs and other pharmaceutical treatments, and relied on the insurance payments from its middle- to upper-class clientele rather than on government support.[89] While government institutes continued to address alcohol and drug problems separately, private centers began treating compulsive alcohol and drug use as different symptoms of the same disease.

The Minnesota treatment center Hazelden, which had been founded for alcoholics and managed by a stalwart AA member until the mid-1960s, expanded both its client base and treatment methods in the 1970s and 1980s. The center integrated treatment for men and women; broadened its focus to the treatment of chemical dependencies and comorbidities such as depression; and added professional staff to individually tailor treatment plans rather than apply a one-size-fits-all AA model.[90] By the 1970s, Hazelden's publishing division had grown from a cottage industry to a cultural force.

It had originally served as an outlet for both AA-approved literature and daily meditation books in keeping with the AA traditions. By the 1980s, however, the publishing company was also doing robust business in meditation books geared to a variety of addictions (such as food) and demographics (including women and teens) as well as in educational materials for families and clinicians. Cultural studies scholar Trysh Travis notes that Hazelden's sales representatives successfully marketed its literature to for-profit hospital chains such as Charter Medical, Hospital Corporation of America, and Psychiatric Institutes of America, which were then expanding into the treatment field.[91]

Hospitals' interest in chemical-dependency treatment was inspired by the expansion of mandatory insurance coverage for addiction treatment in some states in the 1980s.[92] The newfound interest in addiction treatment among mainstream medical providers disrupted the practices of treatment workers, who had preferred to operate outside the medical establishment. Some treatment veterans such as Riley Regan, a state official in New Jersey whose career had begun in the 1960s, argued that managed-care firms and major hospitals confused inpatient and long-term residential care. The result was a system that favored ten days of inpatient treatment at a psychiatric hospital facility over a longer-term stay at a residential program.[93]

To investors in the 1980s, the standard treatment offered in both settings appeared identical: the twelve-step process. "The reality was that, even at $1,500 per day, programs were still providing AA in the morning, AA in the afternoon, and AA in the evening," said Regan.[94] Ironically, thanks in part to marketing by publisher-providers such as Hazelden and CompCare, twelve step had gained a foothold in hospitals and stayed there. Patients' length of stay grew shorter.

The case for TCs as a successful treatment model had relied on evidence that supported longer lengths of stay. The TC model was nearly synonymous with long-term, residential treatment. In order to adapt to the new economic climate, TC advocates began framing the TC as a peer-based treatment "method" rather than a residential-treatment setting.[95] The TC method could be applied in intensive outpatient programs as well as more traditional settings, such as residential centers and correctional facilities.

When the Clinton administration began developing a plan for universal health insurance, treatment leaders cautioned that a quick move to managed care would curtail access to services and widen the gap in the continuum of care. In 1993, 100 million people relied on publicly funded treatment programs. Yet that year an even larger population—160 million people—purchased treatment with private insurance. Regardless of whether the Clinton program became law, publicly funded providers would need to consider how to compete for insured clients.[96]

While pressure from insurers encouraged many residential addiction-treatment providers to adopt an acute-care treatment model, new scientific research in the 1990s began to frame addiction as a "chronic and relapsing brain disease" that should be managed rather than cured. In this new paradigm for addiction, a relapse could be viewed a sign of chronicity, not evidence of the futility of treatment.[97] But the brain-disease model of addiction initially failed to influence treatment financing; although the disease was considered chronic, insurers placed limits on chemical-dependency-treatment coverage. "Treatment works!" became providers' rallying cry even as they demanded more of it.[98]

In the traditional TC treatment philosophy, the community helped bring about a personality shift that was more or less permanent. Successful treatment meant no criminal recidivism and no readmissions. In contrast, the chronic brain-disease definition of addiction suggested that a lifelong cure was unrealistic. The more forgiving attitude came with some drawbacks, argued AA critic Stanton Peele, who was sympathetic to the TC model's emphasis on personal responsibility. In *The Diseasing of America*, Peele endorsed TC-based treatment over twelve step; unlike TCs, he argued, twelve-step programs encouraged adherents to see themselves as "powerless" over their choices and to craft an identity around learned helplessness.[99] Even worse, he later cautioned, the newest brain science funded by the federal government was being used to justify twelve-step philosophy.[100]

The disease model originally proposed in the canonical text *Alcoholics Anonymous* hypothesized that alcoholism was an "allergic reaction" that afflicted a minority of the population. Those who were susceptible experienced an intense compulsion to drink without regard for negative repercussions. The only solution for the condition was total abstinence;

otherwise, the disease would progress, and the compulsion to consume, amount ingested, and attendant consequences would grow.[101] Although the allergy theory was never substantiated, addiction researchers in the 1990s united around a new disease model that included not just alcoholism but other chemical addictions.

The historian David Courtwright calls this model the "NIDA brain disease paradigm" in honor of the federal institute that funded and promoted the research on it. Simply put, the NIDA paradigm frames addiction as a "chronic, relapsing brain disease with a social context, a genetic component, and significant comorbidity with other disorders."[102] Habitual substance use leads to observable changes in brain structure and function. The brain changes lead to behavioral ones—the most conspicuous of which is compulsive substance seeking despite negative consequences. Although the NIDA paradigm emerged under the leadership of institute chiefs Alan Leschner (1994–2001) and Nora Volkow (2003–present), it was a concept that the institute's first director, Robert Dupont, would also endorse.

In *The Selfish Brain*, published in 1997, Robert Dupont linked the brain based NIDA paradigm to the twelve-step treatment model. An addicted brain was imprudent and selfish; a recovering one was resilient and generous. Dupont disagreed with critics of AA who believed the twelve-step model was well supported by government agencies and the medical establishment. In fact, Dupont argued, the history of twelve-step fellowships "was exactly the opposite. Every one of these traditional institutions was initially skeptical" of twelve-step programs. Mutual-aid groups flourished "despite the opposition, or more often the neglect, of major social institutions, not because of their support."[103] But by the end of twentieth century, that negligence also came to an end.

By the 1990s, government officials and policy advocates began to call on people in recovery to publicly disclose their disease status and advocate for treatment. Why was there no "consumer movement" for drug-treatment clients on par with the efforts of breast cancer survivors, AIDS activists, or the National Alliance for the Mentally Ill? Alan Leschner, the NIDA chief, told a panel in 1997 that he was continually "struck by the lack of a public presence of people who have been successfully treated."[104] In the early 2000s, that presence would begin to take shape as the "recovery movement," a constituency committed to combating stigma and advocating for treatment and social services.

For TC pioneers, the claim that there were no successfully treated addicts advocating on their own behalf was another kind of brain malfunction: historical amnesia. The new calls for advocacy overlooked the experiences of TC treatment leaders over the previous three decades. In its earliest stage, the TC was "completely consumer-driven," reflected David Deitch in 2010. The residents shaped the business model and were responsive to social problems in the wider community. But as the model gained legitimacy, the alternative treatment became its own bureaucracy. "Careerists replaced 'change agents.' Staff counselors replaced careerists, and licensing or certification and funder demands created commercialism," said Deitch.[105]

In order to reinvigorate the field, treatment veterans sought to recapture the dynamism of the 1960s and early 1970s. "We have drifted too far from the community recovery model," argued Ken Schonlau, the head of a network of sober-living houses based in southern California, in 1997. Schonlau's editorial to treatment professionals argued that self-governed spaces that support "self-help learning" do a better job of recovery promotion than the traditional health-care system. "Community recovery managers are responsible for creating a 'recovery fever' that influences persons to be responsible for their own recovery," wrote Schonlau.[106] The wider recovery-movement energy would provide a boost to traditional TCs that came to work closely with the new advocacy groups, observed Deitch.[107]

For too long the frenzy that accompanied U.S. drug policies was driven by panic. In the 1980s, the panic played out as renewed calls for punishing and committing drug users. By the 1990s, many policy makers had forgotten the energetic advocacy that accompanied the struggle to establish a new structure for treating addiction just a few decades earlier. The "recovery-oriented" model of care that emerged in the mid-2000s presented community-based resources and recovering counselors or coaches as integral parts of the larger treatment system.[108] The system included hospital-based and residential treatment, but it didn't end there. The "recovery-oriented system of care" looked much like the NARA ideal of the 1960s: it emphasized social integration over incarceration, community-based treatment options over centralized ones, and continuity of service as people in treatment and recovery transition between different levels of care.

This era of treatment looked even more like the 1870s. Whereas the treatment efforts in the 1960s and 1970s had been fixated largely on heroin and marijuana use, both the chemical-dependency and the brain-disease models of addiction, like the inebriety theories of yore, viewed the compulsive use of *any* substance as a manifestation of the same condition. The private treatment industry targeted new markets in old vices, from gambling to gluttony, which professionals relabeled as "behavioral" addictions. Long-split addictions reconciled, and recovering advocates vowed to address every variety of disordered behavior.

THE RECOVERY MOVEMENT

The twelve-step model of mutual aid also expanded to support a variety of philosophical approaches to recovery. Those who found the traditional AA model too religious could find comfort in groups such as Rational Recovery and Secular Organizations for Sobriety. For believers who found AA too ecumenical, Milati Islami, Celebrate Recovery, and the Buddhist Recovery Network offered twelve-step programs adapted for their respective faith traditions. Feminist critics who considered AA male dominated founded Women for Sobriety and drafted "16 Steps for Discovery and Empowerment." The feminist steps began with empowerment, not powerlessness; the Buddhists started with mindfulness.[109] In the end, all the steps led to abstinence.

Although twelve-step groups are often blamed for promoting a prohibitionist agenda,[110] America's complicated relationship with abstinence has deeper roots. Today, the belief that some substances or behaviors should not be enjoyed even in moderation is associated with social conservatives. In actuality, the historian Jessica Warner notes, the ideal of abstinence has long suited radicals of every political persuasion—abolitionist Frederick Douglas, Communist Vladmir Lenin, pacificist and anticolonialist

Mahatma Gandhi, and feminist Andrea Dworkin all praised it—while also maintaining a broad-based American appeal.[111] Synanon members and some second-generation TC leaders may have been self-professed social radicals, but their drug-free treatment model found supporters because "zero tolerance" was far from a fringe idea. Even today, the number of Americans who voluntarily swear off alcohol and drugs surpasses the population of abstainers who identify as being in addiction recovery.[112] Early European observers described the American outlook as practical and unphilosophical; abstinence's appeal in the United States has been, perhaps unsurprisingly, pragmatic.[113]

Nonaddicts and anonymous group members alike commit to abstinence for several common reasons, Warner argues. The "just say no" doctrine is a soothingly simple one that spans faith traditions. Sacrificing baser pleasures creates a yearning that can be filled with more profoundly spiritual experiences. This spiritual experience of abstinence often arrives in the company of true friends and fellow abstainers. Thus, the pursuit of abstinence is also the pursuit of higher-order happiness.[114] "We are going to know a new freedom and a new happiness," AA's program promises. "Keep it simple. It works if you work it."[115]

In treatment and recovery communities, the instructions about which substances should be off-limits were less clear-cut. Could former heroin users learn to drink in moderation? Was opiate-replacement therapy an immature form of recovery? If positively reinforcing behaviors such as gambling, shopping, sex, and food consumption were also addictions, a person committed to abstinence-based recovery would need to be especially vigilant about trading one compulsive habit for another. Did authentic recovery entail abstinence in all things?

In the 1960s and 1970s, some treatment centers, including the TCs Daytop and Gateway, tried teaching "controlled drinking" to treatment clients. Moderate amounts of alcohol were a privilege that clients attained as they progressed in the recovery process. The results were mixed. Some former drug addicts developed alcohol problems, and most treatment centers soon swore off controlled drinking.[116]

Many centers also resisted maintenance medications. Although the anti-methadone rhetoric abated along with the heroin crisis of the late 1960s and early 1970s, the bias against maintenance therapies persisted, with the percentage of drug-treatment centers that offer methadone or bupenor-phine holding steady at about 9 percent well into the twenty-first century.[117] Even after prominent drug-free private treatment centers accepted maintenance, political and criminal-justice leaders often continued to oppose it. While Betty Ford and Hazelden adopted opioid-replacement therapy after their merger in 2012, drug courts often continued to mandate drug-free therapies.[118] In many courts, the bans on maintenance therapies lasted until 2015, when the Substance Abuse and Mental Health Services Administration announced it would refuse to fund states that prohibited maintenance.[119]

But if prescribed medications, properly used, could eventually be accepted by twelve-step and TC treatment providers as part of a recovered life, moderate, recreational use could not. As researchers began to shift their focus from addiction's harms to recovery's promises in the early 2000s, the official definitions of recovery that emerged carried on the abstinence-based tradition. The federal Center for Substance Abuse Treatment, the American Society for Addiction Medicine, and the Betty Ford Institute Consensus Panel made abstinence and sobriety conditions of their respective definitions of recovery.[120]

* * *

At first, the abstinence-based philosophy of recovery appeared incompatible with another grassroots advocacy movement that grew in the 1990s: harm reduction. "Harm reduction," wrote psychologist and supporter Alan Marlatt in 1996, "accepts the practical fact that many people use drugs and engage in other high-risk behaviors and that idealistic visions of a drug-free society are unlikely to become reality."[121] But accepting drug use did not mean accepting the harms often associated with it, and in the 1990s the most pressing public-health threat was AIDS. If actions short of total abstinence could improve the well-being of drug users and protect the public's health, harm reductionists argued, it was socially responsible to take them.

Some of these actions were controversial. To social conservatives, supplying condoms seemed to condone premarital sex, and allowing people to exchange used syringes for clean ones enabled illicit drug use. By the mid-1990s, epidemiological research had established that supplying condoms and clean needles helped bring down rates of human immunodefiency virus (HIV) transmission without driving up rates of drug use.[122] But the debate over harm-reduction activities was not purely academic; the scholars who studied needle-exchange programs did so with the help of radical drug-user allies.

The first needle-exchange programs in the United States were illegal. Government-approved programs led by user-activists were in place in the Netherlands by the mid-1980s, but even in the middle of the AIDS crisis harm reductionists in the United States faced resistance. They found their first partners in AIDS advocacy groups, not in the drug-treatment establishment.

The National AIDS Brigade was founded by the former heroin user and harm-reduction leader Jon Stuen-Parker in the early 1980s. Stuen-Parker had begun his career by distributing clean needles on the streets of New Haven, Connecticut, in 1983 while he was a student at Yale Medical School. The AIDS Brigade's needle-exchange services soon spread along the East Coast to Philadelphia, Boston, and New York. For Stuen-Parker and the first cohort of needle-exchange volunteers, the programs were a form of civil disobedience. Stuen-Parker's activism led to twenty-seven arrests in seven states throughout the 1980s and 1990s. In 1991, eight activists from the AIDS Coalition to Unleash Power were arrested for informally running a needle exchange in Manhattan's Lower East Side.[123]

The AIDS Coalition's program was a response to city leaders' inability to launch an official needle-exchange program. David Sencer, then the city's health commissioner, proposed distributing clean needles to drug users in 1985; Mayor Ed Koch publicly repudiated the idea. The health commissioner who followed Sencer, methadone-maintenance pioneer Herman Joseph, attempted to start a needle-exchange program as part of a clinical trial on the method's effectiveness. The trial, however, was first stymied by city and state leadership, then redesigned several times before opening to participants in 1988, and finally called to a halt in 1990 following criticism by both community groups and the George H. W. Bush administration.[124]

Yet needle-exchange programs gained legitimacy in other locations. In Tacoma, Washington, drug counselor David Purchase began handing out clean syringes in 1988. He had the support of the city's police commissioner, and within five months he had singlehandedly distributed thirteen thousand needles to drug users throughout the region.[125] In the early 1990s, programs popped up elsewhere on the West Coast in places such as the San Francisco Bay Area.[126] "Harm reduction is coming to the USA," University of Washington psychologist Alan Marlatt predicted in 1996.[127] After it arrived, however, it would take on a different character than it had in Europe.

In the Netherlands, state-sponsored needle exchange was a response to a drug-user union, Junkiebond (Junkie League), that was founded in 1980. Government input from the advocacy group led to the first needle-exchange program in Amsterdam in 1984; with the threat of HIV transmission imminent, the number of exchanged syringes grew from 100,000 in 1985 to 720,000 in 1988. That same year the U.S. Congress passed the Health Omnibus Program Extension Act (or HOPE Act), which funded HIV-prevention and treatment programs but prohibited the use of federal funds for needle-exchange programs.[128]

The rationale for opposing needle-exchange programs was based on abstinence. Opinion polls showed that people who attended church at least once a week or identified as conservative, Republican, or southern were significantly more likely to believe needle-exchange programs increase drug use.[129] Distributing clean needles undermines the social message that drug use is "morally wrong," said George H. W. Bush's drug adviser Robert Martinez.[130] Despite his misgivings, Martinez decided to investigate harm reductionists' empirical claims. In 1991, Martinez and Bill Roper, the director of the Centers for Disease Control and Prevention, commissioned a review of the data on needle-exchange programs. The external review was conducted by the Universities of California at Berkeley and San Francisco. Researchers found overwhelming evidence that needle-exchange programs prevented HIV infection, did not inspire higher rates of drug use, and even functioned as an entry point to addiction treatment.[131]

These findings were no more politically tolerable to President Clinton, however, and his administration suppressed the report. In 1998, after suppression of the report became national news, Clinton and Secretary for Health and Human Services Donna Shalala publicly acknowledged the effectiveness of needle-exchange programs but refused to lift the ban on federal funding.[132] Some individuals in the drug-treatment and prevention establishment supported that stance.

Federal funding for needle-exchange programs "enables" drug abuse, wrote Phoenix House president Mitchell Rosenthal to Barry McCaffrey, the director of the Clinton administration's Office of National Drug Control Policy. Rosenthal argued that needle-exchange programs work *against* the goal of bringing users into treatment. He expressed concern that federal funding for harm-reduction programs would draw resources away from comprehensive residential treatment programs.[133] Sue Rusche, the executive director of the antidrug parent group Families in Action, concurred: "We believe federal funds must be spent to move addicts into treatment, which research shows provides the best protection against HIV transmission."[134]

In order to overcome opposition, harm-reduction advocates in the United States made two central arguments. The first framed harm reduction as a public-health issue: preventing the transmission of HIV, by whatever means, protected the body politic from the spread of a fatal disease.[135] Yet critics who accepted the validity of the epidemiological research could still object to needle-exchange programs on moral grounds. The nation could not "allow our concern for AIDS to undermine our determination to win the war on drugs," said drug czar Martinez.[136]

The second argument was abstinence based. Clean needles could be used as a way to attract active drug users to treatment programs and connect them with other health and social services.[137] Unlike in the Netherlands, where users were unionized and drug use a more legitimate lifestyle choice, U.S. supporters presented harm-reduction tactics as the first step on the path to treatment—and, ideally, to abstinence. In a newsletter published by the National Harm Reduction Coalition following its first conference in 1995, the cover article described the "gulf between harm reduction and drug treatment" as "artificial."[138] Harm reduction and drug treatment exist on a continuum, the newsletter claimed. Most treatment programs already employed some form of harm reduction, whether through maintenance therapies or strategies for making small, initial behavioral changes. Harm-reduction programs were beginning to add more comprehensive therapeutic services and reckon with the spiritual and psychological harms that drug use could cause. Although the spiritual orientation of twelve-step programs could alienate some drug users, the article concluded, "for others it has achieved healing, transformation, joy, and community that transcends the often reductive and utilitarian language" of the first argument in favor of harm reduction.[139]

Like twelve-step treatment centers, needle exchanges often enlisted recovered addicts as program workers. Howard Josepher had graduated from Odyssey House and worked in both Phoenix House and Daniel Casriel's private psychotherapy institute before founding a harm-reduction-based treatment project in New York in the late 1980s. Josepher saw harm reduction's "peer counselors" as similar to the "paraprofessional" employees of historical TCs; his first employee was a Phoenix House graduate. In 2015, he spoke proudly of a fifty-year career in treatment advocacy that began with his TC experience. "We spoke up," said Josepher. "We brought the message of successful treatment out to the public through speaking engagements and the media. We wanted people to know [that] addiction could be overcome and [that] we, the early participants in the TCs, were examples of that transcendence. Our advocacy efforts were incredibly successful as treatment centers began opening all over the world."[140]

But as ex-addicts evolved into recovery advocates at the turn of the twenty-first century, Josepher came to view the movement's focus on abstinence as limiting. For Josepher and a growing group of more open-minded advocates, the celebration of abstinence discouraged people from seeking treatment and limited available treatment options.[141] Besides, the population of people who identified as being in long-term, abstinence-based recovery was too small to sustain a social movement alone. Treatment and recovery advocates always had to appeal to political allies.

Most people with substance-use problems resolve them without treatment, twelve-step involvement, or interaction with harm-reduction providers. Yet since the 1960s researchers and policy makers have focused on a subset of serious cases: people in treatment or in need of it. Ex-addict testimonials had highlighted the dire consequences of substance use by graphically portraying the recovery process as a crisis point that led to a transformative treatment experience. When the advocacy group Faces and Voices of Recovery conducted public-opinion research on recovery in the early 2000s, it found that most people did not have a positive view of the term *recovery*. Survey respondents thought "recovery" meant that someone was trying but failing to stop using drugs. They associated it with relapse.[142]

Faces and Voices decided to revise the message. The group's guidelines for "recovery messaging" to the press jettisoned the words *addict* and *alcoholic*, the twelve steps, and the disease concept of addiction. The talking points smoothed over conflicts between treatment and recovery approaches by omitting an academic definition of recovery. The personal definition in Faces and Voices's message, however, was clear. The template provided by the group directed people in recovery to emphasize two key points: long-term abstinence and life fulfillment.[143]

Greg Williams, director of the documentary *The Anonymous People* (2013) and leader of the ManyFaces1Voice public-relations campaign, became a spokesperson after a training session sponsored by Faces and Voices of Recovery. In promotional interviews about his documentary, Williams used the group's template: "Today at the level of press, I identify like this: My name is Greg Williams, and I am a person in long-term recovery, and that means I haven't used alcohol or drugs since I was 17. The goal is to reframe our message for our communities, for our elected officials and for the media. I walked out of that training and for the first time in my life, I felt good about telling someone on a train or telling a reporter my story. I had been given a language of empowerment."[144]

For the new wave of recovering advocates, empowerment included fighting for well-established causes such as access to addiction treatment, insurance parity, and federal funding for peer-support services. As the movement gained ground, advocates also began to call for more politicized drug-policy reforms, such as restoring voting rights for people with drug convictions, changing drug-sentencing laws, and shifting resources from prisons to community-based support services.[145]

According to the Faces and Voices founding statement in 2001, the policy changes would be built on personal stories. "Only when Americans have a sound appreciation of recovery, and fully understand the recovery process, will laws and policies be effectively changed to reduce discrimination and lower barriers to recovery services," the statement concluded.[146] In his keynote address at the organization's founding meeting, Senator Paul Wellstone (D–MN) called the coalition "the beginning of a new civil rights movement."[147] Summit leaders mobilized around a shared identity—being in recovery—and planned to bring about change through media messaging and community organizing.

* * *

Months before the first Faces and Voices summit, George W. Bush was narrowly elected on a platform of "compassionate conservatism," a domestic-policy philosophy that was compatible with support for faith-based community recovery groups. On the campaign trail, Bush anticipated aspects of the activist message. Candidate Bush admitted having problems with alcohol and became an abstainer at the age of forty following his conversion to Southern Baptism and the Reverend Billy Graham's spiritual counseling. At a campaign stop at the faith-based, boot-camp treatment program Teen Challenge, Bush told the audience, "I'm on a walk just like you. I understand. I used to drink too much and I quit drinking. I want you to know that your life's walk is shared by a lot of other people, even some who wear suits."[148]

Only one part of the message was missing: Bush never identified as a person in recovery. His conversion experience and ability to quit cold turkey made him skeptical about investing in Texas's prison-based recovery programs during his tenure as governor. "No program works unless somebody wants it to work, and the question is, how do you create the will in somebody's soul to want to be sober?" he said. As governor of Texas, Bush concluded that you couldn't; "most adult criminals, are, sad to say, beyond much chance of rehabilitation."[149]

As president, Bush continued to support incarceration for drug offenders. He appointed Straight founder Melvin Sembler as ambassador to Italy and William Bennett's former chief of staff John Walters as the director of the Office of National Drug Control Policy. Walters viewed government-supported drug treatment as a liberal folly and publicly denounced the "therapy-only lobby" in the weeks before his confirmation hearings in 2001.[150] But while Bennett and Walters continued to argue that prison was the best solution to the "moral poverty" of substance use and associated crime, Bush's view began to soften during his presidency.[151]

* * *

In the 1980s and 1990s, punitive drug policies and the rise of managed care led to serious disparities in access to addiction treatment. Community-based resources were difficult to come by, and formal treatment outside the criminal-justice system increasingly required public or private insurance coverage.[152] In the 2000s, advocates successfully lobbied to address these gaps with recovery-based resources.

Bush created the Office of Faith Based Initiatives and encouraged giving federal dollars to faith-based recovery groups.[153] In 2003, his State of the Union Address outlined the Access to Recovery program. The program provided block grants to states for peer-based recovery programs and vouchers for addicts to use in the treatment marketplace.[154] By the end of Bush's second term, forty states were reorganizing social services according to a new model called "recovery-oriented systems of care."[155] In 2008, the president signed Paul Wellstone (D–MN) and Pete Domenici's (R–NM) Mental Health Parity and Addiction Act into law, ensuring that most health-insurance plans for addiction treatment would be no more restrictive than plans for other medical or surgical services.[156]

After Democrat Barack Obama took office in 2009, his "drug policy for the 21st century" included another victory for recovery advocates. The Office of National Drug Control Policy presented the president's first three strategic priorities—prevention, treatment, and criminal-justice-system reforms—as a progressive breakthrough in the nation's lengthy drug war.[157] In fact, since Nixon's first term, each of these three strategies had factored into presidential drug policy, with varying degrees of emphasis and alternating tactics for accomplishing each one.

But the fourth strategy established by the Office of National Drug Control Policy under President Obama was unprecedented. The administration aimed to lift the century-old "stigma associated with those in recovery or suffering from substance use disorders."[158] This strategy promised to channel the optimism of the new recovery movement to bring about a cultural shift in society's attitude toward people with substance-use disorders.

A reversal of attitudes about people who use substances would be a radical cultural change; the stigma against illicit substance use remains deeply rooted in American culture. The pejorative term *junkie* hailed from New York in the 1920s, where the heroin users who supported their habit by selling cast-off scrap metal became associated with their disposable wares.[159] In the 1960s, sociologists defined *stigma* as a form of "spoiled" identity, in which an individual's character is discredited through the revelation of previous addictive behaviors or other socially undesirable experiences.[160] Synanon's "dope fiends" and second-generation TC leaders recovered their respectability by marketing a moral model of addiction treatment. But they lost something in the bargain: their campaigns rarely challenged the assumption that they were lesser humans to begin with.

Breakthroughs in brain research aside, most Americans today still do not view the behavior of people who use substances as a purely medical problem. In 2013, a survey of public attitudes about people with drug addiction found respondents were significantly more likely to endorse discriminatory policies, such as unequal access to employment and housing and limited support for treatment, for people with drug addiction than for people with other mental illnesses. A significant majority of respondents (60 percent) believed treatment for addiction to be ineffective, compared to a minority (40 percent) who held that view for mental illness.[161] The stigma associated with this sick population continues to "spoil" the perception of the treatment system that serves them.

If the recovery revolution of the twenty-first century is a new civil rights movement, modeled on campaigns for racial equality, women's rights, and gay rights, then social justice will require dramatic changes in public attitudes. Yet the treatment system's turmoil since the 1960s should make current advocates cautious about symbolic progress. Personal recovery stories can be made to serve almost any political agenda, and, as Faces and Voices researchers discovered, testimonials that were once effective can be turned against the interests of the people who need help.

When Michael Botticelli, a recovering alcoholic and Massachusetts public-health leader, was confirmed as the director of the Office of National Drug Policy under Obama, he accepted "an honor I never dreamed about 26 years ago, when my substance use disorder had become so acute that I was handcuffed to a hospital bed."[162] After Botticelli recovered, the eradication of stigma became the defining goal of his drug policy.

The most significant barrier facing people with substance-use disorders today is no longer the absence of a treatment system, wrote Botticelli. The passage of the Patient Protection and Affordable Care Act in 2010 marked the largest expansion in addiction-treatment access since the 1960s and early 1970s. The law ensured that more than 60 million Americans would have coverage for addiction-treatment services. Yet only one in nine Americans who meets the diagnostic criteria for substance-use disorder receives treatment for it. According to Botticelli, the other eight are held back by shame, not by the availability of treatment.

Treatment-system advancements "are not enough unless we fundamentally change the way we think about people with addiction," Botticelli declared.[163] If this assessment is correct, recovery activists will be engaged in changing cultural stereotypes and connecting with mainstream health-care providers rather than in building new treatment centers. The recovery revolution of the twenty-first century will be postindustrial.

CONCLUSION

The Revolution's Aftermath

S EATED ON A threadbare sofa in a Victorian-style halfway house in Lynn, Massachusetts, Michael Botticelli made a public confession. "I have a criminal record," Botticelli told a *Washington Post* reporter to the applause of the recovering residents.[1] Botticelli explained that he had hit bottom in 1988 after a drunk-driving accident on the Massachusetts turnpike. He thought he lost control of the car while smoking a cigarette but had a hazy memory of the details. When he awoke in the hospital, he was under arrest.

In the coming months, Botticelli found solace in a special-interest twelve-step meeting for gay men and lesbians. After achieving recovery, he met the man who would become his husband and shifted careers, moving from college administration to the Massachusetts Department of Public Health's HIV-prevention and substance-abuse services.[2] By the time the *Washington Post* decided to interview Botticelli in 2014, he had been promoted from deputy to acting director of the Office of National Drug Control Policy under President Barack Obama. The president had promised to abandon drug-war rhetoric and adopt a public-health approach to substance use. Botticelli was the antithesis of Bill Bennett; the *Post* heralded Botticelli as the "embodiment" of the president's treatment-friendly drug policy.[3] Reporters wrote that Botticelli was a "celebrity" and a "rock star" in the recovery community.[4] Even politicians celebrated his personal history; when he was promoted from acting to actual director in February 2015, the congressional confirmation of his nomination was unanimous. Michael Botticelli became the first drug-policy director since the 1970s with direct experience in the addiction-treatment field.

Botticelli's progressive state programs first caught the attention of his predecessor, former Seattle police chief Gil Kerlikowske, toward the end of Obama's first term. Under Botticelli's watch as director of substance-abuse services, Massachusetts carried out a major expansion of addiction treatment in community health centers, a policy that Obama endorsed through his health-care reform legislation, the Patient Protection and Affordable Care Act of 2010. Botticelli also piloted a new naloxone program in which police dispensed the drug to people dangerously close to dying from heroin or prescription-drug overdoses.[5] The naloxone intervention was a novel solution to the rising rate of overdose deaths, which had been growing since the widespread marketing of prescription opioids such as Oxycontin in the 1990s. Nearly two decades later, the public-health problem demanded federal attention. In 2013, the Centers for Disease Control and Prevention announced that prescription-drug overdoses had surpassed car crashes as the nation's leading cause of accidental death.[6]

The expansion of prescription opioid use in the early twenty-first century eventually affected the illicit heroin market as younger, white drug users and middle-class women, for reasons of convenience and cost, shifted substances. As the commissioner of New York City's Department of Health and Mental Hygiene in the early 2000s, future Centers for Disease Control and Prevention director Tom Frieden watched the death toll from both substances climb. New York and Boston, the urban centers where Frieden and Botticelli built their careers, were among the first cities to experience the effects of a resurgent heroin market.[7] Renewed calls for decriminalization and publicly funded addiction treatment invited comparisons to the heroin epidemic of the 1970s, when rising rates of drug use among white, middle-class youth helped inspire government support for treatment.[8] But by the time Barack Obama took office and Frieden took the helm of the Centers for Disease Control and Prevention in 2009, the number of opioid fatalities had surpassed the death count during the influ-ential drug-abuse epidemic a generation earlier. With its medical origins, the new epidemic more closely resembled that of the late 1800s.[9]

In the second half of the nineteenth century, opioid consumption rose by more than 500 percent, reaching a peak in the mid-1890s. Although the epidemic's causes were varied, medicine played a major role. Effective treat-ments were scarce, so physicians relied on morphine to address everything from injuries to diarrhea. By alleviating any form of pain, opiates appealed to both doctors and patients. But catch-all opiate treatment came with a negative side effect: it was also addictive.[10]

In the late 1800s, medical providers even used opiates to treat alcoholism and other addictions. Before modern pharmaceutical regulations, purvey-ors of patent medicines laced their inebriety cures with opium—a recipe for repeat business. As scientific medicine developed and the harms asso-ciated with addiction became evident, medical authorities and progressive policy makers began to rein in drug use. Physicians willingly scaled back their prescribing practices; Victorian reformers in the United States and the United Kingdom called for better market regulations.[11]

But reform efforts took a harsh turn following World War I as regula-tions became prohibitions. Inebriety institutions, tarnished by allegations of quackery and a loss of confidence in their services, closed their doors. Substance use was addressed as a crime, and the demand for medical spe-cialists to treat it diminished.

A century later, the specialized addiction-treatment industry once again became vulnerable. The Affordable Care Act incentivized the inte-gration of substance-abuse services with mainstream medical treatment and threatened the funding structure of addiction-treatment organizations that primarily relied on federal block grants.[12] The $12 billion in Medicaid predicted to go to addiction treatment was poised to help dismantle the current treatment system—not in favor of simple criminal-justice solu-tions, as occurred in the 1920s, but in favor of more traditional medical ones.[13]

DISSOLUTION AND CONSOLIDATION

Addiction-treatment researchers predicted that the Affordable Care Act would "revolutionize" care for substance-use disorders by putting an end to the "segregated" system of behavioral health care.[14] Ex-addicts successfully rebuilt the treatment field in the 1960s, but their separatism meant that the treatment industry of the late twentieth century operated outside traditional medical settings. Even insurance for substance-use disorders was carved out and managed apart from larger plans that covered other medical conditions. "The system and the patients within it were stigmatized, segregated, and marginalized," conclude treatment researchers Thomas McLellan and Abigail Mason Woodworth, who believe that dynamic is due for a shift. "Skeptics may note that mainstream healthcare has never shown either the ability or inclination to integrate care for these stigmatized disorders. Many doubt that true integration will ever happen. This is a bad bet." To McLellan and Woodworth, the best corporate analogy for the contemporary treatment system is Kodak, not Coke: the film camera was a late-nineteenth-century innovation rendered obsolete by technological developments and market changes.[15]

More than one market force threatens the current treatment system. The Affordable Care Act classified addiction as a chronic disease and treatment as an essential health service. The expansion of Medicaid could provide many more individuals with access to health insurance for addiction treatment, yet most traditional addiction-treatment providers are not equipped to bill Medicaid for their services. Traditional addiction-treatment providers also face increased competition from primary-care providers and community health centers that already possess electronic health records and clinicians with medical degrees. Most states have done little to help addiction-treatment programs adapt to these changes.[16]

Researchers predict that the push to integrate substance-abuse treatment with other medical services will place additional pressure on treatment centers to employ credentialed providers and evidence-based treatments. "The era of 'anything goes' in addiction treatment seems to be coming to end," wrote alcoholism treatment researchers William Miller and Theresa

Moyers in 2014.[17] Whether the complete standardization of addiction treatment is possible or desirable is another question. Recent research suggests that treatment matching—the fit between the client and the type of treatment—may be even more important than the treatment model. Outcomes can vary widely between different sites that employ the same "evidence-based" treatment. Relational factors, such as the interactions between the client and clinician, are just as powerful as institutional ones. The possible consolidation of addiction treatment around a single model concerns some providers.[18] A one-size-fits-all medical solution will be ill suited to some populations.

The traditional TC will probably not be tomorrow's treatment standard. The expansion of addiction treatment is predicated on targeting a larger number of preclinical individuals who can modify their behavior after short-term interventions;[19] longer-term TC treatment has historically been tailored to people with acute, chronic substance-abuse histories. To remain relevant, TCs have expanded beyond their historical roots, adding shorter-term treatments, outpatient counseling, and integrated HIV-treatment and prevention services. The trend in the field is to grow or to close.[20] Cenikor recently formed an alliance with Odyssey House; Samaritan Village acquired Daytop.[21] Phoenix House partnered with the twelve-step center Hazelden, which had already merged with Betty Ford.[22]

Yet these institutional developments haven't rendered past efforts by recovering addicts obsolete; in recent years, peer-based care has also emerged as an affordable adjunct to medical treatment. According to the historian William White, as addiction counseling was "colonized" by mainstream medicine, the "recovery coach" began to carry the experiential knowledge that had originally characterized the counseling field.[23]

RECOVERY COACHES AND THE SERVICE ECONOMY

Unlike counselors, who offer credentialed psychological treatment, recovery coaches describe themselves as "cheerleaders" and "beacons of hope."[24] Although the percentage of credentialed addiction counselors in recovery has been declining for decades, according to White, coaches "carr[y] the torch" ignited by the generation of ex-addict counselors in the 1960s.[25] They preserve the tradition of ex-addict counseling by serving as role models and offering practical advice about self-care, employment, and educational pursuits. Unlike twelve-step sponsors, who are unpaid, coaches usually draw a small income and can be counted on to provide support for people reentering society after a treatment episode.[26] They serve as a relatively inexpensive form of relapse prevention (and relapses can be costly).

The potential cost savings has inspired some states to use new Medicaid dollars to pay peer counselors.[27] Even conservative states, such as Texas, which resisted the expansion of Medicaid under the Affordable Care Act, have recently invested in coaching.[28] Coaches' supporters hope that providing extra help during the transition from treatment to aftercare will result in fewer emergency-room visits and better economic prospects for program participants. Promoters present the service as a proven method for coping with a chronic condition; contemporary addiction-recovery support is often modeled on other public-health programs for the self-management of diabetes, HIV, and mental illness.[29]

The self-management programs are part of a larger movement; in the late twentieth century, the chronic-disease burden in the United States grew, and society shifted the responsibility for health-behavior modification from institutions to individuals.[30] Although both insurance for addiction treatment and the treatment marketplace are expected to increase, access to hospital stays and residential centers is no longer the primary goal of treatment reform. Leaders in the treatment field have expressed conflicting responses to this development, either mourning a treatment system lost to "neoliberalism" or celebrating the new system that might replace it.

The new system will be a product of the twenty-first-century service economy. While Synanon and some second-generation TCs created responsible citizens and churned out products to support their therapeutic enterprises, the U.S. economy began to move away from manufacturing and toward services such as health, hospitality, and education. The turn of the twenty-first century saw a decline in corporate benefits and salaried work and a rise in outsourced labor and independent contracting.[31] Recovery coaches might be kindling the spark from the past treatment revolution, but they do so under the conditions of contemporary contract work: Hazelden offers online coaching for people transitioning out of treatment; wealthy New Yorkers put personal coaches on retainer rather than suffer through twelve-step meetings; Odyssey House offers alumnae a small stipend for work as coaches.[32] Unlike the TC leaders of decades past, who were embedded in (and indebted to) their institutional cultures, recovery coaches operate as free agents.

Critics of this recovery movement argue that reorganizing the current treatment system in this way is not an expression of optimism; instead, it represents a lack of political will to provide more long-term, intensive support for a marginalized and chronically ill group.[33] The nation should focus on improving specially designated institutions for addiction and mental-health treatment, not on dismantling them: "Bring back the asylum," argued three bioethicists in the *Journal of the American Medical Association* in 2015.[34]

Some recovery advocates would rather leave the privileged status of specialized treatment institutions in the past. Perhaps, treatment researcher and clinician Keith Humphreys concludes, treatment is not the gateway to recovery, and coaching is more than an exit strategy from in-patient treatment. Many people alter their substance-use behavior with peer support alone, with pastoral counseling, or with short-term criminal-justice programs, writes Humphreys. "Though the idea that treatment is the royal route to change is at one level self-aggrandizing, in the long run it sets us professionals up for failure," he concludes; when a new drug epidemic appears, treatment providers may be blamed for the mounting deaths.[35] In punitive drug-policy cycles, such as the period from the 1920s until the 1960s, treatment can get caught in the crackdown. If history is a reliable guide, rebuilding a treatment system for a third time would probably not be a painless venture.

REVOLUTIONARY CONCLUSIONS

One can define revolution as a return, coming full circle to a point of origin. Revolutionaries are often energized by the notion of starting over again or beginning anew; they are motivated by the nostalgic vision that past ideals will be fulfilled.[36] Synanon promoters overlaid a psychedelic soundtrack on nineteenth-century images of inebriety.[37] Second-generation TC leaders similarly repurposed the previous century's romantic principles. At a conference held at the second-generation TC Walden House, Daytop executive Monsignor O'Brien quoted Henry David Thoreau and then declared, "It is in the therapeutic community that a true revolution of the spirit takes place and we must never lose this."[38] Revolutionary leaders promise to turn a cyclical history into a progressive one.

Historians have more comprehensive criteria for defining revolution. Revolutions need a leader (or leaders) with a clear vision of social justice. A leader needs rhetorical and organizational skills to shape public sentiment and inspire change. But ideology alone isn't revolutionary; revolutionary ideas must translate into forcible attempts to change the government or create new political institutions. Radical social movements that can't win allies or effect institutional change remain on the fringes of society. They fail to qualify as revolutions.[39]

Radical leaders who launch full-scale revolutions go down in history as heroes (if their revolutions are viewed as successful) or villains (if not). The outcome of a revolution, like its heroes and villains, depends on the historical vantage point, and it is not easy to discern when the outcome should be assessed. Every historian's judgment is clouded by the present. Most recent accounts of treatment have been written in the shadow of the global drug war of the 1980s and 1990s. They tend to present abstinence-based treatment as a form of government control and social oppression.[40]

In the end, is the outcome of the recovery revolution a disaster—the worst abuses of the drug-free treatment industry, the punitive antidrug policies of the drug war? Or is it a restoration—the revival of community-based recovery advocacy, the changing public opinions about mass incarceration and minor drug offenses in the 2000s? Recovery revolutionaries are undoubtedly responsible for the growing availability of addiction treatment over the past half century. Are they also accountable for the specialized treatment industry's possible demise?

Revolutionary cycles defy simplistic interpretations. It is still too soon to tell whether the recovery revolution has reached its conclusion.

THE FUTURE OF RECOVERY

Although recovery concepts occasionally appear in popular culture, recovery communities remain subcultures, unified by shared storytelling practices and often-repeated slogans. *"Fake it till you make it." "One day at a time." "Growing old is mandatory; growing up is optional."* The slogans are a kind of indigenous language; like the slang used by other subaltern groups, they reflect larger cultural standards with the wry humor of the exiled.[41] They have been called the "language of the heart" and understood as a primitive form of cognitive behavioral therapy. They have been critiqued as clichés, as brainwashing, and as covert politics—and they may be all of these things.[42] Yet the stories we tell about recovery have repercussions for drug policy. From that perspective, the most promising proverb might be *"We're all recovering from something."*

The term *recovery* can refer to a rebounding stock market after an economic recession, to a period of healing following a sports injury, or to capturing a space capsule after a flight. But say the word, and most audiences associate it with addiction. Activists' current attempt to present the concept in a more positive light is a reactionary strategy for combating the entrenched social stigma of substance-use disorders.

In a recent interview, TC veteran Howard Josepher redefined recovery as a process that includes any movement in a positive, life-affirming direction; abstinence is not a prerequisite.[43] We might also be more open-minded about the negative state that recovery is countering. Addiction, whether its source is the brain or society, is essentially a form of suffering. It is driven by the urge to alter consciousness—a uniquely human compulsion that is not likely to be eradicated anytime soon. Perhaps people struggling with addiction are not subhuman, but rather too human: an uncomfortable reflection of our species' faulty mental wiring, a challenge to our illusion of self-determination, and an expression of naked pain. No wonder their stories are so often sensationalized.

Breaking the tradition of the punitive approaches to addiction needs to begin by abandoning the premise that people who use substances compulsively are constitutional criminals. If addiction treatment is to be successfully integrated into mainstream medicine, providers need to overcome their prejudices: surveys show most physicians still have negative biases about treating people with substance-use disorders.[44] Addiction-treatment professionals and recovery advocates, who are often subject to charges of patient exploitation and therapeutic dogma, should continue to be careful of the company they keep. A fully realized recovery revolution would not only bring about the expansion of treatment access and the repeal of punitive drug laws. It would also result in an enduring reversal of attitudes about people with addiction—in a society that no longer needs the hard sell.

ACKNOWLEDGMENTS

M Y FIRST DEBT of gratitude is to David Courtwright, Charles Devlin, Howard Kushner, and Wendy Williams. This work would not have been possible without their guidance and insight.

I have also benefitted from the assistance of many colleagues, sources, family members, and friends. Some read material and offered feedback; some helped navigate the publication process; some shared resources, records, and memories; and some provided shelter and moral support. I am grateful to Susan Anderson, Bill Bailey, Pat Beachamin, Matthew Bernstein, Peter Bourne, Harold Braswell, Richard Buckman, Nancy Campbell, David Cantor and Barbara Harkins, Marcus Chatfield, Amy Hildreth Chen, Bridget Clark, Ron Clark, Tom Cole, Elena Conis, Michael Darcy, David Deitch, George De Leon, Ted Dibble, Emily Dufton, Sidney Finkelstein, Emily Howorth, Guy Hall, David Herzberg, Jerome Jaffe, Howard Josepher, Warren Katz, Andrew Kolotny, Gary Laderman, Lindsey and Michael Lawrence, Philip Leventhal, Marianne Marcus, Grischa Metlay, Shan Muktar, Rod Mullen, Adam and Colleen November, Simon Padmanabhan, Michael Pickering, Richard Pruss, Paul Roman, Mitchell Rosenthal, Joe Spillane, John Stallone, Luke Walden and J. P. Olsen, Harry Wexler, Bill White, and Ron Williams.

The Synanon Archives Trust is working to preserve a remarkable collection of multimedia material and make it accessible to researchers; I am grateful to the trust and to the National Film Preservation Foundation for funding a proposal for the digitization of a promotional film from the early 1970s.

Portions of chapter 4 originally appeared in the article "'Chemistry Is the New Hope': Therapeutic Communities and Methadone Maintenance, 1965–1971," in *Social History of Alcohol and Drugs: An Interdisciplinary Journal* 26, no. 2 (2012): 192–216, and are republished here with permission.

This research was generously supported by several grants: a Thayer Fellowship from the University of California at Los Angeles, a Pisano Travel Grant from the National Institutes of Health's Office of History, and a Competitive Research Grant from Emory University. I fortunately received fellowship support from Emory University and from the McGovern Center for Humanities and Ethics at the University of Texas. The Department of Behavioral Science in the College of Medicine at the University of Kentucky provided an ideal environment for bringing this book to completion.

Above all, I am grateful to my parents, Mike Clark and Molly Ducharme, for instilling in me a love of learning and a persistent curiosity about the 1960s. This book is dedicated to them.

APPENDIX
HISTORICAL ACTORS

HARRY J. ANSLINGER, antidrug crusader and first commissioner of the Federal Bureau of Narcotics

JAMES "LUKE" AUSTIN, Cenikor founder

ART BARKER, Seed founder

KEN BARUN, Cenikor leader, Nancy Reagan staffer

ABRAHAM BEAME, Democratic mayor of New York City (1974–1977)

WILLIAM "BILL" BENNETT, drug-policy adviser to President George H. W. Bush

MICHAEL BOTTICELLI, public-health leader, primary drug-policy adviser to President Barack Obama

BERTRAM BROWN, psychiatrist, director of the National Institute of Mental Health

GEORGE H. W. BUSH, forty-first president of the United States (1989–1993)

GEORGE W. BUSH, forty-third president of the United States (2001–2009)

DANIEL CASRIEL, psychiatrist, Synanon scholar, Daytop cofounder

FRANK CHURCH, Democratic US senator, Idaho (1957–1980)

BILL CLINTON, forty-second president of the United States (1993–2001)

SIDNEY COHEN, psychiatrist, drug researcher, and first director of the Division of Narcotic Addiction and Drug Abuse at the National Institute of Mental Health

HAROLD T. CONRAD, associate director of the Division of Narcotic Addiction and Drug Abuse, National Institute of Mental Health; hospital chief at the Lexington Narcotic Hospital

CHARLES "CHUCK" DEDERICH, Synanon founder and leader

DAVID DEITCH, Synanon resident, Daytop leader

GEORGE DE LEON, psychologist, therapeutic-community researcher

JUDIANNE DENSEN-GERBER, psychiatrist, Odyssey House founder

THOMAS DODD SR., Democratic US senator, Connecticut (1959–1970)

VINCENT DOLE, MARIE NYSWANDER, researchers, methadone-maintenance pioneers

JEFFREY DONFELD, adviser to President Richard Nixon

ROBERT DUPONT, psychiatrist, first director of the National Institute on Drug Abuse; primary drug-policy adviser to Presidents Richard Nixon and Gerald Ford

SAM ERVIN, Democratic US senator, North Carolina (1954–1974)

WILLIAM FINE, media mogul, Phoenix House board member

BETTY FORD, First Lady of the United States (1974–1977)

THOMAS "BUDDY" GLEATON, SUE RUSCHE, MARTHA "KEITH" SCHUHARD, parent-movement leaders

CHARLIE HAMER, early Synanon member

HAROLD HUGHES, Democratic US senator, Iowa (1969–1974)

JEROME JAFFE, psychiatrist, first chief of the Special Action Office of Drug Abuse Prevention under President Nixon

HOWARD JOSEPHER, Odyssey House and Phoenix House counselor, harm-reduction treatment pioneer

EDWARD "TED" KENNEDY, Democratic US senator, Massachusetts (1969–1974)

JOHN F. KENNEDY, thirty-fifth president of the United States (1961–1963)

EGIL "BUD" KROGH, adviser to President Richard Nixon

CANDY LATSON, Synanon member, later therapeutic-community pioneer

ALAN LESCHNER, director of the National Institute on Drug Abuse

JOHN LINDSAY, Republican and then Democratic mayor of New York City (1966–1973)

DOUGLAS LIPTON, criminologist

DONALD IAN MACDONALD, physician, Straight supporter, drug-policy adviser to President Ronald Reagan

JOHN MAHER, Synanon resident, Delancey Street founder

BOB MARTINEZ, Republican governor of Florida (1987–1991), drug-policy adviser to President George H. W. Bush

ABRAHAM MASLOW, father of humanistic psychology

RICHARD MCGEE, first director of the California Department of Corrections (1944–1961); first administrator of the California Youth and Adult Correctional Agency (1961–1967)

ROD MULLEN AND NAYA ARBITER, Synanon residents, Amity Foundation founders

MILLER NEWTON, drug-treatment counselor, clinical director for Straight, Inc.

RICHARD M. NIXON, thirty-seventh president of the United States (1969–1974)

BARACK OBAMA, forty-fourth president of the United States (2009–2017)

MONSIGNOR WILLIAM O'BRIEN, Catholic priest, Daytop cofounder

EFREN RAMIREZ, first director of New York City's Addiction Services Agency

NANCY REAGAN, First Lady of the United States (1981–1989)

RONALD REAGAN, governor of California (1967–1975), forty-fourth president of the United States (1981–1989)

JANET RENO, attorney general to President Bill Clinton (1993–2001)

NELSON ROCKEFELLER, Republican governor of New York State (1959–1973)

MITCHELL ROSENTHAL, psychiatrist, Synanon scholar, Phoenix House cofounder

GRANT SAWYER, Democratic governor of Nevada (1959–1967), Synanon supporter

MELVIN SEMBLER, businessman, cofounder of Straight, Inc.

CARLTON TURNER, drug researcher, President Ronald Reagan's primary drug-policy adviser

RITA "RICKY" VOLKMAN AND DONALD CRESSEY, criminologists, Synanon supporters

ROBERT F. WAGNER, Democratic mayor of New York City (1954–1965)

ROBERT S. WEPPNER, anthropologist, Matrix House researcher

HARRY WEXLER, psychologist, therapeutic-community researcher

JON WILDES, JAY THERRIEN, VERNON FARRINGTON, CARL SALLEY, Matrix House founders

RON WILLIAMS, Phoenix House resident and leader, Stay N Out cofounder

WALKER WINSLOW, journalist, Synanon supporter

LEWIS YABLONSKY, criminologist, Synanon scholar

ABBREVIATIONS

AA	Alcoholics Anonymous
AIDS	acquired immunodeficiency syndrome
ARC	Addiction Research Center, Lexington Narcotics Hospital
ASA	Addiction Services Administration of New York
CDC	California Department of Corrections
Cenikor	Center of the Core of the Individual
CRC	Clinical Research Center, Lexington Narcotic Hospital/Farm
DATOP or Daytop	Drug Addicts Treated on Probation or Drug Addicts Yield to Persuasion
FBI	Federal Bureau of Investigation
HEW	US Department of Health, Education, and Welfare
HIV	human immunodeficiency virus
IDAP	Illinois Drug Abuse Program
LEAA	Law Enforcement Assistance Administration
LSD	lysergic acid diethylamide
NARA	Narcotic Addict Rehabilitation Act of 1966
NIDA	National Institute on Drug Abuse
NIMH	National Institute of Mental Health

PDFA	Partnership for a Drug-Free America
SAODAP	Special Action Office for Drug Abuse Prevention
SPAN	Special Action Project Against Narcotics, Daytop
SOS	Sponsors of Synanon
TC	therapeutic community
UCLA	University of California at Los Angeles

NOTES

PREFACE

1. Charles Winick, "Maturing Out of Narcotic Addiction," *Bulletin on Narcotics* 14, no. 1 (1962): 1–7.

2. Patrick Biernecki, *Pathways from Heroin Addiction: Recovery Without Treatment* (Philadelphia: Temple University Press, 1986); Dan Waldorf, "Natural Recovery from Opiate Addiction: Some Social-Psychological Processes of Untreated Recovery," *Journal of Drug Issues* 13 (1983): 237–247.

3. William White, *Slaying the Dragon: The History of Addiction Treatment and Recovery in America* (Bloomington, IN: Chestnut Health Systems, 1989); David Rothman, *The Discovery of the Asylum: Social Order and Disorder in the New Republic* (Boston: Little, Brown, 1971).

4. Johann Hari, *Chasing the Scream: The First and Last Days of the War on Drugs* (New York: Bloomsbury, 2015); Michelle Alexander, *The New Jim Crow: Mass Incarceration in the Age of Colorblindness* (New York: New Press, 2009); Elizabeth Hinton, *From the War on Poverty to the War on Crime: The Making of Mass Incarceration in America* (Cambridge, MA: Harvard University Press, 2016).

5. William White, interview, *Points: The Blog of the Alcohol and Drugs History Society*, July 22, 2014, https://pointsadhsblog.wordpress.com/2014/07/22/the-points-interview-special-edition-william-l-white/.

INTRODUCTION: THE ROOTS OF REVOLUTION

1. Quoted in Guy Endore, *Synanon* (New York: Doubleday, 1968), 20. A complete transcript of an oral history with Hamer is available in Oral History Program, Charles E.

Young Special Collections, UCLA. See also Elizabeth Dixon, ed., *Seven Voices from Synanon: Oral History Transcript: Charles Dederich, Charles Hamer, Bettye Coleman, Monte Morton, James Middleton, Arlene Hefner, and Reid Kimball* (Los Angeles: Oral History Program, UCLA, 1964).

2. David Courtwright, *Dark Paradise: A History of Opiate Addiction in America*, 2nd ed. (Cambridge, MA: Harvard University Press, 2001).

3. David Courtwright, Herman Joseph, and Don DesJarlais, *Addicts Who Survived: An Oral History of Narcotic Use in America* (Knoxville: University of Tennessee Press, 1989); David Musto, *The American Disease: The Origins of Narcotic Control* (New Haven, CN: Yale University Press, 1973); Caroline Acker, *Creating the American Junkie: Addiction Research in the Classic Era of Narcotic Control* (Baltimore: Johns Hopkins University Press, 2003).

4. Musto, *The American Disease*, chap. 10; see Narcotics Commission Records, Box 1917-10, California State Archives, Sacramento, for extensive documentation of the state's reassessment of drug policy beginning in the late 1950s.

5. The language used to describe people with addiction histories can reinforce stigma. Although some of the terms I employ throughout this book are now considered dated and politically problematic, I have made every effort to describe people in recovery using historically accurate terminology. For example, *ex-addict* was the label most commonly used by people who had recovered from drug addiction in the 1960s and 1970s; the terms *recovered* and *recovering* began to become the dominant labels in the 1980s and 1990s. In general, I have avoided stigmatizing terms, such as *substance abuser*, that people in treatment and recovery did not commonly use as a means of self-identification.

6. For the lineage of prototypical TC, ex-addict-led form of drug treatment, see Frederick Glaser, "Some Historical Aspects of the Drug-Free Therapeutic Community," *American Journal of Drug and Alcohol Abuse* 1, no. 1 (1974): 37–52. For the rise and fall of ex-addicts as drug-treatment counselors and professionals, see Charles Winick, "The Counselor in Drug Treatment," *International Journal of the Addictions* 25, no. 12A (1990–1991): 1479–1502.

7. *Questions and Answers on Daytop Village*, brochure, Daytop Village Folder 514, Box 29, Papers of Mayor [John] Lindsay, New York City Municipal Archives.

8. The American Association for the Cure of Inebriates was founded on November 29, 1870 (William White, *Slaying the Dragon: The History of Addiction Treatment and Recovery in America* [Bloomington, IN: Chestnut Health Systems, 1989], 25; see also chapters 4 and 5 in White's book, "The Rise and Fall of Inebriate Asylums" and "Inebriate Homes and Asylums: Treatment Philosophies, Methods, and Outcomes").

9. Ibid., chaps. 4 and 5; Barbara Weiner and William White, "*The Journal of Inebriety* (1878–1914): History, Topical Analysis, and Photographic Images," *Addiction* 102 (2007): 15–23.

10. White, *Slaying the Dragon*, chaps. 4 and 5.

11. C. Stoddard, "What of the Drink Cures?" *Scientific Temperance Journal* (1922), quoted in White, *Slaying the Dragon*, 27.

12. Inebriety institutions concentrated on chemical dependency and generally rejected the medicinal use of alcohol or narcotics, then common in insane asylums. For more on

the concept of inebriety and the fate of inebriate asylums, see Sarah Tracy, *Alcoholism in America: From Reconstruction to Prohibition* (Baltimore: Johns Hopkins University Press, 2005). Seminal histories on the history and culture of insane asylums include David J. Rothman, *The Discovery of the Asylum: Social Order and Disorder in the New Republic* (Boston: Little, Brown, 1971); Gerald Grob, *Mental Institutions in America: Social Policy to 1875* (New York: Free Press, 1973); Gerald Grob, *Mental Illness and American Society, 1875–1940* (Princeton, NJ: Princeton University Press, 1983); Benjamin Reiss, *Theaters of Madness: Insane Asylums and Nineteenth Century American Culture* (Chicago: University of Chicago Press, 2008).

13. Acker, *Creating the American Junkie*, 38.

14. White, *Slaying the Dragon*, 28.

15. John C. McWilliams, "Unsung Partner Against Crime: Harry J. Anslinger and the Federal Bureau of Narcotics, 1930–1962," *Pennsylvania Magazine of History and Biography* 113, no. 2 (1989): 211–216.

16. Anslinger's most vehement critic was Alfred Lindesmith of Indiana University. See Alfred R. Lindesmith, "Dope Fiend Mythology," *Journal of Criminal Law and Criminology* 31, no. 2 (1940): 199; John F. Galliher, David P. Keys, and Michael Elsner, "Lindesmith v. Anslinger: An Early Government Victory in the Failed War on Drugs," *Journal of Criminal Law and Criminology* 88, no. 2 (1998): 661–682.

17. Jill Jonnes, *Hep Cats, Narcs, and Pipe Dreams: A History of America's Romance with Illegal Drugs* (Baltimore: Johns Hopkins University Press, 1999), 159–160.

18. David T. Courtwright. "Mr. ATOD's Wild Ride: What Do Alcohol, Tobacco, and Other Drugs Have in Common?" *Social History of Alcohol and Drugs* 20, no. 1 (2005): 105–140.

19. John C. Burnham, *Bad Habits: Drinking, Smoking, Taking Drugs, Gambling, Sexual Misbehavior, and Swearing in American History* (New York: New York University Press, 1993). For more on the clash between Victorian and modern values in the American context, see T. J. Jackson Lears, *No Place of Grace: Antimodernism and the Transformation of American Culture* (Chicago: University of Chicago Press, 1981).

20. American Association for the Study and Cure of Inebriety, *The Disease of Inebriety from Alcohol, Opium, and Other Narcotic Drugs* (New York: E. B. Treat, 1893), 88, 200.

21. Burnham, *Bad Habits*, 42–43.

22. Alan Petigny, *The Permissive Society, 1941–1965* (Cambridge: Cambridge University Press, 2009); Barry Hankins, *Jesus and Gin: Evangelicalism, the Roaring Twenties, and Today's Culture Wars* (New York: St. Martin's Press, 2010); James Monroe, *Hellfire Nation: The Politics of Sin in American History* (New Haven, CT: Yale University Press, 2003).

23. Arthur Toynbee, *A Study of History: Abridgement of Vols. I–VI.* (Oxford: Oxford University Press, 1946). For the conservative contention that American society since the 1960s is in a state of Toynbean decline, see Charles Murray, *Coming Apart: The State of White America, 1960–2010* (New York: Crown, 2012). Of course, the scholars who have pointed out the considerable shortcomings of a repressive Victorian society rigidly structured around hierarchies of gender, race, and class are too numerous to cite in full. See, for example, Lytton Strachey, *Eminent Victorians* (1918; e-book ed., n.p.: Start Publishing,

2012); Elaine Showalter, *The Female Malady: Women, Madness, and English Culture, 1830–1980* (New York: Pantheon Books, 1985); Stephen Jay Gould, *The Mismeasure of Man*, rev. ed. (New York: Norton, 2006).

24. Acker, *Creating the American Junkie.*

25. Ibid.; Timothy Hickman, *The Secret Leprosy of Modern Days: Narcotic Addiction and Cultural Crisis in the United States, 1870–1920* (Amherst: University of Massachusetts Press, 2007); Scott Vrecko, "Civilizing Technologies and the Role of Deviance," *Biosocieties* 5, no. 1 (2010): 36–51.

26. Acker, *Creating the American Junkie*, 157–158.

27. Ibid., 157–161.

28. William F. Conhurst, "A New Deal for the Drug Addict," *Baltimore Sun*, July 14, 1935; for historical interpretation, see Nancy Campbell, "'A New Deal for the Drug Addict': The Addiction Research Center, Lexington, Kentucky," *Journal of the History of the Behavioral Sciences* 42, no. 2 (2006): 135–157.

29. "Iatrogenic" addicts were introduced to addictive substances by physicians and became dependent on those substances as an unintended side effect of medical treatment; in contrast, "psychopathic" addicts supposedly possessed fundamental personality flaws that correlated with compulsive substance use.

30. See Nancy Campbell, *Discovering Addiction: The Science and Politics of Substance Abuse Research* (Ann Arbor: University of Michigan Press, 2007), chaps. 3 and 5–7; Acker, *Creating the American Junkie*, chap. 6.

31. Musto cites these studies as among the most significant in damaging Lexington's reputation (*The American Disease*, 282–283): M. J. Pescor, "Prognosis in Drug Addiction," *American Journal of Psychiatry* 97 (1941): 1419–1433; G. H. Hunt and M. E. Odoroff, "Follow-Up Study of Narcotic Drug Addicts After Hospitalization," *Public Health Reports* 77 (1962): 41–52.

32. Donald F. Bolles, "Doctors Battle Dope at Lexington Hospital," *Courier Times* (city unknown, Associated Press), January 14, 1962, clipping in the folder "Newspapers and Magazine Clippings on Narcotic and Drug Addiction 1962," Box 1 "Clinical Research Center, Lexington, KY, Personnel, 1961–1974," Records of the Alcohol, Drug Abuse, and Mental Health Administrative Office, Record Group 511, National Archives and Records Administration–Southeast, Morrow, GA.

33. Theodore Roszack, *The Making of a Counter-Culture: Reflections on the Technocratic Society and Its Youthful Opposition* (New York: Doubleday, 1969). Compare William Akin, *Technocracy and the American Dream: The Technocrat Movement, 1900–1941* (Berkeley: University of California Press, 1977); John Jordan, *Machine-Age Ideology: Social Engineering and American Liberalism, 1911–1939* (Chapel Hill: University of North Carolina Press, 2010); Frank Fischer, *Technocracy and the Politics of Expertise* (New York: Sage, 1989).

34. Janet Clark and Howard Becker, *The Fantastic Lodge: Autobiography of a Girl Drug Addict* (New York: Houghton Mifflin, 1961), "fantastic lodge" on 232–233. For an interpretation of the farm's impact on addicted identity, as recounted in Clark's memoir, see Campbell, *Discovering Addiction*, 64–69.

35. Endore, *Synanon*, 278–279.

36. John Maher, quoted in ibid., 279.

37. David Deitch and Joan Zweben, "Synanon: A Pioneering Response in Drug Treatment and a Signal for Caution," in *Substance Abuse: Clinical Problems and Perspectives*, ed. Joyce Lowinson and Pedro Ruiz (Baltimore: Williams and Wilkins, 1981), 289–302; Geoffrey Skoll, *Walk the Walk and Talk the Talk: An Ethnography of a Drug Treatment Facility* (Philadelphia: Temple University Press, 1992).

38. R. D. Fox, "Unique Club Seeks to Whip Narcotics," *Santa Monica Evening Outlook*, January 23, 1959.

39. Charles E. Dederich, interview, "The Early History of Synanon," transcript, Box 1, Synanon Collection, Charles E. Young Library, UCLA.

40. Quoted in Rod Janzen, *The Rise and Fall of Synanon: A California Utopia* (Baltimore: Johns Hopkins University Press, 2001), 11. Synanon was technically incorporated as a nonprofit; by concentrating on the development of "social enterprises," it became a wealthy one. The organization's profitable social enterprises (gas stations, advertising specialty business, therapy clubs) retained nonprofit status by functioning as therapy and vocational training for addicts or delinquent youth. For an extensive discussion of Synanon's financials (in 1977, it had a net worth of $12 million and assets of $30 million) and Dederich's corporate approach, see Defendant's Statement of Material Facts, *Synanon Church vs. United States of America*, No. 82-2303, undated, DC District Court, esp. pp. 57–58, Documents: Synanon Church vs. USA, Folder 4, Box 2, Mitchell–Synanon Litigation Papers, University of Tennessee at Knoxville.

41. Yinger partially bases his theory of "contraculture" on the work of criminologist Lewis Yablonsky, who studied juvenile delinquents in New York before becoming Synanon's most eminent researcher. See J. Milton Yinger, "Contraculture and Subculture," *American Sociological Review* 25, no. 5 (1960): 625–635.

42. Roszack, *The Making of a Counter-Culture*.

43. Excessive alcohol consumption emerged as a public-health problem in the late 1960s (Robin Room, "Alcohol Control and Public Health," *Annual Review of Public Health* 5 [May 1984]: 293–317). Likewise, concerns about prescription-tranquilizer abuse—which was negotiated by medical professionals in the late 1950s and early 1960s—came to the national stage in debates surrounding the Drug Abuse Control Amendments of 1965 (David Herzberg, *Happy Pills in America: From Miltown to Prozac* [Baltimore: Johns Hopkins University Press, 2009]). Concerns about illicit drug use in the late 1960s set in motion the federally coordinated national surveys of drug use, such as the National Household Survey on Drug Use, begun in 1971.

44. William Satterfield, testimony, U.S. House of Representatives, Special Subcommittee on Alcoholism and Narcotics of the Committee on Labor and Public Welfare, *Inquiry Into the Problem of Alcoholism and Narcotics*, 91st Cong., 1st sess., October 4, 1969, 713.

45. For more on the 1960s as the beginning of the fragmentation of the Left or an "Age of Fracture" in general, see Daniel T. Rodgers, *The Age of Fracture* (Cambridge, MA: Harvard University Press, 2011); William O'Neill, *Coming Apart: An Informal History of America in the 1960s* (New York: Times Books, 1971); John M. Blum, *Years of Discord* (New York:

Norton, 1991); Maurice Isserman and Michael Kazin, *America Divided: The Civil War of the 1960s* (New York: Oxford University Press, 2000). Although some scholars conflate the counterculture and the New Left or argue that the counterculture took a leftist turn (see, e.g., Doug Rossinow, "The New Left in the Counterculture: Hypotheses and Evidence," *Radical History Review* 67 [1997]: 79–120), the sociologist Rebecca Klatch's interviews with both New Left and New Right revealed that both movements were catalyzed by their members' antagonistic perceptions of the counterculture ("The Counterculture, the New Left, and the New Right," *Qualitative Sociology* 17, no. 3 [1994]: 199–214). Michael Kramer argues in *The Republic of Rock: Music and Citizenship in the Sixties* (New York: Oxford University Press, 2013) that countercultural leisure encouraged both libertarian and communitarian visions (12).

46. The Synanon founder Charles Dederich famously said, "These three syllables will someday be as well known as Coca-Cola" (qtd. in Endore, *Synanon*, 47).

47. Glaser, "Some Historical Aspects of the Drug-Free Therapeutic Community"; George De Leon, *The Therapeutic Community: Theory, Model, Method* (New York: Springer, 2000), 3–33.

48. The most extensive discussion of Synanon's relationship to nineteenth-century religious communes is Janzen, *The Rise and Fall of Synanon*.

49. Barry Sugarman, *Daytop Village: A Therapeutic Community* (New York: Holt, Rinehart, and Winston, 1974), 130–131.

50. For the transportation of the former-addict advocate to the United Kingdom, see Alex Mold and Virginia Berridge, "'The Rise of the User?': Voluntary Organizations, the State, and Illegal Drugs in England Since the 1960s," *Drugs: Education, Prevention, and Policy* 15, no. 5 (2008): 451–461; on transportation to Europe, see Johan Edman, "Red Cottages and Swedish Virtues: Swedish Institutional Drug Treatment as an Ideological Project, 1968–1981," *Social History of Medicine* 3, no. 26 (2013): 510–531; on the similarities between TCs and the recovery model, see William White, "David Deitch, PhD, and George De Leon, PhD, on Recovery Management and the Future of the Therapeutic Community," *Counselor* 11, no. 5 (2010): 38–49.

51. Timothy Miller, *The Sixties Communes: Hippies and Beyond* (Syracuse, NY: Syracuse University Press, 1999), xvii–xx.

52. The story of the growth of TCs complicates the vast literature on the failure of the radicals of the 1960s and 1970s both in general and in terms of antipsychiatry. See Arthur Marwick, *The Sixties: Cultural Revolution in Britain, France, Italy, and the United States, c. 1958–c. 1974* (New York: Oxford University Press, 1998); Peter Collier and David Horowitz, *Destructive Generation: Second Thoughts About the Sixties* (New York: Encounter Books, 2005); Jeremy Varon, *Bringing the War Home: The Weather Underground, the Red Army Faction, and Revolutionary Violence in the Sixties and Seventies* (Berkeley: University of California Press, 2004); Dan Berger, *Outlaws of America: The Weather Underground and the Politics of Solidarity* (Oakland, CA: AK Press, 2006); Joshua Bloom and Waldo Martin, *Black Against Empire: The History and Politics of the Black Panther Party* (Berkeley: University of California Press, 2013); Richard Wolin, *The Wind from the East: French Intellectuals, the Cultural Revolution, and the Legacy of the 1960s* (Princeton, NJ:

Princeton University Press, 2012); Michael Staub, *Madness Is Civilization: When the Diagnosis Was Social, 1948–1980* (Chicago: University of Chicago Press, 2011).

53. Dan Baum, *Smoke and Mirrors: The War on Drugs and the Politics of Failure* (Boston: Little, Brown, 1996); Paul Gootenberg, *Andean Cocaine: The Making of a Global Drug* (Chapel Hill: University of North Carolina Press, 2009); Edward Jay Epstein, *Agency of Fear: Opiate and Political Power in America* (New York: Verso, 1990); Alfred McCoy, *The Politics of Heroin: CIA Complicity in the Global Drug Trade* (Chicago: Chicago Review Press, 2003).

54. Jeremy Kuzmarov, *The Myth of the Addicted Army: Vietnam and the Modern War on Drugs* (Amherst: University of Massachusetts Press, 2009); David T. Courtwright, *No Right Turn: Conservative Politics in a Liberal America* (Cambridge, MA: Harvard University Press, 2010); Michael Massing, *The Fix* (1998; reprint, Berkeley: University of California Press, 2000); Philip Jenkins, *Decade of Nightmares: The End of the Sixties and the Making of Eighties America* (Oxford: Oxford University Press, 2006); Myron Magnet, *The Dream and the Nightmare: The Sixties Legacy to the Underclass* (San Francisco: Encounter Books, 1993).

55. Musto, *The American Disease*; Susanna Reiss, *We Sell Drugs: The Alchemy of U.S. Empire* (Berkeley: University of California Press, 2014); Lisa McGirr, *The War on Alcohol: Prohibition and the Rise of the American State* (New York: Norton, 2015); Matthew Lassiter, "Impossible Criminals: The Suburban Imperatives of America's War on Drugs," *Journal of American History* 102, no. 1 (2015): 126–140.

1. SELLING SYNANON

1. Quoted in Guy Endore, *Synanon* (New York: Doubleday, 1968), 358–360.

2. Zev Putterman, quoted in Lewis Yablonsky, *Synanon: The Tunnel Back* (1965; reprint, Baltimore: Penguin, 1967), 272.

3. Charles E. Dederich, "Changing the World: The New Profession," audio tape of lecture, February 3, 1973, Box 70, Synanon Collection, Charles E. Young Special Collections, UCLA (hereafter UCLA Synanon Collection).

4. Richard Ofshe, "The Social Development of the Synanon Cult: The Managerial Strategy of Organizational Transformation," *Sociological Analysis* 41, no. 2 (1980): 109–127; Dave Mitchell, Cathy Mitchell, and Richard Ofshe, *The Light on Synanon: How a Country Weekly Exposed a Corporate Cult and Won the Pulitzer Prize* (New York: Seaview Books, 1980).

5. "Life at Synanon Is Swinging," *Time*, December 26, 1977, http://content.time.com/time /magazine/article/0,9171,919202,00.html, accessed October 9, 2016.

6. David Deitch and Joan Zweben, "Synanon: A Pioneering Response in Drug Treatment and a Signal for Caution," in *Substance Abuse: Clinical Problems and Perspectives*, ed. Joyce Lowinson and Pedro Ruiz (Baltimore: Williams and Wilkins, 1981), 289–302.

7. Leon Brill, "Some Comments on the Paper 'Social Control in Therapeutic Communities' by Dan Waldorf," *International Journal of the Addictions* 6 (March 1971): 46.

8. For a summary of TC research, see George De Leon, *The Therapeutic Community: Theory, Model, Method* (New York: Springer, 2000).

9. Max Weber, "The Nature of Charismatic Authority and Its Routinization," in *On Charisma and Institution Building: Selected Papers*, ed. Max Weber and Stuart Eisenstadt (Chicago: University of Chicago Press, 1968), 48–65.

10. Rod Janzen, *The Rise and Fall of Synanon: A California Utopia* (Baltimore: Johns Hopkins University Press, 2001), 10.

11. "Charles Dederich," in *Seven Voices from Synanon: Oral History Transcript: Charles Dederich, Charles Hamer, Bettye Coleman, Monte Morton, James Middleton, Arlene Hefner, and Reid Kimball*, ed. Elizabeth Dixon (Los Angeles: Oral History Program, UCLA, 1964), 47–65.

12. Quoted in David Gerstel, *Paradise Incorporated: Synanon* (Novato, CA: Presidio Press, 1982), 35.

13. Ralph Waldo Emerson's essay "Self-Reliance" was published in Emerson's first collection of essays, *Essays: First Series* (Boston: James Munroe), in 1841 and is available online at http://www.emersoncentral.com/selfreliance.htm, accessed December 11, 2015.

14. Charles E. Dederich, "The Early History of Synanon," transcript of interview, Box 1, UCLA Synanon Collection.

15. Endore, *Synanon*, 40–47; Yablonsky, *Synanon*, 54.

16. Dederich, "The Early History of Synanon."

17. Quoted in Endore, *Synanon*, 74; see also Janzen, *The Rise and Fall of Synanon*, 11.

18. Yablonsky, *Synanon*, 61.

19. "Synanon Members as of 11/1/1964," Folder "Population History," Box 81, UCLA Synanon Collection. Several demographic characteristics might help account for Synanon's success with the addicts who stuck with the program in the early 1960s. For example, the average resident's age was twenty-nine years and nine months old; most heroin addicts in this era seriously sought treatment or began the process of "aging out" of use by their thirties (see Charles Winick, "Maturing Out of Narcotic Addiction," *Bulletin on Narcotics* 14, no. 1 [1962]: 1–7). In addition, although the Synanon community was integrated and quite ethnically diverse for its day, the majority of residents (76.77 percent) were white. White, middle-class patients typically had better treatment outcomes than ethnic minorities. For example, an analysis of men committed to California's Civil Addict Program in 1964–1966 found that success in the program was related to ethnic background, with whites highest (21.9 percent), blacks lowest (11.7 percent), and Mexicans intermediate (17.2 percent) (W. H. McGlothlin, M. D. Anglin, and B. D. Wilson, "Outcome of the California Civil Addict Commitments: 1961–1972," *Drug and Alcohol Dependence* 1 [1975–1976]: 165–181).

20. Endore, *Synanon*, 352; for the one thousand figure, see Ofshe, "The Social Development of the Synanon Cult," 112.

21. Timothy Novak, "LSD Before Leary: Sidney Cohen's Critique of 1950s Psychedelic Research," *Isis* 88, no. 1 (1997): 97.

22. "Sidney Cohen Interviews Charles Dederich About His LSD Experience," June 4, 1966, audio recording, Box 614, UCLA Synanon Collection.

23. Timothy Leary endorsed Synanon as the "foremost university of behavioral change in the world." This quote was repeated in Synanon lectures and promotional material (see the lecture by Synanon member Bill Crawford at the University of Nevada, 1963, transcript, Box 1, UCLA Synanon Collection). Leary wrote positively of Synanon's therapeutic methods and implemented them in experiments with prisoners. See Timothy Leary, Ralph Metzner, Madison Presnell, Gunther Weil, Ralph Schwitzgebel, and Sarah Kinne, "A New Behavior Change Program Using Psilocybin," *Psychotherapy* 2, no. 2 (1965): 61–72, and Timothy Leary "The Effects of Consciousness-Expanding Drugs on Prisoner Rehabilitation," *Psychedelic Review* 10 (1969): 29–44.

24. "Sidney Cohen Interviews Charles Dederich About His LSD Experience."

25. U.S. Senate, Subcommittee on Executive Reorganization, *Organization and Coordination of Federal Drug Research and Regulatory Programs: LSD*, 89th Cong., 2nd sess., May 24 and 25, 1966.

26. Ericka Dyck, *Psychedelic Psychiatry: LSD from Clinic to Campus* (Baltimore: Johns Hopkins University Press, 2008).

27. "Sidney Cohen Interviews Charles Dederich About His LSD Experience"; Sidney Finkelstein, interviewed by the author, Safety Harbor, FL, July 23, 2011.

28. Abraham Maslow, "Comments on 'Religions, Values, and Peak Experiences," in *The Farther Reaches of Human Nature* (New York: Penguin, 1971), 331–337.

29. For a description of Maslow's definition of "self-actualization," see Abraham Maslow, *Toward a Psychology of Being* (New York: Van Nostrand, 1962); to understand Dederich's emphasis on self-reliance, see Emerson, "Self-Reliance."

30. Janzen, *Rise and Fall of Synanon*, 11.

31. From a scrapbook of Charles E. Dederich's responses to news articles, Box 83, UCLA Synanon Collection.

32. Endore, *Synanon*, 150.

33. Quoted in Yablonsky, *Synanon*, 254.

34. *Or Die*, short film, Box 572, UCLA Synanon Collection.

35. Richard A. McGee to Anna Kross, May 13, 1963, Narcotics Commission Records, Folder F3717:195, Box F317:192–219, California State Archives, Sacramento.

36. Quoted in Daniel J. Boorstin, *The Image: A Guide to Pseudo Events in America* (1962; reprint, New York: Vintage Books, 1992), 18.

37. T. J. Jackson Lears, *Fables of Abundance: A Cultural History of Advertising in America* (New York: Basic Books, 1995), part 2, 151–275.

38. Ibid.

39. Ibid.

40. Boorstin, *The Image*.

41. Ibid., 10.

42. "Synanon: On the Side of Life," *Manas*, December 25, 1963, http://www.manasjournal.org/pdf_library/VolumeXVI_1963/XVI-52.pdf, accessed December 11, 2015.

43. Gerstel, *Paradise Incorporated*, 40.

44. R. D. Fox, "Unique Club Seeks to Whip Narcotics," *Santa Monica Evening Outlook*, January 23, 1959.

45. R. D. Fox, "Drug Addicts Get a Lift," *Santa Monica Evening Outlook*, January 24, 1959.
46. Ibid.
47. "S.S. Hang Tough," *Time*, April 7, 1961, Synanon offprint, author's personal collection.
48. Quoted in Endore, *Synanon*, 192.
49. Walker Winslow, "Synanon Revisited," *Manas*, February 8, 1961, Synanon offprint, author's personal collection.
50. Walker Winslow, "Experiment for Addicts," *The Nation,* April 29, 1961, Synanon offprint, author's personal collection.
51. For letters to Brown, see Narcotics Commission Records, Folder F3717:195, Box F317:192–219, California State Archives, Sacramento. For letters to the Kennedy administration, see Folder 1 of 2 "Synanon Foundation Correspondence," Box 3 "Public Relations Correspondence 1939–1973, Clinical Research Center (CRC), Lexington, Kentucky," Records of the Alcohol, Drug Abuse, and Mental Health Administration (ADAMHA), Record Group (RG) 511, National Archives and Records Administration–Southeast, Morrow, GA.
52. Charles Hamer to President Kennedy, February 25, 1961, Folder 1 of 2 "Synanon Foundation Correspondence," Box 3 "Public Relations Correspondence 1939–1973, CRC," ADAMHA Records, RG 511, National Archives and Records Administration–Southeast.
53. Winslow, "Experiment for Addicts."
54. Film clip, *Steve Allen Show*, undated, Box 571, UCLA Synanon Collection. The *Steve Allen Show* was produced by NBC and ran from 1956 to 1960.
55. The reported success rate was 90 percent for those who stayed at least three months (Daniel Casriel, *So Fair a House: The Story of Synanon* [Englewood Cliffs, NJ: Prentice-Hall, 1963], 177).
56. Harold Gilman, "Tunnel to the Human Race," *San Francisco Chronicle*, January 26, 1964; for the *Life* feature on Synanon, see Grey Villet and Richard Stolley, "A Tunnel Back to the Human Race," *Life*, March 9, 1962, 52–67.
57. Boorstin, *The Image*, 38.
58. "Synanon Story in *Life*," *Santa Monica Independent*, March 1, 1962.
59. Eugene Ireland to Harry Anslinger, March 6, 1962, Folder 1 of 2 "Synanon Foundation Correspondence," Box "Public Relations Clippings 1939–1973, CRC," ADAMHA Records, RG 511, National Archives and Records Administration–Southeast.
60. Janzen, *The Rise and Fall of Synanon*, 30.
61. Ted Dibble, interviewed by the author, Novato, CA, August 26, 2012.
62. Zev Putterman, June 21, 1965, recording, Box 605, UCLA Synanon Collection.
63. Richard Quine, dir., *Synanon* (Columbia Pictures, 1965), DVD (Sony Pictures Home Entertainment, 2011).
64. Hollis Alpert, review of *Synanon* (Columbia Pictures), *Saturday Review*, May 1, 1965, 4.
65. The article "Film Plugs & Pluggers: Needle Sharp Excitement of the Sell," *Variety*, April 28, 1965, 22, referred to the campaign as "schizoid" because it included contrasting lines that read either "decorously" ("Dope addiction, the topic making headlines across the country") or more "thrillingly" ("cash in on needle sharp excitement . . . !"). The article cheekily suggested alternative slogans for the "basically honest project": "'Synanon'—your

mainline to profit!" "Hypo your box office!" "Watch the kids kick the TV habit!" This marketing approach was characteristic of low-budget "social problem" films; see Eric Schafer, *Bold! Shocking! Daring! True! A History of Exploitation Films, 1919–1959* (Durham, NC: Duke University Press, 1999).

66. *Synanon Program*, film program (Los Angeles: Columbia Pictures, 1965), Folder "Synanon Movie: Quine PR," Box 100, UCLA Synanon Collection.

67. "Do you have a former addict in your community? One that would be willing to stand up and say 'Yes, I was . . .' on radio and television and to the press? Such an individual could be the greatest box office booster that ever came into your showmanship history! To find him (or, preferably, her!) ask the Police Department or welfare agency for assistance" (*Synanon Pressbook* [Los Angeles: Columbia Pictures, 1965], 9, author's personal collection.

68. Richard Stolley, "An Honest Look at the Tunnel Back," *Life*, May 14, 1965, 19.

69. For Time-Life's direct cinema depiction of Synanon, see Bill Ray, dir., *David*, 16-mm film (Time-Life Broadcast and Drew Associates, 1961).

70. Steven Lipkin, *Real Emotional Logic: Film and Television Docudrama as Persuasive Practice* (Carbondale: Southern Illinois University Press, 2002), 5.

71. Villet and Stolley, "A Tunnel Back to the Human Race"; Yablonsky, *Synanon*; *Synanon Pressbook*.

72. Villet and Stolley, "A Tunnel Back to the Human Race," 56–57.

73. Stolley, "An Honest Look at the Tunnel Back," 19.

74. *Synanon Program*.

75. Quoted in Paine Knickerbocker, "Edmund O'Brien's Approach to Synanon," *San Francisco Chronicle*, May 5, 1965.

76. Folder "Stockholder's Report 1968," Box 100, UCLA Synanon Collection

77. Charles Dederich to Richard Quine, October 5, 1964, Folder "Columbia Pictures," Box 102, UCLA Synanon Collection.

78. "A Benefit Preem for 'Synanon,'" *Hollywood Reporter*, May 11, 1965.

79. Folder "Synanon Movie: Quine PR," Box 100, UCLA Synanon Collection.

80. Quoted in Grover Sales Jr., "Critics Choice," column clipping, Folder "Synanon Movie: Quine PR," Box 100, UCLA Synanon Collection.

81. Yablonsky, *Synanon*, 2–3.

82. Daniel Casriel, testimony, U.S. Senate, *Hearings Before the Subcommittee to Investigate Juvenile Delinquency of the Committee of the Judiciary, U.S. Senate*, 87th Cong., 2nd sess., August 6 and 7, 1962, 2785.

83. "A Study in Heroism: Statement of Thomas Dodd to the U.S. Senate Subcommittee to Investigate Juvenile Delinquency," *Congressional Record*, September 6, 1962, Synanon offprint, author's personal collection, no page numbers in the offprint.

84. Quoted in Casriel, *So Fair a House*, 176.

85. Arthur Alarcon to John O'Connell, December 15, 1961, with appended report, Narcotics Commission Records, Folder 3717:196, Box 1917-10, California State Archives.

86. Boorstin, *The Image*, 202. On advertisers' adoption of popular social science concepts beginning in the early twentieth century, see Lears, *Fables of Abundance*, 194–212.

87. Edgar Friedenberg, "The Synanon Solution," *The Nation*, March 8, 1965, 257.

88. David Riesman, with Nathan Glazer and Reuel Denney, *The Lonely Crowd* (New Haven, CT: Yale University Press, 1950).

89. "Synanon: Its Best May Come Last," *Manas,* November 14, 1962, 2,http://www.manas journal.org/pdf_library/VolumeXV_1962/XV-46.pdf, accessed December 11, 2015.

90. Thomas Frank, *The Conquest of Cool: Business Culture, Counterculture, and the Rise of Hip Consumerism* (Chicago: University of Chicago Press, 1997), 93.

91. Yablonsky, *Synanon,* 397.

92. Jim Hoffman, "New Hope for the Addict: Synanon," *Pageant,* January 1964, 123–129; Gilman, "Tunnel to the Human Race."

93. Peter Collier, "The House of Synanon," *Ramparts,* October 1967. The client-retention problem carried over to the TCs inspired by Synanon.

94. "Synanon Members as of 11/1/1964."

95. McGlothlin, Anglin, and Wilson, "Outcome of the California Civil Addict Commitments." For example, the "success rate" for men in California's Civil Addict Program hovered between 15 and 20 percent from 1961 to 1964.

96. Ray, *David*; Dederich quoted in Endore, *Synanon,* 246–247.

97. Guy Endore, *Synanon Is the People Business*, pamphlet, Box 84, Guy Endore Papers, UCLA. According to Peter Collier in a *Ramparts* article, Synanon accepted $100,000 combined state and federal funds for rehabilitation ("The House of Synanon," 54).

98. Folder "Sponsors of Synanon 1964," Box 95, UCLA Synanon Collection.

99. Folder "Industries–Investors," Box 73, UCLA Synanon Collection.

100. Folder "Sponsors of Synanon 1964," Box 95, UCLA Synanon Collection

101. Yablonsky, *Synanon,* 399.

102. Quoted in Grover Sales, *John Maher of Delancey Street: A Guide to Peaceful Revolution in America* (New York: Norton, 1976), 53.

103. William Crawford to Lee Work, December 5, 1964, Folder "Press Releases," Box 83, UCLA Synanon Collection.

104. Advertisement for Synanon Texaco station, Folder "Synanon Industries," Box 489, UCLA Synanon Collection.

105. Kerwin Kaye Brook, "Drug Courts and the Treatment of Addiction: Therapeutic Jurisprudence and Neoliberal Governance," PhD diss., New York University, 2010, 195.

106. Quoted in Yablonsky, *Synanon,* 338.

107. Quoted in Lewis Yablonsky, "The Anti-criminal Society: Synanon," *Federal Probation* 26 (1962): 57.

108. Yablonsky, *Synanon,* 336.

109. Harry Wexler and Craig T. Lowe, "Therapeutic Communities in Prison," in *Therapeutic Community: Advances in Research and Application*, ed. Frank Tims, George De Leon, and Nancy Jainchill (Rockville, MD: National Institute on Drug Abuse, 1994), 188.

110. Yablonsky, *Synanon,* 337.

111. Walter Cronkite, "Synanon in Prison," episode 13, season 9, *Twentieth Century,* CBS, aired March 13, 1966, 16-mm film, Box 580, UCLA Synanon Collection.

112. Dan Garrett to Marin County Board of Supervisors, November 16, 1964, author's personal collection.

113. Synanon press release, November 9, 1964, author's personal collection.

114. Ibid.

115. Folder "Press Releases: 1960–1969," Box 82, UCLA Synanon Collection.

116. Ibid.

117. "Hospital and Community Services for Addicts: A List Compiled by the National Institute of Mental Health," Folder 3 of 4 "Civil Commitment 1966," Box 7 "Administrative Files, CRC," ADAMHA Records, RG 511, National Archives and Records Administration–Southeast.

118. Fox, "Unique Club Seeks to Whip Narcotics."

119. Quoted in Paul Lofty, "A Former Addict Reveals What Goes on Inside Synanon," *True*, May 1967, 55.

120. Ibid.; Collier, "House of Synanon," 52.

121. Quoted in Collier, "House of Synanon," 52.

122. Winslow, "Synanon Revisited," 5.

123. Janzen, *Rise and Fall of Synanon*, 41.

124. "Welcome to Synanon," letter to new game-club members, Folder "Game Club Articles," Box 70, UCLA Synanon Collection.

125. Quoted in Sylvia Glick, "Synanon Game Is Verbal Mayhem," *LA Free Press*, April 21–27, 1967, 3.

126. "Proposal: Public Service Announcements," Folder "PR Information 1965–71," Box 83, UCLA Synanon Collection.

127. Glick, "Synanon Game Is Verbal Mayhem."

128. *The Most Adult Game*, 16-mm film, KRON-TV, San Francisco, 1967.

129. Glick, "Synanon Game Is Verbal Mayhem."

130. "Bill Crawford Addresses San Francisco Synanon," Synanon Foundation news release, April 4, 1968, San Francisco, author's personal collection.

131. Robert Claiborne, "The Potential of Human Potential," *The Nation*, October 19, 1970, 373.

132. "Bill Crawford Addresses San Francisco Synanon."

133. "Tenth Anniversary—What a Party!" *Synanon News*, week ending November 9, 1968, Folder "Newsletters," Box 83, UCLA Synanon Collection.

134. Mike Kaiser to All Media, "Synanon's Ten Year Anniversary," Folder "Synanon 10 and 15 Year Anniversaries," Box 100, UCLA Synanon Collection.

135. Lofty, "A Former Addict Reveals What Goes on Inside Synanon," 114.

136. Synanon's anniversary press release projected that the organization would save society $30 million in 1969 (Mike Kaiser to All Media, "Synanon's Ten Year Anniversary").

137. Ibid.

138. Jessica Grogan, *Encountering America: Humanistic Psychology, Sixties Culture, and the Shaping of the Modern Self* (New York: Harper, 2013), 96.

139. Abraham Maslow, "Synanon and Eupsychia," *Journal of Humanistic Psychology* 7 (1967): 28–35.

140. Grogan, *Encountering America*, 96; Abraham Maslow, *Eupsychian Management* (New York: Irwin, 1965).

141. "Abraham Maslow Speaks at General Meeting in Santa Monica," January 1, 1966, recording, Box 611, UCLA Synanon Collection; Dederich speaks at the beginning of this recording.

142. Ibid.

143. Maslow, "Synanon and Eupsychia," 28.

144. Quoted in Leon Brill, review of *Synanon* by Guy Endore, *Social Work*, July 1969, 119–121.

145. Natasha Zaretsky, *No Direction Home: The American Family and the Fear of National Decline, 1968–1980* (Chapel Hill: University of North Carolina Press, 2007), 140; Zaretsky provides an historical analysis of Maslow's Quality of Work Life programs.

146. *The Most Adult Game.*

147. Maslow, "Synanon and Eupsychia," 32.

148. "Abraham Maslow Speaks at General Meeting in Santa Monica."

149. Synanon Game Poster with poem by Steve Handler, 1972, Synanon website, http://www .synanon.org/synanon/Museum/PhotoDB.cfm?PID=559, accessed October 1, 2016.

150. Janzen, *Rise and Fall of Synanon*, 31–57.

151. Quoted in Endore, *Synanon*, 241.

152. Mike Kaiser to All Media, "Synanon's Ten Year Anniversary," emphasis added.

153. "Synanon: Its Best May Come Last," 1.

2. SYNANON RASHOMON

1. Walker Winslow, "Synanon Revisited," *Manas*, February 8, 1961, emphasis in original.

2. For a survey of a variety of U.S. radical groups in the 1960s and 1970s, see Bryan Burrough, *Days of Rage: America's Radical Underground, the FBI, and the Forgotten Age of Revolutionary Violence* (New York: Penguin, 2015).

3. Winslow, "Synanon Revisited."

4. Walker Winslow, "Experiment for Addicts," *The Nation*, April 29, 1961, Synanon offprint, author's personal collection.

5. In *To Slay a White Horse*, 16-mm film, Box 572, Synanon Collection, Charles E. Young Special Collections, UCLA (hereafter UCLA Synanon Collection).

6. Lee Bernstein, *America Is the Prison: Arts and Politics in Prison in the 1970s* (Chapel Hill: University of North Carolina Press, 2010), 1–15.

7. John C. Burnham and Joseph F. Spillane, "Editors' Introduction," in William Wilkinson, *Prison Work: A Tale of Thirty Years in the California Department of Corrections*, ed. John C. Burnham and Joseph F. Spillane (Columbus: Ohio State University, 2005), x–xi. See also Francis A. Allen, *The Decline of the Rehabilitative Ideal* (New Haven, CT: Yale University Press, 1981), and Eric Cummins, *The Rise and Fall of California's Radical Prison Movement* (Stanford, CA: Stanford University Press, 1994).

8. Gerard DeGroot, "'A Goddamned Electable Person': The 1966 California Gubernatorial Campaign of Ronald Reagan," *History* 82, no. 267 (1997): 429–448; Burnham and Spillane, "Editors' Introduction," xv–xvi.

9. Kerwin Kaye Brook, "Drug Courts and the Treatment of Addiction: Therapeutic Jurisprudence and Neoliberal Governance," PhD diss., New York University, 2010, 177.

10. Ibid., 181–182.

11. Ibid., 193.

12. Interviewed in Walter Cronkite, "Synanon in Prison," episode 13, season 9, *Twentieth Century*, CBS, aired March 13, 1966, 16-mm film, Box 580, UCLA Synanon Collection.

13. Malcolm X, with Alex Haley, *Autobiography of Malcolm X* (New York: Grove Press, 1965); Eldridge Cleaver, *Soul on Ice* (Berkeley, CA: Ramparts Press, 1968); George Jackson, *Soledad Brother: The Prison Letters of George Jackson* (New York: Bantam, 1970).

14. "Mutual Aid in Prison," *Time*, March 1, 1963, 67.

15. Bernstein, *America Is the Prison*, 75–98.

16. "Synanon in Prison," Box 580, UCLA Synanon Collection.

17. In *To Slay a White Horse*.

18. In *Nevada State Prison*, 16-mm film, Box 572, UCLA Synanon Collection.

19. Legislative Commission of the Legislative Counsel Bureau of Nevada, *Illegal Narcotic and Drug Use in Nevada*, Bulletin 80 (Carson City: State of Nevada, January 1969), 12. For an overview of the transition away from behavior-modification programs that use a "level" system of rewards, see Alexandra Rutherford, "The Social Control of Behavior Control: Behavior Modification, Individual Rights, and Research Ethics in America, 1971–1979," *Journal of the History of the Behavioral Sciences* 42, no. 3 (2006): 203–220.

20. Joseph Spillane, *Coxsackie* (Baltimore: Johns Hopkins University Press, 2014).

21. Charles Dederich, "Synanon Foundation," paper read before the Southern California Parole Officers, October 1958, Synanon reprint, 1962 (including Dederich's comments from four years later), author's personal collection, cited in David Deitch and Joan Zweben, "Synanon: A Pioneering Response in Drug Treatment and a Signal for Caution," in *Substance Abuse: Clinical Problems and Perspectives*, ed. Joyce Lowinson and Pedro Ruiz (Baltimore: Williams and Wilkins, 1981), 289–302. See also Geoffrey Skoll, *Walk the Walk and Talk the Talk: An Ethnography of a Drug Treatment Facility*. (Philadelphia: Temple University Press, 1992).

22. Quoted in "Synanon Ordered to Move," *Santa Monica Evening Outlook*, August 13, 1959.

23. Quoted in R. D. Fox, "Unique Club Seeks to Whip Narcotics," *Santa Monica Evening Outlook*, January 23, 1959. See also Harry Nelson, "Synanon Drug Center Condemned, Praised," *Los Angeles Times*, October 8, 1961.

24. "State Parole Officer Praises Synanon," *Santa Monica Evening Outlook*, September 2, 1959.

25. "Dope Addict Flood Into State Feared: Synanon Plan Would Bring in Users from NY," *Los Angeles Times*, November 12, 1964; Sidney Finkelstein, interviewed by the author, Safety Harbor, FL, July 23, 2011.

26. Guy Endore, *Synanon* (New York: Doubleday, 1968), 297–300.

27. Ibid.

28. Synanon information flyer, Folder "Games: Seawall Berkeley," Box 70, UCLA Synanon Collection.

29. CDC presentation, in ibid.

30. Endore, *Synanon*, 297–306; Kenneth Hansen, "State Appeals Ruling: Hearing on Synanon Slated Today," *Los Angeles Times*, June 12, 1967.

31. "Synanon Hails Ruling on Tests for Ex-addicts," *Los Angeles Times*, October 13, 1966.

32. Ibid.

33. The distinction between rehabilitation and habilitation is discussed in Rod Mullen and Naya Arbiter, "Against the Odds: Therapeutic Community Approaches to Underclass Drug Abuse," in *Drug Policy in the Americas*, ed. Peter Smith (Boulder, CO: Westview Press, 1992), 179–201. Mullen and Arbiter are former Synanon members.

34. Michael Staub, *Madness Is Civilization: When the Diagnosis Was Social, 1948–1980* (Chicago: University of Chicago Press, 2011), 3.

35. Ibid., 4. Staub notes that the Cold War gave rise to the National Mental Health Act of 1946, the NIMH in 1949, and the first edition of the *Diagnostic and Statistical Manual of Mental Disorders* in 1952.

36. Milgram's experiments on obedience to authority, conducted in the early 1960s, cast subjects in the role of "teachers" whom the experimenter ordered to administer electric shocks to a "learner" (played by an actor) when the learner failed to answer an academic question correctly. In actuality, no shocks were administered; however, Milgram's experiment apparently showed that more than 50 percent of subjects were willing to administer dangerous doses of voltage when given repeated directions by the authority figure—the experimenter—to do so. Similarly, Philip Zimbardo's Stanford Prison Experiment, initially designed to reveal the dehumanizing conditions of prison, ended after only six days when the psychologically healthy young adult subjects thoroughly adopted their randomly assigned hierarchical roles of prisoners and guards. As punishment for minor infractions, the guards stripped the prisoners, placed them in solitary confinement, and deprived them of food, leading to several nervous breakdowns. The researchers describe the experiments in Stanley Milgram, *Obedience to Authority: An Experimental View* (1974; reprint, New York: Harper, 2009), and Philip Zimbardo, *The Lucifer Effect: Understanding How Good People Turn Evil* (New York: Random House, 2007).

37. Donald R. Cressey, "Changing Criminals: The Application of the Theory of Differential Association," *American Journal of Sociology* 61, no. 2 (1955): 116–120.

38. Ibid., 119.

39. "S.S. Hang Tough," *Time*, April 7, 1961, Synanon offprint, author's personal collection; Rita Volkman and Donald Cressey, "Differential Association and the Rehabilitation of Drug Addicts," *American Journal of Sociology* 69 (1963): 139.

40. Volkman and Cressey, "Differential Association and the Rehabilitation of Drug Addicts," 129.

41. Lewis Yablonsky, *Confessions of a Criminologist: Some of My Best Friends Were Sociopaths* (New York: iUniverse, 2010), chaps. 1 and 2.

42. Lewis Yablonsky, *Synanon: The Tunnel Back* (1965; reprint, Baltimore: Penguin, 1967), 2–3.

43. Ibid.

44. Yablonsky, *Confessions of a Criminologist*, Kindle e-book, location 1363–1380.

45. Ibid.

46. Charles Dederich, Father William Dubay, and Lewis Yablonsky, lecture, San Francisco Valley State College, April 19, 1966, audio recording, Box 611, UCLA Synanon Collection.

47. According to Jennifer Platt, "participant observation" as we understand it today emerged following World War II ("The Development of the 'Participant Observation' Method in Sociology: Origin Myth and History," *Journal of the History of the Behavioral Sciences* 19 [1983]: 379–393).

48. Quoted in Endore, *Synanon*, 241.

49. Daniel Casriel, *So Fair a House: The Story of Synanon* (Englewood Cliffs, NJ: Prentice-Hall, 1963), 4–5.

50. Ibid., 6.

51. Casriel worked in Metropolitan and Riverside Hospitals.

52. Casriel, *So Fair a House*, 3, 6.

53. Ibid., 11, 42–43.

54. Ibid., 208.

55. Daniel Casriel and David Deitch, *New Success in the Cure of Addicts* (Staten Island, NY: Daytop Village, 1967), 3.

56. Mitchell Rosenthal, oral history with David Courtwright, July 23, 1981, Addicts Who Survived Collection, Columbia University Center for Oral History, New York.

57. "Nolan Diller Psychoanalysis," audio recording, Box 614, UCLA Synanon Collection.

58. Rosenthal, oral history with Courtwright, July 23, 1981.

59. Peter Sheehy, "The Triumph of Group Therapeutics: Therapy, the Social Self, and Liberalism in America, 1910–1960," PhD diss., University of Virginia, 2002.

60. Steven Simon, "Synanon: Toward Building a Humanistic Organization," *Journal of Humanistic Psychology* 8, no. 3 (1978): 4.

61. Ibid., 15, 16.

62. Sidney Jo Becker, "Synanon: An Alternate Lifestyle for the Non-addict," PhD diss., UCLA, 1973; Lewis Yablonsky, *Robo-paths: People as Machines* (New York: Penguin, 1972).

63. Jeremy Varon, *Bringing the War Home: The Weather Underground, the Red Army Faction, and Revolutionary Violence in the Sixties and Seventies* (Berkeley: University of California Press, 2004), 74–112.

64. Tom Wolfe, "The 'Me' Decade and the Third Great Awakening" *New York Magazine*, August 23, 1976, 26–40, http://nymag.com/news/features/45938/, accessed December 15, 2015.

65. Tom Snyder, ed., *120 Years of American Education: A Statistical Portrait*, vol. 1 (Alexandria, VA: National Center for Education Statistics, 1993), 66 (in chap. 3, "Higher Education").

66. For this origin story, see William J. Rorabaugh, *Berkeley at War: The 1960s* (Oxford: Oxford University Press, 1989); Seth Rosenfeld, *Subversives: The FBI's War on Student Radicals and Reagan's Rise to Power* (New York: Farrar, Strauss and Giroux, 2012); James Miller, *Democracy Is in the Streets: From Port Huron to the Siege of Chicago* (Cambridge, MA: Harvard University Press, 1987); Kirkpatrick Sale, *SDS: The Rise and Development of the Students for a Democratic Society* (New York: Random House, 1973).

67. Don Lattin, *The Harvard Psychedelic Club: How Timothy Leary, Ram Dass, Huston Smith, and Andrew Weil Killed the Fifties and Ushered in a New Age for America* (New York: Harper Collins, 2010).

68. In Denis Mitchell, dir., *The House on the Beach*, 16-mm film (Canadian Broadcasting Corporation, Westinghouse Broadcasting Corporation, 1965), Box 593, UCLA Synanon Collection.

69. Casriel, *So Fair a House*, 5.

70. Warren Katz, interviewed by the author, Park Ridge, NJ, March 9, 2013.

71. Quoted in Endore, *Synanon*, 167.

72. Wendy Williams, interviewed by the author, Princeton, NJ, March 6, 2013.

73. Wolfe, "The 'Me' Decade."

74. Timothy Miller, *The Sixties Communes: Hippies and Beyond* (Syracuse, NY: Syracuse University Press, 1999), xvii–xx.

75. For an overview of how historians and writers have viewed counterculture history through the lens of Woodstock and Altamont, see the introduction in John McMillian, *Smoking Typewriters: The Sixties Underground Press and the Rise of Alternative Media in America* (Oxford: Oxford University Press, 2011).

76. In Mitchell, *The House on the Beach.*

77. Grace Elizabeth Hale, *The Romance of the Outsider: How the White Middle Class Fell in Love with Rebellion in Postwar America* (Oxford: Oxford University Press, 2011), 7.

78. Howard Becker, *Outsiders: Studies in the Sociology of Deviance* (New York: Free Press, 1963).

79. Quoted in Lynn Grossberg, "Dope Addicts Discover a Cure for Themselves," *Sepia*, August 1961, Synanon offprint, author's personal collection.

80. "Synanon Members as of 11/1/64," Folder "Population History," UCLA Synanon Collection; Rod Janzen, *The Rise and Fall of Synanon: A California Utopia* (Baltimore: Johns Hopkins University Press, 2001), 26.

81. Tom Wolfe, "Radical Chic: That Party at Lenny's," *New York Magazine*, June 8, 1970, http://nymag.com/news/features/46170/, accessed December 11, 2015. Wolfe described a fund-raiser held for the Black Panthers by famous composer Leonard Bernstein. In 1967, a list of twenty-seven Hollywood luminaries supported Synanon's contention that police opponents were "racial bigots." The list included Francis Ford Coppola, Leonard Nimoy, and Synanon supporters who participated in the Columbia Pictures film made in 1965, such as actress Eartha Kitt. See "Synanon Is in Danger," Motion Picture and Television Committee for Synanon, advertisement printed in *Hollywood Reporter*, September 22, 1967, Synanon Folder, Social Movements Collection, microfilm, University of California at Berkeley.

82. Louis Robinson, "Drug Addicts Who Cure Each Other," *Ebony*, February 1963, 120. See also Susan Glass, "Synanon: The Integrated Community," *The Crisis*, June–July 1965, 54–55.

83. Hedda Hopper, "Honors, Film Bids Heaped on Poitier," *Los Angeles Times*, May 2, 1964; Hedda Hopper, "Poitier Quits 'Synanon House,'" *Los Angeles Times*, August 21, 1964.

84. For descriptions of Synanon Oakland's youth and breakfast programs, see Samuel and Edith Grafton, *Youth Report Newsletter*, n.d.; "Hello! This Is Synanon Oakland," brochure; and "Synanon: One Year in Oakland," all in Synanon Folder, Social Movements Collection, microfilm, University of California at Berkeley. For Synanon "games" and Bay Area Black Panthers, see Janzen, *The Rise and Fall of Synanon*, 25, 29, 47, 133. Eldridge Cleaver, the minister of information for the Oakland-based Black Panther Party and an advocate of guerilla revolutionary tactics—until he converted to Christianity and Republicanism in the late 1970s—corresponded with Synanon members over the course of his long career and took note when the San Francisco–area Synanon branch took up arms in 1973. For Cleaver's correspondence and personal collection of Synanon news clippings, see Synanon Folder, Box 13, Eldridge Cleaver Papers, 1963–1988, University of California at Berkeley. On Synanon's decision to take up arms, see Janzen, *The Rise and Fall of Synanon*, 114.

85. "A California Summary," Folder "State Summaries 1967–1968," Microfilm Roll 36, Office of Economic Opportunity Collection, Lyndon Baines Johnson Presidential Library, Austin, TX. For a parody of the movement, see Tom Wolfe, *Radical Chic and Mau-Mauing the Flak Catchers* (New York: Farrar, Strauss and Giroux, 1970).

86. "Job Corps Adviser: Synanon Plan Praised," *Los Angeles Times*, March 4, 1965; "Synanon Slated to Get U.S. Research Windfall," *Santa Monica Evening Outlook*, May 26, 1967, Folder "OEO: Job Corps," Box 489, UCLA Synanon Collection.

87. Folder "OEO: Job Corps," Box 489, UCLA Synanon Collection.

88. Ron Clark, interviewed by the author, Washington, DC, April 23, 2013; David Deitch, interviewed by the author, La Jolla, CA, May 25, 2011; John Maher quoted in Grover Sales, *John Maher of Delancey Street: A Guide to Peaceful Revolution in America* (New York: Norton, 1976), 54. Clark, Deitch, and Maher went on to lead their own socially active TCs.

89. Quoted in Sales, *John Maher of Delancey Street*, 54.

90. In *Synanon on Film Newsreel: Female Boot Camp*, 16-mm film, Box 572, UCLA Synanon Collection.

91. Jane Howard, *Please Touch: A Guided Tour of the Human Potential Movement* (New York: Dell, 1970).

92. Robert Claiborne, "The Potential of Human Potential," *The Nation*, October 19, 1970, 373–374.

93. Wolfe, "The 'Me' Decade."

94. Christopher Lasch, *The Culture of Narcissism: American Life in an Age of Diminishing Expectations* (New York: Norton, 1991).

95. "The American Dream—a Lie," in Folder "Bypass 1974," Box 81, UCLA Synanon Collection. See also "Synanon Methods Being Used to Aid Collegians with Lost Feeling," *Los Angeles Times*, April 3, 1966.

96. Charles Dederich, "Kennedy Talk," December 1963, audio tape, Box 605, UCLA Synanon Collection; William J. Rorabaugh, *Kennedy and the Promise of the Sixties* (Cambridge: Cambridge University Press, 2004); David Musto and Pamela Korsmeyer,

The Quest for Drug Control: Politics and Federal Policy in a Period of Increasing Substance Abuse (1963–1981) (New Haven, CT: Yale University Press, 2002), 7.

97. For an overview of studies highlighting the California Rehabilitation Center's poor results, see John Kramer and Richard Bass, "Institutionalization Patterns Among Civilly Committed Addicts," *Journal of the American Medical Association* 208, no. 12 (1969): 2287–2301. For the story of Riverside Hospital, see William White, "Riverside Hospital: The Birth of Adolescent Treatment," *Counselor* 5, no. 2 (2004): 18–20. An overview of criticisms of New York and California civil-commitment programs can be found in William White, *Slaying the Dragon: The History of Addiction Treatment and Recovery in America* (Bloomington, IN: Chestnut Health Systems, 1989), 250–251.

98. U.S. Department of Health, Education, and Welfare, *Public Health Service News Summary Bulletin*, September 22, 1962, Folder "Narcotic Addiction White House Conference," Box 3 "Clinical Research Center (CRC), Lexington, Kentucky, Public Relations Correspondence, 1939–1973," Records of the Alcohol, Drug Abuse, and Mental Health Administration (ADAMHA), Record Group (RG) 511, National Archives and Records Administration–Southeast, Morrow, GA.

99. "Remarks of the President to White House Conference on Narcotics (as Actually Delivered)," press release, September 27, 1962, Narcotics Commission Records, Folder F3717:198, Box F317:192–219, California State Archives, Sacramento.

100. "Ex-Drug Addicts Convene Here," *Washington Post*, September 27, 1962.

101. "Hospital and Community Service Facilities for Addicts by State," Folder 3 of 4 "Civil Commitment 1966," Box 7 "Administrative Files, CRC," ADAMHA Records, RG 511, National Archives and Records Administration–Southeast.

102. Folder "Study of the Future of the CRC, 1963–1965," Box 11 "Administrative Files, CRC," ADAMHA Records, RG 511, National Archives and Records Administration–Southeast.

103. Charles Dederich to Sidney Cohen, December 29, 1968, Folder "NIMH-NARA," Box 489, UCLA Synanon Collection.

104. Sidney Cohen to Charles Dederich, January 22, 1969, Folder "NIMH-NARA," Box 489, UCLA Synanon Collection.

105. Nancy Campbell, "The History of a Public Science: How the Addiction Research Center Became the NIDA Intramural Program," *Drug and Alcohol Dependence* 107, no. 1 (2007): 108–112.

106. "Nixon, Synanon in Disagreement," *Santa Monica Evening Outlook*, July 11, 1961.

107. Walker Winslow, "Frontiers: A Lesson from Current History," *Manas*, June 17, 1964, 11–13; Yablonsky, *Synanon*, 392; Endore, *Synanon*, 357; Sales, *John Maher of Delancey Street*, 169, quoting John Maher.

108. Manon S. Perry, "Dorthea Dix," *American Journal of Public Health* 96, no. 4 (2006): 624–625.

109. Winslow, "Frontiers," 13.

110. Quoted in Endore, *Synanon*, 357.

3. SELLING THE SECOND GENERATION

1. Guy Endore, "1,000 Words on Synanon," Guy Endore Collection, UCLA; Guy Endore, *Synanon* (New York: Doubleday, 1968), 61.

2. William Safire, "Hang Tough," in *Safire's Political Dictionary* (New York: Oxford University Press, 2008), 304.

3. Thomas Frank, *The Conquest of Cool: Business Culture, Counterculture, and the Rise of Hip Consumerism* (Chicago: University of Chicago Press, 1997), 168–172.

4. Martin Tolchin, "600 Addicts Aided by Ex-users in City Program," *New York Times*, February 4, 1968.

5. In addition to the tours for U.S. professionals described in previous chapters, in 1967 Synanon was also featured on a drug-focused study tour for professionals with Great Britain's newly funded Addiction Research Unit. The researchers visited many of the representatives from treatment centers that are discussed in this chapter and elsewhere: Lexington penitentiary officials; Vincent Dole and Marie Nyswander; Mitchell Rosenthal and Efren Ramirez; and Jerome Jaffe. See Griffith Edwards, "Seeing America— Diary of a Drug-Focused Study Tour Made in 1967," *Addiction* 105 (2010): 984–990.

6. Michael Massing, *The Fix* (1998; reprint, Berkeley: University of California Press, 2000), 102–104.

7. Todd Gitlin, *The Sixties: Years of Hope, Days of Rage* (New York: Bantam, 1993); Jeremy Varon, "Between Revolution 9 and Thesis 11: Or, Will We Learn (Again) to Start Worrying and Change the World?" in *The New Left Revisited*, ed. John McMillian and Paul Buhle (Philadelphia: Temple University Press, 2003), 214–240; Dan T. Carter, *The Politics of Rage: George Wallace, the Origins of the New Conservatism, and the Transformation of American Politics* (New York: Simon and Schuster, 1995); Rick Perlstein, *Nixonland: The Rise of a President and the Fracturing of America* (New York: Scribner, 2009); Mary C. Brennan, *Turning Right in the Sixties: The Conservative Capture of the GOP* (Chapel Hill: University of North Carolina Press, 1995).

8. George De Leon, *The Therapeutic Community: Theory, Model, Method* (New York: Springer, 2000), 24–25.

9. Barry Sugarman, *Daytop Village: A Therapeutic Community* (New York: Holt, Rinehart, and Winston, 1974), 8–9.

10. Ibid., 9.

11. Endore, *Synanon*, 308.

12. Charles Devlin, interviewed by the author, New York, October 6, 2011; Sugarman, *Daytop Village*, 9.

13. Monsignor William O'Brien, oral history with David Courtwright, July 31, 1981, Addicts Who Survived Collection, Columbia University Center for Oral History, New York; Charles Devlin, interviewed by the author, New York, October 6, 2011; Sugarman, *Daytop Village*, 9.

14. David Deitch, interviewed by the author, La Jolla, CA, May 25, 2011.

15. O'Brien, oral history with Courtwright, July 31, 1981.

16. Ibid.

17. Endore, *Synanon*, 297.

18. O'Brien, oral history with Courtwright, July 31, 1981.

19. Ibid.

20. Deitch, interview by the author, May 25, 2011.

21. Ibid.

22. Daniel Casriel and Grover Amen, *Daytop: Three Addicts and Their Cure* (New York: Hill and Wang, 1971), xv.

23. Sugarman, *Daytop Village*, 9.

24. The intention to pursue a variety of sources for funds is described in the news article "Daytop Village Plans 7 Branches," *New York Times*, June 26, 1966. For example, parents donated approximately $100,000 toward the purchase of a new building for Daytop (C. Gerald Fraser, "Ex-addicts' Parents Clean New Daytop Center," *New York Times*, January 7, 1973).

25. Quoted in Peter Collier, "The House of Synanon," *Ramparts*, October 1967, 54.

26. George Gent, "TV: New Hope for Young Addicts," *New York Times*, July 21, 1967.

27. Ernest Pendrell, dir., *Marathon: The Story of Young Drug Users*, 16-mm film, ABC, aired June 8, 1967.

28. Methadone pioneer Vincent Dole later hypothesized that Lindsay selected the Puerto Rican–born Ramirez to lead his treatment efforts for political reasons (Vincent Dole, oral history with David Courtwright, September 13, 1982, Addicts Who Survived Collection, Columbia University Center for Oral History, New York; Samuel Roberts, "'Rehabilitation' as a Boundary Object: Medicalization, Local Activism, and Narcotics Addiction Policy in New York City, 1951–62," *Social History of Alcohol and Drugs* 26, no. 2 (2012): 163.

29. Thomas Buckley, "City Starts Narcotics Plan to Turn Tide of Addiction," *New York Times*, July 27, 1966.

30. Mitchell Rosenthal, oral history with David Courtwright, July 23, 1981, Addicts Who Survived Collection, Columbia University Center for Oral History, New York.

31. In Pendrell, *Marathon*.

32. In *Current Trends in the Therapy for Narcotic Addiction*, VHS (Public Health Service, U.S. Department of Health, Education, and Welfare, 1969).

33. Sugarman, *Daytop Village*, 93.

34. Daniel Casriel and David Deitch, *New Success in the Cure of Addicts* (Staten Island, NY: Daytop Village, 1967); "Daytop Village 1966," Folder 514, Box 29, Papers of Mayor [John] Lindsay, New York City Municipal Archives; Daniel Casriel, testimony, U.S. Senate, *Inquiry Into the Problem of Alcoholism and Narcotics: Hearing Before the Special Subcommittee on Alcoholism and Narcotics of the Committee on Labor and Public Welfare of the United States Senate*, 91st Cong., 1st sess., October 4, 1969, 787.

35. Murdock Head, dir., *The Distant Drummer: Flowers of Darkness*, VHS (George Washington University, the National Institute of Mental Health, District of Columbia Medical Society, and American Academy of General Practice, 1972).

36. Casriel and Amen, *Daytop*, 77.

37. Quoted in Sugarman, *Daytop Village*, 123.

38. David Bird, "Ramirez to Head Addiction Agency," *New York Times*, November 27, 1967.

39. Rosenthal, oral history with Courtwright, July 23, 1981; for Phoenix House numbers, see Barbara Campbell, "Cost and Space Plague Addicts' Centers," *New York Times*, March 4, 1970.

40. For Synanon residency numbers, see Richard Ofshe, "The Social Development of the Synanon Cult: The Managerial Strategy of Organizational Transformation," *Sociological Analysis* 41, no. 2 (1980): 109–127; Lexington and Fort Worth numbers calculating the residents at the end of fiscal year 1970 are given in "February 1971: Folder Statistical Data," Box 1 "Clinical Research Center Administrative Files, Lexington, Kentucky," Records of the Alcohol, Drug Abuse, and Mental Health Administration, Record Group 511, National Archives and Records Administration–Southeast, Morrow, GA.

41. Phoenix House, *Drug Addiction 1969–1972*, brochure, Folder 560, Box 31, Papers of Mayor Lindsay, New York City Municipal Archives.

42. Dan Garrett to Ted Dibble, November 1967, Graduates Folder, Box 70, Synanon Collection, Charles E. Young Special Collections, UCLA (hereafter UCLA Synanon Collection).

43. Walter V. Collier, Edward Hammock, and Charles Devlin, *An Evaluation Report on the Therapeutic Program of Daytop Village* (Staten Island, NY: Daytop Village, February 1970), 63.

44. Charles Devlin, "Daytop History Timeline," September 2011, Charles Devlin's personal papers, author's copy.

45. "Confirmed Individuals of Daytop Village," June 11, 1968, Charles Devlin's personal papers, author's copy.

46. Quoted in Ron Williams, interviewed by the author, New York, March 6, 2013.

47. Ibid.

48. Ibid.

49. Ibid.

50. Ibid.

51. Ibid.

52. "Kenny Talks About the Time He Was in Phoenix House," May 14, 1971, Box 640, UCLA Synanon Collection.

53. Ibid.

54. Vinny Marino, *Journey from Hell* (Kaneohe, HI: Habilitat, 1966), 143.

55. Ibid.

56. Martin Gansberg, "City Acts to Let Foundation Run Addict Program," *New York Times*, October 12, 1970; Buckley, "City Starts Narcotics Plan to Turn Tide of Addiction."

57. Francis Smith, the Democratic New York City Council president, complained in 1969 that "none" of Phoenix House's residents had completed the program in three years (Maurice Carroll, "Smith Terms Mayor's Program on Drugs 'Highly Unsuccessful,'" *New York Times*, October 19, 1969).

58. When an independent evaluator raised questions about Phoenix House's retention rate and cost efficacy, Rosenthal supplied the Lindsay administration with De Leon's internal evaluation studies and publications. See Mitchell Rosenthal to John Lindsay, April 5,

1973, and appended material in "Phoenix House 1973," Folder 1592, Box 85, Papers of Mayor Lindsay, New York City Municipal Archives.

59. William White, "David Deitch, PhD, and George De Leon, PhD, on Recovery Management and the Future of the Therapeutic Community," *Counselor* 11, no. 5 (2010): 38–49.

60. Therapeutic goals included, for example, "long term drug freedom, elimination of antisocial behavior and attitudes, emotional change, psychological insight, job stability" (George De Leon, "Phoenix House Therapeutic Community: The Influence of Time in Program on Change in Resident Drug Addicts," in *Phoenix House: Studies in a Therapeutic Community, 1968–1973*, ed. George De Leon [New York: MSS Information Corporation, 1974], 194; see this collection for additional key studies).

61. Ibid. 194–198.

62. Quoted in James Markham, "Methadone Therapy Programs: Issue and Debate," *New York Times*, April 17, 1973.

63. Judianne Densen-Gerber, *We Mainline Dreams: The Odyssey House Story* (New York: Doubleday, 1973), 33, 34.

64. Ibid., 34, 35.

65. Ibid., 36.

66. Ibid., 37.

67. Ibid., 37, 41.

68. Quoted in ibid.

69. Quoted in ibid., 44.

70. Ibid., 45.

71. Ibid., 69.

72. Ibid., 73.

73. Quoted in Tolchin, "600 Addicts Aided by Ex-users."

74. Densen-Gerber, *We Mainline Dreams*, 282.

75. Judianne Densen-Gerber, oral history with David Courtwright, August 5, 1981, Addicts Who Survived Collection, Columbia University Center for Oral History, New York.

76. "'Funeral' Held for Narcotics Center," *New York Times*, July 22, 1968.

77. Quoted in Israel Shenker, "A Crusader Aiding Addicts: Doctor Leads Crusade for Teen-aged Addicts," *New York Times*, March 6, 1970.

78. Densen-Gerber, *We Mainline Dreams*, 406, 408.

79. Shenker, "A Crusader Aiding Addicts."

80. Quoted in Alfonso Narvaez, "Addict, 12, Tells Enquiry of Mainlining," *New York Times*, February 27, 1970.

81. Quoted in ibid. Ralphie was dismissed from the program a few weeks later. Densen-Gerber explained that the adolescent unit could not accommodate the needs of such a young patient—including bedtime stories (Martin Arnold, "Boy Who Told of Addiction at 12 Is Back Home," *New York Times*, March 11, 1970).

82. "The Odyssey Move," *New York Times*, February 14, 1970.

83. Densen-Gerber testified: "NARA revisions should make clear . . . that the private sector, including non-profit agencies, should take an active role in commitment and rehabilita-

tion programs" (U.S. House of Representatives, *Treatment and Rehabilitation of Narcotic Addicts: Hearing Before the Subcommittee to Amend the Narcotic Rehabilitation Act of 1966 of the Committee on the Judiciary of the United States House of Representatives*, 92nd Cong., 1st sess., June and September 1971, 692).

84. Beatrice Berg, "Television: Real Life Comes to 'One Life to Live,'" *New York Times*, August 2, 1970.

85. Densen-Gerber, *We Mainline Dreams*, 408.

86. Ibid., 186, 392.

87. Vincent Dole and Marie Nyswander, "A Medical Treatment for Diacetylmorphine (Heroin) Addiction," *Journal of the American Medical Association* 193 (August 23, 1965): 646–650.

88. Marie Nyswander, *The Drug Addict as Patient* (New York: Grune and Stratton, 1956).

89. This history is discussed in more detail in David Courtwright, "The Prepared Mind: Marie Nyswander," *Addiction* 92 (1997): 257–265.

90. Ibid., 258.

91. Ibid., 259; Vincent Dole and Marie Nyswander, "Heroin Addiction: A Metabolic Disease," *Archives of Internal Medicine* 120, no. 1 (1967): 19–24.

92. Casriel, testimony, U.S. Senate, *Inquiry Into the Problem of Alcoholism and Narcotics*, 813. Another variation on this metaphor is "shifting an alcoholic from scotch to cheap wine": Densen-Gerber, oral history with Courtwright, August 5, 1981; William L. Claiborne, "A Daily Dose of Methadone Could Be Answer to Crime," *Washington Post*, December 6, 1970.

93. Courtwright, "The Prepared Mind," 260.

94. Vincent Dole, Marie Nyswander, and Alan Warner, "Successful Treatment of 750 Criminal Addicts," *Journal of the American Medical Association* 206 (December 16, 1968): 2708.

95. Dole explained that Trussel was a strong supporter of his methadone program, in stark contrast to Ramirez (Dole, oral history with Courtwright, September 13, 1982). When Lindsay decided to invest in methadone, he placed the treatment under the purview of the Health Services Agency rather than the Addiction Services Agency, which operated (controversially) with little oversight until comptroller and future mayor Abraham Beame released a damning report in 1970 (Tom Buckley, "Medicine: Lindsay Steps Up Methadone Program," *New York Times*, October 4, 1970).

96. Quoted in Charles G. Bennett, "Addiction Agency Called a 'Fraud': Councilman Moskowitz Says Dr. Ramirez Has Failed," *New York Times*, December 11, 1968.

97. Ibid.

98. Ibid.

99. Buckley, "Medicine."

100. Lindsay left office in 1973 after a party switch and a failed bid for the Democratic presidential nomination in 1972. Abraham Beame, a Democrat and vocal critic of Phoenix House, succeeded him from 1973 to 1977.

101. Courtwright, "The Prepared Mind," 260; Robert Newman, "Methadone Maintenance: It Ain't What It Used to Be," *British Journal of Addiction* 71, no. 2 (1976): 183–187.

102. Peter Bourne, interviewed by the author, Washington, DC, April 24, 2013; Peter Bourne, "Alcoholism and Drug Abuse," n.d., http://petergbourne.co.uk/articles10.html, accessed October 21, 2013.

103. Herman Joseph, Sharon Stancliff, and John Langrod, "Methadone Maintenance Treatment: A Review of Historical and Clinical Issues," *Mount Sinai Journal of Medicine* 67, nos. 5–6 (2000): 347–364.

104. Robert DuPont and Richard Katon, "Development of a Heroin-Addiction Treatment Program: Effect on Urban Crime," *Journal of the American Medical Association* 216 (May 24, 1971): 1320–1324.

105. O'Brien, oral history with Courtwright, July 31, 1981.

106. Deitch, interview by the author, May 25, 2011; Sugarman, *Daytop Village*, 124; Joshua Bloom and Waldo Martin, *Black Against Empire: The History and Politics of the Black Panther Party* (Berkeley: University of California Press, 2013).

107. Quoted in O'Brien, oral history with Courtwright, July 31, 1981.

108. Ibid.

109. Will Lissner, "Narcotics Complex Split by Charges of Cultist Activity," *New York Times*, November 17, 1968.

110. Joe Pilati, "Schism on 14th Street: The Daytop Explosion," *Village Voice*, November 21, 1968.

111. Lissner, "Narcotics Complex Split."

112. Ibid.

113. Will Lissner, "Legal Action Planned in Daytop Dispute," *New York Times*, November 18, 1968.

114. Ibid.

115. Quoted in Pilati, "Schism on 14th Street."

116. Ibid.

117. "4-Day Music Fete Aids Ex-addicts," *New York Times*, June 16, 1968.

118. Deitch, interview by the author, May 25, 2011.

119. This observation was made by a theater critic; see Eleanor Lester, ". . . Or the Wave of the Future?" *New York Times*, June 30, 1968.

120. Casriel and Amen, *Daytop*, 82–83.

121. See, for example, the review in Dan Sullivan, "The Theater: 'The Concept' Pictures Narcotics Victims Ordeal: Rescued Addicts Recall Their Cure in Play," *New York Times*, May 7, 1968.

122. Robert Brustein, "New Fads, Ancient Truths," *New York Times*, August 17, 1969.

123. Casriel and Amen, *Daytop*, xxv, citing the *Village Voice* critic.

124. Sullivan, "The Theater."

125. Lawrence Sacharow, "A Carbon Copy 'Concept'?" *New York Times*, September 7, 1969.

126. Ibid.

127. Mortimer Levitt, "A Community 'Concept'?" *New York Times*, September 21, 1969.

128. "Daytop Board Gains Control of Center," *New York Times*, December 3, 1968.

129. Raymond Glasscote, James N. Sussex, Jerome H. Jaffe, John Ball, and Leon Brill, *The Treatment of Drug Abuse: Programs, Problems, Prospects* (Washington, DC: American Psychiatric Association, 1972), 83–103, 242–244.

130. "Daytop Village Gets Grant," *New York Times*, July 30, 1970.

131. Daniel Casriel, *A Scream Away from Happiness* (New York: Grosset and Dunlap, 1972).

132. Griffith Edwards, "Conversation with David Deitch," *Addiction* 94 (1999): 795.

133. Jerome H. Jaffe, "The Nathan B. Eddy Lecture: Science, Policy, Happenstance," in *Problems of Drug Dependence, 1994: Proceedings of the 56th Annual Scientific Meeting, the College on Problems of Drug Dependence*, vol. 1 (Rockville, MD: National Institute on Drug Abuse, 1994), 21.

134. Ibid.

135. Ibid., 21–25.

136. Jerome Jaffe, interviewed by the author, Baltimore, April 23, 2013.

137. Jaffe, "Nathan B. Eddy Lecture," 21–25.

138. Schuster and Hughes later emerged as international leaders in addiction research.

139. Jaffe, "Nathan B. Eddy Lecture," 21–25.

140. Jaffe, interview by the author, April 23, 2013.

141. This debate is recorded in the film *Current Trends in the Therapy for Narcotic Addiction*.

142. Ibid.

143. Jerome Jaffe, oral history with Nancy Campbell, transcript, n.d., Oral History of Substance Abuse Research, William White Papers, Bentley Historical Library, University of Michigan, Ann Arbor, http://www.williamwhitepapers.com/pr/2013%20Dr.%20Jerome%20Jaffe.pdf, accessed December 11, 2015.

144. Jerome Jaffe, Misha S. Zaks, and Edward N. Washington, "Experience with the Use of Methadone in a Multi-modality Program for the Treatment of Narcotics Users," *International Journal of the Addictions* 4 (September 1969): 481–490.

145. Jaffe, interview by the author, April 23, 2013.

146. Ibid.

147. Jaffe, oral history with Campbell, n.d.; Jaffe, "Nathan B. Eddy Lecture," 24.

148. Jaffe, interview by the author, April 23, 2013.

149. Ibid.

150. Ibid.

151. Jaffe, oral history with Campbell, n.d. The new TC, called BRASS, became a corporate shell that was later adopted by another Chicago TC.

152. Darcy, scarcely out of his teens at the time, grew into a leader in the field and president of the Therapeutic Communities of America.

153. Jaffe, "Nathan B. Eddy Lecture," 23.

154. Glasscote et al., *The Treatment of Drug Abuse*, 148; Jaffe, interview by the author, April 23, 2013.

155. Ibid.

156. David Courtwright, *Dark Paradise: A History of Opiate Addiction in America*, 2nd ed. (Cambridge, MA: Harvard University Press, 2001), 165–174.

157. Ibid. Edward Jay Epstein argues that Nixon, unlike campaign opponent and New York governor Nelson Rockefeller, did not link crime and drug use in the 1968 campaign. According to Epstein, it was only later in his first term that Nixon—when he realized that new drug policies could produce data-driven results and powerful, "tough" rhetoric— made drug control a central part of his political agenda (*Agency of Fear: Opiate and Political Power in America* [New York: Verso, 1990], chaps. 4 and 5).

158. Massing, *The Fix*, 102.

159. Ibid., 97.

160. Ibid., 100–101.

161. Ibid., 102.

162. Ibid.

163. Quoted in ibid., 103.

164. Quoted in ibid.

165. Ibid., 104–105.

166. Ibid., 103–112; DuPont and Katon, "Development of a Heroin-Addiction Treatment Program."

167. White House Tapes, OVAL 516–510, June 10, 1971, 3:08–4:24 p.m., Richard Milhaus Nixon Presidential Library, Yorba Linda, CA.

168. Ibid.; see also Massing, *The Fix*, 105.

169. U.S. Senate, *Inquiry Into the Problem of Alcoholism and Narcotics*; U.S. House of Representatives, *Treatment and Rehabilitation of Narcotics Addicts: Hearing Before the Subcommittee to Amend the Narcotic Rehabilitation Act of 1966 of the Committee on the Judiciary of the United States House of Representatives*, 92nd Cong., 1st sess., June 23 and 30 and September 21, 23, 24, 29, 30, 1971.

170. Casriel, testimony, U.S. Senate, *Inquiry Into the Problem of Alcoholism and Narcotics*, 787.

171. For an example of each of these analogies in context, see the congressional testimony of recovered addicts in ibid., 698, 704.

172. Samuel Anglin, testimony, ibid., 698.

173. For the history fetal alcohol syndrome, see Janet Golden, *Message in a Bottle: The Making of Fetal Alcohol Syndrome* (Cambridge, MA: Harvard University Press, 2005); for one example of an article on methadone's effect on infants, see Stuart Auerbach, "Babies Born Addicted to Methadone," *Washington Post*, February 26, 1972.

174. Vincent Dole, testimony, U.S. House of Representatives, *Treatment and Rehabilitation of Narcotic Addicts*, 399.

175. Representative Robert McClory, response in ibid., 399.

176. McClory, response in ibid.

177. Anglin, testimony, U.S. Senate, *Inquiry Into the Problem of Alcoholism and Narcotics*, 700.

178. William O'Brien, "Address to the Ninth World Conference of Therapeutic Communities," San Francisco, 1985, reprinted in Lewis Yablonsky, *The Therapeutic Community: A Successful Approach for Treating Substance Abuse* (Lake Worth, FL: Gardner Press, 1994), 39.

179. For a discussion of "community as method" and an overview of changes in TC structure, see De Leon, *The Therapeutic Community*.

180. Representative Lawrence Hogan (R–MD), statement in U.S. House of Representatives, *Treatment and Rehabilitation of Narcotic Addicts*, 695.

181. A pioneering and influential nationwide study of treatment efficacy began in 1969 when the NIMH contracted with Texas Christian University to produce a large-scale evaluation study of the drug-treatment models employed by fifty-two agencies taking part in the Drug Abuse Reporting Program. See Saul B. Sells, ed., *Studies of the Effectiveness of Treatments for Drug Abuse*, vol. 1 (Cambridge, MA: Ballinger, 1974). It is important to note that other modalities of treatment existed in the late 1960s and early 1970s—such as hospital detoxification programs and religious treatments, including Teen Challenge. However, most comparative academic studies such as Sells's focused on variations of methadone and TC treatments, either independently or in their "multimodal" forms.

182. Douglas K. Spiegel and Saul B. Sells, "Part I: Evaluation of Treatments for Drug Users in DARP," in Sells, *Studies of the Effectiveness of Treatments for Drug Abuse*, 1:170–171.

183. Ibid., 1:191–192.

184. Ibid., 1:170.

185. Edward Jay Epstein, "Methadone: The Forlorn Hope," *Public Interest* 36 (Summer 1974): 14.

186. For an overview of the shifting media coverage, see Ronald Bayer, "Liberal Opinion and the Problem of Heroin Addiction: 1960–1973," *Contemporary Drug Problems* 93 (Summer 1975): 93–112.

187. Quoted in Richard Severo, "Chemistry Is the New Hope," *New York Times*, March 19, 1971.

188. For an overview of the historical significance of the rise in mass incarceration in the United States, see Heather Ann Thompson, "Why Mass Incarceration Matters: Rethinking Crisis, Decline, and Transformation in Postwar America," *Journal of American History* 97, no. 3 (2010): 703–733. For an overview of mass incarceration in relation to punitive drug laws, see Michelle Alexander, *The New Jim Crow: Mass Incarceration in the Age of Colorblindness* (New York: New Press, 2009). For the role that African American antidrug and anticrime community activists played in lobbying for both treatment and harsher penalties, see Michael Javen Fortner, *Black Silent Majority: The Rockefeller Drug Laws and the Politics of Punishment* (Cambridge, MA: Harvard University Press, 2015).

189. Governor Reagan reduced the funding for California's proposed methadone program from $5,020,000 to $20,000 (Associated Press, "Reagan Methadone Veto Draws Sharp Criticism," *Modesto Bee*, August 21, 1972). Although the state reversed course, the history of methadone had different patterns of diffusion in California and New York. See "Differences Between New York and California," in *Federal Regulation of Methadone Treatment*, ed. Richard Retting and Adam Yarmolinsky (Washington, DC: National Academies Press, 1995), 85–89.

4. LEFT, RIGHT, AND CHAOS

1. Robert L. Dupont, "The Drug Abuse Decade," *Journal of Drug Issues* 8, no. 2 (1978): 183. On the Controlled Substances Act as "Big Tent" legislation, see Joseph Spillane,

"Debating the Controlled Substances Act," *Drug and Alcohol Dependence* 76, no. 1 (2004): 17–29, and David Courtwright, "The Controlled Substances Act: How a 'Big Tent' Reform Became a Punitive Drug Law," *Drug and Alcohol Dependence* 76, no. 1 (2004): 9–15.

2. The cover of the first edition of Michael Massing's book *The Fix* (1998; reprint, Berkeley: University of California Press, 2000) read "Nixon Was Right." The College on Problems of Drug Dependence, an organization of addiction researchers, gave Massing a Media Award for his work in 2001. See also Courtwright, "The Controlled Substances Act"; David T. Courtwright, "NIDA: This Is Your Life," *Drug and Alcohol Dependence* 107, no. 1 (2010): 116–118; Nancy Campbell, review of Jeremy Kuzmarov, *The Myth of the Addicted Army: Vietnam and the Modern War on Drugs, Social History of Alcohol and Drugs* 24, no. 2 (2010): 176–177; Kevin Yuill, "Another Take on the Nixon Presidency: The First Therapeutic President?" *Journal of Policy History* 21, no. 2 (2009): 138–162.

3. David Greenberg, *Nixon's Shadow: The History of an Image* (New York: Norton, 2004), 73–125. In *Decade of Nightmares: The End of the Sixties and the Making of Eighties America* (Oxford: Oxford University Press, 2006), Philip Jenkins argues that Watergate ushered in an "age of paranoia" (23).

4. Nancy Campbell, "The History of a Public Science: How the Addiction Research Center Became the NIDA Intramural Research Program," *Drug and Alcohol Dependence* 107, no. 1 (2010): 109.

5. Quoted in Cliff Linedecker, "Escape from Addiction: Drug Addicts Treated, Not Punished," *Philadelphia Inquirer*, March 30, 1970.

6. Robert S. Weppner, *The Untherapeutic Community: Organizational Behavior in a Failed Addiction Treatment Program* (Lincoln: University of Nebraska Press, 1983), 39.

7. Robert S. Weppner, "Matrix House: Its First Year in Lexington," *HSMA Health Reports* 86, no. 9 (1971): 762.

8. Quoted in Cliff Linedecker, "Escape from Addiction: South Phila. 'Hustler' Turns Designer," *Philadelphia Inquirer*, March 31, 1970. A note on identity: It is possible to determine the names of Matrix members through public records such as newspaper articles, court records, and open government archives. However, cofounder "Terry" left relatively early in the history of the organization, and press accounts simply use his first name, as I have done here. Weppner's book *The Untherapeutic Community* uses pseudonyms for Matrix leaders. However, the identities of other leaders such as Jon Wildes and Jay Theirren (called "Ron" and "Ray" in Weppner's book) can be easily determined by cross-referencing Weppner's account with the published newspaper articles cited in the book and with available government documents.

9. Weppner, *The Untherapeutic Community*, 39.

10. Weppner, "Matrix House," 762.

11. Dick Shea, interviewed by Luke Walden and J. P. Olsen (King Love Films), undated transcript, author's personal collection; Joan Roesgen, "After Matrix, Can They Make It?" *Kingsport Times News*, undated clipping from a series published in October 1970, Folder "Clinical Research Center (CRC) Publicity, Lexington, Kentucky," Box 1 "CRC Public Relations 1939–1973, Clippings," Records of the Alcohol, Drug Abuse, and Mental

Health Administration (ADAMHA), Record Group (RG) 511, National Archives and Records Administration–Southeast, Morrow, GA.

12. Margie Smith, interviewed by Luke Walden and J. P. Olsen (King Love Films), undated transcript, author's personal collection.

13. Jack Croughan, interviewed by Luke Walden and J. P. Olsen (King Love Films), undated transcript, author's personal collection.

14. "Matrix Unit Quarterly Report," October–December 1971, Folder "Quarterly Report October–December 1971," Box 4 "Administrative Files, CRC," ADAMHA Records 1957–1974, RG 511, National Archives and Records Administration–Southeast.

15. Joan Roesgen, "Cured Addicts Fall Back Fast," *Kingsport Times News*, undated clipping from a series published in October 1970, Folder "CRC Publicity," Box 1 "Personnel 1961–1971, Administrative Office, CRC," ADAMHA Records, RG 511, National Archives and Records Administration–Southeast. See also Matrix House promotional material republished in Nancy Campbell, Luke Walden, and J. P. Olsen, *The Narcotic Farm: The Rise and Fall of America's First Prison for Drug Addicts* (New York: Abrams, 2008).

16. Weppner, "Matrix House," 767.

17. Ibid., 766.

18. Ibid.

19. Quoted in Linedecker, "Escape from Addiction: South Phila. 'Hustler' Turns Designer."

20. Quoted in "NIMH Clinical Research Center Special Report for 1971 Budget Hearings," Folder "Special Report for 1971 Budget Hearings," Box 2 "CRC Financial Records 1937–1973, Working Capital," ADAMHA Records, RG 511, National Archives and Records Administration–Southeast.

21. "Ex-Addicts Hired by the Federal Government," under "HEW News Press Release," Folder "Lexington Staffing Issues 1969–1971," Box 1 "Personnel 1961–1971, Administrative Office, CRC," ADAMHA Records, RG 511, National Archives and Records Administration–Southeast.

22. Quoted in Weppner, *The Untherapeutic Community*, 45.

23. Harold Conrad, *A Word of Introduction*, Matrix House promotional brochure, digital scan, author's personal collection. Conrad wrote, "Matrix House is being studied intensively from the research point of view."

24. Weppner, "Matrix House," 768.

25. Weppner, *The Untherapeutic Community*, 149–150.

26. Ibid., 67–68, 177.

27. "Emerson, Thoreau, and Yablonsky" is from Weppner, *The Untherapeutic Community*, 89. The Hoffman and Mao reading materials are confirmed in Marty Panone, interviewed by Luke Walden and J. P. Olsen (King Love Films), undated transcript, author's personal collection.

28. Smith, interview by Walden and Olsen. Wildes later claimed his work in Matrix had been a political protest for gay liberation (Weppner, *The Untherapeutic Community*, 149). This claim confirmed Lexington staff's assumptions about his sexual orientation, as

discussed in Sidney Louis, "Matrix House," Folder 22, Box 7, Lexington Collection, Kentucky Historical Society, Lexington.

29. Smith, interview by Walden and Olsen; Weppner, *The Untherapeutic Community*, 149.

30. Wildes told longer-term residents that some of Matrix's new members might be "people that would have been undesirable in the first year and a half," remembered former resident Dick Shea, "people that would bring down the house" (Shea, interview by Walden and Olsen).

31. Weppner, *The Untherapeutic Community*, 149–150.

32. Harold Conrad to Acting Director, Division of Narcotic Addiction and Drug Abuse, "Memo: Annual Report—Fiscal Year 1971," July 1, 1971, Folder "Annual Reports 1971," Box 4 "Administrative Files, CRC," ADAMHA Records 1957–1974, RG 511, National Archives and Records Administration–Southeast.

33. Shea, Smith, and Panone, interviews by Walden and Olsen.

34. Shea, interview by Walden and Olsen.

35. Ibid. Green also charged Wildes with sexual abuse (Weppner, *The Untherapeutic Community*, 150–151; Bob Cooper, "Former Patients Relate Sex, Violence," *Kentucky New Era*, April 13, 1973).

36. Panone, interview by Walden and Olsen.

37. Smith, interview by Walden and Olsen; Weppner, *The Untherapeutic Community*, 153.

38. Weppner, *The Untherapeutic Community*, 179.

39. Smith, interview by Walden and Olsen. Jack Anderson was on a master list of Nixon's political enemies that emerged during the Watergate hearings. The list was compiled by Nixon's special counsel Chuck Colson. For more on the alleged plot to kill Andersen, see Mark Feldstein, *Poisoning the Press: Richard Nixon, Jack Anderson, and the Rise of Washington's Scandal Culture* (New York: Farrar, Strauss and Giroux, 2008).

40. Cooper, "Former Patients Relate Sex, Violence."

41. Associated Press, "Indictments Returned in Probe of Drug Center," *Harlan Daily Enterprise*, April 19, 1973; Weppner, *The Untherapeutic Community*, 165.

42. Quoted in "Ex-Matrix Head Derelict in Duties—Grand Jury," *Lexington Leader*, April 22, 1975.

43. Labor–Management Committee Meeting, June 18, 1970, minutes, Folder "Lexington Staffing Issues 1969–1971," Box 1 "Personnel 1961–1971, Administrative Office, CRC," ADAMHA Records, RG 511, National Archives and Records Administration–Southeast.

44. In fact, Matrix House established storefronts, began a new initiative in Pee Wee Valley Women's Prison, and even had plans to expand to Australia ("Matrix House Annual Report—Fiscal Year–1971," Folder "Annual Reports 1971," Box 4 "Administrative Files, CRC," ADAMHA Records 1957–1974, RG 511, National Archives and Records Administration–Southeast; Shea, interview by Walden and Olsen.

45. Campbell, "The History of a Public Science," 109.

46. "Ex-addicts Hired by the Federal Government." In a private letter to Conrad, Brown encouraged the Lexington chief's speaking engagements with Matrix members and suggested using images in promotional material: "You are in tune with the times! Equal

employment and consumer participation are recurrent themes in the daily life of the Washington branch of the Institute" (Bertram Brown to Harold T. Conrad, October 13, 1970, Folder "Special Report for 1971 Budget Hearings," Box 2 "CRC Financial Records 1937–1973, Working Capital," ADAMHA Records, RG 511, National Archives and Records Administration–Southeast.

47. Weppner, *The Untherapeutic Community*, 103.

48. "Matrix House Annual Report—Fiscal Year–1971."

49. Harold Conrad to Director, Division of Narcotic Addiction and Drug Abuse, March 9, 1971, Folder "CRC Publicity," Box 1 "CRC Public Relations 1939–1973, Clippings," ADAMHA Records, RG 511, National Archives and Records Administration–Southeast.

50. Harold Conrad to Sidney Cohen, May 5, 1970, Folder "CRC Publicity," Box 1 "CRC Public Relations 1939–1973, Clippings," ADAMHA Records, RG 511, National Archives and Records Administration–Southeast.

51. Sidney Louis, "The Ex-addict Speaker," n.d., Folder 10, Box 6, Lexington Collection, Kentucky Historical Society.

52. Cliff Linedecker, "Escape from Addiction: Local Center Needed to Aid Victims," *Philadelphia Inquirer*, April 2, 1970; Matrix House informational booklet attached to a memo from Harold Conrad to All Clinical Research Center Employees, "Subject: Open House," July 27, 1970, Folder 22, Box 7, Lexington Collection, Kentucky Historical Society.

53. Weppner, *The Untherapeutic Community*, 175.

54. Harold Conrad to All Clinical Research Center Employees, "Subject: Open House," July 27, 1970.

55. Jack Miller, Synanon Speaker's Bureau, to Charles Dederich, April 1, 1971, Folder "Public Relations Information 1965–1971," Box 83, Synanon Collection, Charles E. Young Special Collections, UCLA (hereafter UCLA Synanon Collection).

56. "NARA II Quarterly Report: Jan–March 31, 1970," Folder "Quarterly Reports thru March 1970," Box 1 "Administrative Files, CRC," ADAMHA Records 1957–1974, RG 511, National Archives and Records Administration–Southeast.

57. Sidney Louis, "Matrix House," n.d., Folder 22, Box 7, Lexington Collection, Kentucky Historical Society.

58. Croughan, interview by Walden and Olsen; Glynn Tucker, Lexington guard, interviewed by Luke Walden and J. P. Olsen (King Love Films), undated transcript, author's personal collection.

59. Folder "Organization Charts," Box 12 "Administrative Files, CRC," ADAMHA Records 1957–197, RG 511, National Archives and Records Administration–Southeast.

60. Croughan, interview by Walden and Olsen.

61. Louis, "Matrix House."

62. This was during a period of transition between SAODAP and NIDA when Dupont was heading both of them and supervising the transition.

63. Bertram Brown, NIMH director, to HEW secretary, December 13, 1972, Folder "Memos and Correspondence," Box 7 "Administrative Files, CRC," ADAMHA Records 1957–1974, RG 511.

64. Nancy Campbell, *Discovering Addiction: The Science and Politics of Substance Abuse Research* (Ann Arbor: University of Michigan Press, 2007), 136–137.

65. Ibid., 57–58.

66. Ibid., 136.

67. Campbell, "The History of a Public Science," 111.

68. Robert L. Dupont, "Reflections on the Early History of National Institute on Drug Abuse (NIDA): Implications for Today," *Journal of Drug Issues* 39, no. 5 (2009): 9.

69. Campbell, *Discovering Addiction*, 169.

70. For a detailed discussion of the "crisis of legitimacy" in the prison system, see Jessica Neptune, "The Making of the Carceral State: Street Crime, the War on Drugs, and Punitive Politics in New York, 1951–1973," PhD diss., University of Chicago, 2012, esp. chap. 6.

71. "NARA I Quarterly Report—Jan, Feb, March 1970," Folder "Quarterly Reports thru 1970," Box 1 "Administrative Files, CRC," ADAMHA Records 1957–1974, RG 511, National Archives and Records Administration–Southeast.

72. On Attica, see Neptune, "The Making of the Carceral State," chap. 6; Tom Wicker, *A Time to Die: The Attica Prison Revolt* (New York: Haymarket Books, 1975); Heather Ann Thompson, *Blood in the Water: The Attica Uprising of 1971 and Its Legacy* (New York: Pantheon Books, 2016).

73. James Q. Whitman, *Harsh Justice: Criminal Punishment and the Widening Divide Between America and Europe* (New York: Oxford University Press, 2003); Naomi Murakawa, *The First Civil Right: How Liberals Built Prison America* (New York: Oxford University Press, 2014).

74. For a summary of the trajectory of this argument, see Gerald Klerman, "Behavior Control and the Limits of Reform," *Hastings Center Report*, August 1975, 40–45.

75. David Garland, *The Culture of Control: Crime and Social Order in Contemporary Society* (Chicago: University or Chicago Press, 2001), chap. 1.

76. Jessica Neptune, "Harshest in the Nation: The Rockefeller Drug Laws and the Widening Embrace of Punitive Politics," *Social History of Alcohol and Drugs* 26, no. 2 (2012): 170–191.

77. Jessica Mitford, *Kind and Usual Punishment: The Prison Business* (New York: Random House, 1973).

78. Tina Stevens argues that the emergence of bioethics was influenced by leftist critiques of science and medicine in the 1960s—specifically by scholars such as Theodore Roszack and Herbert Marcuse—but the institutionalization of bioethics ultimately diffused those critiques (*Bioethics in America: Origins and Cultural Politics* [Baltimore: Johns Hopkins University Press, 2000]).

79. Max Holland, *Leak: Why Mark Felt Became Deep Throat* (Lawrence: University of Kansas Press, 2012).

80. Radley Balko, *Rise of the Warrior Cop: The Militarization of America's Police Forces* (New York: Public Affairs, 2012), 101.

81. Ibid., 105.

82. Kathleen Frydl, *Drug Wars in America, 1940–1973* (New York: Cambridge University Press, 2013), 290.

83. Balko, *Rise of the Warrior Cop*, 95.

84. Matthew P. Dumont, "The Junkie as Political Enemy," *American Journal of Orthopsychiatry* 43 (1973): 539.

85. U.S. Senate, *Individual Rights and the Federal Role in Behavior Modification: A Study Prepared by the Staff of the Subcommittee on Constitutional Rights of the Committee on the Judiciary*, 93rd Cong., 2nd sess., November 1974 (Washington, DC: U.S. Government Printing Office, 1974). Popular articles submitted with the report included, for example, Jessica Mitford, "The Torture Cure," *Harper's*, August 1973, 16–30, and Stephen L. Chorover, "The Pacification of the Brain," *Psychology Today*, May 1974, 59–69.

86. U.S. Senate, *Individual Rights*, 35–36.

87. Ibid., 1–2.

88. Klerman, "Behavior Control," 45.

89. Ibid. See also the special issue of the National Caucus of Labor Committees periodical *The Campaigner* published in February–March 1974, featuring articles such as L. Marcus, "Editorial: Rockefeller's 1984-Plot," 5–18, and Carol Menzel, "Coercive Psychology: Capitalism's Monster Science," 33–54.

90. Leaders in the TC field and other treatment enterprises engaged in the debate. See Dan Waldorf, "Social Control in Therapeutic Communities for Drug Addicts," *International Journal of the Addictions* 6 (March 1971): 29–43; Leon Brill, "Some Comments on the Paper 'Social Control in Therapeutic Communities' by Dan Waldorf," *International Journal of the Addictions* 6 (March 1971): 45–50.

91. Helene Kloth, North Miami High School guidance counselor, recorded statement in U.S. Senate, *Individual Rights*, 190.

92. Robert J. Fournier to Florida governor Rueben Askew, May 23, 1973, Surviving Straight Inc. website, http://www.survivingstraightinc.com/SeedFloridaGovernmentDocs/SeedLetters/Seed-Governors-Office-GovAskew_Combine.pdf, accessed October 8, 2016.

93. National Commission for the Protection of Human Subjects of Biomedical and Behavioral Research, Department of Health, Education, and Welfare, *Belmont Report: Ethical Principles and Guidelines for the Protection of Human Subjects of Research* (Washington, DC: U.S. Government Printing Office, September 30, 1978).

94. Campbell, "The History of a Public Science."

95. Daniel Casriel, *So Fair a House: The Story of Synanon* (Englewood Cliffs, NJ: Prentice-Hall, 1963), 176.

96. Maia Szalavitz, *Help at Any Cost: How the Troubled-Teen Industry Cons Parents and Hurts Kids* (New York: Riverhead Books, 2006), 35.

97. U.S. Senate, *Individual Rights*, 183–184.

98. Judith Miller, "The Seed: Reforming Drug Users with Love," *Science* 182, no. 4107 (1973): 41.

99. Statistical Review of the Seed, Inc., February 20, 1973, Surviving Straight Inc. website, http://www.survivingstraightinc.com/SeedFloridaGovernmentDocs/SeedInternalDocs/1973-SEED-In-House-Statistical-Review-of-the-Seed_Combine.pdf, accessed October 8, 2016.

100. Robert S. Weppner and James A. Inciardi, "Decriminalizing Marijuana," *International Journal of Offender Therapy and Comparative Criminology* 22, no. 2 (1978): 120.

101. Ibid., 117.

102. Ibid., 123.

103. Robert S. Weppner and Duane C. McBride, "Comprehensive Drug Programs: The Dade County Example," *American Journal of Psychiatry* 132 (1975): 734–738.

104. Dade, for example, followed a typical New Right voting pattern. After voting for Hubert Humphrey in the presidential election in 1968, the county helped elect Nixon in 1972, Carter in 1976, Reagan in 1980 and 1984, and Bush in 1988. Beauty-queen Anita Bryant launched a Christian crusade against gay rights in Dade County in 1977. It served as a model for similar campaigns in Kansas, Oregon, Washington, and Minnesota. She also protested an "indecent" Jim Morrison concert in 1969 (see "Anita Bryant," in *Culture Wars: An Encyclopedia of Issues, Viewpoints, and Voices*, ed. Roger Chapman [Armonk, NY: M. E. Sharpe, 2010], 55–56).

105. Miller, "The Seed," 40.

106. Ibid., 41.

107. Ibid.

108. Ibid., 40.

109. The governor's eventual investigation of the Seed concluded that it "has isolated itself from the mainstream of the Drug Rehabilitation Community by failing to establish and maintain a cooperative relationship with that community. We recommend the establishment of that relationship to the Seed" (Florida Governor's Office, press release, April 10, 1974, Surviving Straight Inc. website, http://www.survivingstraightinc.com /SeedFloridaGovernmentDocs/SeedInvestigations/April10-1974-gov-askew-releases -drug-abuse-state-advisory-council-report_Combine.pdf, accessed October 8, 2016. This statement echoes the NIMH initial grant review, which required the Seed to put a referral system in place ("Narcotic Addict Rehabilitation Branch Ad Hoc Review Committee Recorder's Report for The Seed, Fort Lauderdale, FL," no. 1 HBO MH 618-01, September 23, 1971, NIDA Grant Microfiche Collection, Office of History, National Institutes of Health, Bethesda, MD.

110. Mr. and Mrs. Don Lund to the Dade County Health Planning Council, April 12, 1973, Surviving Straight Inc. website, http://www.survivingstraightinc.com/SeedFlorida GovernmentDocs/SeedLetters/Seed-Miscellaneous-letters3_Combine.pdf, accessed October 8, 2016.

111. U.S. Senate, *Individual Rights*, 192.

112. Elaine Murphy, clinical-treatment specialist, Technical Assistance Branch, to Robert J. Robertson, acting director of community assistance, "Review and Comment on the Seed Documents," April 22, 1974, NIDA Grant Microfiche Collection, Office of History, National Institutes of Health.

113. "Recorder's Report for the Seed," September 23, 1971, NIDA Grant Microfiche Collection, Office of History, National Institutes of Health.

114. The NIDA Grant Microfiche Collection documents Barker's steps: he hired an in-house evaluator, organized a list of referral organizations, and made a new organization

chart. Despite these steps, the Seed continued to exhibit "serious" and "obvious" weaknesses such as "the lack of documentation of physical complications or medical care," reported by an evaluator after a site visit in August 1972 (Lucille Kester to Robert J. Robertson, "Trip Report to The Seed," September 21, 1972, NIDA Grant Microfiche Collection, Office of History, National Institutes of Health).

115. Murphy to Robertson, "Review and Comment on the Seed Documents," April 22, 1974.

116. Quoted in U.S. Senate, *Individual Rights*, 192–193.

117. Quoted in ibid., 195.

118. Ibid., 199–200.

119. Lois Chatham, Narcotic Addict Rehabilitation Branch chief, to Bertram Brown, NIMH director, "The Seed Inc," May 2, 1972, NIDA Grant Microfiche Collection Office of History, National Institutes of Health.

120. Florida Governor's Office, press release, April 10, 1974.

121. Szalavitz, *Help at Any Cost*, 51–53.

122. Miller, "The Seed," 40.

123. Szalavitz, *Help at Any Cost*, 51–53.

124. George De Leon and George Beschner, "Introduction," in *The Therapeutic Community: Proceedings of the Therapeutic Communities of America Planning Conference January 29–30, 1976*, comp. and ed. George De Leon and George Beschner (Rockville, MD: National Institute on Drug Abuse, 1976), 2.

125. Ibid., 3.

126. Odyssey House Grant Review, "Engagement and Success in a Therapeutic Community," no. 1 H81 DA 01109-01, March 19, 1973, NIDA Grant Microfiche Collection, Office of History, National Institutes of Health.

127. Robert D. McFadden, "Beame Accuses Drug Unit of Losing Local Control," *New York Times*, August 12, 1973; New York Comptroller's Office, *Addiction Services Agency: A Study of Mismanagement* (New York: The Unit, 1973). Phoenix House was not the only organization that suffered public criticism about its cost and efficacy. See the editorial discussion in John E. Imhof, "Is Odyssey House the Tiffany of TC's?" *Contemporary Drug Problems* 3 (1974): 443–456.

128. "Results of the NIDA Special Review of ASA Treatment Services Grant FY 1974," NIDA Grant Microfiche Collection, Office of History, National Institutes of Health.

129. George De Leon and George Beschner, "Epilogue," in De Leon and Beschner, *The Therapeutic Community*, 109.

130. Quoted in David MacDonald, "The Little Paper That Dared," *Reader's Digest*, July 1981, 65, copy in Box 1, Folder 6, Mitchell–Synanon Litigation Papers, University of Tennessee at Knoxville. This collection of papers documents a detailed chronology of Synanon's devolution.

131. De Leon and Beschner, "Epilogue," 109.

132. "An institution is but the lengthened shadow of one man" (Ralph Waldo Emerson, "Self-Reliance," in *Essays: First Series* [Boston: James Munroe, 1841], http://www.emerson central.com/selfreliance.htm, accessed December 11, 2015).

5. SELLING A DRUG-FREE AMERICA

1. Douglas Martin, "William L. Fine, Who Shaped Narcotics Laws in New York, Dies at 86," *New York Times*, May 20, 2013; Joseph Perisco, *Imperial Rockefeller: A Biography of Nelson A. Rockefeller* (New York: Simon and Schuster, 1982), 142.

2. Martin, "William L. Fine."

3. Michael Massing, *The Fix* (1998; reprint, Berkeley: University of California Press, 2000), 157; "Just Say No, 1982–1987," Ronald Reagan Presidential Library and Museum website, http://www.reaganfoundation.org/nancy-reagan-life-and-times.aspx, accessed May 30, 2013.

4. Claire D. Clark and Emily Dufton, "Peter Bourne's Drug Policy and the Perils of a Public Health Ethic," *American Journal of Public Health* 105, no. 2 (2015): 283–292.

5. Quoted in Massing, *The Fix*, 148.

6. Quoted in Daniel T. Rodgers, *The Age of Fracture* (Cambridge, MA: Harvard University Press, 2011), 34.

7. Doug Rossinow, *The Reagan Era: A History of the 1980s* (New York: Columbia University Press), 61–62.

8. Arnold Trebach, *Why We Are Losing the Great Drug War and Radical Proposals That Could Make America Safe Again* (New York: Macmillan, 1987), 133–135; Massing, *The Fix*, 157; Donnie Radcliffe, "The First Lady Reshapes Her Royal Image," *Washington Post*, January 21, 1985.

9. Mitchell Rosenthal, interviewed by the author, New York City, June 2, 2014.

10. Massing, *The Fix*, 157–162.

11. Ann Wrobleski, exit interview by Terry Good, March 18, 1985, White House Staff Exit Interviews, Ronald Reagan Presidential Library and Museum, Simi Valley, CA.

12. Ann Wrobleski to Staff, "Re: Drug Initiatives, January/June, 1982," June 14,1981, Folder "Mrs. Reagan Drug Program," Box 14, OA 16995, Richard Williams Files, Ronald Reagan Presidential Library and Museum.

13. Wrobleski, exit interview, March 18, 1985.

14. "Program Overview of Second Genesis Inc," Folder "Second Genesis/Rehabilitation (1)," Box 6, OA 15003, and *"To Begin Again: A Second Chance* (Second Genesis Pamphlet)," Folder "Second Genesis/Rehabilitation (2)," Box 6, OA 15003, Drug Abuse Policy Office Records, Ronald Reagan Presidential Library and Museum.

15. Carlton Turner, "Memo: Meetings with Mrs. Reagan July 15, 1981," Folder "Mrs. Reagan's Report," Box 57, Carlton E. Turner Files, Ronald Reagan Presidential Library and Museum; Donnie Radcliffe, "The First Lady at Second Genesis," *Washington Post*, July 14, 1981.

16. *Nancy Reagan at Gateway House*, videotape, May 10, 1982, R826, White House Communications Agency Videotape Collection, Ronald Reagan Presidential Library and Museum.

17. Quoted in William Overend, "Treatment Program Officials Critical: First Lady's Drug War Hit," *Los Angeles Times*, March 30, 1982.

18. Quoted in ibid.

19. Quoted in Richard Pruss, president of Therapeutic Communities of America, to Otto Moulton, September 26, 1983, Folder "Therapeutic Communities of America," Box 64, Carlton E. Turner Files, Ronald Reagan Presidential Library and Museum.

20. Rosenthal, interview by the author, June 2, 2014.

21. *Phoenix House Annual Report, 1984–1985* (New York: Phoenix House, 1985), author's personal collection.

22. Quoted in Lois Romano, "New Starts and the First Lady: At Second Genesis, Ex-addicts Say Thanks," *Washington Post*, April 4, 1984.

23. Robert L. Dupont, "A Fresh Perspective for the War on Drugs," *Washington Star*, July 2, 1981, Tobacco Documents Library, University of California at Berkeley, http://legacy .library.ucsf.edu/tid/hyv39boo, last accessed May 6, 2015.

24. Carlton Turner to Ann Wrobleski, "Memo: Mrs. Reagan's Drug Program," August 11, 1981, Folder "Mrs. Reagan's Report," Box 57, Carlton E. Turner Files, Ronald Reagan Presidential Library and Museum.

25. Maia Szalavitz, *Help at Any Cost: How the Troubled-Teen Industry Cons Parents and Hurts Kids* (New York: Riverhead Books, 2006), 52.

26. Ibid., 35–37.

27. Steven L. Schlossman, *Love and the American Delinquent: The Theory and Practice of Progressive Juvenile Justice* (Chicago: University of Chicago Press, 1977).

28. Trustees of the State Industrial School for Girls at Lancaster, *First Annual Report* (Boston: State Printers, 1857), 203, quoted in Schlossman, *Love and the American Delinquent*, 41, emphasis in original.

29. Schlossman, *Love and the American Delinquent*.

30. Gregory Kutz and Andy O'Connell, testimony, U.S. House of Representatives, *Residential Treatment Programs: Concerns Regarding Abuse and Death in Certain Programs for Troubled Youth: Hearings Before the Committee on Education and Labor of the United States House of Representatives*, 110th Cong., 1st sess., October 7, 2007, 3–5.

31. Miller Newton, *Gone Way Down: Teenage Drug Use Is a Disease* (Tampa, FL: American Studies Press, 1981), 11–12.

32. William O'Brien to the World Federation of Therapeutic Communities, December 5, 1988, Surviving Straight Inc. website, http://www.thestraights.net/images/obrien -letter.gif, accessed October 8, 2016

33. Andrew I. Malcolm, "An Examination of Straight Incorporated," Folder "Straight Inc. (3)," Box 62, Carlton E. Turner Files, Ronald Reagan Presidential Library and Museum.

34. Straight, Inc., *The Dream for Every Parent*, pamphlet, Folder "Straight Inc. (1)," Box 3, OA 15002, Drug Abuse Policy Office Records, 1981–1987, Ronald Reagan Presidential Library and Museum.

35. "Prevention: Protecting the Family Dream," *Epidemic* (Straight newsletter), no. 2, n.d., Surviving Straight Inc. website, http://www.survivingstraightinc.com/FederalGovern mentStraightDocs/GeorgeBushPresidentialLibraryDocs/11-Straight-inc-2_PartB _Combined.pdf, accessed October 8, 2016

36. Szalavitz, *Help at Any Cost*, 23.

37. Robert Dupont, "Sometimes Coercion Is the Only Way," *Washington Post*, June 11, 1983.

38. Szalavitz, *Help at Any Cost*, 49.

39. Ibid., 60–61.

40. Rand McNutt, "Nancy Reagan Moved by Tales of Drug Abuse," *Cincinnati Enquirer*, September 19, 1984; Nancy Berlier, "First Lady Issues Call to Youths," *Cincinnati Post*, September 18, 1984.

41. Susanne M. Schafer, "Princess Diana and Nancy Reagan Visit Drug Abuse Center," Associated Press, November 11, 1985, http://www.apnewsarchive.com/1985/Princess -Diana-and-Nancy-Reagan-Visit-Drug-Abuse-Center-With-AM-Royalty-Bjt/id -4c71bd0262e7de3bbedda286e562f446, last accessed May 6, 2015; Trebach, *Why We are Losing the Great Drug War*, 145.

42. Pierre-Marie Loizeau, *Nancy Reagan: The Woman Behind the Man* (Hauppaugue, NY: New History Publications, 2004), 106.

43. "Letters from Straight Parents," *St. Petersburg Times*, May 15, 1983.

44. David and Deborah Fontaine to President George H. W. Bush, n.d., Folder "Straight Incorporated," Series "White House Office of Records Management Alphabetical Files S [Sowkes–Sullivan]," Surviving Straight Inc. website, http://www.survivingstraightinc .com/FederalGovernmentStraightDocs/GeorgeBushPresidentialLibraryDocs/6 -Straight-Incorporated-for-website-part1_combine.pdf, accessed October 8, 2016.

45. Ronald Reagan, "Remarks on Signing the Anti–Drug Abuse Act of 1986," October 27, 1986, Ronald Reagan Presidential Library and Museum website, http://www.reagan .utexas.edu/archives/speeches/1986/102786c.htm, last accessed May 6, 2015.

46. William D. Oliver, "Philosophy Statement: The Straight Foundation Inc," *Epidemic*, no. 10 (n.d.), Folder "Straight Inc. (1)," Box 62, Carlton E. Turner Files, Ronald Reagan Presidential Library and Museum.

47. Reagan, "Remarks on Signing the Anti–Drug Abuse Act of 1986."

48. Quoted in David T. Courtwright, *No Right Turn: Conservative Politics in a Liberal America* (Cambridge, MA: Harvard University Press, 2010), 164.

49. Lee Atwater to Republican leaders, September 5, 1989, Folder "Drug Strategy: RNC Meeting," Kirsten Gear Files, Box 1, George Herbert Walker Bush Presidential Library, College Station, TX.

50. Ronald and Nancy Reagan, "Radio Address to the Nation on Federal Drug Policy," October 2, 1982, Ronald Reagan Presidential Library and Museum website, http:// www.reagan.utexas.edu/archives/speeches/1982/100282a.htm, last accessed May 6, 2015.

51. "Letters from Straight Parents."

52. Courtwright, *No Right Turn*, 140.

53. Memo: Summary of Mrs. Reagan's Activities Against Drug and Alcohol Abuse, October 31, 1984, Folder "Mrs. Reagan's Program," Box 57, Carlton E. Turner Files, Ronald Reagan Presidential Library and Museum.

54. Cenikor, *Cenikor Annual Report, 1983* (Houston: Cenikor, 1983).

55. Cenikor, *Cenikor Foundation Inc. Agency Profile Book, 1989* (Houston: Cenikor, 1989), 1; John Dunning, "Self-Help Rehabilitation: Cenikor Offers Convict a Path Back to Society," *Denver Post*, May 19, 1968.

56. Cenikor, *Cenikor Foundation Inc. Agency Profile Book, 1989*, 1.

57. Ibid., 1–2.

58. Ibid., 2–3.

59. Ibid.

60. Cenikor, *Cenikor Annual Report, 1983*, 6–7.

61. Quoted in ibid.

62. Quoted in ibid. In *Age of Fracture*, Daniel T. Rodgers also discusses how Reagan's speechwriters blended "the self-actualization psychology handbooks of the 1970s" with references to an idyllic American past (22–37).

63. *White House Report to Students: Special Edition*, 4, Folder "Miscellaneous 3844 (5)," Box 13, Ian MacDonald Series III: Division of Adult Parole Operations Subject Files, Ronald Reagan Presidential Library and Museum.

64. Joel Brinkley, "Fighting Narcotics Is Everyone's Issue Now," *New York Times*, August 10, 1986.

65. Drug Enforcement Administration, *DEA History Book, 1985–1990* (Washington, DC: Drug Enforcement Agency, n.d.), http://web.archive.org/web/20060823024931/http://www.usdoj.gov/dea/pubs/history/1985-1990.html, accessed April 29, 2015.

66. Peter McKillop, "An Inferno of Craving, Dealing, and Despair," *Newsweek*, June 16, 1986, 18.

67. Keith Harriston and Sally Jenkins, "Maryland Basketball Star Len Bias Is Dead at 22: Traces of Cocaine Found in System," *Washington Post*, June 20, 1986; Sam McManis, "When Rights Go Wrong: Before June 27 Drug Death, Don Rogers Was Troubled; Maybe He Cared Too Much," *Los Angeles Times*, August 3, 1986; Michael White, "Crack at Prime Time for Ron and Nancy," *Guardian*, September 15, 1986.

68. Quoted in Brinkley, "Fighting Narcotics Is Everyone's Issue Now."

69. Reagan, "Remarks on Signing the Anti–Drug Abuse Act of 1986."

70. Jacqueline Cohen, *Incapacitating Criminals: Recent Research Findings: National Institute of Justice Brief* (Washington, DC: U.S. Department of Justice, December 1983), 1, Folder "National Institute of Justice," Box 16, Ian MacDonald Series III: Division of Adult Parole Operations Subject Files, Ronald Reagan Presidential Library and Museum.

71. David R. Buchanan and Lawrence Wallack, "This Is the Partnership for a Drug-Free America: Any Questions?" *Journal of Drug Issues* 28, no. 2 (1998): 329–356.

72. Quoted in Philip H. Dougherty, "Advertising: The War on Drugs Begins," *New York Times*, March 6, 1987.

73. Buchanan and Wallack, "This Is the Partnership for a Drug-Free America," 347–348.

74. William O'Brien and Ellis Henican, *You Can't Do It Alone: The Daytop Way to Make Your Child Drug Free* (New York: Simon and Schuster, 1993), 185.

75. *White House Conference for a Drug Free America: Final Report June 1988*, 82–83, Folder "White House Conference for a Drug Free America—June 1988," Box 20, OA 16997, Richard Williams Files, Ronald Reagan Presidential Library and Museum.

76. Victoria Churchville, "First Lady Opens New Front in Drug War, Attacking Casual Users," *Washington Post*, March 1, 1988; Mrs. Reagan's statement is recorded in *White House Conference on Drug Abuse*, videotape, March 1, 1988, R074B, White House Communications Agency Videotape Collection, Ronald Reagan Presidential Library and Museum.

77. Introduction to *White House Conference for a Drug Free America: Final Report June 1988*, 7.

78. "The Reagan Record on the Crusade for a Drug Free America," White House Office of Public Affairs, June 6, 1988, Folder "Crusade for a Drug Free America (5)," Box 2, Ian MacDonald Series II Subject Files, Ronald Reagan Presidential Library and Museum.

79. Ronald Reagan, "Remarks on Signing the Anti-Drug Abuse Act of 1988," November 18, 1988, https://reaganlibrary.gov/archives/photographs/36-archives/speeches/1988/8737 -111888c, accessed October 13, 2016.

80. Michael Isikoff, "Reagan Signs Sweeping Anti-drug Bill," *Washington Post*, November 19, 1988.

81. Michael Isikoff, "Search Underway for a 'Drug Czar,'" *Washington Post*, November 17, 1988.

82. John Harwood, "Former Florida Doctor Hoping for Bush's Call," *St. Petersburg Times*, January 17, 1989.

83. Robert DuPont, "Suggestions for President Bush for a Personal Approach to Drug Abuse," February 2, 1989, Folder "Robert Dupont," White House Office of Records Management, Alphabetical Files (D), George Herbert Walker Bush Presidential Library.

84. Quoted in S. Frederick Starr, "Bennett's Ideology of Education," *Washington Post*, October 18, 1988.

85. Mike Royko, "We Can't Call Bush Impetuous," *St. Petersburg Times*, May 24, 1988.

86. C. Boyden Gray to David Q. Bates, "Comparison of Director Bennett's Draft Anti-drug Strategy with the President's Campaign Statements," August 14, 1989, emphasis in original, Folder HE000-01 [065373–066634], White House Office of Records Management, Health Subject Files, HE006-001 Case Nos. 065236–068864, George Herbert Walker Bush Presidential Library.

87. Charles Paul Freund, "Rhetorical Questions: A Czar Who Leads with His Lip," *Washington Post*, January 17, 1989.

88. William J. Bennett, "Drugs: Consequences and Confrontation," speech to the Washington Hebrew Congregation, Washington, DC, May 3, 1989, emphasis in original, Folder "Drug Strategy: William Bennett Speech," Box 1, Kirsten Gear Files, George Herbert Walker Bush Presidential Library.

89. Richard Cohen, "New Strategy Needed to Fight Drug War," *St. Louis Post-Dispatch*, January 17, 9189.

90. "Briefing by William J. Bennett and Richard G. Darman," press release, September 5, 1989, Folder "Drugs [1]," Box 8, Judy Smith Subject Files, George Herbert Walker Bush Presidential Library.

91. White House, *National Drug Control Strategy* (Washington, DC: U.S. Government Printing Office, September 1989), 37, Folder "Drug Strategy: Drug Control Strategy Book," Box 1, Kirsten Gear Files, George Herbert Walker Bush Presidential Library.

92. Ibid., 37.

93. Ibid., 38.

94. Peter Kilborn, "Budget Deficit Up in '88, Despite Forecast of Drop," *New York Times*, October 29, 1988.

95. Nikil Saval, *Cubed: A Secret History of the Modern Workplace* (New York: Doubleday, 2014), Kindle e-book, location 3991.

96. Jerald Bachman, Lloyd Johnston, and Patrick O'Malley, "Explaining Recent Increases in Students' Marijuana Use: Impacts of Perceived Risks and Disapproval, 1976 Through 1996," *American Journal of Public Health* 88, no. 6 (1998): 887–892.

97. Courtwright, *No Right Turn*, 205–208.

98. "Remarks by the President and Governor Bob Martinez," press release, November 30, 1990, Folder "Drugs OA/ID 12713," Box 3, Press Release Subject Files, George Herbert Walker Bush Presidential Library.

99. Joel Brinkley, "4-Year Fight in Florida 'Just Can't Stop Drugs,'" *New York Times*, September 4, 1986.

100. Quoted in Joseph Treaster, "Drug Office Would Have New Voice Under Florida's Low-Key Governor," *New York Times*, November 30, 1990.

101. "Remarks by the President and Governor Bob Martinez"; Governor's Drug Policy Task Force, *Toward a Drug Free Florida: Report to the Governor*, February 1989, Folder HE 006-01 [062335] (1), White House Office of Records Management, Health Subject Files, Case Numbers 045770–062335, George Herbert Walker Bush Presidential Library.

102. Ruth Wilson Gilmore, *Golden Gulag: Prisons, Surplus, Crisis, and Opposition in Globalizing California* (Berkeley: University of California Press, 2007); Mona Lynch, *Sunbelt Justice: Arizona and the Transformation of American Punishment* (Palo Alto, CA: Stanford Law Books, 2009).

103. "Talking Points Re Governor Martinez," January 8, 1990, Folder FG0006-17, Document Range 194825 to 218265, Box "Federal Government Series Subseries FG006-17, Office of National Drug Control Policy Scanned 218700 to CF 156911," Series: Subject Files— Federal Government Subseries: Office of National Drug Control Policy, George Herbert Walker Bush Presidential Library.

104. Neal R. Peirce, "Martinez's Record Is Bad News for the War on Drugs," *St. Petersburg Times*, January 7, 1991.

105. Lauren Kirchner, "Remembering the Drug Court Revolution," *Pacific Standard*, April 25, 2014, http://www.psmag.com/politics-and-law/remembering-drug-court-revolution-80034, last accessed May 6, 2015.

6. COURTS AND MARKETS

1. Quoted in Ronald Smothers, "Miami Tries Treatment, Not Jail, in Drug Cases," *New York Times*, February 19, 1993.

2. Quoted in Michael Isikoff and William Booth, "Miami 'Drug Court' Demonstrates Reno's Unorthodox Approach," *Washington Post*, February 20, 1993.

3. Quoted in David Lauter, "Clinton Arkansas Record: He Won a Few, Lost a Few," *Los Angeles Times*, May 23, 1992.

4. Ibid.

5. Ibid.

6. Michelle Alexander, *The New Jim Crow: Mass Incarceration in the Age of Colorblindness* (New York: New Press, 2010), 55.

7. Tracy L. Snell, *Correctional Populations in the United States, 1991* (Rockville, MD: Bureau of Justice Statistics, U.S. Department of Justice, August 1993), 5.

8. Julilly Kohler-Hausmann, "Guns and Butter: The Welfare State, the Carceral State, and the Politics of Exclusion in the Postwar United States," *Journal of American History* 102, no. 1 (2015): 87–99.

9. In Jeremy Diamond, "Bill Clinton Concedes Role in Mass Incarceration," CNN.com, May 7, 2015, http://www.cnn.com/2015/05/06/politics/bill-clinton-crime-prisons-hillary -clinton, accessed October 8, 2016

10. William J. Clinton, foreword to *Solutions: American Leaders Speak Out on Criminal Justice*, ed. Inimai Chettiar and Michael Waldman (New York: Brennan Center for Justice, 2015), v–vi.

11. Quoted in Douglas Jehl, "Clinton to Use Drug Plan to Fight Crime," *New York Times*, February 10, 1994.

12. Ibid.

13. Sam Vincent Meddis, "'Break with the Past': Reno Offers Creative Tactics," *USA Today*, March 12, 1993.

14. Quoted in ibid.

15. Quoted in Isikoff and Booth, "Miami 'Drug Court.'"

16. "Talking Points on 1994 Drug Strategy: Demanding That More Hardcore Drug Users Be Treated," Clinton Administration History Project and History of the Office of National Drug Control Policy, "ONDCP–National Drug Control Strategy, 1993–200 [4]," William Jefferson Clinton Digital Library, http://clinton. presidentiallibraries.us /items/show/4911, accessed May 16, 2015.

17. Meddis, "'Break with the Past.'"

18. U.S. Department of Justice, *Indexed Legislative History of the Anti–Drug Abuse Act of 1986* (Washington, DC: U.S. Department of Justice, October 27, 1986), https://www .ncjrs.gov/pdffiles1/Digitization/126728NCJRS.pdf, accessed December 8, 2014.

19. Quoted in "Offender Programs Take Spotlight, with Drug Courts the Focus," *Alcoholism and Drug Abuse Weekly*, January 5, 1998, 1–2.

20. For the papers presented at the conference, see Alfonso P. Acampora and Ethan Nebelkopf, eds., *Bridging Services: Proceedings of the 9th World Conference of Therapeutic Communities, September 1–6, 1985, San Francisco, California* (San Francisco: Walden House, 1986).

21. Nancy Campbell, *Discovering Addiction: The Science and Politics of Substance Abuse Research* (Ann Arbor: University of Michigan Press, 2007), 145–146; Francis A. Allen, *The Decline of the Rehabilitative Ideal* (New Haven, CT: Yale University Press, 1981).

22. Douglas Lipton, Robert Martinson, and Judith Wilks, *Effectiveness of Correctional Treatment: A Survey of Treatment Evaluation Studies* (Westport, CT: Praeger, 1975); Robert Martinson, "What Works? Questions and Answers About Prison Reform," *Public Interest*, Spring 1974, 22–54; Francis Cullen, "The Twelve People Who Saved Rehabilitation: How the Science of Criminology Made a Difference," *Criminology* 43 (2005): 1–42.

23. Douglas Lipton, Gregory Falkin, and Harry Wexler, "Correctional Drug Abuse Treatment in the United States: An Overview," in *Drug Abuse Treatment in Prisons and Jails*, National Institute on Drug Abuse (NIDA) Research Monograph 118 (Rockville, MD: NIDA, 1992), 11.

24. Fred Scaglione, "New York Therapeutic Communities: Still Stay'n Out After Thirty Years," *New York Nonprofit Press*, July–August 2007, 10–11.

25. D. C. DesJarlais and H. K. Wexler, "A Reanalysis of Nash's Findings," internal report to the New York State Division of Substance Abuse Services, 1979, cited in Lipton, Falkin, and Wexler, "Correctional Drug Abuse Treatment in the United States," 14.

26. Douglas Lipton, *The Effectiveness of Treatment for Drug Abusers Under Criminal Justice Supervision: National Institute of Justice Research Report* (Rockville, MD: U.S. Department of Justice, 1995); Harry Wexler, "The Success of Therapeutic Communities for Substance Abusers in American Prisons," *Journal of Psychoactive Drugs* 27 (1995): 57–66; Harry K. Wexler and Douglas S. Lipton, "From REFORM to RECOVERY: Advances in Prison Drug Treatment," in *Drug Treatment and Criminal Justice*, ed. James A. Inciardi (Thousand Oaks, CA: Sage, 1993), 209–227.

27. Lipton, *The Effectiveness of Treatment*, 1–10.

28. "The Clinton Administration Strategy to Break the Cycle of Crime and Drugs, Pueblo, Colorado, September 11, 1996," and "Recent Studies on the Effectiveness of Residential Substance Abuse Treatment Programs," Domestic Policy Council, Bruce Reed, and Crime Series, "Drug Testing," William Jefferson Clinton Digital Library, http://clinton.presidentiallibraries.us/items/show/22561, accessed September 1, 2015.

29. Douglas Lipton, "Prison-Based Therapeutic Communities: Their Success with Drug-Abusing Offenders," *National Institute of Justice Journal*, February 1996, 12–20.

30. Ibid., 14.

31. Lipton, *The Effectiveness of Treatment*, 24–27.

32. Lipton, "Prison-Based Therapeutic Communities," 17.

33. Quoted in Katharine Q. Seelye, "The Crime Bill: Overview; House Approves Crime Bill After Days of Bargaining, Giving Victory to Clinton," *New York Times*, August 22, 1994.

34. Michelle S. Phelps, "Rehabilitation in the Punitive Era: The Gap Between Rhetoric and Reality in U.S. Prison Programs," *Law and Society Review* 45, no. 1 (2011): 33–68; Teresa Gowan and Sarah Whetstone, "Making the Criminal Addict: Subjectivity and Social Control in a Strong-Arm Rehab," *Punishment and Society* 14, no. 1 (2012): 69–93; Jill McCorkel, *Breaking Women: Gender, Race, and the New Politics of Imprisonment* (New York: New York University Press, 2013).

35. Quoted in "Offender Programs Take Spotlight," 1–2.

36. Therapeutic Communities of America, Criminal Justice Committee, *Therapeutic Communities in Correctional Settings: The Prison-Based TC Standards Development Project (Final Report of Phase II)*, prepared for the White House Office of National Drug Control Policy (Washington, DC: White House Office of National Drug Control Policy, 1999), 2.

37. Dale G. Parent, *Shock Incarceration: An Overview of Existing Programs* (Rockville, MD: Office of Justice Program, U.S. Department of Justice, June 1989), xi.

38. Quoted in Richard Pruss, "Drug Treatment Facilities for Offenders Better Than Work Camps," *New York Times*, March 18, 1987.

39. "Social Issues," *Businessweek*, November 27, 1989; Paul M. Barrett, "Prison Treatment Attracts Interest as Evidence Mounts That It's Successful," *Wall Street Journal*, May 20, 1991.

40. Scaglione, "New York Therapeutic Communities."

41. Sam Roberts, "Metro Matters; Out of Prison and Off of Drugs: This Way Works," *New York Times*, December 17, 1990.

42. Scaglione, "New York Therapeutic Communities," 10.

43. Quoted in Sam Howe Verhovek, "Warehouse of Addiction: A Change in Governors Stalls Model Drug Program in Texas," *New York Times*, July 4, 1995.

44. Mona Lynch, *Sunbelt Justice: Arizona and the Transformation of American Punishment* (Palo Alto, CA: Stanford Law Books, 2009), Kindle e-book, location 3064.

45. Ruth Wilson Gilmore, *Golden Gulag: Prisons, Surplus, Crisis, and Opposition in Globalizing California* (Berkeley: University of California Press, 2007), 73.

46. Lynch, *Sunbelt Justice*, Kindle e-book, location 2185–2194.

47. Eric Cummins, *The Rise and Fall of California's Radical Prison Movement* (Stanford, CA: Stanford University Press, 1994), 265.

48. Ibid., 269; Eldridge Cleaver, *Soul on Ice* (Berkeley, CA: Ramparts Press, 1968).

49. Quoted in Dan Weikel, "In Prison, a Drug Rehab That Pays Off," *Los Angeles Times*, April 25, 1997.

50. Rod Mullen, James Rowland, Naya Arbiter, Lew Yablonsky, and Bette Fleishman, *Building and Replicating an In-Prison Therapeutic Community That Reduces Recidivism: Amity Foundation's TC in the Richard J. Donovan Correctional Facility* (Los Angeles: Amity Foundation, 2001), http://www.amityfdn.org/wp-content/uploads/2016/09/1999-09-Rowland-et-al.-Building-Replicating-In-Prison-TC.pdf, accessed October 8, 2016; Lewis Yablonsky, *Juvenile Delinquency: Into the 21st Century* (Belmont, CA: Wadsworth, 2000).

51. Rod Mullen, James Rowland, Naya Arbiter, Lew Yablonsky, and Bette Fleishman, "California's First Prison Therapeutic Community: A 10-Year Review," *Offender Substance Abuse Report* 1, no. 2 (2001): 1–6, quote on 3.

52. David Corn, "Throwing Away the Key: Justice's War on Drug Treatment," *The Nation*, May 14, 1990, 659–662.

53. Columbia University Center on Addiction and Substance Abuse, *Behind Bars: Substance Abuse and America's Prison Population* (New York: Columbia University, January 1998), 114.

54. Mullen et al., *Building and Replicating an In-Prison Therapeutic Community*.

55. Rod Mullen, John Ratelle, Elaine Abraham, and Jody Boyle, "California Program Reduces Recidivism and Saves Tax Dollars," *Corrections Today*, August 1996, 121.

56. Griffith Edwards, "A Conversation with Robert Dupont," *Addiction* 100 (2005): 1406.

57. John S. Goldkamp, *Justice and Treatment Innovation: The Drug Court Movement. A Working Paper of the First National Drug Court Conference, December 1993* (Washington, DC: Office of Justice Programs, U.S. Department of Justice, 1994), 11.

58. Ibid.

59. Deborah Sharp, "Innovative Ideas Win Praise in Florida," *USA Today*, March 9, 1993.

60. Ibid.

61. Quoted in Jennifer L. Stevenson, "Drug Court Pushes Treatment Over Jail," *St. Petersburg Times*, June 28, 1990.

62. James L. Nolan, "Therapeutic Adjudication," *Society* 39, no. 2 (2002): 34–35.

63. Ibid., 34–36.

64. Quoted in "Drug Courts: A Blessing and a Curse for Treatment Agencies," *Alcoholism and Drug Abuse Weekly*, May 9, 1994, 2–3.

65. Ibid.

66. Frank S. Taxman and Jeffrey Bouffard, "Treatment Inside the Drug Treatment Court: The Who, What, Where, and How of Treatment Services," *Substance Use and Misuse* 37, nos. 12–13 (2002): 1665–1688.

67. National Treatment Accountability for Safer Communities, *Treatment Services in Adult Drug Courts: Report on the 1999 National Drug Court Treatment Survey: Executive Summary May 2001*, prepared for the Drug Courts Program Office, Office of Justice Programs, and Center for Substance Abuse Treatment at the Substance Abuse and Mental Health Services Administration (Washington, DC: Office of Justice Programs, U.S. Department of Justice, May 2001), 7.

68. Peggy Fulton Hora, "Trading One Drug for Another?" *Journal of Maintenance in the Addictions* 2, no. 4 (2005): 71–76. For recent sociological and anthropological critiques of drug courts, see Rebecca Tiger, *Judging Addicts: Drug Courts and Coercion in the Justice System* (New York: New York University Press, 2013), and Jennifer Murphy, *Illness or Deviance? Drug Courts and the Ambiguity of Addiction* (Philadelphia: Temple University Press, 2016).

69. David Cole, "Doing Time—in Rehab: Drug Courts Keep Addicts Out of Jail," *The Nation*, September 20, 1999, 30–31.

70. J. Scott Sanford and Bruce A. Arrigo, "Lifting the Cover on Drug Courts: Evaluation Findings and Policy Concerns," *International Journal of Offender Therapy and Comparative Criminology* 49, no. 3 (2005): 239–259.

71. Goldkamp, *Justice and Treatment Innovation*, 23.

72. John S. Goldkamp, "The Impact of Drug Courts," *Criminology and Public Policy* 2, no. 2 (2003): 197–206.

73. Drug Court Clearinghouse and Technical Assistance Project, *Looking at a Decade of Drug Courts* (Rockville, MD: Office of Justice Programs, U.S. Department of Justice, 1998), https://www.ncjrs.gov/html/bja/decade98.htm, accessed October 8, 2016.

74. U.S. House of Representatives, *Drug Treatment Options for the Justice System: Hearing Before the Subcommittee on Criminal Justice, Drug Policy, and Human Resources of the Committee on Government Reform*, 106 Cong., 2nd sess., April 4, 2000.

75. Steven Belenko, statement, in ibid., 56–57.

76. Judge Jeffrey Tauber, statement in ibid., 13–26, quotes on 19.

77. Sally Satel, statement, in ibid., 62, 68.

78. Jeffrey A. Eisenach and Andrew J. Cowin, "The Case Against More Funds for Drug Treatment," *Backgrounder: Heritage Foundation Newsletter*, May 17, 1991, 1, 13.

79. Jack Alexander, "Alcoholics Anonymous," *Saturday Evening Post*, May 1941, and "The History of How the Article Came to Be," *AA Grapevine*, May 1945, both at http://www.barefootsworld.net/aajalexpost1941.html, accessed September 2, 2015.

80. "Timeline of AA History," AA Group Directories, General Services Office Archives, AA, New York, http://www.aa.org/pages/en_US/aa-timeline, accessed September 15, 2015.

81. Stanton Peele, *The Diseasing of America: Addiction Treatment Out of Control* (Lexington, MA: Lexington Books, 1989); Charles Bufe, *Alcoholics Anonymous: Cult or Cure?* (San Francisco: Sharp Press, 1991); Herbert Fingarette, *Heavy Drinking: The Myth of Alcoholism as a Disease* (Berkeley: University of California Press, 1988).

82. Anne Fletcher, *Inside Rehab: The Surprising Truth About Addiction Treatment—and How to Get the Help That Works* (New York: Viking, 2013), 218.

83. William White, *Slaying the Dragon: The History of Addiction Treatment and Recovery in America*, 2nd ed. (Bloomington, IN: Chestnut Health Systems, 2014), 261–278, quote on 264.

84. Ibid., 275–277.

85. Grischa Metlay, "Federalizing Medical Campaigns Against Alcoholism and Drug Abuse," *Milbank Quarterly* 91, no. 1 (2013): 155.

86. Ibid.

87. Ibid.

88. Quoted in Barbara Gamarekian, "Mrs. Ford Criticizes Neglect of Alcohol in U.S. Drug Efforts," *New York Times*, March 26, 1991.

89. Betty Ford, *The Times of My Life* (New York: Harper Collins, 1978); Betty Ford and Chris Chase, *A Glad Awakening* (New York: Doubleday, 1987).

90. White, *Slaying the Dragon*, 271–273.

91. Trysh Travis, *The Language of the Heart: A Cultural History of the Recovery Movement from Alcoholics Anonymous to Oprah Winfrey* (Chapel Hill: University of North Carolina Press, 2010), 166.

92. Bob Curley, "Minnesota Looks at Dr. Managed and Mr. Care," *Alcoholism and Drug Abuse Weekly*, April 10, 1995, 5.

93. Bob Curley, "Jurassic Spark: Predictions of New Life for Ancient Treatment Ideas," *Alcoholism and Drug Abuse Weekly*, June 5, 1995, 5; Michael Abramowitz, "Need for Hospital Stays Questioned," *Washington Post*, July 1, 1989.

94. Quoted in Curley, "Jurassic Spark," 5.

95. "Why Does the TC Work?" *Alcoholism and Drug Abuse Weekly*, July 21, 1997, 5.

96. Legal Action Center, National Association of Addiction Treatment Providers, National Association of Alcoholism and Drug Abuse Counselors, National Council on Alcoholism and Drug Dependence, and Therapeutic Communities of America, *Healthcare Reform and Substance Abuse Treatment: The Cost of Financing Under Alternative Approaches: Final Report* (Fairfax, VA: Lewin-VHI, February 2, 1994), 13; White House Health Care Task Force, Task Force on National Health Care, and Ira Magaziner, *Legal Action Center Final Report*, William Jefferson Clinton Digital Library, http://clinton presidentiallibraires.us/items/show/39657, accessed May 16, 2015.

97. Alan I. Leschner, "Addiction Is a Brain Disease, and It Matters," *Science* 278, no 5335 (1997): 45.

98. White, *Slaying the Dragon*, 494–495.

99. Peele, *The Diseasing of America*, 263–272.

100. Stanton Peele, "Addicted to Brain Scans," *Reason*, March 2014, http://reason.com /archives/2014/02/26/addicted-to-brain-scans/, accessed September 3, 2015.

101. *Alcoholics Anonymous: The Story of How Many Thousands of Men and Women Have Recovered from Alcoholism*, 3rd ed. (New York: Alcoholics Anonymous World Services, 1976), xxiii–xxx.

102. David T. Courtwright, "The NIDA Brain Disease Paradigm: History, Resistance, and Spin-offs," *BioSocieties* 5, no. 1 (2010): 137.

103. Robert L. Dupont, *The Selfish Brain: Learning from Addiction* (Washington, DC: American Psychiatric Press, 1997), 400.

104. Quoted in "Speakers Say Consumer Input Holds Key to Treatment Success," *Alcoholism and Drug Abuse Weekly*, September 29, 1997, 1–2.

105. David Deitch and George De Leon, interviewed by William White, 2010, William White Papers, http://www.williamwhitepapers.com/papers/topics/pioneer_interviews/, accessed September 3, 2015.

106. Ken Schonlau, "We Have Drifted Too Far from the Community Recovery Model," *Alcoholism and Drug Abuse Weekly*, July 28, 1997, 5.

107. Deitch and De Leon, interview by White, 2010.

108. William White, *Recovery Management and Recovery-Oriented Systems of Care: Scientific Rationale and Promising Practices* (Chicago: Northeast Addiction Technology Transfer Center and Great Lakes Addiction Technology Transfer Center; Philadelphia: Philadelphia Department of Behavioral Health and Mental Retardation Services, 2008).

109. For histories of each group and relevant links, see William White's website, http:// www.williamwhitepapers.com/recovery_mutual_aid_history/overview/, accessed September 3, 2015.

110. Philip McGowan, "AA and the Redeployment of Temperance Literature," *Journal of American Studies* 48, no. 1 (2014): 51–78; Kevin Kaufman, "Rigorous Honesty: A Cultural History of Alcoholics Anonymous 1935–1960," PhD diss., Loyola University Chicago, 2011, 20–54; Craig Reinarman, "The Twelve Step Movement and Advanced Capitalist Culture: The Politics of Self-Control in Post-modernity," in *Cultural Politics and Social Movements*, ed. Marcy Darnovsky, Barbara Epstein, and Richard Flacks (Philadelphia: Temple University Press, 1995), 90–109.

111. Jessica Warner, *All or Nothing: A Short History of Abstinence in America* (Toronto: McClelland and Stewart, 2008), 1–2.

112. Jessica Warner, "Temperance, Alcohol, and the American Evangelical: A Reassessment," *Addiction* 104 (2009): 1075–1084.

113. On the American outlook over time, see, for example, Alexis de Tocqueville, *Democracy in America*, trans. Arthur Goldhammer (New York: Penguin Books, 2004), 478–649, and Max Weber, *The Protestant Ethics and the Spirit of Capitalism*, trans. Talcott Parsons (New York: Routledge, 2001).

114. Warner, *All or Nothing*, 3–8.

115. *Alcoholics Anonymous*, 83–84.

116. William White, "Can Recovering Drug Addicts Drink? A Historical Footnote," *Counselor* 8, no. 6 (2007): 36–41.

117. Substance Abuse and Mental Health Services Administration, Center for Behavioral Health Statistics and Quality, *The N-SSTATS Report: Trends in the Use of Methadone and Buprenorphine at Substance Abuse Treatment Facilities: 2003 to 2011* (Washington, DC: Substance Abuse and Mental Health Services Administration, April 23, 2013), http://archive .samhsa.gov/data/2k13/NSSATS107/sr107-NSSATS-BuprenorphineTrends.htm, accessed October 8, 2016; Harlan Matusow, Samuel L. Dickman, Josiah D. Rich, Chunki Fong, Dora M. Dumont, Carolyn Hardin, Douglas Marlowe, and Andre Rosenblum, "Medication Assisted Treatment in U.S. Drug Courts: Results from a Nationwide Survey of Availability, Barrier, and Attitudes," *Journal of Substance Abuse Treatment* 44, no. 5 (2013): 473–480.

118. "It's Official: Hazelden, Betty Ford Center Have Merged," Hazelden press release, February 10, 2014, http://www.hazelden.org/web/public/hazelden-betty-ford-press-release.page, accessed September 3, 2015; Maia Szalavitz, "Hazelden Introduces Anti-addiction Medications to Recovery for First Time," *Time*, November 5, 2012, http:// healthland.time.com/2012/11/05/hazelden-introduces-antiaddiction-medications-in -recovery-for-first-time/, accessed September 3, 2015.

119. Substance Abuse and Mental Health Services Administration, "SAMHSA Treatment Drug Courts, Request for Applications (RFA) T1-15-002," issued for grant deadline April 10, 2015, pp. 8–13, http://www.samhsa.gov/sites/default/files/grants/pdf/ti-15-002 -modified-due.pdf, accessed October 9, 2016.

120. Faces and Voices of Recovery, "Definitions of Recovery" and "Frequently Asked Questions," http://www.facesandvoicesofrecovery.org/who/faqs#5, accessed September 5, 2015.

121. G. Alan Marlatt, "Harm Reduction: Come as You Are," *Addictive Behaviors* 20, no. 6 (1996): 785–786.

122. Elizabeth A. Bowen, "Clean Needles and Bad Blood: Needle Exchange as Morality Policy," *Journal of Sociology and Social Welfare* 39, no. 2 (2012): 121–141; David Vlahov, Don C. DesJarlais, Eric Goosby, Paula C. Hollinger, Peter G. Lurie, Michael D. Shriver, and Steffanie A. Strathdee, "Needle Exchange Programs for the Prevention of Human Immunodeficiency Virus Infection: Epidemiology and Policy," *American Journal of Epidemiology* 154, no. 12 (2001): S70–S77.

123. Katherine Mclean, "The Biopolitics of Needle Exchange in the United States," *Critical Public Health* 21, no. 1 (2011): 73.

124. Warwick Anderson, "The New York Needle Trial: The Politics of Public Health in the Age of AIDS," *American Journal of Public Health* 81, no. 11 (1991): 1506–1517.

125. Ibid., 1512.

126. Marlatt, "Harm Reduction," 782; San Francisco AIDS Foundation, "History of Health: Needle Exchange in San Francisco," n.d., http://sfaf.org/client-services/syringe-access /history-of-needle-exchange.html, accessed December 11, 2015.

127. Marlatt, "Harm Reduction," 779.

128. Ibid., 784; Daliah Heller and Denise Paone, "Access to Sterile Syringes for Injecting Drug Users in New York City: Politics and Perception (1984–2010)," *Substance Use and Misuse* 46 (2011): 141.

129. Sandra Crouse Quinn, "Public Attitudes Towards Needle Exchange Programs," *AIDS* 13, no. 11 (1999): 1428.

130. Quoted in Arthur Benavie, *Drugs: America's Holy War* (New York: Routledge, 2009), 46.

131. Vlahov et al., "Needle Exchange Programs," S71–S72.

132. Ibid., S72.

133. Mitchell Rosenthal to Barry McCaffrey, April 10, 1998, Domestic Policy Council, Bruce Reed, and Subject Files, "Needle Exchange [2]," William Jefferson Clinton Digital Library, http://clintonpresidentiallibraries.us/items/show/31476, accessed May 16, 2015.

134. Sue Rusche to Barry McCaffrey, April 9, 1998, Domestic Policy Council, Bruce Reed, and Subject Files, "Needle Exchange [2]," William Jefferson Clinton Digital Library, http://clintonpresidentiallibraries.us/items/show/31476, accessed May 16, 2015.

135. Kelly Szott, "Governing Through Health: The Biomedical and Public Health Management of Drug Using Bodies," PhD diss., Syracuse University, 2015, 17–34.

136. Quoted in Benavie, *Drugs*, 46–47.

137. Marlatt, "Harm Reduction," 787–788.

138. Paul Carvajal, "Integration of Harm Reduction and Other Treatment Approaches," *Harm Reduction Communication*, Fall 1995, 1.

139. Ibid.

140. Howard Josepher, interviewed by William White, 2015, William White Papers, http://www.williamwhitepapers.com/pr/2015%20Howard%20Josepher.pdf, accessed October 8, 2016.

141. Ibid.

142. Faces and Voices of Recovery, "Recovery Messaging from Faces and Voices of Recovery," http://www.facesandvoicesofrecovery.org/sites/default/files/Recovery_Messaging.pdf, accessed September 4, 2015.

143. Ibid.

144. Quoted in John Lavitt, "A Language of Empowerment," *The Fix*, March 13, 2014, http://www.thefix.com/content/language-empowerment, accessed September 4, 2015.

145. See policy-position papers on the Faces and Voices of Recovery website, http://www.facesandvoicesofrecovery.org: for example, "Policy Position Paper on Criminal Justice Recovery Advocacy," http://www.facesandvoicesofrecovery.org/sites/default/files/3.12.13_Criminal_Justice_Policy_Position.pdf, accessed September 4, 2015, and "Policy Position Paper on Discrimination," http://www.facesandvoicesofrecovery.org/sites/default/files/10.24.11_Discrimination_Policy_Position_Paper.pdf, accessed September 4, 2015.

146. Faces and Voices of Recovery, "Core Positioning Document," 2001, http://www.facesandvoicesofrecovery.org/sites/default/files/core_positioning.pdf, accessed September 4, 2015.

147. Senator Paul Wellstone, keynote address, in Johnson Institute Foundation, *Faces and Voices Summit 2001 Proceedings* (St. Louis Park, MN: Johnson Institute Foundation,

2001), 5, http://www.facesandvoicesofrecovery.org/sites/default/files/2001_summit
_report.pdf, accessed September 4, 2015.

148. Quoted in Ron Hutcheson, "Bush Tells Addicts About His Drinking in Highly Personal Terms: The Candidate Talked to People in a Treatment Facility About His Experience with Alcohol," *Philadelphia Inquirer*, January 22, 2000.

149. Quoted in Verhovek, "Warehouse of Addiction."

150. David E. Sanger, "Bush Names a Drug Czar and Addresses Criticism," *New York Times*, May 11, 2001.

151. For Bennett and Walters's view, see William J. Bennett, John DiIulio, and John P. Walters, *Body Count: Moral Poverty . . . and How to Win America's War Against Crime and Drugs* (New York: Simon and Schuster, 1996).

152. White, *Slaying the Dragon*, 398–403.

153. George W. Bush, "Remarks at the Office of Faith-Based and Community Initiatives National Conference, June 26, 2008," in *Public Papers of the Presidents of the United States, George W. Bush, 2004: Book 3* (Washington, DC: U.S. Government Printing Office, 2007), 884–886.

154. Peter Gaumond and Melanie Whitter, *Access to Recovery (ATR) Approaches to Recovery-Oriented Systems of Care: Three Case Studies* (Rockville, MD: Center for Substance Abuse Treatment, Substance Abuse and Mental Health Services Administration, 2009).

155. Substance Abuse and Mental Health Services Administration, *Recovery-Oriented Systems of Care (ROSC) Resource Guide (Working Draft)* (Rockville, MD: Substance Abuse and Mental Health Services Administration, September 2010), 12, http://www.samhsa .gov/sites/default/files/rosc_resource_guide_book.pdf, accessed September 4, 2015.

156. Colleen L. Barry, Haiden A. Huskamp, and Howard H. Goldman, "A Political History of Federal Mental Health and Addiction Insurance Parity," *Milbank Quarterly* 88, no. 3 (2010): 404–433.

157. The Obama administration announced the "21st century drug control strategy" in 2012 and included "giving a voices to people in recovery" as a component in 2013. In 2014, "supporting Americans in recovery by lifting stigma" was made the fourth point in the president's "Plan to Reform Drug Policy." Plans are available at https://www.white house.gov/ondcp/national-drug-control-strategy, accessed September 4, 2015.

158. Ibid.

159. Erving Goffman, *Stigma: Notes on the Management of Spoiled Identity* (Englewood Cliffs, NJ: Prentice-Hall, 1963), 1.

160. Ibid.

161. Colleen L. Barry, Emma E. McGinty, Bernice Pescosolido, and Howard H. Goldman, "Stigma, Discrimination, Treatment Effectiveness, and Policy: Public Views About Drug Addiction and Mental Illness," *Psychiatric Services* 65, no. 10 (2014): 1271.

162. Michael Botticelli, "The Work Before Us: A Message from Michael Botticelli," *White House Blog*, February 9, 2015, https://www.whitehouse.gov/blog/2015/02/09/work-us -message-michael-botticelli, accessed September 4, 2015.

163. Ibid.

CONCLUSION: THE REVOLUTION'S AFTERMATH

1. Quoted in Katie Zezima, "Drug Czar Approaches Challenge from a Different Angle: As a Recovering Alcoholic," *Washington Post*, August 26, 2014.

2. Ibid.

3. Ibid.

4. Ibid.; Brian MacQuarrie, "Substance Help from One Who Struggled," *Boston Globe*, June 23, 2014; Alan Schwarz, "Michael Botticelli Is a Drug Czar Who Knows Addiction Firsthand," *New York Times*, April 25, 2015.

5. MacQuarrie, "Substance Help from One Who Struggled."

6. Nick Wing, "America, It's Time for an Intervention: Drug Overdoses Are Killing More People Than Cars, Guns," *Huffington Post*, August 30, 2013, http://www.huffingtonpost .com/2013/08/30/drug-overdose-deaths_n_3843690.html, accessed October 8, 2016; Centers for Disease Control and Prevention, "Prescription Drug Overdose Data," October 16, 2015, http://www.cdc.gov/drugoverdose/data/overdose.html, accessed October 20, 2015.

7. Centers for Disease Control and Prevention, "Today's Heroin Epidemic," July 7, 2015, http://www.cdc.gov/vitalsigns/heroin, accessed October 9, 2016, accessed October 20, 2015; Katharine Q. Seelye, "Heroin in New England, More Abundant and Deadly," *New York Times*, July 18, 2013.

8. Michael Durfee, "Framing Heroin Addiction: Then and Now," *Points: The Blog of the Alcohol and Drugs History Society*, May 15, 2014, https://pointsadhsblog.wordpress. com/2014/05/15/framing-addiction-heroin-then-and-now/, accessed December 11, 2015; Jason Cherkis, "Dying to Be Free," *Huffington Post*, January 28, 2015, http://projects .huffingtonpost.com/dying-to-be-free-heroin-treatment, accessed October 8, 2016; Elijah Wolfson, "Prescription Drugs Have Pushed Heroin Into the Suburbs," *Newsweek*, May 28, 2014.

9. Andrew Kolodny, David T. Courtwright, Catherine S. Hwang, Peter Kreiner, John L. Eadie, Thomas W. Clark, and G. Caleb Alexander, "The Prescription Opioid and Heroin Crisis: A Public Health Approach to an Epidemic of Addiction," *Annual Reviews of Public Health* 36 (2015): 559–574.

10. Ibid., 561–562.

11. David T. Courtwright, "The Cycles of American Drug Policy," *American Historian*, August 2015, http://digitalcommons.unf.edu/ahis_facpub/25, accessed October 19, 2015.

12. Community Anti-Drug Coalitions of America, *Coalitions and Community Health: Integration of Behavioral Health and Primary Care* (Washington, DC: Substance Abuse and Mental Health Services Administration, Health Resources and Service Administration Center for Integrated Health Solutions, April 2013); David Mechanic, "More People Than Ever Before Are Receiving Behavioral Health Care in the United States, but Gaps and Challenges Remain," *Health Affairs* 33, no. 8 (2014): 1416–1424.

13. Christina Andrews, Colleen M. Grogan, Marianne Brennan, and Harold A. Pollack, "Lessons from Medicaid's Divergent Paths on Mental Health and Addiction Services," *Health Affairs* 34, no. 7 (2015): 1131–1138.

14. Keith Humphreys and Richard G. Frank, "The Affordable Care Act Will Revolutionize Care for Substance Use Disorders in the United States," *Addiction* 109 (2014): 1957–1958; A. Thomas McLellan and Abigail Mason Woodworth, "The Affordable Care Act and Treatment for 'Substance Use Disorders': Implications of Ending Segregated Behavioral Healthcare," *Journal of Substance Abuse Treatment* 46 (2014): 541–545.

15. McLellan and Woodworth, "The Affordable Care Act and Treatment for 'Substance Use Disorders,'" 545, 544.

16. Christina Andrews, Amanda Abraham, Colleen M. Grogan, Harold A. Pollack, Clifford Bersamira, Keith Humphreys, and Peter Friedmann, "Despite Resources from the ACA, Most States Do Little to Help Addiction Treatment Programs Implement Health Care Reform," *Health Affairs* 34, no. 5 (2015): 828–835.

17. William R. Miller and Theresa B. Moyers, "The Forest and the Trees: Relational and Specific Factors in Addiction Treatment," *Addiction* 110 (2014): 401.

18. Ibid.; George De Leon, "'The Gold Standard' and Related Considerations for a Maturing Science of Substance Abuse Treatment: Therapeutic Communities, a Case in Point," *Substance Use and Misuse* 50, nos. 8–9 (2015): 1106–1109.

19. McLellan and Woodworth, "The Affordable Care Act and Treatment for 'Substance Use Disorders.'"

20. Meredith Huey Dye, Lori J. Ducharme, J. Aaron Johnson, Hannah K. Knudsen, and Paul M. Roman, "Modified Therapeutic Communities and Adherence to Traditional Elements," *Journal of Psychoactive Drugs* 41, no. 3 (2009): 275–283; "TCs Positioning Themselves for New Healthcare Environment," *Alcoholism and Drug Abuse Weekly*, February 25, 2013, 1–3.

21. "Cenikor Foundation Teams with Odyssey House," InsideDP.com, July 29, 2010, http://insidedp.com/news/dp-news/715-cenikor-foundation-teams-with-odyssey-house; Samaritan Daytop Village, "Samaritan Village: History," http://www.samaritanvillage.org/about-good/history, accessed October 20, 2015.

22. "Phoenix House Announces New CEO and Clinical Initiatives Agreement with Hazelden Betty Ford Foundation," July 9, 2015, http://www.phoenixhouse.org/news-and-views/news-and-events/phoenix-house-announces-new-ceo-and-clinical-initiatives-agreement-with-hazelden-betty-ford-foundation/, accessed October 20, 2015.

23. William White, "Recovery Coaching: A Lost Function of Addiction Counseling?" *Counselor* 5, no. 6 (2004): 20–22.

24. "Recovery Coach Helps an Addict Resist Heroin's Lure," National Public Radio, August 10, 2014, http://www.npr.org/sections/health-shots/2014/08/10/332352845/recovery-coach-helps-an-addict-resist-heroins-lure, accessed October 8, 2016.

25. White, "Recovery Coaching." The percentage of counselors in recovery declined from roughly 70 percent in the 1970s to 30 percent in 2008 (William White, *Peer-Based Addiction Recovery Support: History, Theory, Practice, and Scientific Evaluation* [Chicago: Lakes Addiction Technology Transfer Center; Philadelphia: Philadelphia Department of Behavioral Health and Mental Retardation Services, 2009], 165–171).

26. White, "Recovery Coaching," 20–22.

27. New York State Office of Alcoholism and Substance Abuse Services, *Statewide Comprehensive Plan 2012–2016: 2013 Interim Report* (Albany: State of New York, February 15, 2013), 6–8, http://www.oasas.ny.gov/pio/commissioner/documents/5YPIntReport2013.pdf, accessed October 20, 2015; Martha Bebinger, "To Beat Heroin Addiction, a Turn to Coaches," WBUR, June 2014, http://commonhealth.wbur.org/2014/06/heroin-recovery-coaches, accessed October 20, 2015.

28. Texas Recovery Initiative Criminal Justice Workgroup, *Criminal Justice Population Resource Guide 2013* (Austin: State of Texas, 2013), https://www.tdcj.state.tx.us/documents/rpd/RPD_TRI_Resource_Guide_English.pdf, accessed October 20, 2015.

29. William White and Arthur C. Evans Jr., "The Recovery Agenda: The Shared Role of Peers and Professionals," *Public Health Reviews* 35, no. 2 (2014): 1–15.

30. Simon Szreter, "Rethinking McKeown: The Relationship Between Public Health and Social Change," *American Journal of Public Health* 92, no. 5 (2002): 722–735; Nikolas Rose, *Governing the Soul: The Shaping of the Private Self*, 2nd ed. (London: Free Association Books, 1999).

31. Alaine Touraine, *The Post-industrial Society, Tomorrow's Social History: Classes, Conflicts, and Culture in the Programmed Society* (New York: Random House, 1971); Jefferson Cowie, *Stayin' Alive: The 1970s and the Last Days of the Working Class* (New York: New Press, 2010); Arlie Russell Hochschild, *The Outsourced Self: Intimate Life in Market Times* (New York: Macmillan, 2012).

32. "Hazelden's New Post-treatment Program Offers Recovery Coaching and More," *Voice*, Spring 2011, https://www.hazelden.org/web/public/1104connection.page, accessed October 8, 2016; "Odyssey House Offers New Peer-Run Services for People in Early Recovery," press release, October 8, 2010, http://odysseyhousenyc.org/odyssey-house-offers-new-peer-run-services-people-early-recovery/, accessed October 8, 2016; Marisa Fox, "Mothers Find a Helping Hand in Sobriety Coaches," *New York Times*, July 11, 2014.

33. Joel Braslow, "The Manufacture of Recovery," *Annual Review of Clinical Psychology* 9 (2013): 781–809; Nancy Laurenzo Myers, *Recovery's Edge: An Ethnography of Mental Health Care and Moral Agency* (Nashville: Vanderbilt University Press, 2015).

34. Dominic Sisti, Andrea G. Segal, and Ezekiel J. Emanuel, "Improving Long-Term Psychiatric Care: Bring Back the Asylum," *Journal of the American Medical Association* 313, no. 3 (2015): 243–244.

35. Keith Humphreys, "Addiction Treatment Professionals Are Not the Gatekeepers of Recovery," *Substance Use and Misuse* 50, nos. 8–9 (2015): 1026.

36. Frederic Jameson, "Walter Benjamin, or Nostalgia," *Salmagundi*, nos. 10–11 (Fall 1969–Winter 1970): 52–68; Michael Lowy, "Revolution Against 'Progress': Walter Benjamin's Romantic Anarchism," *New Left Review* 152 (July–August 1985): 42–59.

37. *Instant Guide to Synanon*, 16-mm film (1973), Box 580, Synanon Collection, Charles E. Young Special Collections, UCLA.

38. Quoted in Lewis Yablonsky, *The Therapeutic Community: A Successful Approach for Treating Substance Abusers* (Lake Worth, FL: Gardner Press, 1994), 40.

39. Eric Selbin, *Revolution, Rebellion, Resistance: The Power of Story* (New York: Zed Books, 2010); Jack A. Gladstone, *Revolutions: A Very Short Introduction* (Oxford: Oxford University Press, 2014), 1–9.

40. See, for example, Johann Hari, *Chasing the Scream: The First and Last Days of the War on Drugs* (New York: Bloomsbury, 2015).

41. James C. Scott, *Domination and the Arts of Resistance: Hidden Transcripts* (New Haven, CT: Yale University Press, 1992).

42. Trysh Travis, *The Language of the Heart: A Cultural History of the Recovery Movement from Alcoholics Anonymous to Oprah Winfrey* (Chapel Hill: University of North Carolina Press, 2010); David Sheff, *Clean: Overcoming Addiction and Ending America's Greatest Tragedy* (New York: Houghton Mifflin, 2013), 226; Alexander Bassin, "Proverbs, Slogans, and Folk Sayings in the Therapeutic Community: A Neglected Therapeutic Tool," *Journal of Psychoactive Drugs* 16, no. 1 (1984): 51–56; Stephen Kent, *From Slogans to Mantras: Social Protest and Religious Conversion in the Late Vietnam Era* (Syracuse, NY: Syracuse University Press, 2001); E. Summerson Carr, *Scripting Addiction: The Politics of Therapeutic Talk and American Sobriety* (Princeton, NJ: Princeton University Press, 2010).

43. Howard Josepher, interviewed by William White, 2015, William White Papers, http://www.williamwhitepapers.com/pr/2015%20Howard%20Josepher.pdf, accessed October 8, 2016.

44. Leonieke C. van Boeke, Evelien P. M. Brouwers, Jaap van Weeghel, and Henk F. L. Garretsen, "Stigma Among Health Professionals Towards Patients with Substance Use Disorders and Its Consequences for Healthcare Delivery: Systematic Review," *Drug and Alcohol Dependence* 131, nos. 1–2 (2013): 23–35.

BIBLIOGRAPHY

PRIMARY SOURCES

Archives and Special Collections

Alcoholics Anonymous. General Services Office Archives, New York.

California State Archives, Sacramento. Narcotics Commission Records.

Charles Devlin Personal Papers. New York.

Columbia University Center for Oral History, New York. Addicts Who Survived Collection.

George Herbert Walker Bush Presidential Library, College Station, TX. Judy Smith Subject Files.

——. Kirsten Gear Files.

——. Press Release Subject Files.

——. White House Office of Records Management, Alphabetical Files.

——. White House Office of Records Management, Health Subject Files.

Kentucky Historical Society, Lexington, KY. Lexington Collection.

Lyndon Baines Johnson Presidential Library, Austin, TX. Office of Economic Opportunity Collection.

National Archives and Records Administration–Southeast, Morrow, GA. Records of the Alcohol, Drug Abuse, and Mental Health Administration, Record Group 511.

National Institutes of Health, Office of History, Bethesda, MD. National Institute on Drug Abuse Grant Microfiche Collection.

New York City Municipal Archives, New York. Papers of Mayor [John] Lindsay.

Richard Milhaus Nixon Presidential Library, Yorba Linda, CA. White House Tapes.

Ronald Reagan Presidential Library and Museum, Simi Valley, CA. Carlton E. Turner Files.

——. Drug Abuse Policy Office Files, 1981–1987.

——. Drug Abuse Policy Office Records.

——. Ian MacDonald Series II Subject Files.

——. Ian MacDonald Series III: Division of Adult Parole Operations Subject Files.

——. Richard Williams Files.

——. White House Communications Agency Videotape Collection.

——. White House Staff Exit Interviews.

University of California at Berkeley. Eldridge Cleaver Papers, 1963–1988.

——. Social Movements Collection.

——. Tobacco Documents Library.

University of California at Los Angeles.Guy Endore Papers.

——. Synanon Collection, Charles E. Young Special Collections.

University of Tennessee at Knoxville. Mitchell–Synanon Litigation Papers.

Online Archives and Websites

Alcoholics Anonymous. www.aa.org.

Amity Foundation Library. www.amityfdn.org/Library/index.php.

Centers for Disease Control and Prevention. www.cdc.gov.

Faces and Voices of Recovery. www.facesandvoicesofrecovery.org/.

Ronald Reagan Presidential Library and Museum. www.reaganfoundation.org.

Surviving Straight Inc. www.survivingstraightinc.com.

Synanon Online Archive. www.synanon.org.

White House Office of National Drug Control Strategy, www.whitehouse.gov/ondcp.

William Jefferson Clinton Digital Library, clinton.presidentiallibraries.us.

William White Papers. www.williamwhitepapers.com.

Government Documents

Bush, George W. *Public Papers of the Presidents of the United States, George W. Bush, 2004: Book 3.* Washington, DC: U.S. Government Printing Office, 2007.

Cohen, Jacqueline. *Incapacitating Criminals: Recent Research Findings: National Institute of Justice Brief.* Washington, DC: U.S. Department of Justice, December 1983.

Community Anti-Drug Coalitions of America. *Coalitions and Community Health: Integration of Behavioral Health and Primary Care.* Washington, DC: Substance Abuse and Mental Health Services Administration, Health Resources and Service Administration Center for Integrated Health Solutions, April 2013.

Drug Court Clearinghouse and Technical Assistance Project. *Looking at a Decade of Drug Courts.* Rockville, MD: Office of Justice Programs, U.S. Department of Justice, 1998. https://www.ncjrs.gov/html/bja/decade98.htm.

Drug Enforcement Administration. *DEA History Book, 1985–1990.* Washington, DC: Drug Enforcement Agency, n.d. http://web.archive.org/web/20060823024931/http://www.usdoj .gov/dea/pubs/history/1985-1990.html.

Gaumond, Peter and Melanie Whitter. *Access to Recovery (ATR) Approaches to Recovery-Oriented Systems of Care: Three Case Studies.* Rockville, MD: Center for Substance Abuse Treatment, Substance Abuse and Mental Health Services Administration, 2009.

Goldkamp, John S. *Justice and Treatment Innovation: The Drug Court Movement. A Working Paper of the First National Drug Court Conference, December 1993.* Washington, DC: Office of Justice Programs, U.S. Department of Justice, 1994.

Legal Action Center, National Association of Addiction Treatment Providers, National Association of Alcoholism and Drug Abuse Counselors, National Council on Alcoholism and Drug Dependence, and Therapeutic Communities of America. *Healthcare Reform and Substance Abuse Treatment: The Cost of Financing Under Alternative Approaches: Final Report.* Fairfax, VA: Lewin-VHI, February 2, 1994.

Legislative Commission of the Legislative Counsel Bureau of Nevada. *Illegal Narcotic and Drug Use in Nevada: Bulletin 80.* Carson City: State of Nevada, January 1969.

Lipton, Douglas. *The Effectiveness of Treatment for Drug Abusers Under Criminal Justice Supervision: National Institute of Justice Research Report.* Rockville, MD: U.S. Department of Justice, 1995.

Lipton, Douglas, Gregory Falkin, and Harry Wexler. "Correctional Drug Abuse Treatment in the United States: An Overview." In *Drug Abuse Treatment in Prisons and Jails,* National Institute on Drug Abuse (NIDA) Research Monograph 118, 8–30. Rockville, MD: NIDA, 1992.

National Commission for the Protection of Human Subjects of Biomedical and Behavioral Research, Department of Health, Education, and Welfare. *Belmont Report: Ethical Principles and Guidelines for the Protection of Human Subjects of Research.* Washington, DC: U.S. Government Printing Office, September 30, 1978.

National Treatment Accountability for Safer Communities. *Treatment Services in Adult Drug Courts: Report on the 1999 National Drug Court Treatment Survey: Executive Summary May 2001.* Prepared for the Drug Courts Program Office, Office of Justice Programs, and Center for Substance Abuse Treatment, Substance Abuse and Mental Health Services Administration. Washington, DC: Office of Justice Programs, U.S. Department of Justice, May 2001.

New York Comptroller's Office. *Addiction Services Agency: A Study of Mismanagement.* New York: The Unit, 1973.

New York State Office of Alcoholism and Substance Abuse Services. *Statewide Comprehensive Plan 2012–2016: 2013 Interim Report.* Albany: State of New York, February 15, 2013. http://www.oasas.ny.gov/pio/commissioner/documents/5YPIntReport2013.pdf.

Parent, Dale G. *Shock Incarceration: An Overview of Existing Programs.* Rockville, MD: Office of Justice Program, U.S. Department of Justice, June 1989.

Reagan, Ronald. "Remarks on Signing the Anti–Drug Abuse Act of 1986." October 27, 1986. http://www.reagan.utexas.edu/archives/speeches/1986/102786c.htm.

——. "Remarks on Signing the Anti-Drug Abuse Act of 1988." November 18, 1988. https://reaganlibrary.gov/archives/photographs/36-archives/speeches/1988/8737-111888c.

Snell, Tracy L. *Correctional Populations in the United States, 1991.* Rockville, MD: Bureau of Justice Statistics, U.S. Department of Justice, August 1993.

Snyder, Tom, ed. *120 Years of American Education: A Statistical Portrait.* Vol. 1. Alexandria, VA: National Center for Education Statistics, 1993.

"Study in Heroism: Statement of Thomas Dodd to the U.S. Senate Subcommittee to Investigate Juvenile Delinquency, A." *Congressional Record,* September 6, 1962, no page numbers.

Substance Abuse and Mental Health Services Administration. *Recovery-Oriented Systems of Care (ROSC) Resource Guide (Working Draft)*. Rockville, MD: Substance Abuse and Mental Health Services Administration, September 2010. http://www.samhsa.gov/sites/default/files/rosc_resource_guide_book.pdf.

Substance Abuse and Mental Health Services Administration, Center for Behavioral Health Statistics and Quality. *The N-SSTATS Report: Trends in the Use of Methadone and Buprenorphine at Substance Abuse Treatment Facilities: 2003 to 2011*. Washington, DC: Substance Abuse and Mental Health Services Administration, April 23, 2013. http://archive.samhsa.gov/data/2k13/NSSATS107/sr107-NSSATS-BuprenorphineTrends.htm.

Texas Recovery Initiative Criminal Justice Workgroup. *Criminal Justice Population Resource Guide 2013*. Austin: State of Texas, 2013. https://www.tdcj.state.tx.us/documents/rpd/RPD_TRI_Resource_Guide_English.pdf.

Therapeutic Communities of America, Criminal Justice Committee. *Therapeutic Communities in Correctional Settings: The Prison-Based TC Standards Development Project (Final Report of Phase II)*. Prepared for the White House Office of National Drug Control Policy. Washington, DC: White House Office of National Drug Control Policy, 1999.

U.S. Department of Justice. *Indexed Legislative History of the Anti–Drug Abuse Act of 1986*. Washington, DC: U.S. Department of Justice, October 27, 1986. https://www.ncjrs.gov/pdffiles1/Digitization/126728NCJRS.pdf.

U.S. House of Representatives. *Drug Treatment Options for the Justice System: Hearing before the Subcommittee on Criminal Justice, Drug Policy, and Human Resources of the Committee on Government Reform*. 106th Cong., 2nd sess., April 4, 2000.

——. *Residential Treatment Programs: Concerns Regarding Abuse and Death in Certain Programs for Troubled Youth: Hearing Before the Committee on Education and Labor of the United States House of Representatives*. 110th Cong., 1st sess., October 7, 2007.

——. *Treatment and Rehabilitation of Narcotics Addicts: Hearing Before the Subcommittee to Amend the Narcotic Rehabilitation Act of 1966 of the Committee on the Judiciary of the United States House of Representatives*. 92nd Cong., 1st. sess., June 23, 30, and September 21, 23, 24, 29, 30, 1971.

U.S. House of Representatives, Special Subcommittee on Alcoholism and Narcotics of the Committee on Labor and Public Welfare. *Inquiry Into the Problem of Alcoholism and Narcotics*. 91st Cong., 1st sess., October 4, 1969.

U.S. Senate. *Hearings Before the Subcommittee to Investigate Juvenile Delinquency of the Committee of the Judiciary, U.S. Senate*. 87th Cong., 2nd sess., August 6 and 7, 1962.

——. *Individual Rights and the Federal Role in Behavior Modification: A Study Prepared by the Staff of the Subcommittee on Constitutional Rights of the Committee on the Judiciary, United States Senate*. 93rd Cong., 2nd sess., November 1974. Washington, DC: U.S. Government Printing Office, 1974.

——. *Inquiry Into the Problem of Alcoholism and Narcotics: Hearing Before the Special Subcommittee on Alcoholism and Narcotics of the Committee on Labor and Public Welfare of the United States Senate*. 91st Cong., 1st sess., October 4, 1969.

U.S. Senate, Subcommittee on Executive Reorganization. *Organization and Coordination of Federal Drug Research and Regulatory Programs: LSD*. 89th U.S. Cong., 2nd sess., May 24 and 25, 1966.

White House. *National Drug Control Strategy*. Washington, DC: U.S. Government Printing Office, September 1989.

White House Health Care Task Force, Task Force on National Health Care, and Ira Magaziner. *Legal Action Center Final Report*. William Jefferson Clinton Digital Library. http://clintonpresidentiallibraires.us/items/show/39657.

Theses and Dissertations

Becker, Sidney Jo. "Synanon: An Alternate Lifestyle for the Non-addict." PhD diss., University of California at Los Angeles, 1973.

Brook, Kerwin Kaye. "Drug Courts and the Treatment of Addiction: Therapeutic Jurisprudence and Neoliberal Governance." PhD diss., New York University, 2010.

Cleeker, Patricia. "Dealing with Mister Jones: An Exploration of the Boundary Between Addict and Non-addict in the Street and in Rehabilitation." PhD diss., Cornell University, 1974.

Kaufman, Kevin. "Rigorous Honesty: A Cultural History of Alcoholics Anonymous 1935–1960." PhD diss., Loyola University Chicago, 2011.

Levenstein, Phyllis. "The Synanon: Some Dimensions of Its Impact in Two Settings." Master's thesis, University of California at Los Angeles, 1963.

Neptune, Jessica. "The Making of the Carceral State: Street Crime, the War on Drugs, and Punitive Politics in New York, 1951–1973." PhD diss., University of Chicago, 2012.

Patterson, Carlos, Jr. "Synanon: An Anti-poverty Community." Master's thesis, University of California at Los Angeles, 1974.

Sheehy, Peter. "The Triumph of Group Therapeutics: Therapy, the Social Self, and Liberalism in America, 1910–1960." PhD diss., University of Virginia, 2002.

Szott, Kelly. "Governing Through Health: The Biomedical and Public Health Management of Drug Using Bodies." PhD diss., Syracuse University, 2015.

Interviews and Oral Histories

Selected Interviews by Claire Clark

Bourne, Peter. Washington, DC, April 24, 2013.

Clark, Ron. Washington, DC, April 23, 2013.

Deitch, David. La Jolla, CA, May 25, 2011.

Devlin, Charles. New York, October 6, 2011.

Dibble, Ted. Novato, CA, August 26, 2012.

Finkelstein, Sidney. Safety Harbor, FL, July 23, 2011.

Jaffe, Jerome. Baltimore, April 23, 2013.

Katz, Warren. Park Ridge, NJ, March 9, 2013.

Rosenthal, Mitchell. New York, June 2, 2014.

Williams, Ron. New York, March 6, 2013.

Williams, Wendy. Princeton, NJ, March 6, 2013.

Miscellaneous

Croughan, Jack. Interviewed by Luke Walden and J. P. Olsen (King Love Films). Undated transcript in author's files.

Deitch, David and George De Leon. Interviewed by William White, 2010. William White Papers. http://www.williamwhitepapers.com/papers/topics/pioneer_interviews/.

Densen-Gerber, Judianne. Oral history with David Courtwright, August 5, 1981. Addicts Who Survived Collection. Columbia University Center for Oral History, New York.

Dixon, Elizabeth, ed. *Seven Voices from Synanon: Oral History Transcript: Charles Dederich, Charles Hamer, Bettye Coleman, Monte Morton, James Middleton, Arlene Hefner, and Reid Kimball.* Los Angeles: Oral History Program, University of California at Los Angeles, 1964.

Dole, Vincent. Oral history with David Courtwright, September 13, 1982. Addicts Who Survived Collection. Columbia University Center for Oral History, New York.

Jaffe, Jerome. Oral history with Nancy Campbell, undated transcript. Oral History of Substance Abuse Research, Bentley Historical Library, University of Michigan, Ann Arbor. http://www.williamwhitepapers.com/pr/2013%20Dr.%20Jerome%20Jaffe.pdf.

Josepher, Howard. Interviewed by William White, 2015. William White Papers. http://www.williamwhitepapers.com/pr/2015%20Howard%20Josepher.pdf.

O'Brien, Monsignor William. Oral history with David Courtwright, July 31, 1981. Addicts Who Survived Collection. Columbia University Center for Oral History, New York.

Panone, Marty. Interviewed by Luke Walden and J. P. Olsen (King Love Films). Undated transcript in author's files.

Rosenthal, Mitchell. Oral history with David Courtwright, July 23, 1981. Addicts Who Survived Collection. Columbia University Center for Oral History, New York.

Shea, Dick. Interviewed by Luke Walden and J. P. Olsen (King Love Films). Undated transcript in author's files.

Smith, Margie. Interviewed by Luke Walden and J. P. Olsen (King Love Films). Undated transcript in author's files.

Tucker, Glynn. Interviewed by Luke Walden and J. P. Olsen (King Love Films). Undated transcript in author's files.

Magazines, Newspapers, Periodicals, and News Sites

Alcoholism and Drug Abuse Weekly
Baltimore Sun
Boston Globe
Businessweek
The Campaigner
CNN.com
The Crisis
Ebony
The Fix
Guardian
Harlan Daily Enterprise

Harper's
Hollywood Reporter
Huffington Post
Kentucky New Era
LA Free Press
Lexington Leader
Life
Los Angeles Times
Manas
Modesto Bee
The Nation
National Public Radio
Newsweek
New York Magazine
New York Nonprofit Press
New York Times
Pacific Standard
Pageant
Philadelphia Inquirer
Psychology Today
Ramparts
Reader's Digest
Reason
San Francisco Chronicle
Santa Monica Evening Outlook
Santa Monica Independent
Saturday Review
Sepia
St. Louis Post-Dispatch
Time
True
USA Today
Variety
Village Voice
Wall Street Journal
Washington Post

Radio, Television, and Film

Cronkite, Walter. "Synanon in Prison." Episode 13, season 9, *Twentieth Century*, CBS, aired March 13, 1966.
Current Trends in the Therapy for Narcotic Addiction. VHS. Public Health Service, U.S. Department of Health, Education, and Welfare, 1969.

Head, Murdock, dir. *The Distant Drummer: Flowers of Darkness.* VHS. George Washington University, National Institute of Mental Health, District of Columbia Medical Society, and American Academy of General Practice, 1972.

Mitchell, Dennis, dir. *The House on the Beach.* 16-mm film. Canadian Broadcasting Corporation, Westinghouse Broadcasting Corporation, 1965.

Most Adult Game, The. 16-mm film. KRON-TV, San Francisco, 1967.

Pendrell, Ernest, dir. *Marathon: The Story of Young Drug Users.* 16-mm film. ABC, 1967.

Quine, Richard, dir. *Synanon.* Columbia Pictures, 1965. DVD. Sony Pictures Home Entertainment, 2011.

Ray, Bill, dir. *David.* 16-mm film. Time-Life Broadcast and Drew Associates, 1961.

Seven Former Drug Addicts Recount Their Experiences as Addicts in 60 and 30 Second Spots. LP. U.S. Department of Health, Education, and Welfare, 1969.

SECONDARY SOURCES

Acampora, Alfonso P. and Ethan Nebelkopf, eds. *Bridging Services: Proceedings of the 9th World Conference of Therapeutic Communities, September 1–6, 1985, San Francisco, California.* San Francisco: Walden House, 1986.

Acker, Caroline. *Creating the American Junkie: Addiction Research in the Classic Era of Narcotic Control.* Baltimore: Johns Hopkins University Press, 2003.

Akin, William. *Technocracy and the American Dream: The Technocrat Movement, 1900–1941.* Berkeley: University of California Press, 1977.

Alcoholics Anonymous: The Story of How Many Thousands of Men and Women Have Recovered from Alcoholism. 3rd ed. New York: Alcoholics Anonymous World Services, 1976.

Alexander, Michelle. *The New Jim Crow: Mass Incarceration in the Age of Colorblindness.* New York: New Press, 2009.

Allen, Francis A. *The Decline of the Rehabilitative Ideal.* New Haven, CT: Yale University Press, 1981.

American Association for the Study and Cure of Inebriety. *The Disease of Inebriety from Alcohol, Opium, and Other Narcotic Drugs.* New York: E. B. Treat, 1893.

Anderson, Patrick. *High in America: The True Story Behind NORML and the Politics of Marijuana.* New York: Viking Press, 1981.

Anderson, Warwick. "The New York Needle Trial: The Politics of Public Health in the Age of AIDS." *American Journal of Public Health* 81, no. 11 (1991): 1506–1517.

Andrews, Christina, Amanda Abraham, Colleen M. Grogan, Harold A. Pollack, Clifford Bersamira, Keith Humphreys, and Peter Friedmann. "Despite Resources from the ACA, Most States Do Little to Help Addiction Treatment Programs Implement Health Care Reform." *Health Affairs* 34, no. 5 (2015): 828–835.

Andrews, Christina, Colleen M. Grogan, Marianne Brennan, and Harold A. Pollack. "Lessons from Medicaid's Divergent Paths on Mental Health and Addiction Services." *Health Affairs* 34, no. 7 (2015): 1131–1138.

"Anita Bryant." In *Culture Wars: An Encyclopedia of Issues, Viewpoints, and Voices*, edited by Roger Chapman, 55–56. Armonk, NY: M. E. Sharpe, 2010.

Bachman, Jerald, Lloyd Johnston, and Patrick O'Malley. "Explaining Recent Increases in Students' Marijuana Use: Impacts of Perceived Risks and Disapproval, 1976 Through 1996." *American Journal of Public Health* 88, no. 6 (1998): 887–892.

Balko, Radley. *Rise of the Warrior Cop: The Militarization of America's Police Forces*. New York: Public Affairs, 2012.

Barry, Colleen L., Haiden A. Huskamp, and Howard H. Goldman. "A Political History of Federal Mental Health and Addiction Insurance Parity." *Milbank Quarterly* 88, no. 3 (2010): 404–433.

Barry, Colleen L., Emma E. McGinty, Bernice Pescosolido, and Howard H. Goldman. "Stigma, Discrimination, Treatment Effectiveness, and Policy: Public Views About Drug Addiction and Mental Illness." *Psychiatric Services* 65, no. 10 (2014): 1269–1272.

Bassin, Alexander. "Proverbs, Slogans, and Folk Sayings in the Therapeutic Community: A Neglected Therapeutic Tool." *Journal of Psychoactive Drugs* 16, no. 1 (1984): 51–56.

Baum, Dan. *Smoke and Mirrors: The War on Drugs and the Politics of Failure*. Boston: Little, Brown, 1996.

Bayer, Ronald. "Liberal Opinion and the Problem of Heroin Addiction: 1960–1973." *Contemporary Drug Problems* 93 (Summer 1975): 93–112.

Becker, Howard. *Outsiders: Studies in the Sociology of Deviance*. New York: Free Press, 1963.

Bellah, Robert N., Richard Madsen, William M. Sullivan, Ann Swidler, and Steven M. Tipton. *Habits of the Heart: Individualism and Commitment in American Life*. Berkeley: University of California Press, 1985.

Benavie, Arthur. *Drugs: America's Holy War*. New York: Routledge, 2009.

Bennett, William J., John DiIulio, and John P. Walters. *Body Count: Moral Poverty . . . and How to Win America's War Against Crime and Drugs*. New York: Simon and Schuster, 1996.

Berger, Dan. *Outlaws of America: The Weather Underground and the Politics of Solidarity*. Oakland, CA: AK Press, 2006.

Bernstein, Lee. *America Is the Prison: Arts and Politics in Prison in the 1970s*. Chapel Hill: University of North Carolina Press, 2010.

Biernecki, Patrick. *Pathways from Heroin Addiction: Recovery Without Treatment*. Philadelphia: Temple University Press, 1986.

Bloom, Joshua and Waldo Martin. *Black Against Empire: The History and Politics of the Black Panther Party*. Berkeley: University of California Press, 2013.

Blum, John M. *Years of Discord*. New York: Norton, 1991.

Boorstin, Daniel J. *The Image: A Guide to Pseudo Events in America*. 1962. Reprint. New York: Vintage Books, 1992.

Bourne, Peter. "Alcoholism and Drug Abuse." n.d. http://petergbourne.co.uk/articles10.html.

Bowen, Elizabeth A. "Clean Needles and Bad Blood: Needle Exchange as Morality Policy." *Journal of Sociology and Social Welfare* 39, no. 2 (2012): 121–141.

Braslow, Joel. "The Manufacture of Recovery." *Annual Review of Clinical Psychology* 9 (2013): 781–809.

Brennan, Mary C. *Turning Right in the Sixties: The Conservative Capture of the GOP.* Chapel Hill: University of North Carolina Press, 1995.

Brill, Leon. Review of *Synanon* by Guy Endore. *Social Work*, July 1969, 119–121.

——. "Some Comments on the Paper 'Social Control in Therapeutic Communities' by Dan Waldorf." *International Journal of the Addictions* 6 (March 1971): 45–50.

Buchanan, David R. and Lawrence Wallack. "This Is the Partnership for a Drug-Free America: Any Questions?" *Journal of Drug Issues* 28, no. 2 (1998): 329–356.

Bufe, Charles. *Alcoholics Anonymous: Cult or Cure?* San Francisco: Sharp Press, 1991.

Burnham, John C. *Bad Habits: Drinking, Smoking, Taking Drugs, Gambling, Sexual Misbehavior, and Swearing in American History.* New York: New York University Press, 1993.

Burnham, John C., and Joseph F. Spillane. "Editor's Introduction." In William Wilkinson, *Prison Work: A Tale of Thirty Years in the California Department of Corrections*, edited by John C. Burnham and Joseph F. Spillane, ix–xx. Columbus: Ohio State University, 2005.

Burrough, Bryan. *Days of Rage: America's Radical Underground, the FBI, and the Forgotten Age of Revolutionary Violence.* New York: Penguin, 2015.

Campbell, Nancy. *Discovering Addiction: The Science and Politics of Substance Abuse Research.* Ann Arbor: University of Michigan Press, 2007.

——. "The History of a Public Science: How the Addiction Research Center Became the NIDA Intramural Program." *Drug and Alcohol Dependence* 107, no. 1 (2007): 108–112.

——. "'A New Deal for the Drug Addict': The Addiction Research Center, Lexington, Kentucky." *Journal of the History of the Behavioral Sciences* 42, no. 2 (2006): 135–157.

——. Review of *The Myth of the Addicted Army: Vietnam and the Modern War on Drugs* by Jeremy Kuzmarov. *Social History of Alcohol and Drugs* 24, no. 2 (2010): 176–177.

Campbell, Nancy, Luke Walden, and J. P. Olsen, *The Narcotic Farm: The Rise and Fall of America's First Prison for Drug Addicts.* New York: Abrams, 2008.

Carr, E. Summerson. *Scripting Addiction: The Politics of Therapeutic Talk and American Sobriety.* Princeton, NJ: Princeton University Press, 2010.

Carter, Dan T. *The Politics of Rage: George Wallace, the Origins of the New Conservatism, and the Transformation of American Politics.* New York: Simon and Schuster, 1995.

Carvajal, Paul. "Integration of Harm Reduction and Other Treatment Approaches." *Harm Reduction Communication*, Fall 1995, 1.

Casriel, Daniel. *A Scream Away from Happiness.* New York: Grosset and Dunlap, 1972.

——. *So Fair a House: The Story of Synanon.* Englewood Cliffs, NJ: Prentice-Hall, 1963.

Casriel, Daniel and Grover Amen. *Daytop: Three Addicts and Their Cure.* New York: Hill and Wang, 1971.

Casriel, Daniel and David Deitch. *New Success in the Cure of Addicts.* Staten Island, NY: Daytop Village, 1967.

Cenikor. *Cenikor Annual Report, 1983.* Houston: Cenikor, 1983.

——. *Cenikor Foundation Inc. Agency Profile Book, 1989.* Houston: Cenikor, 1989.

Chandler, Alfred D. *The Visible Hand: The Managerial Revolution in American Business.* Cambridge, MA: Belknap Press of Harvard University Press, 1977.

Chapman, Roger, ed. *Culture Wars: An Encyclopedia of Issues, Viewpoints, and Voices.* Armonk, NY: M. E. Sharpe, 2010.

Chatfield, Marcus. *Institutionalized Persuasion: The Technology of Persuasion in Straight Incorporated and the Residential Teen Treatment Industry.* N.p.: Marcus Chatfield, 2014.

Clark, Claire D. and Emily Dufton. "Peter Bourne's Drug Policy and the Perils of a Public Health Ethic." *American Journal of Public Health* 105, no. 2 (2015): 283–292.

Clark, Janet and Howard Becker. *The Fantastic Lodge: Autobiography of a Girl Drug Addict.* New York: Houghton Mifflin, 1961.

Cleaver, Elridge. *Soul on Ice.* Berkeley, CA: Ramparts Press, 1968.

Clinton, William J. Foreword to *Solutions: American Leaders Speak Out on Criminal Justice,* edited by Inimai Chettiar and Michael Waldman, v–vi. New York: Brennan Center for Justice, 2015.

Collier, Peter, and David Horowitz. *Destructive Generation: Second Thoughts About the Sixties.* New York: Encounter Books, 2005.

Collier, Walter V., Edward Hammock, and Charles Devlin. *An Evaluation Report on the Therapeutic Program of Daytop Village.* Staten Island, NY: Daytop Village, February 1970.

Columbia University Center on Addiction and Substance Abuse. *Behind Bars: Substance Abuse and America's Prison Population.* New York: Columbia University, January 1998.

Courtwright, David T. "The Controlled Substances Act: How a 'Big Tent' Reform Became a Punitive Drug Law." *Drug and Alcohol Dependence* 76, no. 1 (2004): 9–15.

——. "The Cycles of American Drug Policy" *American Historian,* August 2015. http://digitalcommons.unf.edu/ahis_facpub/25.

——. *Dark Paradise: A History of Opiate Addiction in America.* 2nd ed. Cambridge, MA: Harvard University Press, 2001.

——. "Morality, Religion, and Drug Use." In *Morality and Health,* edited by Allan M. Brandt and Paul Rozin, 231–250. New York: Routledge, 1997.

——. "Mr. ATOD's Wild Ride: What Do Alcohol, Tobacco, and Other Drugs Have in Common?" *Social History of Alcohol and Drugs* 20, no. 1 (2005): 105–140.

——. "The NIDA Brain Disease Paradigm: History, Resistance, and Spin-offs." *BioSocieties* 5, no. 1 (2010): 137–147.

——. "NIDA: This Is Your Life." *Drug and Alcohol Dependence* 107, no. 1 (2010): 116–118.

——. *No Right Turn: Conservative Politics in a Liberal America.* Cambridge, MA: Harvard University Press, 2010.

——. "The Prepared Mind: Marie Nyswander." *Addiction* 92 (1997): 257–265.

Courtwright, David T., Herman Joseph, and Don DesJarlais. *Addicts Who Survived: An Oral History of Narcotic Use in America.* Knoxville: University of Tennessee Press, 1989.

Cowie, Jefferson. *Stayin' Alive: The 1970s and the Last Days of the Working Class.* New York: New Press, 2010.

Cressey, Donald R. "Changing Criminals: The Application of the Theory of Differential Association." *American Journal of Sociology* 61, no. 2 (1955): 116–120.

——. "Contradictory Theories in Correctional Group Therapy Programs." *Federal Probation* 18 (1954): 20–26.

Cullen, Francis. "The Twelve People Who Saved Rehabilitation: How the Science of Criminology Made a Difference." *Criminology* 43 (2005): 1–42.

Cummins, Eric. *The Rise and Fall of California's Radical Prison Movement.* Stanford, CA: Stanford University Press, 1994.

Dederich, Charles. "Synanon Foundation." Paper read before the Southern California Parole Officers, October 1958, place not identified. Author's personal collection.

DeGroot, Gerard. "'A Goddamned Electable Person': The 1966 California Gubernatorial Campaign of Ronald Reagan." *History* 82, no. 267 (1997): 429–448.

Deitch, David. "Developmental Feature of the Therapeutic Community: Imprints—Actions and Discoveries." *Journal of Psychoactive Drugs* 29, no. 2 (1997): 145–148.

Deitch, David and Joan Zweben. "Synanon: A Pioneering Response in Drug Treatment and a Signal for Caution." In *Substance Abuse: Clinical Problems and Perspectives*, edited by Joyce Lowinson and Pedro Ruiz, 289–302. Baltimore: Williams and Wilkins, 1981.

De Leon, George. "'The Gold Standard' and Related Considerations for a Maturing Science of Substance Abuse Treatment: Therapeutic Communities, a Case in Point." *Substance Use and Misuse* 50, nos. 8–9 (2015): 1106–1109.

——, ed. *Phoenix House: Studies in a Therapeutic Community, 1968–1973*. New York: MSS Information Corporation, 1974.

——. "Phoenix House Therapeutic Community: The Influence of Time in Program on Change in Resident Drug Addicts." In *Phoenix House: Studies in a Therapeutic Community, 1968–1973*, edited by George De Leon, 194–198. New York: MSS Information Corporation, 1974.

——. *The Therapeutic Community: Theory, Model, Method*. New York: Springer, 2000.

De Leon, George and George Beschner. "Introduction." In *The Therapeutic Community: Proceedings of the Therapeutic Communities of America Planning Conference January 29–30, 1976*, compiled and edited by George De Leon and George Beschner, 1–5. Rockville, MD: National Institute on Drug Abuse, 1976.

——. "Epilogue." In *The Therapeutic Community: Proceedings of the Therapeutic Community of America Planning Conference January 29–30, 1976*, compiled and edited by George De Leon and George Beschner, 109–110. Rockville, MD: National Institute on Drug Abuse, 1976.

——, comps. and eds. *The Therapeutic Community: Proceedings of the Therapeutic Communities of America Planning Conference January 29–30, 1976*. Rockville, MD: National Institute on Drug Abuse, 1976.

Densen-Gerber, Judianne. *We Mainline Dreams: The Odyssey House Story*. New York: Doubleday, 1973.

"Differences Between New York and California." In *Federal Regulation of Methadone Treatment*, edited by Richard Retting and Adam Yarmolinsky, 85–89. Washington, DC: National Academies Press, 1995.

Dole, Vincent and Marie Nyswander. "Heroin Addiction: A Metabolic Disease." *Archives of Internal Medicine* 120, no. 1 (1967): 19–24.

——. "A Medical Treatment for Diacetylmorphine (Heroin) Addiction." *Journal of the American Medical Association* 193 (August 23, 1965): 646–650.

Dole, Vincent, Marie Nyswander, and Alan Warner. "Successful Treatment of 750 Criminal Addicts." *Journal of the American Medical Association* 206 (December 16, 1968): 2708–2711.

Dumont, Matthew P. "The Junkie as Political Enemy." *American Journal of Orthopsychiatry*, 43 (1973): 533–540.

Dupont, Robert L. "The Drug Abuse Decade." *Journal of Drug Issues* 8, no. 2 (1978): 173–187.

——. "Reflections on the Early History of National Institute on Drug Abuse (NIDA): Implications for Today." *Journal of Drug Issues* 39, no. 5 (2009): 5–14.

——. *The Selfish Brain: Learning from Addiction*. Washington, DC: American Psychiatric Press, 1997.

DuPont, Robert and Richard Katon. "Development of a Heroin-Addiction Treatment Program: Effect on Urban Crime." *Journal of the American Medical Association* 216 (May 24, 1971): 1320–1324.

Duster, Troy. *The Legislation of Morality: Law, Drugs, and Moral Judgment*. New York: Free Press, 1970.

Dyck, Ericka. *Psychedelic Psychiatry: LSD from Clinic to Campus*. Baltimore: Johns Hopkins University Press, 2008.

Dye, Meredith Huey, Lori J. Ducharme, J. Aaron Johnson, Hannah K. Knudsen, and Paul M. Roman. "Modified Therapeutic Communities and Adherence to Traditional Elements." *Journal of Psychoactive Drugs* 41, no. 3 (2009): 275–283.

Edman, Johan. "Red Cottages and Swedish Virtues: Swedish Institutional Drug Treatment as an Ideological Project 1968–1981." *Social History of Medicine* 3, no. 26 (2013): 510–531.

Edwards, Griffith. "Conversation with David Deitch." *Addiction* 94 (1999): 791–800.

——. "A Conversation with Robert Dupont." *Addiction* 100 (2005): 1402–1411.

——. "Seeing America—Diary of a Drug-Focused Study Tour Made in 1967." *Addiction* 105 (2010): 984–990.

Eisenach, Jeffrey A. and Andrew J. Cowin. "The Case Against More Funds for Drug Treatment." *Backgrounder: Heritage Foundation Newsletter*, May 17, 1991, 1–14.

Emerson, Ralph Waldo. "Self-Reliance." In *Essays: First Series*. Boston: James Munroe, 1841. http://www.emersoncentral.com/selfreliance.htm.

Endore, Guy. *Synanon*. New York: Doubleday, 1968.

Epstein, Edward Jay. *Agency of Fear: Opiate and Political Power in America*. New York: Verso, 1990.

——. "Methadone: The Forlorn Hope." *Public Interest* 36 (Summer 1974): 3–24.

Feldstein, Mark. *Poisoning the Press: Richard Nixon, Jack Anderson, and the Rise of Washington's Scandal Culture*. New York: Farrar, Strauss and Giroux, 2008.

Fingarette, Herbert. *Heavy Drinking: The Myth of Alcoholism as a Disease*. Berkeley: University of California Press, 1988.

Finney, Graham S. *Drugs: Administering Catastrophe*. Washington, DC: Drug Abuse Council, 1975.

Fischer, Frank. *Technocracy and the Politics of Expertise*. New York: Sage, 1989.

Fletcher, Anne. *Inside Rehab: The Surprising Truth About Addiction Treatment—and How to Get the Help That Works*. New York: Viking, 2013.

Ford, Betty. *The Times of My Life*. New York: Harper Collins, 1978.

Ford, Betty and Chris Chase. *A Glad Awakening*. New York: Doubleday, 1987.

Fortner, Michael Javen. *Black Silent Majority: The Rockefeller Drug Laws and the Politics of Punishment*. Cambridge, MA: Harvard University Press, 2015.

Frank, Thomas. *The Conquest of Cool: Business Culture, Counterculture, and the Rise of Hip Consumerism*. Chicago: University of Chicago Press, 1997.

Frankel, B. Gail, Robert C. Brook, and Paul C. Whitehead, with the assistance of Linda L. Adamtau and Carol M. Chamberlain. *Therapeutic Communities for the Management of Addictions: A Critically Annotated Bibliography.* Toronto: Addiction Research Foundation, 1976.

Frydl, Kathleen. *Drug Wars in America, 1940–1973.* New York: Cambridge University Press, 2013.

Galliher, John F., David P. Keys, and Michael Elsner. "Lindesmith v. Anslinger: An Early Government Victory in the Failed War on Drugs." *Journal of Criminal Law and Criminology* 88, no. 2 (1998): 661–682.

Garland, David. *The Culture of Control: Crime and Social Order in Contemporary Society.* Chicago: University of Chicago Press, 2001.

Gerstel, David. *Paradise Incorporated: Synanon.* Novato, CA: Presidio Press, 1982.

Gilmore, Ruth Wilson. *Golden Gulag: Prisons, Surplus, Crisis, and Opposition in Globalizing California.* Berkeley: University of California Press, 2007.

Gitlin, Todd. *The Sixties: Years of Hope, Days of Rage.* New York: Bantam, 1993.

Gladstone, Jack A. *Revolutions: A Very Short Introduction.* Oxford: Oxford University Press, 2014.

Glaser, Frederick. "Some Historical Aspects of the Drug-Free Therapeutic Community." *American Journal of Drug and Alcohol Abuse* 1, no. 1 (1974): 37–52.

Glasscote, Raymond, James N. Sussex, Jerome H. Jaffe, John Ball, and Leon Brill. *The Treatment of Drug Abuse: Programs, Problems, Prospects.* Washington, DC: American Psychiatric Association, 1972.

Goffman, Erving. *Asylums: Essays on the Social Situation of Mental Patients and Other Inmates.* Garden City, NY: Anchor Books, 1961.

——. *Stigma: Notes on the Management of Spoiled Identity.* Englewood Cliffs, NJ: Prentice-Hall, 1963.

Golden, Janet. *Message in a Bottle: The Making of Fetal Alcohol Syndrome.* Cambridge, MA: Harvard University Press, 2005.

Goldkamp, John S. "The Impact of Drug Courts." *Criminology and Public Policy* 2, no. 2 (2003): 197–206.

Gootenberg, Paul. *Andean Cocaine: The Making of a Global Drug.* Chapel Hill: University of North Carolina Press, 2009.

Gould, Stephen Jay. *The Mismeasure of Man.* Rev. ed. New York: Norton, 2006.

Gowan, Teresa and Sarah Whetsone. "Making the Criminal Addict: Subjectivity and Social Control in a Strong-Arm Rehab." *Punishment and Society* 14, no. 1 (2012): 69–93.

Greenberg, David. *Nixon's Shadow: The History of an Image.* New York: Norton, 2004.

Grob, Gerald. *Mental Illness and American Society, 1875–1940.* Princeton, NJ: Princeton University Press, 1983.

——. *Mental Institutions in America: Social Policy to 1875.* New York: Free Press, 1973.

——. "Rediscovering Asylums: The Unhistorical History of the Mental Hospital." *Hastings Center Report* 7, no. 4 (1977): 33–41.

Grogan, Jessica. *Encountering America: Humanistic Psychology, Sixties Culture, and the Shaping of the Modern Self.* New York: Harper, 2013.

Gusfield, Joseph. *Symbolic Crusade: Status Politics and the American Temperance Movement.* Urbana: University of Illinois Press, 1963.

Hale, Grace Elizabeth. *The Romance of the Outsider: How the White Middle Class Fell in Love with Rebellion in Postwar America.* Oxford: Oxford University Press, 2011.

Hankins, Barry. *Jesus and Gin: Evangelicalism, the Roaring Twenties, and Today's Culture Wars.* New York: St. Martin's Press, 2010.

Hari, Johann. *Chasing the Scream: The First and Last Days of the War on Drugs.* New York: Bloomsbury, 2015.

Heller, Daliah and Denise Paone. "Access to Sterile Syringes for Injecting Drug Users in New York City: Politics and Perception (1984–2010)." *Substance Use and Misuse* 46 (2011): 140–149.

Herzberg, David. *Happy Pills in America: From Miltown to Prozac.* Baltimore: Johns Hopkins University Press, 2009.

Hickman, Timothy. *The Secret Leprosy of Modern Days: Narcotic Addiction and Cultural Crisis in the United States, 1870–1920.* Amherst: University of Massachusetts Press, 2007.

Hinton, Elizabeth. *From the War on Poverty to the War on Crime: The Making of Mass Incarceration in America.* Cambridge, MA: Harvard University Press, 2016.

Hochschild, Arlie Russell. *The Outsourced Self: Intimate Life in Market Times.* New York: Macmillan, 2012.

Holland, Max. *Leak: Why Mark Felt Became Deep Throat.* Lawrence: University of Kansas Press, 2012.

Hora, Peggy Fulton. "Trading One Drug for Another?" *Journal of Maintenance in the Addictions* 2, no. 4 (2005): 71–76.

Howard, Jane. *Please Touch: A Guided Tour of the Human Potential Movement.* New York: Dell, 1970.

Hughes, Patrick. *Behind the Wall of Respect: Community Experiments in Heroin Addiction Control.* Chicago: University of Chicago Press, 1977.

Humphreys, Keith. "Addiction Treatment Professionals Are Not the Gatekeepers of Recovery." *Substance Use and Misuse* 50, nos. 8–9 (2015): 1024–1027.

Humphreys, Keith and Richard G. Frank. "The Affordable Care Act Will Revolutionize Care for Substance Use Disorders in the United States." *Addiction* 109 (2014): 1957–1958.

Hunt, G. H. and M. E. Odoroff. "Follow-Up Study of Narcotic Drug Addicts After Hospitalization." *Public Health Reports* 77 (1962): 41–52.

Imhof, John E. "Is Odyssey House the Tiffany of TC's?" *Contemporary Drug Problems* 3 (1974): 443–456.

Isserman, Maurice and Michael Kazin. *America Divided: The Civil War of the 1960s.* New York: Oxford University Press, 2000.

Jackson, George. *Soledad Brother: The Prison Letters of George Jackson.* New York: Bantam, 1970.

Jaffe, Jerome H. "The Nathan B. Eddy Lecture: Science, Policy, Happenstance." In *Problems of Drug Dependence, 1994: Proceedings of the 56th Annual Scientific Meeting, the College on Problems of Drug Dependence,* vol. 1, 18–32. Rockville, MD: National Institute on Drug Abuse, 1994.

Jaffe, Jerome, Misha S. Zaks, and Edward N. Washington. "Experience with the Use of Methadone in a Multi-modality Program for the Treatment of Narcotics Users." *International Journal of the Addictions* 4 (September 1969): 481–490.

Jameson, Frederic. "Walter Benjamin, or Nostalgia." *Salmagundi*, nos. 10–11 (Fall 1969–Winter 1970): 52–68.

Janzen, Rod. *The Rise and Fall of Synanon: A California Utopia*. Baltimore: Johns Hopkins University Press, 2001.

Jenkins, Philip. *Decade of Nightmares: The End of the Sixties and the Making of Eighties America*. Oxford: Oxford University Press, 2006.

Johnson Institute Foundation. *Faces and Voices Summit 2001 Proceedings*. St. Louis Park, MN: Johnson Institute Foundation, 2001. http://www.facesandvoicesofrecovery.org/sites /default/files/2001_summit_report.pdf.

Jonnes, Jill. *Hep Cats, Narcs, and Pipe Dreams: A History of America's Romance with Illegal Drugs*. Baltimore: Johns Hopkins University Press, 1999.

Jordan, John. *Machine-Age Ideology: Social Engineering and American Liberalism, 1911–1939*. Chapel Hill: University of North Carolina Press, 2010.

Joseph, Herman, Sharon Stancliff, and John Langrod. "Methadone Maintenance Treatment: A Review of Historical and Clinical Issues." *Mount Sinai Journal of Medicine* 67, nos. 5–6 (2000): 347–364.

Kent, Stephen. *From Slogans to Mantras: Social Protest and Religious Conversion in the Late Vietnam Era*. Syracuse, NY: Syracuse University Press, 2001.

Kerr, David. *The Voices of Integrity: Compelling Portrayals of Addiction and Recovery*. N.p.: XLibris, 2015.

Klatch, Rebecca. "The Counterculture, the New Left, and the New Right." *Qualitative Sociology* 17, no. 3 (1994): 199–214.

Klerman, Gerald. "Behavior Control and the Limits of Reform." *Hastings Center Report*, August 1975, 40–45.

Kohler-Hausmann, Julilly. "Guns and Butter: The Welfare State, the Carceral State, and the Politics of Exclusion in the Postwar United States." *Journal of American History* 102, no. 1 (2015): 87–99.

Kolodny, Andrew, David T. Courtwright, Catherine S. Hwang, Peter Kreiner, John L. Eadie, Thomas W. Clark, and G. Caleb Alexander. "The Prescription Opioid and Heroin Crisis: A Public Health Approach to an Epidemic of Addiction." *Annual Reviews of Public Health* 36 (2015): 559–574.

Kramer, John and Richard Bass. "Institutionalization Patterns Among Civilly Committed Addicts." *Journal of the American Medical Association* 208, no. 12 (1969): 2287–2301.

Kramer, Michael. *The Republic of Rock: Music and Citizenship in the Sixties*. New York: Oxford University Press, 2013.

Kuzmarov, Jeremy. *The Myth of the Addicted Army: Vietnam and the Modern War on Drugs*. Amherst: University of Massachusetts Press, 2009.

Lasch, Christopher. *The Culture of Narcissism: American Life in an Age of Diminishing Expectations*. New York: Norton, 1991.

Lassiter, Matthew. "Impossible Criminals: The Suburban Imperatives of America's War on Drugs." *Journal of American History* 102, no. 1 (2015): 126–140.

Lattin, Don. *The Harvard Psychedelic Club: How Timothy Leary, Ram Dass, Huston Smith, and Andrew Weil Killed the Fifties and Ushered in a New Age for America.* New York: Harper Collins, 2010.

Lears, T. J. Jackson. *Fables of Abundance: A Cultural History of Advertising in America.* New York: Basic Books, 1995.

——. "From Salvation to Self-Realization: Advertising and the Therapeutic Roots of the Consumer Culture, 1880–1930." In *The Culture of Consumption: Critical Essays in American History, 1880–1980,* edited by Richard Wightman Fox and T. J. Jackson Lears, 1–38. New York: Pantheon Books.

——. *No Place of Grace: Antimodernism and the Transformation of American Culture.* Chicago: University of Chicago Press, 1981.

Leary, Timothy. "The Effects of Consciousness-Expanding Drugs on Prisoner Rehabilitation." *Psychedelic Review* 10 (1969): 29–44.

Leary, Timothy, Ralph Metzner, Madison Presnell, Gunther Weil, Ralph Schwitzgebel, and Sarah Kinne. "A New Behavior Change Program Using Psilocybin." *Psychotherapy* 2, no. 2 (1965): 61–72.

Leschner, Alan I. "Addiction Is a Brain Disease, and It Matters." *Science* 278, no. 5335 (1997): 45–47.

Lindesmith, Alfred R. "Dope Fiend Mythology." *Journal of Criminal Law and Criminology* 31, no. 2 (1940): 199–208.

Lipkin, Steven. *Real Emotional Logic: Film and Television Docudrama as Persuasive Practice.* Carbondale: Southern Illinois University Press, 2002.

Lipton, Douglas. "Prison-Based Therapeutic Communities: Their Success with Drug-Abusing Offenders." *National Institute of Justice Journal,* February 1996, 12–20.

Lipton, Douglas, Robert Martinson, and Judith Wilks. *Effectiveness of Correctional Treatment: A Survey of Treatment Evaluation Studies.* Westport, CT: Praeger, 1975.

Loizeau, Pierre-Marie. *Nancy Reagan: The Woman Behind the Man.* Hauppauge, NY: New History Publications, 2004.

Lowy, Michael. "Revolution Against 'Progress': Walter Benjamin's Romantic Anarchism." *New Left Review* 152 (July–August 1985): 42–59.

Lynch, Mona. *Sunbelt Justice: Arizona and the Transformation of American Punishment.* Palo Alto, CA: Stanford Law Books, 2009.

Magnet, Myron. *The Dream and the Nightmare: The Sixties Legacy to the Underclass.* San Francisco: Encounter Books, 1993.

Malcolm X, with Alex Haley. *Autobiography of Malcolm X.* New York: Grove Press, 1965.

Marino, Vinny. *Journey from Hell.* Kaneohe, HI: Habilitat, 1966.

Marlatt, G. Alan. "Harm Reduction: Come as You Are." *Addictive Behaviors* 20, no. 6 (1996): 779–788.

Martinson, Robert. "What Works? Questions and Answers About Prison Reform." *Public Interest,* Spring 1974, 22–54.

Marwick, Arthur. *The Sixties: Cultural Revolution in Britain, France, Italy, and the United States, c. 1958–c. 1974.* New York: Oxford University Press, 1998.

Maslow, Abraham. "Comments on 'Religions, Values, and Peak Experiences.'" In *The Farther Reaches of Human Nature,* 331–337. New York: Penguin, 1971.

——. *Eupsychian Management.* New York: Irwin, 1965.

——. "Synanon and Eupsychia." *Journal of Humanistic Psychology* 7 (1967): 28–35.

——. *Toward a Psychology of Being.* New York: Van Nostrand, 1962.

Massing, Michael. *The Fix.* 1998. Reprint. Berkeley: University of California Press, 2000.

Matusow, Harlan, Samuel L. Dickman, Josiah D. Rich, Chunki Fong, Dora M. Dumont, Carolyn Hardin, Douglas Marlowe, and Andre Rosenblum. "Medication Assisted Treatment in U.S. Drug Courts: Results from a Nationwide Survey of Availability, Barrier, and Attitudes." *Journal of Substance Abuse Treatment* 44, no. 5 (2013): 473–480.

McCorkel, Jill. *Breaking Women: Gender, Race, and the New Politics of Imprisonment.* New York: New York University Press, 2013.

McCoy, Alfred. *The Politics of Heroin: CIA Complicity in the Global Drug Trade.* Chicago: Chicago Review Press, 2003.

McGee, Micki. *Self-Help, Inc: Makeover Culture in American Life.* New York: New York University Press, 2005.

McGirr, Lisa. *The War on Alcohol: Prohibition and the Rise of the American State.* New York: Norton, 2015.

McGlothlin, W. H., M. D. Anglin, and B. D. Wilson. "Outcome of the California Civil Addict Commitments: 1961–1972." *Drug and Alcohol Dependence* 1 (1975–1976): 165–181.

McGowan, Philip. "AA and the Redeployment of Temperance Literature." *Journal of American Studies* 48, no. 1 (2014): 51–78.

Mclean, Katherine. "The Biopolitics of Needle Exchange in the United States." *Critical Public Health* 21, no. 1 (2011): 71–79.

McLellan, A. Thomas and Abigail Mason Woodworth. "The Affordable Care Act and Treatment for 'Substance Use Disorders': Implications of Ending Segregated Behavioral Healthcare." *Journal of Substance Abuse Treatment* 46 (2014): 541–545.

McMillian, John. *Smoking Typewriters: The Sixties Underground Press and the Rise of Alternative Media in America.* Oxford: Oxford University Press, 2011.

McWilliams, John C. "Unsung Partner Against Crime: Harry J. Anslinger and the Federal Bureau of Narcotics, 1930–1962." *Pennsylvania Magazine of History and Biography* 113, no. 2 (1989): 211–216.

Meacham, Andrew. *Selling Serenity: Life Among the Recovery Stars.* Boca Raton, FL: Upton Books, 1999.

Mechanic, David. "More People Than Ever Before Are Receiving Behavioral Health Care in the United States, but Gaps and Challenges Remain." *Health Affairs* 33, no. 8 (2014): 1416–1424.

Metlay, Grischa. "Federalizing Medical Campaigns Against Alcoholism and Drug Abuse." *Milbank Quarterly* 91, no. 1 (2013): 123–162.

Milgram, Stanley. *Obedience to Authority: An Experimental View.* 1974. Reprint. New York: Harper, 2009.

Miller, James. *Democracy Is in the Streets: From Port Huron to the Siege of Chicago.* Cambridge, MA: Harvard University Press, 1987.

Miller, Judith. "The Seed: Reforming Drug Users with Love." *Science* 182, no. 4107 (1973): 40–42.

Miller, Timothy. *The Sixties Communes: Hippies and Beyond.* Syracuse, NY: Syracuse University Press, 1999.

Miller, William R. and Theresa B. Moyers. "The Forest and the Trees: Relational and Specific Factors in Addiction Treatment." *Addiction* 110 (2014): 401–413.

Mitchell, Dave, Cathy Mitchell, and Richard Ofshe. *The Light on Synanon: How a Country Weekly Exposed a Corporate Cult and Won the Pulitzer Prize.* New York: Seaview Books, 1980.

Mitford, Jessica. *Kind and Usual Punishment: The Prison Business.* New York: Random House, 1973.

Mold, Alex and Virginia Berridge. "'The Rise of the User?': Voluntary Organizations, the State, and Illegal Drugs in England Since the 1960s." *Drugs: Education, Prevention, and Policy* 15, no. 5 (2008): 451–461.

Monroe, James. *Hellfire Nation: The Politics of Sin in American History.* New Haven, CT: Yale University Press, 2003.

Morantz, Paul. *From Miracle to Madness: The True Story of Charles Dederich and Synanon.* N.p.: Cresta Publications, 2014.

Moreno, Jonathan D. *Impromptu Man: J. L. Moreno and the Origins of Psychodrama, Encounter Culture, and the Social Network.* New York: Bellevue Literary Press, 2014.

Mullen, Rod and Naya Arbiter. "Against the Odds: Therapeutic Community Approaches to Underclass Drug Abuse." In *Drug Policy in the Americas,* edited by Peter Smith, 179–201. Boulder, CO: Westview Press, 1992.

Mullen, Rod, John Ratelle, Elaine Abraham, and Jody Boyle. "California Program Reduces Recidivism and Saves Tax Dollars." *Corrections Today,* August 1996, 118–123.

Mullen, Rod, James Rowland, Naya Arbiter, Lew Yablonsky, and Bette Fleishman. *Building and Replicating an In-Prison Therapeutic Community That Reduces Recidivism: Amity Foundation's TC in the Richard J. Donovan Correctional Facility.* Tucson, AZ: Amity Foundation, 2001. http://www.amityfdn.org/wp-content/uploads/2016/09/1999-09-Rowland-et.-al.-Building-Replicating-In-Prison-TC.pdf.

——. "California's First Prison Therapeutic Community: A 10-Year Review." *Offender Substance Abuse Report* 1, no. 2 (2001): 1–6.

Murakawa, Naomi. *The First Civil Right: How Liberals Built Prison America.* New York: Oxford University Press, 2014.

Murphy, Jennifer. *Illness or Deviance? Drug Courts and the Ambiguity of Addiction.* Philadelphia: Temple University Press, 2016.

Murray, Charles. *Coming Apart: The State of White America, 1960–2010.* New York: Crown, 2012.

Musto, David. *The American Disease: The Origins of Narcotic Control.* New Haven, CT: Yale University Press, 1973.

Musto, David and Pamela Korsmeyer. *The Quest for Drug Control: Politics and Federal Policy in a Period of Increasing Substance Abuse (1963–1981).* New Haven, CT: Yale University Press, 2002.

Myers, Nancy Laurenzo. *Recovery's Edge: An Ethnography of Mental Health Care and Moral Agency.* Nashville: Vanderbilt University Press, 2015.

Neptune, Jessica. "Harshest in the Nation: The Rockefeller Drug Laws and the Widening Embrace of Punitive Politics." *Social History of Alcohol and Drugs* 26, no. 2 (2012): 170–191.

Newman, Robert. "Methadone Maintenance: It Ain't What It Used to Be." *British Journal of Addiction* 71, no. 2 (1976): 183–187.

Newton, Miller. *Gone Way Down: Teenage Drug Use Is a Disease.* Tampa, FL: American Studies Press, 1981.

Nolan, James L. "Therapeutic Adjudication." *Society* 39, no. 2 (2002): 31–38.

Novak, Timothy. "LSD Before Leary: Sidney Cohen's Critique of 1950s Psychedelic Research." *Isis* 88, no. 1 (1997): 87–110.

Nyswander, Marie. *The Drug Addict as Patient.* New York: Grune and Stratton, 1956.

O'Brien, William and Ellis Henican. *You Can't Do It Alone: The Daytop Way to Make Your Child Drug Free.* New York: Simon and Schuster, 1993.

Ofshe, Richard. "The Social Development of the Synanon Cult: The Managerial Strategy of Organizational Transformation." *Sociological Analysis* 41, no. 2 (1980): 109–127.

O'Neill, William. *Coming Apart: An Informal History of America in the 1960s.* New York: Times Books, 1971.

Peele, Stanton. *The Diseasing of America: Addiction Treatment Out of Control.* Lexington, MA: Lexington Books, 1989.

Perisco, Joseph. *Imperial Rockefeller: A Biography of Nelson A. Rockefeller.* New York: Simon and Schuster, 1982.

Perlstein, Rick. *Nixonland: The Rise of a President and the Fracturing of America.* New York: Scribner, 2009.

Perry, Manon S. "Dorthea Dix." *American Journal of Public Health* 96, no. 4 (2006): 624–625.

Pescor, M. J. "Prognosis in Drug Addiction." *American Journal of Psychiatry* 97 (1941): 1419–1433.

Petingy, Alan. *The Permissive Society, 1941–1965.* Cambridge: Cambridge University Press, 2009.

Phelps, Michelle S. "Rehabilitation in the Punitive Era: The Gap Between Rhetoric and Reality in U.S. Prison Programs." *Law & Society Review* 45, no. 1 (2011): 33–68.

Phoenix House Annual Report 1984–1985. New York: Phoenix House, 1985.

Platt, Jennifer. "The Development of the 'Participant Observation' Method in Sociology: Origin Myth and History." *Journal of the History of the Behavioral Sciences* 19 (1983): 379–393.

Quinn, Sandra Crouse. "Public Attitudes Towards Needle Exchange Programs." *AIDS* 13, no. 11 (1999): 1428–1429.

Reinarman, Craig. "The Twelve Step Movement and Advanced Capitalist Culture: The Politics of Self-Control in Post-modernity." In *Cultural Politics and Social Movements*, edited by Marcy Darnovsky, Barbara Epstein, and Richard Flacks, 90–109. Philadelphia: Temple University Press, 1995.

Reiss, Benjamin. *Theaters of Madness: Insane Asylums and Nineteenth-Century American Culture.* Chicago: University of Chicago Press, 2008.

Reiss, Susanna. *We Sell Drugs: The Alchemy of U.S. Empire*. Berkeley: University of California Press, 2014.

Riesman, David, with Nathan Glazer and Reuel Denney. *The Lonely Crowd*. New Haven, CT: Yale University Press, 1950.

Roberts, Samuel. "'Rehabilitation' as a Boundary Object: Medicalization, Local Activism, and Narcotics Addiction Policy in New York City, 1951–62." *Social History of Alcohol and Drugs* 26, no. 2 (2012): 147–169.

Rodgers, Daniel T. *The Age of Fracture*. Cambridge, MA: Harvard University Press, 2011.

Room, Robin. "Alcohol Control and Public Health." *Annual Review of Public Health* 5 (May 1984): 293–317.

Rorabaugh, William J. *Berkeley at War: The 1960s*. Oxford: Oxford University Press, 1989.

——. *Kennedy and the Promise of the Sixties*. Cambridge: Cambridge University Press, 2004.

Rose, Nikolas. *Governing the Soul: The Shaping of the Private Self*. 2nd ed. London: Free Association Books, 1999.

Rosenfeld, Seth. *Subversives: The FBI's War on Student Radicals and Reagan's Rise to Power*. New York: Farrar, Strauss and Giroux, 2012.

Rosenthal, Mitchell and Ira Mothner. *Drugs, Parents, and Children: The Three-Way Connection*. Boston: Houghton Mifflin, 1972.

Rossinow, Doug. "The New Left in the Counterculture: Hypotheses and Evidence." *Radical History Review* 67 (1997): 79–120.

——. *The Reagan Era: A History of the 1980s*. New York: Columbia University Press.

Roszack, Theodore. *The Making of a Counter-Culture: Reflections on the Technocratic Society and Its Youthful Opposition*. New York: Doubleday, 1969.

Rothman, David J. *The Discovery of the Asylum. Social Order and Disorder in the New Republic*. Boston: Little, Brown, 1971.

Rutherford, Alexandra. "The Social Control of Behavior Control: Behavior Modification, Individual Rights, and Research Ethics in America, 1971–1979." *Journal of the History of the Behavioral Sciences* 42, no. 3 (2006): 203–220.

Safire, William. *Safire's Political Dictionary*. New York: Oxford University Press, 2008.

Sale, Kirkpatrick. *SDS: The Rise and Development of the Students for a Democratic Society*. New York: Random House, 1973.

Sales, Grover. *John Maher of Delancey Street: A Guide to Peaceful Revolution in America*. New York: Norton, 1976.

Sanford, J. Scott and Bruce A. Arrigo. "Lifting the Cover on Drug Courts: Evaluation Findings and Policy Concerns." *International Journal of Offender Therapy and Comparative Criminology* 49, no. 3 (2005): 239–259.

Saval, Nikil. *Cubed: A Secret History of the Modern Workplace*. New York: Doubleday, 2014.

Scaglione, Fred. "New York Therapeutic Communities: Still Stay'n Out After Thirty Years." *New York Nonprofit Press*, July–August 2007, 10–11.

Schafer, Eric. *Bold! Shocking! Daring! True! A History of Exploitation Films, 1919–1959*. Durham, NC: Duke University Press, 1999.

Schlossman, Steven L. *Love and the American Delinquent: The Theory and Practice of Progressive Juvenile Justice*. Chicago: University of Chicago Press, 1977.

Schneider, Eric. *Smack: Heroin and the American City*. Philadelphia: University of Pennsylvania Press, 2009.

Schur, Edwin M. *The Awareness Trap: Self-Absorption Instead of Social Change*. New York: Quadrangle, New York Times Book Company, 1976.

Scott, James C. *Domination and the Arts of Resistance: Hidden Transcripts*. New Haven, CT: Yale University Press, 1992.

Scull, Andrew, Charlotte MacKenzie, and Nicholas Harvey. *Masters of Bedlam: The Transformation of the Mad-Doctoring Trade*. Princeton, NJ: Princeton University Press, 1996.

Selbin, Eric. *Revolution, Rebellion, Resistance: The Power of Story*. New York: Zed Books, 2010.

Sells, Saul B., ed. *Studies of the Effectiveness of Treatments for Drug Abuse*. Vol. 1. Cambridge, MA: Ballinger, 1974.

Sheff, David. *Clean: Overcoming Addiction and Ending America's Greatest Tragedy*. New York: Houghton Mifflin, 2013.

Showalter, Elaine. *The Female Malady: Women, Madness, and English Culture, 1830–1980*. New York: Pantheon Books, 1985.

Simon, Steven. "Synanon: Toward Building a Humanistic Organization." *Journal of Humanistic Psychology* 8, no. 3 (1978): 3–20.

Sisti, Dominic, Andrea G. Segal, and Ezekiel J. Emanuel. "Improving Long-Term Psychiatric Care: Bring Back the Asylum." *Journal of the American Medical Association* 313, no. 3 (2015): 243–244.

Skoll, Geoffrey. *Walk the Walk and Talk the Talk: An Ethnography of a Drug Treatment Facility*. Philadelphia: Temple University Press, 1992.

Spiegel, Douglas K., and Saul B. Sells. "Part I: Evaluation of Treatments for Drug Users in DARP." In *Studies of the Effectiveness of Treatments for Drug Abuse*, vol. 1, edited by Saul B. Sells, 3–234. Cambridge, MA: Ballinger, 1974.

Spillane, Joseph. *Coxsackie*. Baltimore: Johns Hopkins University Press, 2014.

——. "Debating the Controlled Substances Act." *Drug and Alcohol Dependence* 76, no. 1 (2004): 17–29.

Staub, Michael. *Madness Is Civilization: When the Diagnosis Was Social, 1948–1980*. Chicago: University of Chicago Press, 2011.

Stevens, Tina. *Bioethics in America: Origins and Cultural Politics*. Baltimore: Johns Hopkins University Press, 2000.

Strachey, Lytton. *Eminent Victorians*. 1918. E-book ed. N.p.: Start Publishing, 2012.

Sugarman, Barry. *Daytop Village: A Therapeutic Community*. New York: Holt, Rinehart, and Winston, 1974.

Szalavitz, Maia. *Help at Any Cost: How the Troubled-Teen Industry Cons Parents and Hurts Kids*. New York: Riverhead Books, 2006.

Szreter, Simon. "Rethinking McKeown: The Relationship Between Public Health and Social Change." *American Journal of Public Health* 92, no. 5 (2002): 722–735.

Taxman, Frank S. and Jeffrey Bouffard. "Treatment Inside the Drug Treatment Court: The Who, What, Where, and How of Treatment Services." *Substance Use and Misuse* 37, nos. 12–13 (2002): 1665–1688.

Thompson, Heather Ann. *Blood in the Water: The Attica Uprising of 1971 and Its Legacy.* New York: Pantheon Books, 2016.

——. "Why Mass Incarceration Matters: Rethinking Crisis, Decline, and Transformation in Postwar America." *Journal of American History* 97, no. 3 (2010): 703–733.

Tiger, Rebecca. *Judging Addicts: Drug Courts and Coercion in the Justice System.* New York: New York University Press, 2013.

Tipton, Steven. *Getting Saved from the Sixties: Moral Meaning and Conversion in Cultural Change.* Berkeley: University of California Press, 1982.

Tocqueville, Alexis de. *Democracy in America.* Translated by Arthur Goldhammer. New York: Penguin Books, 2004.

Touraine, Alaine. *The Post-industrial Society, Tomorrow's Social History: Classes, Conflicts, and Culture in the Programmed Society.* New York: Random House, 1971.

Toynbee, Arthur. *A Study of History: Abridgement of Vols. I–VI.* Oxford: Oxford University Press, 1946.

Tracy, Sarah. *Alcoholism in America: From Reconstruction to Prohibition.* Baltimore: Johns Hopkins University Press, 2005.

Travis, Trysh. *The Language of the Heart: A Cultural History of the Recovery Movement from Alcoholics Anonymous to Oprah Winfrey.* Chapel Hill: University of North Carolina Press, 2010.

Trebach, Arnold. *Why We are Losing the Great Drug War and Radical Proposals That Could Make America Safe Again.* New York: Macmillan, 1987.

Van Boeke, Leonieke C., Evelien P. M. Brouwers, Jaap van Weeghel, and Henk F. L. Garretsen. "Stigma Among Health Professionals Towards Patients with Substance Use Disorders and Its Consequences for Healthcare Delivery: Systematic Review." *Drug and Alcohol Dependence* 131, nos. 1–2 (2013): 23–35.

Varon, Jeremy. "Between Revolution 9 and Thesis 11: Or, Will We Learn (Again) to Start Worrying and Change the World?" In *The New Left Revisited*, edited by John McMillian and Paul Buhle, 214–240. Philadelphia: Temple University Press, 2003.

——. *Bringing the War Home: The Weather Underground, the Red Army Faction, and Revolutionary Violence in the Sixties and Seventies.* Berkeley: University of California Press, 2004.

Vlahov, David, Don C. DesJarlais, Eric Goosby, Paula C. Hollinger, Peter G. Lurie, Michael D. Shriver, and Steffanie A. Strathdee. "Needle Exchange Programs for the Prevention of Human Immunodeficiency Virus Infection: Epidemiology and Policy." *American Journal of Epidemiology* 154, no. 12 (2001): S70–S77.

Volk, Kyle. *Moral Minorities and the Making of American Democracy.* New York: Oxford University Press, 2014.

Volkman, Rita and Donald Cressey. "Differential Association and the Rehabilitation of Drug Addicts." *American Journal of Sociology* 69 (1963): 129–142.

Vrecko, Scott. "Civilizing Technologies and the Role of Deviance." *Biosocieties* 5, no. 1 (2010): 36–51.

Waldorf, Dan. "Natural Recovery from Opiate Addiction: Some Social-Psychological Processes of Untreated Recovery." *Journal of Drug Issues* 13 (1983): 237–247.

——. "Social Control in Therapeutic Communities for Drug Addicts." *International Journal of the Addictions* 6 (March 1971): 29–43.

Warner, Jessica. *All or Nothing: A Short History of Abstinence in America*. Toronto: McClelland and Stewart, 2008.

——. "Temperance, Alcohol, and the American Evangelical: A Reassessment." *Addiction* 104 (2009): 1075–1084.

Weber, Max. "The Nature of Charismatic Authority and Its Routinization." In *On Charisma and Institution Building: Selected Papers*, edited by Max Weber and Stuart Eisenstadt, 48–65. Chicago: University of Chicago Press, 1968.

——. *The Protestant Ethic and the Spirit of Capitalism*. Translated by Talcott Parsons. New York: Routledge, 2001.

Weiner, Barbara and William White. "*The Journal of Inebriety* (1878–1914): History, Topical Analysis, and Photographic Images." *Addiction* 102 (2007): 15–23.

Weppner, Robert S. "Matrix House: Its First Year in Lexington." *HSMA Health Reports* 86, no. 9 (1971): 761–768.

——. *The Untherapeutic Community: Organizational Behavior in a Failed Addiction Treatment Program*. Lincoln: University of Nebraska Press, 1983.

Weppner, Robert S. and James A. Inciardi. "Decriminalizing Marijuana." *International Journal of Offender Therapy and Comparative Criminology* 22, no. 2 (1978): 115–126.

Weppner, Robert S. and Duane C. McBride. "Comprehensive Drug Programs: The Dade County Example." *American Journal of Psychiatry* 132 (1975): 734–738.

Wexler, Harry. "The Success of Therapeutic Communities for Substance Abusers in American Prisons." *Journal of Psychoactive Drugs* 27 (1995): 57–66.

Wexler, Harry K. and Douglas S. Lipton. "From REFORM to RECOVERY: Advances in Prison Drug Treatment." In *Drug Treatment and Criminal Justice*, edited by James A. Inciardi, 209–227. Thousand Oaks, CA: Sage, 1993.

Wexler, Harry and Craig T. Lowe. "Therapeutic Communities in Prison." In *Therapeutic Community: Advances in Research and Application*, edited by Frank Tims, George De Leon, and Nancy Jainchill, 181–208. Rockville, MD: National Institute on Drug Abuse, 1994.

White, William. "Can Recovering Drug Addicts Drink? A Historical Footnote." *Counselor* 8, no. 6 (2007): 36–41.

——. "David Deitch, PhD, and George De Leon, PhD, on Recovery Management and the Future of the Therapeutic Community." *Counselor* 11, no. 5 (2010): 38–49.

——. Interview. *Points: The Blog of the Alcohol and Drugs History Society*, July 22, 2014. https://pointsadhsblog.wordpress.com/2014/07/22/the-points-interview-special-edition-william-l-white/.

——. *Peer-Based Addiction Recovery Support: History, Theory, Practice, and Scientific Evaluation*. Chicago: Lakes Addiction Technology Transfer Center; Philadelphia: Philadelphia Department of Behavioral Health and Mental Retardation Services, 2009.

——. "Recovery Coaching: A Lost Function of Addiction Counseling?" *Counselor* 5, no. 6 (2004): 20–22.

——. *Recovery Management and Recovery-Oriented Systems of Care: Scientific Rationale and Promising Practices*. Chicago: Northeast Addiction Technology Transfer Center and the

Great Lakes Addiction Technology Transfer Center; Philadelphia: Philadelphia Department of Behavioral Health and Mental Retardation Services, 2008.

———. "Riverside Hospital: The Birth of Adolescent Treatment." *Counselor* 5, no. 2 (2004): 18–20.

———. *Slaying the Dragon: The History of Addiction Treatment and Recovery in America.* Bloomington, IN: Chestnut Health Systems, 1989. 2nd ed. Bloomington, IN: Chestnut Health Systems, 2014.

White, William and Arthur C. Evans Jr. "The Recovery Agenda: The Shared Role of Peers and Professionals." *Public Health Reviews* 35, no. 2 (2014): 1–15.

Whitman, James Q. *Harsh Justice: Criminal Punishment and the Widening Divide Between America and Europe.* New York: Oxford University Press, 2003.

Wicker, Tom. *A Time to Die: The Attica Prison Revolt.* New York: Haymarket Books, 1975.

Wilkinson, William. *Prison Work: A Tale of Thirty Years in the California Department of Corrections.* Edited by John C. Burnham and Joseph F. Spillane. Columbus: Ohio State University, 2005.

Winick, Charles. "The Counselor in Drug Treatment." *International Journal of the Addictions* 25, no. 12A (1990–1991): 1479–1502.

———. "Maturing Out of Narcotic Addiction." *Bulletin on Narcotics* 14, no. 1 (1962): 1–7.

Wolfe, Tom. *Radical Chic and Mau-Mauing the Flak Catchers.* New York: Farrar, Strauss and Giroux, 1970.

Wolin, Richard. *The Wind from the East: French Intellectuals, the Cultural Revolution, and the Legacy of the 1960s.* Princeton, NJ: Princeton University Press, 2012.

Yablonsky, Lewis. "The Anti-criminal Society: Synanon." *Federal Probation* 26 (1962): 50–57.

———. *Confessions of a Criminologist: Some of My Best Friends Were Sociopaths.* New York: iUniverse, 2010.

———. *Juvenile Delinquency: Into the 21st Century.* Belmont, CA: Wadsworth, 2000.

———. *Robo-paths: People as Machines.* New York: Penguin, 1972.

———. *Synanon: The Tunnel Back.* 1965. Reprint. Baltimore: Penguin, 1967.

———. *The Therapeutic Community: A Successful Approach for Treating Substance Abuse.* Lake Worth, FL: Gardner Press, 1994.

Yinger, J. Milton. "Contraculture and Subculture." *American Sociological Review* 25, no. 5 (1960): 625–635.

Yuill, Kevin. "Another Take on the Nixon Presidency: The First Therapeutic President?" *Journal of Policy History* 21, no. 2 (2009): 138–162.

Zaretsky, Natasha. *No Direction Home: The American Family and the Fear of National Decline, 1968–1980.* Chapel Hill: University of North Carolina Press, 2007.

Zimbardo, Philip. *The Lucifer Effect: Understanding How Good People Turn Evil.* New York: Random House, 2007.

INDEX